Encyclopedia of Multicultural Education

Bruce M. Mitchell
and Robert E. Salsbury

GREENWOOD PRESS
Westport, Connecticut • London

Library of Congress Cataloging-in-Publication Data

Mitchell, Bruce M.
Encyclopedia of multicultural education / Bruce M. Mitchell and Robert E. Salsbury.
p. cm.
Includes bibliographical references (p.) and index.
ISBN 0–313–30029–1 (alk. paper)
1. Multicultural education—United States—Encyclopedias.
2. Multicultural education—Encyclopedias. I. Salsbury, Robert E.
II. Title.
LC1099.3.M58 1999
370.117'0973—dc21 98–44222

British Library Cataloguing in Publication Data is available.

Library of Congress Catalog Card Number: 98–44222
ISBN: 0–313–30029–1

First published in 1999

Greenwood Press, 88 Post Road West, Westport, CT 06881
An imprint of Greenwood Publishing Group, Inc.
www.greenwood.com

Printed in the United States of America

The paper used in this book complies with the Permanent Paper Standard issued by the National Information Standards Organization (Z39.48–1984).

10 9 8 7 6 5 4 3 2 1

Contents

Preface

The *Encyclopedia of Multicultural Education* has been created to provide educators with an easy-to-use, single-volume reference work. The encyclopedia consists of more than 400 terms, phrases, concepts, U.S. Supreme Court decisions, significant contributors to the American macroculture from the country's various racial and/or ethnic backgrounds and key events, and court cases related to multicultural education. Arranged alphabetically, each entry is defined and/or discussed in keeping with its relationship to multicultural education.

The entries were chosen by the authors and an advisory group consisting of persons who have played prominent roles in various areas of multicultural education. Advisory group members include Dr. Felix Boateng from Vanderbilt University, Dr. Roberto Ponce, ex-Assistant Superintendent of Public Instruction in California, Al and Sally Miller, educators from the Colville Indian Reservation, Mr. Mike Cantlon, an elementary school teacher in Spokane, Washington, and Mr. Joe Franklin, a secondary social studies teacher in Portland, Oregon.

Encyclopedia entries were selected based on their relationship to the content and method of multicultural education, rather than simply on the basis of historical prominence or celebrity of the individual or event cited. For example, Louis Armstrong was not only an internationally famous musician, but he also spoke out against racial insensitivities, such as the government's handling of the Little Rock, Arkansas, school desegregation issue, an important topic in multicultural education. The biographical information on Armstrong places him in an historical context which lends further credence to his views on the need for racial equity in American education. As with Armstrong, other exemplary persons of color were included in the encyclopedia based on their perceived importance and relationship to multicultural education. Others, equally worthy of inclusion in a more general work, were not included in this encyclopedia if there was not a clear connection to multicultural education. For these latter figures, the reader might wish to consult one of the numerous available biographical dictionaries.

Sources consulted in the preparation of this work were chosen according to three criteria: relevance to the context of multicultural education, value as authoritative sources, and currency of scholarship. Although the latter criterion was an overall concern throughout the encyclopedia, occasionally an older work contained more definitive information about a given entry. For example, the end-of-entry bibliography for "Traditional Jazz" contains references to three works dated 1946, 1963, and 1964. These sources, although not within the 1995–1998 time frame, are nevertheless among the most important in the chronicling of the traditional jazz idiom. This encyclopedia is designed to be a handy reference for social scientists and educators who are interested in ensuring equity, reducing prejudice, and helping young persons learn to appreciate persons who are different from themselves. Each item will provide a brief description of the entry, along with cited references related to the topic. In addition, a selected bibliography is provided at the end of the encyclopedia.

While the entries relate directly to issues which are particularly germane to American history, many of them relate to issues of multicultural education which are being addressed the world over. For example, many countries have attempted to provide special instruction for students who speak a language other than the predominant language of instruction in the schools. Consequently, the issue of "bilingual education" is being dealt with everywhere in an attempt to provide the best possible education for all children.

In summary, the authors hope that this work will help the reader gain access to a more complete and higher level of understanding of the topics, issues, and opportunities residing within the field of multicultural eduation. We are grateful to our advisory group and to the various authors in the field who have stimulated our thoughts regarding the selection and describing of timely and useful entries. Most importantly, we hope that this encyclopedia will assist educators the world over to craft more enlightened and informed instructional programs, with the result of helping young people acquire more positive attitudes about all the people who dwell on Planet Earth, our island home.

Encyclopedia of Multicultural Education

A

ABOLITIONISTS, active in the United States since the very beginning of the slave era, opposed the concept of human ownership by virtue of the belief that the practice constituted a violation of basic human rights. The Spaniards were among the first Europeans to take African slaves, using them on ships which traveled to the Caribbean and American territories. Some of the first African slaves were involved in the construction of forts along the coastal regions of the Americas. One of the early forts was constructed at St. Augustine in present-day Florida.

Among the first abolitionist groups were church organizations such as the Quakers, Presbyterians, Methodists, and Congregationalists. These groups started the Amistad Committee, which later became known as the American Missionary Association. The Amistad Committee was named after the Spanish slave ship *La Amistad*, which was captured by Spanish slaves and taken to Connecticut. The incident culminated in a Supreme Court decision which allowed the slaves to return to their native lands.

With the publication of William Lloyd Garrison's *Liberator* in 1831, the southern states grew increasingly resentful of the increase in anti-slavery resentment among the northern abolitionists. This motivated southern legislatures to enact resolutions demanding the suppression of abolitionist organizations, arguing that the U.S. Constitution guaranteed the practice of slavery.

One of the more militant abolitionist societies was the American Anti-slavery Society. A nagging problem for pro-slavery advocates and abolitionists alike was the issue of slavery in Washington, DC. While voting against the Gott amendment to abolish slavery in the nation's capitol, Abraham Lincoln believed that the ''Congress of the United States has the power, under the Constitution, to abolish slavery in the District of Columbia; but that power should not be exercised unless at the request of the people.''

Among the prominent abolitionists were Frederick Douglass, John Brown, Robert Purvis, Henry Highland Garnett, John Quincy Adams, Horace Mann, Salmon P. Chase, Joshua Giddings, and Cassius M. Clay, the Kentuckian. But perhaps the most famous of all was Sojourner Truth, who, after being sold three times on the auction block, escaped to freedom and afterward helped other fugitives to make successful use of the Underground Railroad. After visiting President Lincoln, she commented on his kindness and his ultimate commitment to the abolitionist cause. Understanding the abolitionist movement is normally part of the fifth grade social studies curriculum, as well as a common U.S. history topic.

References: James A. Banks, *Teaching Strategies for Ethnic Studies*, 6th ed. (Boston: Allyn and Bacon, 1997); David Herbert Donald, *Lincoln* (London: Jonathan Cape, 1995); Bruce M. Mitchell, et al., *The Dynamic Classroom*, 5th ed. (Dubuque, IA: Kendall/Hunt, 1995).

ACCESS is a term used by American educators to determine whether schools and school programs are open to students regardless of their gender, race, ethnicity, social status, or other factors. One example of access denial is in the area of special programs for gifted/talented students who tend to overrepresent affluent European-American youngsters.

Since the U.S. Constitution guarantees equal education opportunities to all American children regardless of race, gender, or socioeconomic status, access to schools and special programs is based on population demographics in given communities and the appropriate ratio of students who reflect the approximate proportion of children from all of a given community's microcultures. The concept of educational equity was challenged during the middle of the century as a result of the 1954 *Brown v. Board of Education* Supreme Court decision, which legally terminated segregated facilities in the United States. Segregation denied certain students ''access'' to appropriate schools on the basis of race. The U.S. Supreme Court ordered the Topeka, Kansas, school district to terminate segregated schools ''with all deliberate speed.''

However, during recent years, the concept of ''access'' seems to have received diminished attention among educators and the American public alike. In fact, there is ample research evidence that shows an increased level of segregation, which some sociologists have referred to as ''the re-segregation of America.'' This implies some limitations on the accessibility of schools and school programs by students from certain racial, ethnic, and socioeconomic backgrounds. Moreover, the anti–affirmative action movement by conservative groups in the United States during the decades of the 1980s and 1990s may have an even greater limitation on the equal education opportunities and program access of non–European-American K–12 and higher education students during the twenty-first century.

References: Bruce M. Mitchell, et al., *The Dynamic Classroom*, 5th ed. (Dubuque, IA: Kendall/Hunt, 1995); Joan Thrower Timm, *Four Perspectives in Multicultural Education* (Belmont, CA: Wadsworth, 1996).

ACCULTURATION is a term which relates to the manner in which people from different racial and/or ethnic groups are able to exchange cultural characteristics. For example, if a Native American becomes interested in African-American literature, it can be said that a significant level of acculturation has occurred. Another example might be when a European American develops an interest in the African contributions to the American jazz art form.

One of the most critical issues in the understanding of this concept has to do with the level of acceptance and adoption of behaviors and values from the new culture. It is usually perceived as a multidimensional concept. It pertains to the level of understanding of the values, languages, knowledge, and behavior of a person from a microcultural background which is different from that of the first person.

It can be used in several different ways. It can refer to language acquisition, where a person learns to speak a second language. It could also refer to the adoption of cultural values by a person who has previously had little knowledge of the second culture, or it could refer to the impact of one culture on another in regard to the extent that one culture adapts the language and values of a different culture through occupation or colonization. For example, Brazil is a Portuguese-speaking nation as a result of the occupation of the Portuguese. In this example, the native Brazilians learned to speak the language of the conquering Portuguese.

References: James A. Banks, *Multiethnic Education: Theory and Practice*, 3d ed. (Boston: Allyn and Bacon, 1994); Carl A. Grant (Ed.), *Educating for Diversity* (Boston: Allyn and Bacon, 1995); Hilda Hernandez, *Multicultural Education* (Columbus, OH: Merrill, 1989); Joan Thrower Timm, *Four Perspectives in Multicultural Education* (Belmont, CA: Wadsworth, 1996).

AFFIRMATIVE ACTION refers to any programs which have been designed to increase employment opportunities for women and minorities. The most common procedures for addressing affirmative action issues have related to "good faith efforts" and quotas. Many communities have adopted affirmative action programs in an attempt to compensate women and minorities for years of racist and sexist hiring practices, admission to educational programs, and appointments to special positions.

Some quotas have specified percentages of persons from racial and/or ethnic backgrounds who must be employed or permitted entrance to special school programs. One notable U.S. Supreme Court decision related to the issue of quotas focused on the case of Alan Bakke, an applicant to the University of California, Davis, Medical School. Bakke was denied admission to the program after failing to be admitted to a number of other medical schools. He sued the

University for "reverse discrimination" on the grounds that he was not allowed to apply for one of the University's quota slots which had been set aside for applicants who were not white males.

In a rather unique decision, the U.S. Supreme Court ruled that his constitutional rights were violated because he had been disallowed to petition for one of the quota slots. He was later admitted to the U.C. Davis School of Medicine. However, the Supreme Court did not disallow the use of quotas as a means of compensating women and minorities for years of blatant discrimination. The Court ruled that whenever quotas are used, the institution in question must allow *all* candidates who were denied admission to special programs the chance to reapply for one of the quota slots.

Consequently, quotas are acceptable as long as they are applied in a constitutionally acceptable manner. However, the issue of affirmative action has become heavily politicized. The political right wing has sought to overturn affirmative action programs on the grounds that they discriminate against White males. It is important for all educators to understand what constitutionally acceptable procedures must be in place for any quota programs which might be employed.

References: James A. Banks, *Teaching Strategies for Ethnic Studies*, 6th ed. (Boston: Allyn and Bacon, 1997); Bruce M. Mitchell, et al., *The Dynamic Classroom*, 5th ed. (Dubuque, IA: Kendall/Hunt, 1995).

AFRICAN AMERICANS, comprising about 12 percent of the population of American people, include all U.S. persons who came from Africa or whose ancestors came to the United States from the continent of Africa. African Americans have been involved in the post-Columbian history of the United States since 1502, when Diego el Negro sailed with Columbus on his last voyage to the United States. Others were involved with the Coronado expeditions which went as far as the state of Kansas. Most present-day African Americans can trace their lineage to the slave era, when Africans were brought to the United States against their will to provide a source of cheap labor for entrepreneurs in the tobacco and cotton plantations. By the time this slave trade peaked in the 1700s, the English were the most heavily involved. European countries prospered greatly, obtaining many raw materials from Africa, which helped them acquire an industrial base. For example, the Gold Coast area of western Africa provided the English with cocoa, gold, and timber. European slavers helped create fortunes in Portugal, Spain, Holland, Britain, and Denmark.

During the 1970s, 1980s and 1990s, an increased number of African Americans migrated to the United States from the various African nations of north Africa and sub-Saharan Africa alike. Some were facing persecution in their own countries, while others became part of a "brain drain," receiving their education in the United States and choosing to stay in the United States after receiving their degrees.

Some African Americans' ancestors extend to the period before the Civil War, when about 5 percent of the nation's African residents consisted of free African Americans who lived north of the Mason–Dixon line.

The term African American is quite generic in nature since, technically, it can refer to a variety of racial and ethnic groups whose ancestral roots are traced back to the continent of Africa. For example, there are great ethnic and racial differences between the Ashanti of Ghana and the Copts of North Africa.

Historically, African-American children have often struggled academically. Denied access to literacy during slavery and ravaged by poverty, these youngsters have often encountered educational difficulties in the schools.

References: James A. Banks, *Teaching Strategies for Ethnic Studies*, 6th ed. (Boston: Allyn and Bacon, 1997); Bruce M. Mitchell and Robert E. Salsbury, *Multicultural Education: An International Guide to Research, Policies, and Programs* (Westport, CT: Greenwood Press, 1996); Joan Thrower Timm, *Four Perspectives in Multicultural Education* (Belmont, CA: Wadsworth, 1996).

AFRICAN CANADIANS is a term which refers to Canadian citizens who came to that country from the continent of Africa. Thus, African Canadians could have migrated to Canada from South Africa, Ghana, Libya, Ethiopia, or any of the other locations in the continent of Africa.

Many African Canadians actually had their original roots in the United States. This resulted because of the Dred Scott decision, which ruled that African-American slaves would not be considered free when they crossed the Mason–Dixon line. This ruling helped create the famous Underground Railroad, which extended from the southern tobacco-growing regions clear to the Canadian border. The runaway slaves were forced to travel on the underground railway clear to Canada where they were provided with citizenship, something that never happened in the United States until after the abolition of slavery. Obviously, these concepts must be part of any serious study of American history.

In addition to the African Canadians who originally came to the country through the United States, there are also many people who have come to Canada in more recent times, directly from the continent of Africa.

References: Bruce M. Mitchell, et al., *The Dynamic Classroom*, 5th ed. (Dubuque, IA: Kendall/Hunt, 1995); Bruce M. Mitchell and Robert E. Salsbury, *Multicultural Education: An International Guide to Research, Policies, and Programs* (Westport, CT: Greenwood Press, 1996).

AFRICAN STUDIES ASSOCIATION is an organization of professional educators, sociologists, and anthropologists who are responsible for higher education programs which focus on the continent of Africa. The primary goal of the group is to help students acquire a more realistic conceptual understanding about the African continent. For years and years, people the world over have harbored a number of distorted notions about the continent. The concept of African Studies became embodied in the curriculum of higher education institutions as a result of issues which occurred during the American civil rights movement.

Many educators involved in multicultural education have become convinced that these misconceptions have helped to generate deep-seated racist feelings among non-Africans the world over. For centuries, people have believed such myths as lions in the jungle, the mysterious "dark continent," "inferior savages," "the land of constant upheaval," "people who are unprepared to govern themselves," "primitive religious systems," and so on.

The hope of the African Studies Association is that through a more aggressive information system and better education about Africa, some of these racist notions can be overturned. Also, the goal of this and other similar organizations is that the continent of Africa deserves better treatment by educators. In fact, the writings of early Muslim scholars who traveled throughout the continent in the tenth and eleventh centuries have revealed that African civilization was quite well advanced by that time. In fact, some scholars have argued that the African civilizations were as advanced, in some cases, as the civilizations in many parts of Europe.

References: B. Davidson, "The Forgotten People," *Christian Science Monitor*, March 6, 1969; Christine I. Bennett, *Comprehensive Multicultural Education: Theory and Practice*, 3d ed. (Boston: Allyn and Bacon, 1995); B. Davidson, *African Kingdoms* (New York: Time-Life Books, 1966).

AFROCENTRISM in educational circles has referred to the attempts of some school districts to create educational sequences that incorporate the accomplishments of Africans and African Americans throughout history. Educators argue that the problems in some school districts throughout the United States are so severe that there is a need for monoethnic curriculums. While this concept may be quite different from the ideals of many multicultural education advocates, it is a perception that seems to be attracting greater attention.

Two Milwaukee schools in 1991 focused on the education and human development of black males. In a similar manner, school districts such as the Portland, Oregon, Public Schools have created a curriculum that integrates multicultural education in such a way that African history, knowledge, and values provide the core of the curriculum.

However, this concept is not without its critics. Albert Shanker, president of the American Federation of Teachers, has argued that the Portland School District's "African-American Baseline Essays" go beyond discussing Egypt as an African society. As he says, they suggest that the inhabitants of ancient Egypt were black Africans which, Shanker argues, is a position that is inconsistent with the best scholarship.

References: James A. Banks, *Multiethnic Education*, 3d ed. (Boston: Allyn and Bacon, 1994); Leonard Davidman with Patricia T. Davidman, *Teaching with a Multicultural Perspective* (New York: Longman, 1994).

AGEISM, a notion pertaining to the inherent capabilities of individuals on the basis of age, also relates to the extent of discrimination against older Americans. Some multicultural education experts have pointed to factors in American society which tend to illustrate the acts of discrimination against older Americans. In fact, one of the most powerful lobbies in the United States is the American Association of Retired Persons (AARP).

The notion of discrimination against older Americans seems to undergird the definition of ''ageism.'' Indeed, AARP has become a lobbying organization that constantly monitors the progress of legislative actions which might jeopardize the position of older Americans, who are often on ''fixed'' incomes and worry about the possibility of inflation and other economic conditions threatening their well-being.

Persons who are concerned with problems of ageism also investigate actions that seem to be prejudicial against older Americans as far as employment equity and other facets of American life, which are protected by the United States Constitution.

References: Pamela L. Tiedt and Iris M. Tiedt, *Multicultural Teaching* (Boston: Allyn and Bacon, 1995); Joan Thrower Timm, *Multicultural Education* (Columbus, OH: Merrill, 1989).

ALAMBRISTAS **(Wire Crossers)** is a Spanish term which has been used to characterize the Mexican nationals who took risks to cross the border into the United States. The metaphor refers to the various strategies that were often employed to gain entrance to the United States. These were not always legally recognized by the U.S. government.

After World War II, crossing the border became more highly regulated by the U.S. Border Patrol. The use of ''coyotes,'' hired border-crossing guides, became a problem for Mexican nationals who attempted to cross the American border. Tragedies befell many of the persons who took advantage of their services.

The number of *Alambristas* has continued to remain rather high because of the continual economic woes of Mexico and the common perception that life in the United States would improve the welfare of Mexican nationals. During 1996, the issue became a major point of contention between Democrats and Republicans in the United States. These ideas can be incorporated into studies of American history and political science.

References: Carey McWilliams, *North from Mexico: The Spanish-Speaking People of the United States* (Westport, CT: Greenwood Press, 1990); James A. Banks, *Teaching*

Strategies for Ethnic Studies, 6th ed. (Boston: Allyn and Bacon, 1997); Christine I. Bennett, *Multicultural Education: Theory and Practice*, 3d ed. (Boston: Allyn and Bacon, 1995).

ALEXIE, SHERMAN (1966–), a Spokane/Coeur d'Alene Indian, won the PEN/Hemingway award for Best First Book of Fiction. He also won the 1994 Lila Wallace-Reader's Digest Writers' Awards. He is the author of three books of poetry: *I Would Steal Horses, Old Shirts and New Skins*, and *The Business of Fancydancing*. His first novel, *Reservation Blues*, received excellent reviews from the *Chicago Tribune*, the *Boston Globe*, and the *New York Times Book Review*.

In his writing, he has depicted life on his own Spokane Indian Reservation. He has been termed a "modern mythmaker" with the ability to describe the ironies of modern Native American life in the United States. In his writing, he has created a formula for mixing narrative, newspaper excerpts, songs, journal entries, visions, and drama. Moreover, he has successfully explored the effects of Christianity on Native Americans in the late twentieth century.

Perhaps his most unique writing quality is his ability to craft stories that combine the pain and bitterness, which has characterized the life of Native Americans, with a refreshing humor and irony.

One of the most critical multicultural teaching strategies requires that students learn to appreciate the cultural contributions of all Americans, one of the underpinnings of any good multicultural education program.

References: Sherman Alexie, *The Lone Ranger and Tonto Fistfight in Heaven* (New York: The Atlantic Monthly Press, 1993); Sherman Alexie, *Reservation Blues* (New York: The Atlantic Monthly Press, 1995).

ALI, MUHAMMAD (1942–), originally named Cassius Clay, was one of the greatest boxers in history. Adopting the flamboyant antics of the famous wrestler, "Gorgeous George," Ali immediately became a crowd-pleasing pugilist during the 1960s and 1970s. He was one of the most exciting athletes in the history of modern sports as he won the heavyweight championship of the world by dethroning Sonny Liston who, most boxing experts believed, was invincible.

He was born in Louisville, Kentucky, in 1942. He won the AAU heavyweight championship in 1959 and went on to become the Olympic light-heavyweight champion. Truly a unique champion, he fought bouts in North America, Europe, Africa, Asia, and the Philippines. One of his trainers said that Ali could "float like a butterfly, sting like a bee." His style was consistent with this phrase.

Physical education teachers and social studies instructors could use the situation encountered by Ali as an example of the discrimination against black athletes, which has plagued the history of the United States.

After bucking the system when he refused to become a member of the United States armed forces, he was stripped of his title during the Vietnam War. He argued that "No Cong ever called me 'nigger.' " His decision not to serve his country was centered around his religious beliefs as a black Muslim. His decision was eventually upheld by the United States Supreme Court, which exonerated him for his actions.

Ali became a symbol of the 1970s. He was a man who bucked the "system" and won. His "Ali shuffle" and the "rope-a-dope" strategy became famous. He set a record for fighting more championship rounds than any other boxer in history. He lit the Olympic torch to begin the 1996 Olympic Games.

References: Bert Randolph Sugar, *The Greatest Boxers of All Time* (New York: Bonanza Books, 1984).

ALLOTMENT is a term used in referring to the actions taken to fit Native Americans into the habits and occupations of civilized life. Included in the concept are such ethnic values as work and education. During the latter part of the twentieth century, the U.S. government allotted Native Americans parcels of land.

In 1887, the Dawes Severalty Act was passed by Congress. The goal of this legislation was to help Native Americans become independent and terminate their special relationship with the U.S. government. This piece of federal legislation authorized the president to allot 160 acres of tribal lands to family heads. Family heads were granted citizenship when they received their allotments.

Many tribes opposed the action from the outset, and the results of the legislation proved to be disastrous for many Native American people. For example, some Indians sold their allotment lands to European Americans for extremely low prices, and these lands were sometimes obtained in illegal ways. Many Indians became poverty stricken during the time the legislation was in effect.

Finally, in 1934, the U.S. Congress passed the Wheeler–Howard Act, which terminated the allotment of Indian lands. In effect, the bill also made it possible for Native Americans to create local governments based on their traditional cultures. It also resulted in the federal government taking a more active role in Indian affairs and helped Native Americans re-establish their cultural value systems.

References: James A. Banks, *Teaching Strategies for Ethnic Studies*, 6th ed. (Boston: Allyn and Bacon, 1997); Brian W. Dippie, *The Vanishing American* (Middletown, CT: Wesleyan University Press, 1982); George F. Hoar and Henry L. Dawes, *Congressional Record* (January 24, 1881, 46th Congress, 3d Session); Cesare Marino, *The American Indian: A Multimedia Encyclopedia* (New York: Facts on File, 1993).

AMERICAN CIVIL LIBERTIES UNION (ACLU) is an organization devoted to defending the civil rights of people in the United States. Founded in 1920 by civil libertarians, including Jane Addams and Helen Keller, the organization provides legal advice for individuals in local, state, and federal courts. Officials from the organization also testify before state and federal legislative bodies, advise government officials, and conduct a variety of educational programs that deal with various constitutional issues pertaining to the civil liberties of American people.

Many of the issues addressed by the ACLU pertain to freedom of speech and protection against various punishments for persons accused of crimes for actions that are guaranteed in the Bill of Rights. Throughout its history, the ACLU has defended poor persons, minorities, and white supremacist organizations alike.

The ACLU also has taken a strong stance on such issues as school desegregation and the right of women to choose abortions. In addition, the organization has championed the abolition of capital punishment and has sought greater protection for immigrants to the country. Finally, the ACLU has taken strong positions for the rights of homosexuals and mental patients and has argued consistently for the separation of church and state.

References: William A. Donohue, *The Politics of the American Civil Liberties Union* (New Brunswick, NJ: Transaction Books, 1985); Samuel E. Walker, *In Defense of American Liberties: A History of the ACLU* (New York: Oxford University Press, 1990).

AMERICAN INDIAN MOVEMENT (AIM) is a United States/Canada civil rights organization that is committed to improving the living conditions of Native Americans and Native Canadians. Another primary goal has been to assist Indian persons establish land ownership rights. One of the major targets of the American Indian Movement has been the Bureau of Indian Affairs (BIA). AIM feels that the BIA has failed to eliminate poverty, job, and housing discrimination.

Founded in 1968, AIM's original goals were to improve the lives of Native Americans in Minneapolis and protect them from certain police actions which they felt were unfair. During the 1970s the organization created a number of groups that were designed to help develop a sense of self-determination among Native Americans. Composed only of Indians, the goals of these groups were to improve education, employment services, legal programs, and health services.

References: Cesare Marino, *The American Indian: A Multimedia Encyclopedia* (New York: Facts on File, 1993); Harvey Markowitz (Ed.), *American Indians* (Pasadena, CA: Salem Press, 1995).

AMISTAD EVENT was the name for an 1839 incident concerning a Spanish slave ship, *La Amistad*. Leaving from Havana, it was taken over by its captive slaves. The leader of the mutiny was named Sengbe, pronounced ''Cinque'' by the Spaniards. The event occurred on the way to Puerto Principe, Cuba. The slaves ordered the Spanish sailors to return them to Africa.

The crew sailed east by night when the stars were out, then gradually turned the ship west during the daytime in an attempt to fool the African mutineers. However, the U.S. Coast Guard commenced receiving reports of a ship which was taking a curious zig-zagging route. Eventually, the U.S. Coast Guard intercepted the ship, and it was taken to New London, Connecticut.

The Spaniards were anxious to retrieve their cargo and sell their slaves for a profit. However, New Haven was in the anti-slavery section of the country. Nonetheless, President Martin Van Buren was anxious for the Spaniards to prevail, and the incident went to litigation.

The case attracted a great deal of pro-slavery and anti-slavery attention and eventually it reached the U.S. Supreme Court. John Quincy Adams argued the case before the United States Supreme Court, and the slaves were granted their freedom as a result of the Court's decision.

The Amistad event also aroused the curiosity of religious groups, such as the Quakers, Methodists, Congregationalists, and Presbyterians, who had adopted strong anti-slavery positions by this time. Eventually, an organization known as the Amistad Committee was formed, and ultimately it became known as the American Missionary Association, the nation's first anti-slavery missionary society.

This group campaigned vigorously for abolition and was instrumental in providing an education for African-American children. After the end of the Civil War, they became heavily involved in the development of teacher education programs and in the establishment of education institutions such as Fisk University, Talladega College, Dillard University, and Le Moyne–Owen College.

References: Bruce M. Mitchell, et al., *The Dynamic Classroom*, 5th ed. (Dubuque, IA: Kendall/Hunt, 1995).

ANASAZI was a Native American culture that flourished some 2,000 years ago in the southwestern region of the United States. This group of early American residents had no known written history, and information about their life has come largely from archaeological evidence, the traditions of their descendants, and written records of Spanish explorers who came into contact with them.

Their land includes the present-day states of New Mexico, Arizona, and parts of Utah and Colorado. These regions are still extremely arid, and no navigable rivers drain the area. The known history of the Anasazis began during the sixteenth century when the Spanish conquerors of Mexico came into contact with them. Their history became recorded through the letters and other writings of those Spanish explorers. They were referred to as *Pueblos* or town dwellers by the Spaniards. The best available information shows that the Anasazis organized themselves into small bands that moved to hunting and food-gathering locations to sustain themselves.

Many of the famous Anasazi monuments were created during the Classic Pueblo Period, which lasted roughly from the eleventh century into the fourteenth century. The amazing buildings at Chaco Canyon and the inspiring cliff houses at Mesa Verde were constructed during this time period. Two of the best known cliff houses were Pueblo Bonito, which had between 600 and 800 rooms, and Cliff Palace at Mesa Verde, which had 220 rooms and 23 kivas. It is thought to have housed between 250 and 350 people.

A study of the Anasazi culture can help teachers create courses of study to help students understand the differences between the pre-and post-Columbian cultures in the United States.

References: Steven H. Lekson, et al., ''The Chaco Canyon Community,'' *Scientific American* 259 (1988); Robert P. Powers, ''Cutliers and Roads in the Chaco System,'' in David G. Noble (Ed.), *New Light on Chaco Canyon* (Santa Fe, NM: School of American Research, 1984); Gordon E. Willey and Jeremy Sabloff, *A History of American Archaeology* (San Francisco: W. H. Freeman, 1980).

ANDERSON, MARIAN (1897–1993), an important biographical study for music educators interested in multicultural education, was the first African-American soloist to appear in the Metropolitan Opera in New York City. Born on February 27, 1897, she had a deep, rich, contralto voice which allowed her to master everything from spirituals to operatic works. Toscanini once remarked that ''a voice like hers comes only once in a century.''

Her appearance with the New York Philharmonic in 1925 was the result of winning a competition against 300 other vocalists. Due to a lack of singing engagements in the United States, she went to Europe to study and perform. After a number of successful European engagements, she returned to the United States in 1935 for a recital in New York and a national tour.

Because of her race, the Daughters of the American Revolution (DAR) would not allow her to sing at Constitution Hall in 1939. The incident sparked a national controversy, and Eleanor Roosevelt resigned from the DAR, assisting in the sponsorship of a Marian Anderson concert at the Lincoln Memorial in Washington, DC. More than 75,000 persons were in attendance, while millions listened on the radio.

Marian Anderson debuted with the Metropolitan Opera Company in 1955. She played the role of Ulrice in *Un Ballo in maschera* by Verdi. She then sang around the world, giving her last recital at Carnegie Hall in 1965. Anderson was an alternative delegate for the United States during the 13th General Assembly of the United Nations. She was also presented awards, including the presidential Medal of Freedom in 1963 and the National Medal of Art in 1986. She died in Portland, Oregon, in 1993.

ANGELOU, MAYA (1928–) is one of the most gifted writers, composers, and stage performers in the United States. Born in 1928, in St. Louis, Missouri, this African-American woman became known for such brilliant pieces of literature as *I Know Why the Caged Bird Sings*, her highly famous autobiography. In addition to this famous work, she also wrote autobiographical sequels such as *The Heart of A Woman* and *All God's Children Need Traveling Shoes*. Critics have argued that this work is one of the most successful attempts by any American author to describe the meaning of being an African American in the United States.

In an attempt to return to her roots, Angelou lived in Africa for a period of time but had difficulty in adapting to some of the African cultural patterns. She was unable to accept being the "second wife" in a marriage proposal. The language differences also constituted a major problem for her.

As a result of her musical contributions, educators can use her creative works to help students develop a more sophisticated understanding of American pluralism.

Included in her books of poetry are *Now Sheba Sings the Song* and *I Shall Not Be Moved*.

Reference: Joan Thrower Timm, *Four Perspectives in Multicultural Education* (Belmont, CA: Wadsworth, 1996).

ANGLO AMERICAN is an ethnic concept that refers to present-day residents of the United States whose roots extend back to Great Britain and whose native language is English. Technically, the term is not generic in the sense that it refers to all persons from the northern sections of Europe who have Caucasian racial characteristics.

Persons referred to as "Anglos" or Anglo-Saxons probably settled in Britain from around the middle of the fifth century. Several kingdoms were established in Kent, Sussex, Essex, Wessex, Mercia, East Anglia, and Northumbria.

In 597, St. Augustine established a cathedral church at Canterbury for the education of future ministers. As Christianity spread throughout the land, so did the need for education. Thus, Anglo-Saxons became one of the more highly educated groups of people in Europe.

As a result of this high level of education and the victory of the English in the French and Indian War in the United States, English became the dominant language in the United States, and Anglo Americans became one of the most powerful ethnic groups in the United States of America. This is a crucial concept for multicultural education educators.

References: Marshall Cavendish Corporation, *Cultures of the World* (North Bellmore, NY: Marshall Cavendish Corporation, 1991); Bruce M. Mitchell and Robert E. Salsbury, *Multicultural Education: An International Guide to Research, Policies, and Programs* (Westport, CT: Greenwood Press, 1996).

ANTI-DEFAMATION LEAGUE OF B'NAI B'RITH is a civil rights organization in the United States. Founded in 1913 by Sigmund Livingston, an Illinois lawyer, the goal of the organization was to stop the persecution and defamation of Jews. In recent years, the objectives of the organization were expanded to act as an agency that seeks to secure fair treatment and justice for all Americans.

The Anti-Defamation League has a national office in New York City and 28 regional offices in strategic parts of the country.

According to studies by ADL, arson attempts and anti-Semitic acts, such as the desecration of tombstones or synagogues and vandalism, have been increasing dramatically. During 1991, there were 950 attacks on Jewish individuals and 49 acts of vandalism against Jewish-owned property, including synagogues. One hundred and one of these acts occurred on 60 different college campuses.

Judaism is one of the world's oldest religions and was one of the first religious sects to teach the existence of one Supreme Being. Prior to the Christianization of the Holy Roman Empire, Jews were persecuted along with the early Christians. They were attacked as heretics during the Middle Ages by Christians, and these attacks would persist throughout history. Probably the worst time for the Jewish religion was during the period of the holocaust, when 6 million Jews were exterminated by the Nazis during World War II. The organization has excellent materials which are available for teachers.

References: J. R. Feagin and C. B. Feagin, *Racial and Ethnic Relations* (Englewood Cliffs, NJ: Prentice-Hall, 1978); T. Sowell, *Ethnic America: A History* (New York: Basic Books, 1980).

ANTI-SEMITISM refers to a stereotypical, anti-Jewish attitude, which has persisted throughout history. Attacked as heretics by Christians during the Middle Ages, Renaissance, and Enlightenment, Jews have been the victims of blatant discrimination. During the Nazi Holocaust, historians have estimated that about 6 million Jews were exterminated. This represented well over one-half of the European Jewish population.

One of the reasons for this anti-Jewish racism may have been the tendencies of Jews to maintain their religion, language, and traditions. Moreover, Jews tended to live in segregated communities, and they sometimes became a target for persons who needed specific microcultures to hate. For example, in the United States, the Ku Klux Klan and the Aryan Nations organizations have taken strong stands against Jewish Americans, and their doctrines of Aryan supremacy have been extremely harmful.

Racist actions against Jews have increased dramatically in recent years. During 1991, a record 1,897 racist, anti-Jewish incidents were reported in the United States. Moreover, in newly unified Germany, anti-Semitic incidents have also increased at a dramatic pace. The acts of violence against German Jews has become a major problem for the German government.

One challenge for teachers is to help students understand the hopelessness of intercultural hatred. For years, educators have argued that ignorance feeds acts of intolerance and hatred. Religious and racial tolerance are critical goals for multicultural educators.

References: J. R. Feagin and C. B. Feagin, *Racial and Ethnic Relations* (Englewood Cliffs, NJ: Prentice-Hall, 1978); T. Sowell, *Ethnic America: A History* (New York: Basic Books, 1980).

APACHE TRIBE consisted of Native Americans who resided in New Mexico and Arizona. These Indians were divided into three groups named the Jicarillas, Mescaleros, and Chiricahuas. Their most famous leader was Cochise, a powerful chief of the Chiricahua Apaches. After surviving years of warfare against Mexico and the United States, Cochise became one of the most important Native American leaders in the United States.

A rather warlike and nomadic people, these residents of the American Southwest are divided into seven different groups. The eastern division includes the Kiowa-Apache, Lipan, and Jicarille. The western division consists of the Navajo, Western Apache, Chiricahua, and Mescalero tribes.

When his brother was executed at Apache Pass by European Americans, Cochise declared war and his forces fought the European-American settlers for about a decade. Apaches were often referred to as ''rattlesnakes'' by the European Americans involved in these conflicts. After a decade of intermittent war, which ended in the surrender of Naiche and Geronomo in 1886, most of the Chiricahua Apaches were removed to Florida. However, after an ill-fated venture at farming, most of the Apaches walked back to their original homeland, finally settling on the Mescalero Reservation in New Mexico.

References: Amiram Gonen (Ed.), *The Encyclopedia of the Peoples of the World* (New York: Henry Holt, 1993); Edwin R. Sweeney, *Cochise* (Norman: University of Oklahoma Press, 1991).

APARTHEID is a concept that refers to regulated racial separation. The term has referred specifically to the South African policy of racial separation. This apartheid policy resulted in the separation of black South Africans and European South Africans. In 1948, the white electorate prevailed in voting into power the National Party with a mandate to introduce policies of apartheid. Finally, as a result of intense international pressure and the influence of the African National Congress (ANC), the apartheid policies were terminated in 1991. During 1994, Nelson Mandella, representing the ANC, was voted into office in the country's first non-racial elections, which were based on the principle of one person, one vote.

South Africa schools were affected by these apartheid actions. Essentially, three separate school districts existed: one for Whites, one for Blacks, and one for children of mixed races and Indians. The program for black children received 50% of the funding for Whites, while the third program (for mixed-race children and Indians) received two-thirds as much as the schools for Whites.

References: Steven Anzovin, *South Africa: Apartheid and Divestiture* (New York: H. W. Wilson, 1987); Harold Nelson, *South Africa: A Country Study* (Washington, DC: U.S. Government Printing Office, 1981).

ARAWAK is a group of diverse Indian peoples who inhabit the South American forests, primarily north of the Amazon River. Prior to the Spanish conquest of

1540, an Arawak group called the Tiano established a sophisticated political organization in the Greater Antilles. The Taino exploited their rich maritime resources and relied heavily on their agricultural production.

The Caribs drove the Arawaks off the Lesser Antilles before the Spanish occupation of the Caribbean. The Arawaks and Caribs were assimilated into Spanish society. However, the mainland Arawaks, who survived the Spanish conquest, continued to practice slash-and-burn agricultural techniques. The Arawaks were culturally diverse but linguistically related.

Reference: Amiram Gonen (Ed.), *The Encyclopedia of the Peoples of the World* (New York: Henry Holt, 1993).

ARMSTRONG, LOUIS (1900–1971), also known by his nickname Satchmo, became one of the great icons of American jazz. Born in 1900, he grew up in a segregated neighborhood on Perdido Street in New Orleans. At the age of 13, he was arrested for shooting off a gun during a New Year's celebration. Because of the infraction, he was forced to spend a year and a half in a waif's home for boys. Since the home had a band, he learned to play the cornet.

In addition to his cornet-playing prowess, Armstrong was a talented vocalist who became America's first ''scat'' singer. He participated in a quartet called the Singing Fools, which would often sing in the evenings on the banks of the Mississippi. Louis Armstrong's talent on the cornet was enhanced by Joe (King) Oliver, who gave young Louis cornet lessons in return for helping his wife with her errands and shopping chores.

After performing in New Orleans with Kid Ory and Tom Anderson, Armstrong went to Chicago to play second cornet with King Oliver, who was performing at the Lincoln Gardens. In 1924, he accepted an invitation to play in Fletcher Henderson's orchestra in Harlem. He was an enormous success.

During the 1930s and 1940s, Armstrong's popularity soared, and during the middle 1950s, he completed a highly successful tour to Europe. Columbia Records released an LP entitled Ambassador Satch (after his nickname, Satchmo). He was then considered to be an American ambassador because of his music.

Armstrong was outspoken over some of the racial insensitivities that have plagued American history. He criticized the U.S. government for its handling of the Little Rock High School desegregation issue. He was angry with President Eisenhower and Governor Orville Faubus, in particular.

Armstrong was always sensitive to his African roots. In 1960, he traveled to Ghana with the blessing of the U.S. State Department. He also went to Kenya and did extensive tours in Europe, Australia, Korea, Japan, Hong Kong, Iceland, India, Canada, and South America. He died in 1971.

References: Max Jones and John Chilton, *Louis: The Louis Armstrong Story* (Boston: Little, Brown, 1971); Hugues Panassie, *Louis Armstrong* (New York: Charles Scribner's Sons, 1956).

ARYAN NATIONS CHURCH is a white supremacist religious body located north of Coeur d'Alene, Idaho. Headed by the "Reverend" Richard Butler, it is a white supremacist, anti-semitic body that believes in the superiority of the white race. The term "Aryan" applies to the belief that Teutons were the purest modern representatives of the Aryans.

The Aryan Nations Church, also referred to as the Church of Jesus Christ Christian, openly advocates the creation of a "Whites only" state, and has repeatedly denounced Jews and African Americans as being inferior to the Teutonic Aryans.

The concept of Aryan supremacy has been traced back to 1854 and a book published by a French writer, Count Joseph Arthur de Gobineau, who gave a racial meaning to Aryan. De Gobineau declared that the Aryan race was supreme among Whites. Adolf Hitler equated Aryan with the Nordic race and used his theory to persecute the Jews. Ashley Montagu and other anthropologists have rejected the theory of the pure or inherently superior racial groups of human beings.

Reference: Southern Poverty Law Center, "Aryan National Congress Focuses on Revolutionary Tactics," in *Intelligence Report* 74 (Montgomery, AL: Southern Poverty Law Center, August 1994).

ASIAN AMERICANS have lived in the United States for more than 150 years and constitute one of the nation's most significant ethnic groups. The total Asian-American population is about 5 million persons. The largest of the highly diverse Asian-American groups are the Chinese, Filipinos, and Japanese. All three groups came to the United States to enter the cheap labor market. Chinese Americans came to work on the construction of railroads and mines, Japanese Americans were recruited as contract laborers, and Filipinos came to the United States during the 1920s to work in the fields as laborers.

Historically, they have often been recognized as the model American minority microculture. However, they have been subjected to intense discrimination through such measures as the Chinese Exclusion Act of 1882 and the World War II internment of Japanese Americans as a result of Executive Order 6066 in 1942. The United States government eventually compensated Japanese Americans for property losses at about ten cents on the dollar.

Among the newest Asian immigrants are the Vietnamese and Hmong from Southeast Asia. Many of the Vietnamese families that migrated to the United States toward the end of the United States–North Vietnamese War did so by bribing the airport guards for seats on airplanes. Consequently, a skewed number of affluent Vietnamese families arrived in the United States as refugees. On the other hand, the Hmong were mostly illiterate tribal farmers from the Laotian highlands. They were recruited by the United States CIA to apply pressure on the Ho Chi Minh Trail in Vietnam.

Asian Americans have contributed greatly toward the development of the nation. The strong education values have helped these students excel in their schooling, and during World War II, a Japanese-American unit became the most highly decorated military group in history.

References: James A. Banks, *Teaching Strategies for Ethnic Studies*, 6th ed. (Boston: Allyn and Bacon, 1997); Robert W. Gardner, et al., *Asian Americans: Growth, Change, and Diversity* (Washington, D.C.: Population Reference Bureau, 1985); Joan Thrower Timm, *Four Perspectives in Multicultural Education* (Belmont, CA: Wadsworth, 1996); United States Bureau of the Census, *Asian and Pacific Islander Population by State* (Washington, DC: U.S. Bureau of the Census, Supplementary Report, 1980).

ASSIMILATION is a term that refers to attempts to incorporate one microculture into another or efforts to make one group more homogeneous in relation to another. Throughout history, United States policy has been accused of attempting to assimilate microcultures through the educational system. Other countries have also crafted aggressive assimilation programs. Educationally, it has not always been clear as to the extent of assimilation that is desirable. In fact, some microcultures have feared that they could be in danger of seeing their groups disappear.

The issue of assimilation has been extremely controversial. Sometimes referred to as ''the melting pot theory,'' the notion is that new immigrants should be expected to jump into the cauldron, shed their native ethnicity, and adapt the ethnic values of the European-American majority. The term first surfaced during colonial times and re-emerged at the turn of the century as a result of a Broadway play by Israel Zangwill entitled *The Melting Pot.*

However, strong objections have been voiced as to the requirement of assimilation. Many American microcultures have argued against this philosophy, claiming that to assimilate means being forced to give up their native culture and become something else. A counter position has been articulated, using the analogy of a stew or salad. The argument has been that in a stew or salad, the total product is unique because of each individual item. Take the meat away from the stew and some of the total essence is lost. Remove the tomatoes from the salad and the total product suffers.

Reference: Christine I. Bennett, *Comprehensive Multicultural Education: Theory and Practice*, 3d ed. (Boston: Allyn and Bacon, 1995).

ATTUCKS, CRISPUS (1723–1770), an African-American colonial patriot, ran away from his master in Framington, Massachusetts, in 1750. He was tall, about 6'3". He led a small group of men who clashed with British troops stationed in Boston. The British troops had been moved to Boston in 1768 and two years later, in 1770, this volatile atmosphere resulted in encounters between the street mobs and the British troops.

The British opened fire on the mob and Attucks was the first of five men to be killed in the skirmishes. This incident became known as the Boston Massacre, and many Americans became convinced that the British would attempt to maintain control over the American colonies regardless of the consequences. It was one of the events that led to the beginning of the American Revolution against the British.

Reference: James C. Stone and Donald P. DeNevi (Eds.), *Teaching Multicultural Populations* (New York: D. Van Nostrand, 1971).

AUSCHWITZ, established in 1940 as a concentration camp for Polish political prisoners, became Nazi Germany's central murder installation in 1943. Jews were sent to Auschwitz from all over Nazi Europe. Prior to that time, the Germans had crowded Jews into ghettos, but between 1941 and 1943, they were brought to Auschwitz in large numbers.

The Auschwitz gas chambers were dynamited and dismantled in 1944. However, during the annihilation period, more than 6 million European Jews had been murdered by the Nazis. The Nazi goal of exterminating all of the Jewish people had been partially achieved. Very few people were able to escape from Auschwitz.

The Nazi party came to power in 1933 as a result of a lack of any working majority in the German parliament. Right-wing politicians believed that the Nazis were no longer a danger, and so they called them to power, believing that with Hitler on their side they could rule the country. Once in power, Hitler rejected these right-wing allies and put together a dictatorship.

Originally, the Nazi movement was not anti-semitic. However, the Nazis eventually articulated a belief that it was necessary to reorder Europe and later, the entire world. The central figures would be the Nordic people of the Aryan race. The Germans, the purest Nordics, would lead the way. It was the view of the Nazis that Jews were trying to disallow the Germans their rightful leadership role in the development of the new order. Thus, it was felt that in order for the Nazis to achieve their goals, it was necessary to exterminate the Jews.

References: Erick Kulka, *Escape from Auschwitz* (South Hadley, MA: Bergin & Garvey, 1986); Primo Levi, *The Drowned and the Saved* (New York: Simon and Schuster, 1986).

AUTONOMOUS MINORITIES are microcultures possessing distinctive religious, linguistic, and cultural characteristics. The members of such groups may belong to families whose roots extend far back into history. However, they are sometimes newcomers to a specific territory, in the case of Jewish immigrants to the United States or Israel. In addition to the religious beliefs of such groups, the language patterns are distinct and are used to express the cultural values and feelings of the microculture.

Reference: Joan Thrower Timm, *Four Perspectives in Multicultural Education* (Belmont, CA: Wadsworth, 1966).

B

BAKKE, ALLAN (1940–) was the central figure of the famous ''reverse discrimination'' case of 1978. Bakke, originally an electrical engineer, decided to become a doctor and attend medical school. After being turned down by a number of medical schools, he applied for admission to the University of California, Davis. He was rejected at that institution, as well, and was not allowed to apply for the quota slot because of his male gender and his European-American racial background.

Bakke decided to sue the University of California, Davis, on the basis of ''reverse discrimination'' because of being a white male. The case reached the U.S. Supreme Court, which ruled in Bakke's favor. He was admitted to the University's medical school. However, the Court also ruled that quota systems for women and minorities were acceptable as long as there were no restrictions on who would be allowed to apply for the limited number of quota slots.

References: Alexander Kern and M. David Alexander, *American Public School Law* (Belmont, CA: Wadsworth, 1998); Bruce M. Mitchell, et al., *The Dynamic Classroom*, 5th ed. (Dubuque, IA: Kendall/Hunt, 1995).

BALDWIN, JAMES (1924–1987) was a New York City writer who became an important literary figure among black American authors. Born in 1924, Baldwin became known for his literary works that depicted the problems of African Americans residing in a white-dominated society. He was the son of a minister and, at a very early age, he became the minister of a small Evangelical church in Harlem, New York.

In 1948, Baldwin spent most of his time residing in France, although he returned periodically to the United States to teach and lecture. His first novel,

Go Tell It on the Mountain, was published in 1953 and chronicled the life of his youth. Other novels included *Giovanni's Room* (1956) and *Another Country* (1962), which addressed racial and sexual problems of New York intellectuals. Perhaps his most famous work was *Blues for Mister Charlie*, which was a play published in 1964. A critical voice during the American Civil Rights era, he died in 1987.

Reference: *Black Americans of Achievement* (Yeadon, PA: Chelsea Curriculum Publications, 1993).

BANNEKER, BENJAMIN (1731–1806) was a free, black, tobacco farmer who acquired fame as a tobacco farmer and a creator of almanacs. Born in 1731, he became a self-educated man by reading books and other documents that he borrowed from George Ellicott, a Quaker mill owner in Maryland. He participated in the survey of the Territory of Columbia (now the District of Columbia).

His maternal grandparents were a freed slave and a white English indentured servant. While surveying the ten-mile-square for the Territory of Columbia, he became known by Maryland and Pennsylvania abolition societies, which supported the almanacs he had created. The almanacs became quite widely distributed. However, due to poor health and new interests in scientific fields, Banneker abandoned his interests in tobacco farming and lived on the income from his farm, where he died in 1806. His life story is a valuable biography for multicultural education programs at the 5th–12th grade levels.

Reference: Silvio A. Bedini, *The Life of Benjamin Banneker* (New York: Charles Scribner's Sons, 1971).

***BARRIO*,** a Spanish word meaning "district" or "quarter," has acquired much more significance since the beginning of the American civil rights movement of the 1960s. It is a term that has been used to characterize a Latino, largely Catholic, ethnic environment where Spanish is the mother tongue of many of the residents. Beyond these characteristics, *barrios* are sometimes considered to be ethnic enclaves, populated by large numbers of low-income persons. But many view *barrios* as havens from oppression, while some feel that they must move out of the *barrio* in order to achieve the "good life."

The largest *barrios* in the United States can be found in communities such as San Antonio, Texas, and East Los Angeles, California. Historically, *barrios* have rather high rates of unemployment and the types of problems that people address in other low-income communities. Often the *barrio* schools have instituted bilingual education programs to upgrade the school performance of Latino students.

Reference: Denis Lynn Daly Heyck (Ed.), *Barrios and Borderlands* (New York: Routledge, 1993).

BECHET, SIDNEY (1897–1959) was a jazz clarinetist and soprano saxophonist who became one of the most important figures in the evolution of American jazz. Born in 1897 in New Orleans, Bechet was one of the first exponents of the jazz idiom to achieve recognition on the soprano saxophone. After World War I, he made his first trip to Europe, playing with Will Marion Cook's Southern Syncopated Orchestra.

During the 1930s, he performed throughout the United States and Europe before forming his own trio. He made several trips to France, where he was so warmly received that he performed in that country for extended periods of time. He felt that as an African American he was treated more favorably in that country than in the country of his birth.

Reference: William Carter, *Preservation Hall* (New York: W. W. Norton, 1991).

BEREA v. KENTUCKY was a significant U.S. Supreme Court decision that related to the segregation of private schools. The case was related to the *Plessy v. Ferguson* decision of 1896, which pertained to the concept of ''separate but equal'' facilities in educational circles.

Berea College, in Kentucky, was a higher educational institution that had a mission to meet the needs of low-income students. A private college, Berea recruited students of all racial and religious backgrounds. Ordered to segregate its student population, the institution argued that it could not be forced to do so, because it was a private institution and the *Plessy v. Ferguson* decision pertained to the public sector. However, the U.S. Supreme Court ruled in favor of the state of Kentucky, thus establishing a Supreme Court precedent for the racial segregation of the private sector.

References: Alexander Kern and M. David Alexander, *American Public School Law* (Belmont, CA: Wadsworth, 1998); Bruce M. Mitchell, et al., *The Dynamic Classroom*, 5th ed. (Dubuque, IA: Kendall/Hunt, 1995).

BETHUNE, MARY McLEOD (1875–1955) was a prominent African-American educator, civic leader, and school founder, who left the cotton fields of her early life to become the only African-American woman to attend Scotia College in North Carolina and Chicago's Moody Bible Institute. In 1904, she founded a normal and industrial school for young African-American women in Daytona Beach, Florida.

Starting with just five students and a rented cottage, her school eventually became known as the Bethune-Cookman College in 1923. She served as the school's president until 1947. Her school was viewed with disfavor by many southern Whites who feared that African Americans would not be content to hold the traditional low-education jobs if they became well educated.

Bethune was president of the National Association of Colored Women, founder-president of the National Council of Negro Women, a member of the

Hoover Committee for Child Welfare, and director of the National Business League. A national monument was erected in her honor in Washington, D.C. in 1974.

References: John H. Franklin and August Meier (Eds.), *Black Leaders of the Twentieth Century* (Urbana: University of Illinois Press, 1982); Milton Meltzer, *Mary McLeod Bethune* (New York: Vanguard Press, 1951).

BIAS is a term that describes an attitude harbored by an individual based on a considerable level of information. Thus, a person may exhibit a positive or negative attitude about an issue or event based on substantial information or experiences. A bias differs from a prejudice in that a prejudice is a belief or attitude based on ignorance.

Biases can pertain to much more than race or ethnicity. For example, a jury can be biased because of information that the members have already acquired before the trial. But biases can also be harbored because of misinformation.

Reference: Joan Thrower Timm, *Four Perspectives in Multicultural Education* (Belmont, CA: Wadsworth, 1996).

BILINGUAL EDUCATION pertains to the efforts of educators to provide instruction in the student's native language, when it is warranted. Two languages are utilized in the instructional sequences to help the learner acquire the necessary understandings as effectively as possible. The goal is to expand on the mother tongue language patterns of the learner to ensure the best possible education.

Bilingual education has been deemed important the world over, since educators are anxious to make certain that their students acquire the necessary learning concepts regardless of their stages of language development. Perhaps the greatest fear among educators is that children will fail in school because of language difficulties and that the reason for the failure will be perceived as a lack of intelligence. This is a major problem for younger students. Consequently, the notion is that if the learner can receive instruction in the language, which he or she understands, there is a higher probability of initial success in the acquisition of basic concepts.

Virtually, every country has either a legal language or a language of primary use that all students must master to achieve success. For example, in the United States, the language of use (not a legal language) is English. Thus, students whose mother tongue is a language other than English may receive initial instruction in that language while concurrently receiving instruction in English. These programs are usually referred to as English as a Second Language (ESL). In most schools, the goal is to get students to the point where they are bilingual in both languages so the need for bilingual instruction terminates. At this point, English becomes the language of instruction.

References: Rosalie Pedalino Porter, *Forked Tongue* (New York: Basic Books, 1990); Arnulfo G. Ramirez, *Bilingualism Through Schooling* (Albany: State University of New York Press, 1985); James Williams and Grace Capizzi Snipper, *Literacy and Bilingualism* (White Plains, NY: Longman, 1990).

BITCH-100 is a test of "intelligence" created by William Williams. The acronym stands for Black Intelligence Test for Cultural Homogeneity, and it was designed specifically for inner-city, African-American youngsters. The creation of the test was based on the argument that racial biases have had an affect on the school performance of African-American children and children from other minority microcultures.

Consequently, the questions were crafted in such a manner that the words, terms, and phrases are familiar to children who grow up in African-American, inner-city areas. Children and adults who were raised in other locales would probably have a difficult time with the questions, since they might not coincide with the frames of reference with which they are familiar.

Reference: M. Lee Manning and Leroy G. Baruth, *Multicultural Education of Children and Adolescents* (Boston: Allyn and Bacon, 1996).

BLACK CODES were slave laws that were established and revised many times during the history of American slavery. During the first half of the 19th century, each state established a set of laws pertaining to the treatment of slaves. For example, some states, such as Mississippi, forbid slaves to beat drums because it was known that in Africa the drum was used to broadcast messages. The fear was that drumming could help foment rebellions and/or uprisings.

Other black codes or slave laws related to such transactions as marriage agreements. Slaves could not enter into such arrangements without the approval of their masters. Slaves could not assemble unless a European-American person was present, nor could they use alcohol or conduct religious services without the involvement of a European-American person. Perhaps the most debilitating black code pertained to reading. Slaves were usually forbidden to read because of the fear that this would increase the communication potential, which might lead to dissatisfaction or revolt. Consequently, many African Americans were illiterate at the termination of the Civil War.

Reference: W. A. Low and Virgil A. Slift (Eds.), *Encyclopedia of Black America* (New York: McGraw-Hill, 1981).

BLACK COLLEGES, as the term implies, are institutions of higher education that cater to African-American students. They can be traced back to the period of Reconstruction, following the termination of the Civil War. Due to the segregation of educational institutions in the southern states, there was a need for higher education institutions that were accessible to African-American students.

One such school was Grambling College, a state-supported educational institution in Louisiana. Opened in 1901 as an industrial education school, it became a four-year college in 1940 and later, a teacher-preparation institution. Its early program was patterned after Tuskegee Institute, founded by Booker T. Washington.

Historically, black colleges struggled financially and were woefully underfunded compared to the higher education institutions for European-American students. Most black colleges originated in the South, as a result of mandated racial segregation. Consequently, African-American students from the South either attended black colleges or went north to schools that would allow them to matriculate. During recent years, many African-American students have chosen to attend black colleges to escape the racism that still exists in various forms.

Reference: Marshall Cavendish Corporation, *African-American Encyclopedia* (Bellmore, NY: Marshall Cavendish Corporation, 1992).

BLACK EDUCATION refers to educational programs that have been created to focus directly on the accomplishments of African-Americans and to offset the Eurocentric approaches to the social sciences that, some critics argue, are prevalent in many of the books and curriculum materials used in American schools.

Many colleges and universities have established Black Studies Departments, which provide courses and/or academic degrees. Frequently, institutions of higher education have initiated graduation requirements which involve students in the study of African-American issues. In many cases, black educational classes rely on a study of the African continent in order for students of all racial backgrounds to acquire a more in-depth understanding of the historical and social issues that have African and African-American roots.

Reference: Marshall Cavendish Corporation, *African-American Encyclopedia* (Bellmore, NY: Marshall Cavendish Corporation, 1992).

BLACK ENGLISH is an English dialect used by many people in the United States. In general, it tends to be used in the southern states and urban regions. The dialect utilizes many distinctive syntax patterns and often makes use of unique vocabulary. Although many of the language patterns have persisted for many years, some people still associate the dialect with poor grammar and a lack of intelligence.

Black English usage has no effect on the capacity of students to learn in school. Most school districts in the United States have done little to change the dialects of children who learn this language at an early age. However, attempts are made to teach students standard English so that children are able to utilize both language patterns with equal facility.

Reference: Christine I. Bennett, *Comprehensive Multicultural Education: Theory and Practice*, 3d ed. (Boston: Allyn and Bacon, 1995).

BLACK HISTORY MONTH was first observed in 1926 and sponsored by the Association for the Study of Negro Life and History. This group was founded by African-American historian Carter G. Woodson, and the goal is to help people from all racial backgrounds become more familiar with the achievements of African Americans during American history.

Schools throughout the United States have created special programs in the month of February to help students acquire more positive information about the accomplishments of persons from this microculture. Requests for special materials can be made to the Association for the Study of Negro Life and History, 1538 Ninth Street, NW, Washington, DC 20001.

Reference: Pamela L. Tiedt and Iris M. Tiedt, *Multicultural Teaching* (Boston: Allyn and Bacon, 1995).

BLACK PANTHERS is a social action organization dedicated to achieving equal rights for African-American people. Organized in 1966 by Huey Newton and Bobby Seale in Oakland, the group became a revolutionary movement that provided an alternative to the non-violent concepts of Dr. Martin Luther King. The Black Panthers believed that the police needed to be monitored by African Americans.

The primary goals of the organization were self-defense and self-determination for members of African-American communities around the country. The Black Panthers believed that a revolution against the white establishment was the quickest way for African Americans to achieve their civil rights. Consequently, the Panthers were often embroiled in armed confrontations with law enforcement officials. Believing that education was their salvation, they organized classes to train young African Americans to carry on their ''revolution.'' Also, they undertook special programs to improve the education of African-American students.

Eventually, the skirmishes with police groups took their toll and many of the leaders of the group received prison sentences, were on probation, exiled to other countries, or killed. The group had chapters around the United States, and the Black Panthers represented the country's first black political movement. But even though the Black Panthers were an extremist organization, their efforts pointed out the many problems of African-American people who were forced to dwell in American ghettos.

References: Edward M. Keating, *Free Huey: The True Story of the Trial of Huey P. Newton for Murder* (New York: Ramparts Press, 1971); Gail Sheehy, *Panthermania: The Clash of Black Against Black in One American City* (New York: Harper and Row, 1971).

BLACK POWER is a term used during the American Civil Rights Movement. The phrase was first uttered by Stokely Carmichael (Kwame Ture) during a march through Mississippi in 1966. European Americans objected to the phrase because they felt that it referred to physical power. However, according to Carmichael, it actually referred to black economic power. It was felt by Carmichael and others that the only way for African Americans to succeed in the United States was to control their economic destiny and to acquire an education that would enable them to compete for jobs.

Reference: Ronald Takaki, *A Different Mirror: A History of Multicultural America* (Boston: Little, Brown, 1993).

BLAKE, EUBIE (1883–1983), along with Scott Joplin, helped to pioneer the American jazz movement. Ragtime became an important exponent in the evolution of jazz, and Blake, along with Scott Joplin, Thomas Turpin, James Scott, and Willie ''The Lion'' Smith, were key figures. In addition to his legendary ragtime musicianship, Blake was also a songwriter. In 1921, he and Noble Sissie wrote the musical score for *Shuffle Along*, which became a highly successful Broadway show.

Reference: W. A. Low and Virgil A. Clift, *Encyclopedia of Black America* (New York: McGraw-Hill, 1981).

BLOCKBUSTING is a term that was used to describe the efforts of persons of color, particularly African Americans, in purchasing homes throughout the United States. Housing in the United States historically has been racially segregated. Many people have been reluctant to sell houses to minority persons. Thus, to acquire more desirable housing, groups of persons from minority backgrounds have pooled their resources to purchase a house at an inflated value. Then, when the sales prices of other houses would diminish, other persons of color would be able to purchase homes at a reasonable price.

Many of the ''blockbusting'' participants became involved in such endeavors, because adequate housing was impossible to acquire due to ''redlining'' practices by realtors. These strategies made it virtually impossible for persons of color to purchase desirable homes in the more affluent sections of a community. Consequently, it sometimes made it difficult for African-American students to have access to ''good'' schools.

Reference: Robert M. Jiobu, *Ethnicity and Assimilation* (Albany: State University of New York Press, 1988).

BOND, JULIAN (1940–), the son of prominent educators, became famous for his election to the Georgia state legislature in 1965. However, the Georgia legislature refused to seat him because of his anti-Vietnam war rhetoric. In 1966, the U.S. Supreme Court ruled the exclusion to be unconstitutional. He was finally seated in 1967.

In 1968, he became the first African American to have his name placed in nomination for the vice-presidency of a major political party. He also seconded the nomination of Eugene McCarthy for the Democratic party. He served in the Georgia House of Representatives from 1967 to 1975 and in the Georgia Senate from 1975 to 1987. He also served as president of the Southern Poverty Law Center.

Reference: Marshall Cavendish Corporation, *African-American Encyclopedia* (North Bellmore, NY: Marshall Cavendish Corporation, 1992).

BORDER PATROL refers to the U.S. Congress action of 1924 that created an organization responsible for keeping out illegal immigrants, particularly Mexicans. The patrol was an arm of the Bureau of Immigration. However, during the Roosevelt administration, the Border Patrol became part of the Immigration and Naturalization Service (INS).

The Border Patrol has had a controversial history. Some people welcomed undocumented workers who provided a source of cheap labor for the California agriculture industry. However, others were interested in keeping the immigrants out. Border agents had a great deal of power in search, seizure, and arrest authority. Consequently, they were not all well received by the border communities. Throughout history, the conflict over their proper role has persisted, often assuming deep political implications. These issues are important factors connected with the economic history of the United States

Reference: L. H. Gann and Peter J. Duignan, *The Hispanics in the United States: A History* (Boulder, CO: Westview Press, 1986).

BRACERO PROGRAM, an effort to provide the United States with cheap labor from Mexico, began after World War II. The word comes from the word "brazo" which means "arm" in the Spanish language. Thus, the word "bracero" refers to the concept of working with one's arms. The program was the result of an agreement between the governments of the United States and Mexico to allow the use of Mexican laborers to work in the United States.

The first Bracero Program was initiated in 1942 and terminated in 1947. The second one started in 1948 and lasted until 1964. The first program began as a result of labor needs in the United States agricultural industry when many American males were involved in the armed forces. During the second program, about 4.5 million Mexican men worked for specific periods of time in the United States. Most of the jobs were designed to provide a labor force in the seasonal agricultural industries in the United States.

Reaching its peak in 1956, the second Bracero Program processed nearly one-half million Mexican agricultural laborers under Public Law 78. This work force constituted about one-fourth of all the agricultural workers in the United States. These laborers were employed in the states of California, Arizona, Colorado, New Mexico, Texas, Arkansas, and Michigan.

Reference: Himilce Novas, *Everything You Wanted to Know About Latino History* (New York: Penguin Books, 1994).

BRANDEIS, LOUIS (1856–1941), the son of sophisticated Bohemian Jewish parents, was the first Jew to sit on the U.S. Supreme Court. Born in Louisville, Kentucky, in 1856, he was appointed to the court by Woodrow Wilson in 1916 and served until 1939. As a member of the Court, he supported the constitutional validity of the majority of Franklin Roosevelt's New Deal legislation. Moreover, he believed in the preservation of federalism, although he also subscribed to the notion of state legislatures being able to draft laws in accordance with changing needs.

Prior to becoming a member of the U.S. Supreme Court, Brandeis established a reputation for being the people's attorney. He attended the public schools of Louisville and the Annen Realschule in Dresden, Germany. Graduating from Harvard Law School in 1877, he was first in his class. He practiced law in Boston for most of his pre-Supreme Court career. While serving on the Supreme Court, he often sided with Oliver Wendell Holmes in the minority. Brandeis University, located in Waltham, Massachusetts, was named after him.

Reference: Homer C. Hockett and Arthur M. Schlesinger, *Land of the Free* (New York: Macmillan, 1944).

BROWN, H. RAP (1943–), a prominent member of the militant Black Panther Party, became famous for his uniform that consisted of combat boots, beret, and sunglasses. He became popular among young African Americans because of his militant rhetoric and became the head of the Student Non-Violent Coordinating Committee (SNCC), succeeding Stokely Carmichael.

Accused of inciting a race riot in Maryland, he was convicted of transporting arms across state lines and was later wounded by police after the holdup of a tavern in New York City. In 1973, he began serving a prison term. During his incarceration, he changed his name to Jamil Abdullah Al-Amin and became a Muslim minister. Following his release from prison, he became the proprietor of an Atlanta grocery store. H. Rap Brown's biography is a necessary ingredient in the U.S. Civil Rights Movement.

References: Clayborn Carson, et al. (Eds.), *Eyes on the Prize: Civil Rights Reader* (New York: Penguin Books, 1991); Charles M. Christian, *Black Saga* (Boston: Houghton Mifflin, 1995).

BROWN, JOHN (1800–1859), a militant American abolitionist, became a martyr to the anti-slavery movement in the United States with his raid on the federal arsenal at Harper's Ferry, Virginia, in 1859. Although he was a European American, he settled with his family in an African-American community at North Alba, New York, in 1849. The land was donated by Gerrit Smith, an anti-slavery philanthropist.

Brown had long been a foe of the concept of slavery. He became obsessed with the idea of taking action to terminate this practice and win justice for enslaved African Americans. He followed his five sons to Kansas in 1855 to become involved in the work of anti-slavery factions in that part of the United States. He became the leader of anti-slavery guerrilla forces there.

During the summer of 1859, with a band of sixteen Whites and five Blacks, he took a federal armory. With augmented forces, he led a rebellion with the hope that escaped slaves would join them. However, he and his forces eventually surrendered to a force of U.S. Marines. He was found guilty of insurrection and treason against the state. He was hanged after his conviction. His biography is an important component of the Civil War history. See HARPER'S FERRY.

Reference: David Herbert Donald, *Lincoln* (London: Jonathan Cape, 1995).

BROWN v. BOARD OF EDUCATION was one of the most significant decisions in the history of the U.S. Supreme Court. The case dealt with the issue of school segregation and centered around racial segregation in the city of Topeka, Kansas. The plaintiff, a fourth grade student, was not allowed to attend the school in her neighborhood, since it was for Whites only.

Declaring that racially segregated schools were unconstitutional, the case nullified the 1896 *Plessy v. Ferguson* Supreme Court decision which upheld the notion of "separate but equal" facilities being constitutionally acceptable. The 1954 *Brown v. Board of Education* decision ordered segregated schools to be integrated "with all deliberate speed."

Prominent in the case was Thurgood Marshall, the NAACP lawyer who argued the case in front of the U.S. Supreme Court. Marshall later became a member of the Supreme Court. The decision stipulated that the plaintiffs had been denied equal protection of the laws guaranteed by the Fourteenth Amendment. The 9–0 decision also maintained that it was illegal for a governmental power to enforce racial segregation.

This reversal of the *Plessy v. Ferguson* decision was a landmark case and had dramatic effects on the social fabric of the United States. More than any other single incident, it motivated the American civil rights movement, which created massive changes in the nation forever after.

References: Harry Ashmor, *Civil Rights and Wrongs* (New York: Pantheon Books, 1994); Ronald Takaki, *A Different Mirror: A History of Multicultural America* (Boston: Little, Brown, 1993); Joan Thrower Timm, *Four Perspectives in Multicultural Education* (Belmont, CA: Wadsworth, 1996).

BUFFALO SOLDIERS is a term used in referring to African Americans who participated in frontier Indian campaigns. Records show that they faced off against Native Americans in about 100 battles. Most of the African Americans were part of the 9th and 10th Cavalry. In addition, the 24th and 25th infantry units also included African-American troops.

Their primary task was to guard American settlers who were moving west. Despite discrimination, they had the lowest desertion rate of all American military units and also the highest re-enlistment rates. The name "Buffalo Soldiers" was given them by the Kiowa, Cheyenne, and Apache tribes who thought their dust and sweat-matted hair resembled buffalo hair.

References: Charles M. Christian, *Black Saga* (Boston: Houghton Mifflin, 1995); John Hope Franklin and Alfred A. Moss, Jr., *From Slavery to Freedom* (New York: Alfred A. Knopf, 1994); Sharon Harley, *The Timetables of African-American History* (New York: Simon and Schuster, 1995).

BUNCHE, RALPH (1904–1971) was the first African American to win the Nobel Prize. He received the award for his role in negotiating a settlement between the Arabs and Israelis the year before getting the award in 1950. After earning graduate degrees at Harvard University, he was hired by Howard University to establish a department of political science. The recipient of a Rosenwald field fellowship, he traveled through French West Africa, studying the organizational structure of Togoland. He later returned to Africa after doing postdoctoral research at Northwestern University. In 1938, he spent two years with Gunnar Myrdal. He and the Swedish sociologist published an epic work on American race relations, *An American Dilemma.*

During World War II, Bunche served in the State Department, the Office of Strategic Services, and the U.S. War Department. During the planning stages of the United Nations in San Francisco, Bunche played a prominent role for the United States interests. In 1955, he became the undersecretary for special political affairs.

However, Bunche received criticism from some African Americans for what they perceived to be a lack of involvement in the American civil rights movement, although he spent 22 years of his life as a board member for the National Association for the Advancement of Colored People (NAACP). Consequently, he began to become more directly involved in helping African-American people in their struggle for equity. He participated in civil rights marches in Selma and Montgomery.

References: Harry S. Ashmor, *Civil Rights and Wrongs* (New York: Pantheon Books, 1994); Ronald Takaki, *A Different Mirror: A History of Multicultural America* (Boston: Little, Brown, 1993).

BUREAU OF INDIAN AFFAIRS (BIA) was first created in 1824 and housed in the War Department. Transferred to the Department of the Interior in 1849, the goal of the organization was to assist Native Americans to develop to their fullest by managing their own affairs and finding ways to reach their maximum potential as human beings.

Many of the BIA's activities are directly related to education. Throughout the history of this organization, attempts have been made to help make education available to all Native Americans in public and/or BIA schools, helping Native Americans in managing their own school systems, and providing appropriate social support services.

Since the early years of the BIA, special schools for Native American children have been conducted by this body. Often, these educational attempts were severely criticized by Native American people. In fact, many of the BIA directors have been accused of attempting to force Native American youth to abandon their Native American traditions and assume the cultural values of the European-American majority.

One of the BIA directors who has been given credit for reversing some of these trends is John Collier, who was considered to have a keen understanding of Native American peoples. During his term of office, many of the Eurocentric trends were reversed.

References: Vine Deloria, Jr., *God Is Red* (New York: Dell, 1973); Barry Klein (Ed.), *Reference Encyclopedia of the American Indians*, vol. 1, 3d ed. (Rye, NY: Todd Publications, 1978); Office of Education, Department of HEW, *A Brief History of the Federal Responsibility to the American Indian* (Washington, DC: U.S. Government Printing Office, 1979); Office of the Federal Register, National Archives and Records Service, General Services Administration, *United States Government Manual, 1978/1979* (Washington, DC: U.S. Government Printing Office, 1978).

BURLINGAME TREATY was a negotiated settlement between the United States and China granting the Chinese unlimited immigration to the United States. The measure was signed by Secretary of State William Seward and Anson Burlingame. After serving as a Massachusetts senator, Burlingame became a member of Congress from 1855–1861. When Lincoln was elected to the presidency, he appointed Burlingame the U.S. Minister to China in 1861. The treaty between the two countries later assumed his name.

However, the unlimited immigration clause of the treaty strained relations between the two countries, and it was eventually rescinded with the passage of the Chinese Exclusion Act of 1822 and the Scott Act of 1888. Anti-Chinese riots in Denver, Los Angeles, and other western localities precipitated these two measures, which ended most Chinese migration to the United States for some time. Chinese laborers were perceived as a threat to European-American laborers, who were often competing in the same work forces.

References: Christine I. Bennett, *Comprehensive Multicultural Education: Theory and Practice*, 3d ed. (Boston: Allyn and Bacon, 1995); Ronald Takaki, *A Different Mirror: A History of Multicultural America* (Boston: Little, Brown, 1993).

BUSSING, also spelled ''busing'' in the multicultural literature, refers to attempts to transport children to integrated schools from the time of the *Brown v. Board of Education* Supreme Court decision to the present. The Brown decision required American schools, which were racially segregated, to become integrated ''with all deliberate speed.'' Since about half of all American school children were bus riders to school at the time of the decision, the school bus was viewed as the obvious method by which the schools could become integrated.

One of the most common strategies used in desegregating the schools was the ''pairing'' method. This model called for mixing the populations of two schools, one being predominantly African American and another consisting of predominantly European-American children. In some communities, such as Athens, Georgia, the use of the school bus for integrating children proceeded rather smoothly. However, in other locales, attempts to desegregate schools sometimes were met with hostility, demonstrations, and rioting. One such incident occurred in Arkansas with the attempt to integrate Little Rock High School. It was necessary for President Eisenhower to finally call in the 101st Airborne Infantry to replace the Arkansas National Guard units, which Governor Orville Faubus had utilized to prevent the integration of the school.

In other communities, such as Flint, Michigan, European-American parents burned busses and endangered their lives to prevent utilizing busses to integrate the schools. Bussing American children to other schools to desegregate the schools helped lead to the so-called ''white flight,'' which resulted in European-American families moving away from communities where the schools were in danger of becoming racially integrated.

References: Harry S. Ashmore, *Civil Rights and Wrongs* (New York: Pantheon Books, 1994); Bruce M. Mitchell and Robert E. Salsbury, *A Multicultural Handbook for School Administrators* (Cheney, WA: Department of Education, 1992).

C

CARLOS, JOHN (1945–) attracted national attention as a premier Olympic sprinter after he won the bronze medal for the United States in the 1968 Olympic Games. While on the victory stand with Tommy Smith, the gold medal winner, he raised a clenched fist skyward during the playing of the national anthem. The gesture served to illustrate the inequalities that afflicted African Americans and became known as the ''clenched-fist salute.''

This gesture became a symbol that was used by persons of color throughout the remainder of the American Civil Rights Movement. The criticism was that persons of color had been persecuted in a variety of ways throughout American history. The clenched fist salute was a way of attracting attention to the problems that existed. The clenched fist salute became an icon for the protest movements during the American Civil Rights era. An understanding of the civil rights era is a basic educational necessity if students are to acquire accurate perceptions about the value of America's pluralistic macroculture.

Reference: Bruce M. Mitchell, et al., *The Dynamic Classroom*, 5th ed. (Dubuque, IA: Kendall/Hunt, 1995).

CARMICHAEL, STOKELY (Kwame Ture, 1941–1998), an important figure during the American Civil Rights movement, attracted national attention for his rhetoric about black power. European Americans were largely convinced that his concept referred to violent, militant actions on the part of African Americans. However, Carmichael was convinced that African Americans needed to control their own destiny through the establishment of economic power and political activity in which they could assume positions of power.

President of the Student Non-violent Coordinating Committee (SNCC), he changed his name to Kwame Ture. Actively involved in the march on Selma, Carmichael was convinced that African Americans needed to overcome their fear of European Americans. He organized a number of civil rights activities in southern European-American strongholds in such areas as Lowndes County in Alabama. He was instrumental in establishing the Lowndes County Freedom Organization, which initiated an aggressive program designed to get African Americans elected to political offices. He died in Guinea in 1998.

Understanding Carmichael's work will help students to become fully functional, literate citizens through understanding race and ethnicity in American society.

References: Clayborn Carson, et al., *Eyes on the Prize: Civil Rights Reader* (New York: Penguin Books, 1991); John Hope Franklin and Alfred A. Moss, *From Slavery to Freedom* (McGraw-Hill, 1994); David Hilliard and Lewis Cole, *This Side of Glory* (Boston: Little, Brown, 1993).

CARPETBAGGERS were northern politicians and adventurers who went to the South in order to secure political advantages after the end of the American Civil War. They were able to acquire political positions because of their ability to attract the votes of freed slaves and low-income European Americans. Most historians painted them as being incompetent, wasteful, and corrupt. Eventually they were driven out because of a loss of voting support. Terrorist activities by the Ku Klux Klan were successful in denying freed slaves the right to vote. The issue of voting in a participatory democracy is a key factor in the U.S. social studies curriculum.

References: Allan Nevis and Henry Steele Commager, *America: The Story of a Free People* (Boston: Little, Brown, 1942).

CARVER, GEORGE WASHINGTON (1888–1949), born in slavery on a plantation belonging to Moses Carver in Missouri, was seized along with his mother during the Civil War and taken to Arkansas. Weakened from whooping cough, he was allowed to roam the woods by his new owner. His travels through the forests helped him to develop his consuming interest in plants and flowers. His work attracted a great deal of attention because of his ability to make difficult plants grow and prosper. A deeply religious man, he also gained a reputation as an outstanding singer.

He received his degree at Iowa State University in Ames, where he was eventually appointed to the faculty as a botany instructor in the Horticulture Department. He was also placed in charge of the University's greenhouses.

His next stop was the Tuskegee Institute where he worked with Booker T. Washington. He developed a strong loyalty to that school and refused other lucrative offers. As an agricultural chemist, his research on the peanut and sweet potato brought a large number of major changes in southern farming. In 1896,

Booker T. Washington persuaded the Alabama legislature to pass enabling legislation for the establishment of the Tuskegee Experimental Station. Later, Carver became its director. His creative mind and his scientific knowledge helped him enhance the reputation of the Tuskegee Institute.

Reference: Basil Mathews, *Booker T. Washington* (College Park, MD: McGrath, 1969).

CASTE originally referred to any of the Indian social classes into which Hindus were divided. The social rank is usually defined by descent, marriage, and occupation. The concept is deeply ingrained in Indian history and dictates the types of social interactions people are able to have. The word is of Spanish origin and means "race," "breed," or "lineage." India's top caste is the Brahmans (priests and warriors), followed by the Kshatriyas (warriors and rulers), Vaisyas (merchants, traders, and farmers), and the Sudras (artisans, laborers, servants, and slaves). Caste members usually marry within their own group. In fact, women who marry below their own caste can be excommunicated.

Due to the efforts of Mohandas K. Gandhi, the caste system in India has undergone many changes during the last four decades. Also, the Indian government has made an effort to abolish caste rituals, remove legal restrictions on untouchables, and promote the general welfare of the lower castes.

While the normal caste system has flourished in India throughout the country's history, other nations have been accused of having quasi-caste systems. For example, in the United States one of the civil rights issues pertained to equity in social programs and economic endeavors regardless of race, gender, ethnicity, or income level.

Reference: Ved Mahta, *Mahatma and His Apostles* (New York: Viking Press, 1976).

CASTRO, FIDEL (1927–), born on a Cuban farm in 1926, received a law degree from the University of Havana in 1950. During his early years, he was greatly opposed to the regime of Juan Batista. After a failed attack on the Moncada army barracks in 1953, he received a fifteen-year sentence but was given amnesty by Batista in 1955 with the provision that he leave the country. He was exiled to Mexico where he formulated a plan for the overthrow of Batista. He returned to Cuba, established a revolutionary army with Che Guevara (a revolutionary from Argentina), and succeeded in overthrowing the Batista regime in 1959. Two years later, he declared himself to be a Marxist/Leninist.

Shortly after his victory, he allied himself with Nikita Kruschev, the Russian leader, and received substantial military aid from that country. Kruschev was anxious to establish a military presence in the backyard of the United States. The alliance evolved into a dangerous missile crisis when the Russians attempted to introduce nuclear warheads into the Cuban defense system. President Kennedy blockaded the island, resulting in the withdrawal of offensive missiles.

Castro placed a great deal of attention on the country's educational system, which resulted in one of the highest literacy rates in Latin America. Twenty-five percent of the nation's annual budget went to education and health services. This policy reversed the Batista policies that made health care almost non-existent for low-income persons.

References: Himilce Novas, *Everything You Need to Know About Latino History* (New York: Penguin Books, 1994); Earl Shorris, *Latinos: A Biography of the People* (New York: W. W. Norton, 1992).

CASTRO, SAL was the leader of a 1968 student walkout at Garfield High School in East Los Angeles. A teacher in the Los Angeles Unified School District, Castro was protesting what he perceived to be inadequate educational offerings for Latino students in East Los Angeles high schools. The walkouts coincided with the issuance of the Kerner Commission report, which stipulated that white racism was the main cause of race riots in American cities.

A list of demands was issued to the Los Angeles Unified School District. Included in the demands was bilingual/bicultural education. The feeling was that Latino students needed to learn more about their own culture. Another of the demands pertained to a perception that the European-American teachers had little knowledge of and even negative attitudes toward their Latino culture.

Reference: Earl Shorris, *Latinos: A Biography of the People* (New York: W. W. Norton, 1992).

CHAVEZ, CESAR (1927–1993), the son of a migrant farm worker, moved to California during the Great Depression, picking carrots and cotton whenever he was able to locate employment. He attended 65 elementary schools as a result of being in the migrant stream. Eventually, he settled in Delano, California, after serving in the United States Navy. He became involved in politics as a result of his participation in the Community Service Organization (CSO). His activities in the CSO included voter registration for farm workers.

He became active in organizing migrant farm workers in California and establishing the National Farm Workers Association, which later became affiliated with the AFL-CIO. By 1965, the Chavez Union had become successful in persuading two of the major growers in Delano to raise the wages of their farm laborers. He also organized a march to Sacramento to protest the problems encountered by migrant farm workers during Ronald Reagan's terms of office.

Chavez adapted the non-violent protest strategies of Gandhi and Martin Luther King, Jr. He organized grape boycotts, a five-year strike (*la huelga*), and participated in several hunger strikes in hopes of improving the working conditions of migrant farm laborers. Finally, in 1970, a number of California grape growers signed a contract that improved wages and working conditions for farm workers.

Throughout the years, he became the symbolic leader of Latino people *(la raza)*, although he was viewed as a major problem by political conservatives and agricultural corporations in California. In addition to helping improve the salaries of farm workers, the Chavez Union turned its attention to the improvement of working conditions. Successful efforts included the requirements that field toilets be provided along with shaded rest areas and safer pesticide usage. Chavez died at the age of 66 in 1993.

References: L. H. Gann and Peter J. Duignan, *The Hispanics in the United States: A History* (Boulder, CO: Westview Press, 1986); Himilce Novas, *Everything You Need to Know About Latino History* (New York: Penguin Books, 1991); Earl Shorris, *Latinos: A Biography of the People* (New York: W. W. Norton, 1992).

CHEROKEE TRIBE, a member of the Eastern Woodland Tribes, is the largest member of that group. At the time of their first encounters with European Americans, their population was estimated at about 25,000. Because of these early interactions with Europeans, the Cherokees acquired many of the European traditions and utilized a syllabary, invented by Sequoyah, that enabled them to read their own language. Thus, they became one of the first literate tribes in the United States. This helped foster a unity among the various Cherokee factions.

The Cherokees sided with the United States during the War of 1812. Fighting in Alabama were the Creeks, one of their traditional enemies. During the battle at Horseshoe Bend, Yonaguska, who became a Cherokee chief, saved the life of Andrew Jackson, who later became president of the United States.

However, due to the demands for land by European Americans, Congress passed the Indian Removal Act of 1830, which allowed the government to relocate the Cherokee tribe to areas west of the Mississippi River. Another reason for passing this legislation was the discovery of gold on the Cherokee land. This action became known as the Cherokee Trail of Tears.

Presently, Oklahoma has the largest number of registered Cherokee members with more than 90,000 people. California has nearly 44,000 with Texas (15,721), Florida (9,918), and Michigan (8,907) being the other large-population states.

References: Leonard Dinnerstein, et al., *Natives and Strangers* (Oxford: Oxford University Press, 1990); Harvey Markowitz (Ed.), *American Indians* (Pasadena, CA: Salem Press, 1995); Ronald Takaki, *A Different Mirror: A History of Multicultural America* (Boston: Little, Brown, 1993).

CHICANO is a term that has been used in referring to Latinos. Some historians have argued that the term dates back to the first Spanish interests in occupied Mexico. When the Spaniards arrived, the native residents called their land ''Meshico'' and the Spaniards referred to them as ''Meshicanos.'' Eventually, the term was pronounced ''Mechicano,'' which finally became ''Chicano.''

However, during the American Civil Rights Movement, the term ''Chicano'' acquired a special significance. Eventually, the term became associated with Latino people, who were involved in and/or sympathetic to causes designed to improve the welfare of Latino people. The term usually implies that a person is sympathetic to the Mexican-American macroculture and is somehow involved in the attempt to enhance liberty, freedom, justice, and equal educational opportunities for all Chicanos.

Not all Latino people prefer to be called "Chicanos." For example, some Spanish-speaking people of northern Colorado may prefer to be called "Espanoles" because of their direct linkage with Spain. People from Cuba may wish to be referred to as "Cubanos" or Cuban Americans. Consequently, it can be seen that the term "Chicano" may not be an accurate term to use when referring to all Latino people.

References: Newlon Clark, *Famous Mexican Americans* (New York: Dodd, Mead, 1968); Ernesto Flores, *The Nature of Leadership for Hispanics and Other Minorities* (Saratoga, CA: Century Twenty-One, 1981); L. H. Gann and Peter J. Duignan, *The Hispanics in the United States: A History* (Boulder, CO: Westview Press, 1986); Himilce Novas, *Everything You Needed to Know About Chicano History* (New York: Penguin Books, 1994); Earl Shorris, *Latinos: A Biography of the People* (New York: W. W. Norton, 1992).

CHICANO MOVEMENT is a concept relating to the civil rights efforts on behalf of Latinos. Motivated by Martin Luther King's efforts during the earlier stages of the American Civil Rights Movement, the Chicano movement became active during the mid-1960s, largely due to the efforts of Cesar Chavez, who fought for the development of the farm workers union. While European Americans sometimes perceived the Chicano movement to be a violent one, Cesar Chavez used the non-violent protest tactics of Ghandi and King. While Chavez has generally been viewed as the inspirational leader of the Chicano movement, other Latinos also played major roles.

Rodolfo "Corky" Gonzalez, a professional boxer, was active in Denver where he founded the Crusade for Justice and authored a classic poem titled *Yo Soy Joaquin*, which helped motivate Latino youth to seek an education and improve their lives. Gonzalez created a motto, "*venceremos,*" meaning "we shall overcome." He was active in trying to improve the education of Latino children, helped develop better health and education programs, and assisted in providing legal aid and employment opportunities for Latinos.

Another activist in the Chicano movement was a Texan, Jose Angel Gutierrez, who established a political party called La Raza Unida, which attempted to end discrimination against Latinos by becoming actively involved in the political system. One of La Raza's key goals was to improve the percentage of Latino children to achieve a higher level of success in the schools.

References: L. H. Gann and Peter J. Duignan, *The Hispanics in the United States: A History* (Boulder, CO: Westview Press, 1986); Earl Shorris, *Latinos: A Biography of the People* (New York: W. W. Norton, 1992).

CHINESE AMERICANS, first arriving in the United States to work in the mines during the California gold rush, became one of the United States' most important laboring forces. By 1870, their numbers had increased to 63,000, and most of them resided in California. During the early days of their residence in California, they had to pay a foreign miner's tax which accounted for between 25 and 50 percent of the state's taxes. The tax was voided by the state's 1870 Civil Rights Act.

Eventually, the mining profits decreased and the Chinese Americans left. However, Charlie Crocker of the Central Pacific Railroad commenced hiring them to work on the transcontinental railroad. Spurred on by Leland Stanford, president, Crocker ended up hiring 12,000 Chinese laborers who constituted about 90 percent of the entire work force. They toiled under excruciating conditions, including the notorious winter of 1866, during which time 60-foot snow drifts plagued the laborers as they scratched and crawled their way through the Sierra. The completion of the line through the Sierra was definitely a Chinese-American victory.

Following the completion of the rail lines, the Chinese Americans returned to San Francisco and to California's agricultural industry. They constructed dikes, ditches, and irrigation canals in the San Joaquin and Sacramento deltas. Many Chinese people opened wash houses and laundries because to do so required a relatively small amount of capital. However, eventually they were perceived as a threat to white laborers and several ugly anti-Chinese riots occurred in San Francisco and Los Angeles.

These activities led to the enactment of the Chinese Exclusion Act of 1882, which greatly reduced the supply of farm labor in the Pacific states, particularly California. The Act was later repealed. Throughout the history of the United States, Chinese Americans have played a significant role. In addition to their involvement in mining, railroading, and agriculture, Chinese Americans took an active role during World War II and have become actively involved in the formation of tongs, organizations composed of family and village members. In addition, Chinese Americans created their own communities and celebrated traditional holidays, thus keeping their microcultural values intact. Ultimately, the *Lau v. Nichols* Supreme Court decision involved a Chinese-American student. See *LAU v. NICHOLS.*

References: Leonard Dinnerstein, et al., *Natives and Strangers* (Oxford: Oxford University Press, 1990); Robert M. Jiobu, *Ethnicity and Assimilation* (Albany: State University of New York Press, 1988) Ronald Takaki, *A Different Mirror: A History of Multicultural America* (Boston: Little, Brown, 1993).

CHINESE EXCLUSION ACT, occurring in 1882, was an act of Congress that resulted in the first U.S. immigration bill designed to exclude a particular race. Many Americans viewed the immigration of Chinese people to be different from the immigration of Europeans. But the action served to exacerbate the anti-foreigner attitudes of many American people.

The Chinese Exclusion Act was motivated by a growing anti-Chinese attitude in the western parts of the United States. Toward the end of the nineteenth century, many European-American and African-American laborers viewed the Chinese immigrants as a threat to their acquisition of suitable employment. Moreover, since the Chinese Americans were not Christians, they were often viewed as not being worthy to be called "Americans." The Chinese Exclusion Act was eventually repealed when anti-Japanese sentiment intended to paint the Chinese-American population in a more favorable light. Textbooks with a positive multicultural focus are still attempting to help students acquire a more positive perception about this microculture.

References: James A. Banks, *Teaching Strategies for Ethnic Studies*, 6th ed. (Boston: Allyn and Bacon, 1997); Joan Thrower Timm, *Four Perspectives in Multicultural Education* (Belmont, CA: Wadsworth, 1996).

CHOCTAW TRIBE was located in present-day Mississippi, Arkansas, and Alabama. Compared to other tribes, they were rather quick to acquire many of the cultural traits of European Americans. As a result of the Removal Act of 1830, they were relocated to Indian Territory (Oklahoma) in 1831 and 1833. The 1990 census listed the Choctaws as having a population of over 82,200 people, making them the fifth largest tribe in the United States.

At the present time, the tribal headquarters of the Choctaws are located at Durant, Mississippi. The tribal lands and businesses of the Choctaw people provide fine examples of sophisticated farming techniques and many industrial developments. The tribal members have long prided themselves on their intellectual and educational pursuits. Helping students acquire valid concepts about the Native American tribes is a crucial component of multicultural education for students of all ages.

References: Angie Debo, *The Rise and Fall of the Choctaw Republic* (Norman: University of Oklahoma Press, 1934); Arthur DeRosier, Jr., *The Removal of the Choctaw Indians* (Knoxville: University of Tennessee Press, 1970); James D. Morrison, *The Social History of the Choctaw Nation, 1865–1907* (Durant, OK: Creative Informatics, 1987).

CHURCH–STATE RELATIONS IN EDUCATION, often referred to as the separation of church and state, has become one of the most volatile issues in American education since the writing of the U.S. Constitution. The Establishment Clause of the United States Constitution provides that "Congress shall make no law respecting an establishment of religion." This clause, through the Fourteenth Amendment, clearly extends to school districts and universities.

Throughout the years, this clause has related to such issues as prayer in the schools and religious instruction. In *Lemon v. Kurtzman*, 403 U.S. 602, 91 S.Ct.

2105, 29 L.Ed.2d 745 (1971), a three-part test was established for determining whether governmental practices or enactments violate the Establishment Clause. This "Lemon Test" requires that any government practice or requirement must have a secular reason, its basic principles must not advance or inhibit religion, and it must not motivate any excessive government involvement with religion.

Consequently, the issue of organized prayers in the schools has been declared to be clearly unconstitutional by virtue of *Wallace v. Jaffree* (1985), *Steele v. Van Buren Public School District* (1988), and *Doe v. Duncanville Independent School District* (1993). These court cases related to all phases of school activity, including both in-school and out-of-school events. However, it should be noted that these court decisions only relate to organized prayers. Students, like all other American citizens, are entitled to pray whenever and wherever they wish.

The U.S. Constitution, as interpreted by court decisions, has also declared other religious activities to be unconstitutional in public schools. Some of these unconstitutional acts include religious activities such as religious choirs (*Sease v. School District of Philadelphia*, 1993), the "Creationism Act" (*Edwards v. Aguillard*, 1993), and use of textbooks that might conflict with students' religious beliefs (*Mozert v. Hawkins County Board of Education*, 1987) and (*Grove v. Mead School District*, 1985). However, the courts have ruled that studying about religion is constitutionally acceptable. But religious exercises, rituals, and celebrations are against the law. Also, a Virginia case ruled that public funds could be used on a limited basis to publish religious materials in the schools.

Thus, it can be seen that the United States judicial system has continuously ruled in favor of the separation of church and state clause, as stipulated in the Fourteenth Amendment to the U.S. Constitution.

References: Alexander Kern and M. David, *American Public School Law* (Belmont, CA: Wadsworth, 1998); Data Research, *Deskbook Encyclopedia of American School Law* (Rosemount, MN: Data Research, 1994); Louis Fischer, et al., *Teachers Law* (White Plains, NY: Longman, 1995).

CINCO DE MAYO, meaning "fifth of May" in Spanish, refers to the victory over the invading Napoleonic forces by General Zaragosa in 1862. It was one of the major victories in Mexico's history and helped the country on its road to becoming a fully independent nation. The battle, occurring at Pueblo, Mexico, was a significant event in the country's struggle for independence.

Since that time, it has become an important event in Mexican-American communities in the United States and is celebrated with fiestas, parades, dancing, and many other activities. In the schools, it has often become a major part of the multicultural curriculum and provides all students with the opportunity of learning to appreciate the rich Latino microcultures that have become so important in the United States.

References: Pamela L. Tiedt and Iris M. Tiedt, *Multicultural Teaching* (Boston: Allyn and Bacon, 1995).

CIVIL RIGHTS ACT OF 1964 was a Congressional act stipulating that federal funds cannot be expended on enterprises where there is discrimination on the basis of race. It terminated the federal funding for schools and/or school districts that were racially segregated. The act was passed during the presidency of Lyndon Johnson, who was instrumental in moving the measure through the House of Representatives (290 to 130) and the Senate (73 to 27).

The Civil Rights Act of 1964 had the effect of adding legislative clout to the 1954 *Brown v. the Board of Education* Supreme Court decision. In addition to ending federal funding for racially segregated school districts, it also authorized the federal government to initiate legal action against school districts that refused to become racially integrated.

References: Harry S. Ashmore, *Civil Rights and Wrongs* (New York: Pantheon Books, 1994); James A. Johnson, et al., *Introduction to the Foundations of American Education* (Boston: Allyn and Bacon, 1996); Perry A. Zirkel, *Supreme Court Decision* (Bloomington, IN: Phi Delta Kappa Educational Foundation, 1988).

CIVIL RIGHTS MOVEMENT, perhaps more than any other series of American events, changed the social fabric for years to come. Motivated by the *Brown v. Board of Education* Supreme Court decision and the Civil Rights Act of 1964, the American Civil Rights movement is commonly thought to have occurred from the mid-1950s through the mid-1970s. However, some historians argue that it can also be traced back to the early part of the twentieth century when W.E.B. Du Bois started the Niagara Movement, an attempt to help African Americans acquire civil rights in American institutions. The movement later evolved into the National Association for the Advancement of Colored People (NAACP).

The Civil Rights Movement, which began shortly after the mid-century, addressed issues such as voter registration for persons of color, the termination of segregated schools, fair housing and other public and private social institutions, the war on poverty, the termination of the "melting pot" philosophy, and bilingual/bicultural education in the schools.

It was a period of non-violent protest marches led by such civil rights leaders as Martin Luther King, Jr. and Cesar Chavez, and ugly riots such as those which occurred in Watts, California. It was necessary to utilize the Arkansas National Guard and the 101st Airborne Infantry to safely escort African-American children to Little Rock High School over the protests of Governor Orville Faubus. In Flint, Michigan, parents chained themselves to school busses to prevent school integration, and students in East Los Angeles walked out of their high schools, presenting the Board of Trustees with a list of demands.

The Civil Rights Movement peaked during the Vietnam War when many Americans argued that the country's involvement in the confrontation was immoral, unwarranted, and even unconstitutional. The numerous incidents during that period of time were instrumental in persuading President Lyndon Johnson to reject a run for re-election to the presidency. And toward the end of the Movement, President Richard Nixon became the first president to resign from office.

References: Clayborne Carson, et al., *Eyes on the Prize: Civil Rights Reader* (New York: Penguin Books, 1991); John Hope Franklin, *From Slavery to Freedom* (New York: Alfred A. Knopf, 1994).

CIVIL WAR (UNITED STATES), sometimes referred to as the War Between the States, began in January 9, 1861 when the *Star of the West* attempted to reinforce the Sumter Garrison at Charleston, South Carolina. The ship was also attempting to land 200 more troops, and when fired upon, it was forced to retreat. The incident triggered the bloody war which ended up taking the lives of more than 600,000 Americans, most of them from the northern states.

At the time of the initial confrontation, there was no thought of the incident evolving into the resulting four-year battle. As young men fired at each other with fury, the real reasons for the war were not often clear but the bitterness acquired through the various confrontations would have a major effect on the nation as a whole for years to come. Soon after the Fort Sumter incident, the states of Florida, South Carolina, Mississippi, Georgia, Texas, and Louisiana seceded from the Union and eventually formed the Confederate States of America.

Abraham Lincoln, the newly elected president, was firm in his commitment to maintain the Union. He believed that the real object of the secessionists was to change the nature of the American government. Lincoln also knew that any attempts to spread slavery into the areas that were not yet states would alienate the party which had elected him.

Since the battles were fought mostly in the South, the terrible losses inflicted by Generals Sheridan and Sherman did enormous damage to the southern states and the ensuing destitution resulted in the creation of an enormous poverty culture among southern European Americans and freed slaves. The Confederate soldiers returned to ruined towns, hunger, and major suffering. Moreover, the war obliterated the educational system in the South, resulting in rapidly increasing illiteracy among European Americans. But the lack of education among freed slaves was also acute. Since the slave states demanded that African Americans be kept illiterate, African-American children were at severe risk and remained so, even during the Reconstruction Period.

References: David Herbert Donald, *Lincoln* (London: Jonathan Cape, 1995); S. Alexander Rippa, *Education in a Free Society* (New York: Longman, 1992).

CLARK, KENNETH (1914–), a psychologist, was a key figure in the unanimous Supreme Court decision in *Brown v. Topeka Board of Education.* Kenneth Clark's research pertained to the issue of how prejudice and discrimination affects the personality development of children. His testimony in the *Brown v.*

Board of Education trial related to his clinical studies of children that focused on the issue of racial preferences in young children.

Clark's studies were done with racially different dolls. Specifically, Clark asked his young subjects to choose among dolls. Seventy-five percent of the young subjects, between 3 and 7 years of age, were conscious of the differences in "white" and "colored" dolls. Moreover, when African-American children were asked about their racial preferences, a statistically significant number of African-American children preferred the white doll over the brown doll. The results of the study were significant in leading to the decision in the *Brown v. Topeka Board of Education* case.

Reference: Kenneth B. Clark, *Prejudice and Your Child* (Boston: Beacon Press, 1955).

CO-FIGURATIVE CULTURE is a concept that focuses attention on the present. People in the same generation share their values, mores, and basic understandings and make an attempt to adapt to the constant changes that confront human beings. The concept also refers to situations in which people from one culture come into contact with persons from another culture or when persons move to a new location where the dominant culture is different from their own.

For example, African Americans came to the United States against their will, finding themselves in contact with European Americans who spoke another language and had different religious values and world views. In order to survive, the African slaves were forced to adapt to a brand new situation. Thus, it can be seen that the phrase also related to the manner in which human beings must change to survive in changing circumstances.

Reference: Joan Thrower Timm, *Four Perspectives in Multicultural Education* (Belmont, CA: Wadsworth, 1996).

COLEMAN REPORT, published in 1969, related to the issue of equality in education. The report, titled *Equality of Educational Opportunity*, was an important document that was often quoted in the American debate between equity and excellence in education. The document was partially a response to the nagging question of the meaning of a popular slogan, "equality of educational opportunity," which is a constitutional guarantee for all American children.

Section 402 of the Civil Rights Act of 1964 directed the U.S. Commissioner of Education to conduct a survey concerning the lack of availability of equal educational opportunities for students by virtue of their race, color, religion, or national origin. The report had to be made to the President of the United States and the U.S. Congress.

Among other things, the Coleman Report declared that in the 1960s the concept of equality of educational opportunity changed from school resource inputs to the effects of the schooling process itself. Thus, the report argued that the emphasis should be on the equality of students' achievement rather than equality in the distribution of educational resources.

Reference: James S. Coleman, "The Concept of Equality of Educational Opportunity," *Harvard Educational Review* (Cambridge, MA: Board of Editors, Equal Educational Opportunity, 1969).

COLLIER, JOHN (1884–1968) was appointed by Franklin Roosevelt to become the Indian Affairs Commissioner. When he took over his duties, the Allotment Program was in effect. Since the passage of the Dawes Act, also referred to as the Indian Emancipation Act, Native Americans were urged to assimilate and become part of the European American macroculture. However, Collier created the Indian Reorganization Act. He admired the sense of community he found among the Native American tribes of New Mexico and felt that European Americans could learn a great deal from them.

Collier believed that the allotment concept was destroying the Native American communal way of life. In addition to becoming an enormous land grab for European Americans, breaking tribal lands into individual holdings through the Allotment Program was a blow to Native American tribal existence. Moreover, he believed that the allotment strategy was a deliberate plan by conservative European Americans to terminate Native American tribal existence. In short, Collier believed strongly that government policy should attempt to help Native Americans establish workable systems of self-government and preserve the Native American microcultural value systems. He felt that this could be accomplished by ending the allotment system. President Roosevelt signed the Allotment Act in 1934.

References: Frederick E. Hoxie, *A Final Promise: The Campaign to Assimilate the Indians, 1880 to 1920* (Lincoln: University of Nebraska Press, 1984); Harvey Markowitz (Consulting Ed.), *American Indians*, Vol. 1 (Pasadena, CA: Salem Press, 1995).

***COLONIA*,** the Spanish word for "colony," originally referred to communities of Mexican refugees who had left their country and were traveling to major United States cities. Later, the term acquired a more permanent flavor when residents of *colonias* settled in locales which were primarily residential areas for persons who had jobs in nearby communities.

Over the years, the term *barrio* was used when referring to communities in which large populations of Mexican Americans and Latinos resided. Sometimes, the two terms tend to be used interchangeably. The *colonias* provide people with a community of common ethnic characteristics where many Latino people choose to live.

One example of a *colonia* is La Colonia of Oxnard, California. Located in Southern California, just a few miles from the Pacific Ocean, La Colonia is a Spanish speaking, largely Catholic community. Considered to have a large proportion of low-income residents, people from La Colonia are employed in the nearby agricultural industries and hold other jobs in nearby communities. La Colonia provides its Latino residents with an environment which many people are reluctant to leave, even when they could become upwardly mobile from an economic standpoint. Educationally, students from such *barrios* tend to struggle, due to poverty and language factors.

Reference: Himilce Novas, *Everything You Wanted to Know About Latino History* (New York: Penguin Books, 1994).

COLORED, originally a non-derogatory term for referring to African Americans, the word became viewed as "less-than positive" after the American Civil Rights Movement. The term was actively used in entertainment circles when it was necessary to identify African-American people. Sometimes it would be used in titles; many groups and publications actually had the term "colored" in the title. One example is the National Association for the Advancement of Colored People (NAACP), a group responsible for improving civil rights for African Americans.

During the American Civil Rights era, some African-American leaders avoided use of the term, feeling that it was condescending at best and blatantly racist at its worst. However, the term later became used in the phrase "persons of color," which referred to anyone who was not of the "Caucasian" race. At this time in history, many African-American leaders argued for using the term "Black" as a means of identifying African Americans. In fact, the phrase "Black is beautiful" became popular as a means of helping young African-American people develop a higher level of pride about their race.

However, it has also been argued that the use of color as a means of referring to racial background is inaccurate, since few human beings are truly "black" or "white." Consequently, writers have often attempted to use the original place of origin for immigrating groups of people, such as "Mexican American," "African Canadian," or "Portuguese Brazilian."

COMANCHE TRIBE, an offshoot of the Shoshone Tribe, originally resided in present-day Texas, New Mexico, Oklahoma, Kansas, and Colorado. According to tribal legends, they split off from the Shoshones who ended up in the Wyoming and Montana mountains. The 1990 census revealed that there are 11,322 Comanches residing in the United States.

Because of their equestrian prowess, the Comanches controlled a large section of land. In the eighteenth century, they became allies of the Kiowas, another tribe with outstanding military horsemanship. Their main enemies were the Apaches, Osages, Navajos, Pawnees, and Utes. Comanche bands had secret societies for men, and the tribal deities were a Creator, the Sun, Earth, and Moon.

The Comanche weapons included strong buffalo-hide battle shields, long war lances, heavy war clubs, and bows and arrows. They were viewed as fierce warriors. The resistance against the United States ended in 1875. The Oklahoma Indian Welfare Act finally dealt with some of the tribal grievances against the U.S. government. Comanches have started a number of successful businesses, and the Tribe is also working hard to keep their cultural traditions intact.

References: William T. Hagen, *United States–Comanche Relations: The Reservation Years* (New Haven, CT: Yale University Press, 1976); Ernest Wallace and E. Adamson Hoebel, *The Comanches: Lords of the South Plains* (Norman: University of Oklahoma Press, 1952).

COMPENSATORY EDUCATION, a term that originated during the American Civil Rights Movement, refers to any educational programs designed to compensate young students for various deficiencies, which might result in a student not having access to equal educational opportunities, a Constitutional guarantee for all American school children. The deficiencies were thought to be a result of the poverty circumstances they may have encountered in their formative years.

The concept was discussed in James B. Conant's book, *Slums and Suburbs: A Commentary on Schools in Metropolitan Areas*, published in 1961. He argued that severe problems in the major cities would occur as a result of the ''white flight'' to the suburbs as a result of the *Brown v. Topeka Board of Education* U.S. Supreme Court decision. This action made it necessary to provide transportation to schools other than the child's neighborhood, in some cases.

Examples of compensatory programs are Headstart and bilingual education, along with the school lunch and breakfast programs.

Reference: James B. Conant, *Slums and Suburbs: A Commentary on Schools in Metropolitan Areas* (New York: McGraw-Hill, 1961).

CONFUCIANISM, one of the great religions of China, became the official philosophy of China during the Han Dynasty from 206 B.C.–220 A.D. Confucius never thought of himself as being the originator of a religious philosophy. The founder of the Han Dynasty, Emperor Kao Tsu, visited Confucius' tomb and offered sacrifices. When Chinese laborers were recruited to work in U.S. mines and railroads, many of them brought their philosophy of humanity to the United States. The philosophy was also part of the Korean-American culture as a result of their emigration from Asia.

While it has been argued that Confucianism is not really a true ''religion,'' it has devised five moral codes governing human relationships: intimacy between father and son; orders between elders and children; loyalty between the king and the subject; distinction in duties between husband and wife; and faith between friends.

References: Harold Chu, "The Korean Learner in an American School," in Edward L. Lake (Ed.), *Teaching for Cross-Cultural Understanding* (Arlington, VA: Arlington Public Schools, 1978); Carl L. Grant (Ed.), *An Anthology of Multicultural Voices* (Boston: Allyn and Bacon, 1995).

CONGRESS OF RACIAL EQUALITY (CORE) is a northern anti-discrimination organization which became prominent during the American Civil Rights Movement. CORE became quite well-known under the leadership of James Farmer, an African-American Quaker pacifist. One of the well-publicized activities of CORE was their participation in the Freedom Riders, who challenged the Jim Crow laws and behaviors south of the Mason–Dixon line in the South.

The organization had its roots in the North and originally was composed of interracial members. However, a faction of African-American members eventually was successful in forcing the resignation of Farmer, who refused to purge CORE of its European-American officials and board members. A study of CORE is a necessary portion of America's multicultural history.

Reference: Harry Ashmore, *Civil Rights and Wrongs* (New York: Random House, 1994).

CONNOR, EUGENE (BULL) was a Public Safety Commissioner from Birmingham, Alabama, who was determined to maintain the southern segregationist ideals during the Civil Rights episodes of the 1960s. During the spring of 1962, African-American students in Birmingham and the Alabama Christian Movement for Human Rights (ACMHR) staged a selective buying program against the downtown stores, which eventually had a major economic effect on those entrepreneurial enterprises. They demanded the desegregation of public institutions, as well as the increased employment of African-American clerks. Connor retaliated against the boycott by cutting off the city relief payments, most of which went to low-income African Americans.

During the Birmingham, Alabama, marches emanating from the 16th Street Baptist Church, Bull Connor ordered that police dogs be turned loose against the assembly. He also ordered the fire department to turn fire hoses against the marchers. Martin Luther King, Jr. was successful in encouraging the protesters to continue the crusade.

Reference: Clayborn Carson, et al., *Eyes on the Prize: Civil Rights Reader* (New York: Penguin Books, 1991).

CONSERVATISM is a term describeing a philosophical position that attempts to keep things as they were. During the American Civil Rights Movement, the term related to a philosophy not committed to achieving the kinds of social changes that were sought. Specifically, conservative organizations often fought against efforts to acquire equity in various educational endeavors, including the abolishment of segregated schools.

Religious conservatives have often taken strong stands against multicultural educational programs that attempted to address issues of equity and the empowerment of persons of color. Moreover, ''Christian'' conservatives have also fought for the institution of prayer and religious instruction in the public schools, practices that are forbidden under the separation of church and state clause of the U.S. Constitution. Moreover, religious right organizations have attempted to initiate legislation allowing parents to receive ''vouchers'' which they could use to send their children to private schools without paying special tuitions. Public school educators argue that such actions might result in the demise of the American public school system.

COOPERATIVE LEARNING, an organizational scheme for classroom instruction, was popularized during the 1980s and early 1990s. Based on the premise that ''all of us are smarter than one of us,'' it is a cooperation model which requires students to pool their intellectual resources to solve educational problems. The research has shown it to be quite successful as a strategy for improving the educational performance of ''at risk'' children.

The learning groups are structured to ensure they are equal in terms of collective intellectual talent. Moreover, they are organized so that racial and ethnic diversity exists in each group. Consequently, students from diverse groups learn to cooperate to solve problems, resulting in more positive attitudes about pluralism. This organizational strategy has been criticized by the religious right on the grounds that it inhibits individual competition because of the cooperation philosophy.

References: David Johnson, *Learning Together and Alone* (Englewood Cliffs, NJ: Prentice-Hall, 1986); Richard Slavin, *Cooperative Learning: Student Teams* (Washington, DC: National Education Association, 1987); Richard Slavin, ''Cooperative Learning and Student Achievement,'' *Educational Leadership* (October 1988).

CROCKER, CHARLES (1822–1888) was one of the key entrepreneurs involved in the construction of the Central Pacific Railroad, the western segment of the transcontinental line leading east from Sacramento, California. Crocker left his home in New York to try his hand in the gold fields after the 1849 strike in California. In partnership with Colis Huntington, Mark Hopkins and Leland Stanford, Crocker was successful in recruiting more than 12,000 Chinese laborers, mostly from Kwangtung Province. By paying these laborers $31 per month, the Central Pacific Railroad line was able to save enormous amounts in its labor costs.

However, despite Crocker's enthusiasm about the performance of his Chinese recruits, he never intended for them to become citizens of the United States. He argued that the use of Chinese laborers would upgrade the white laborers. Moreover, he proposed that the more intelligent of the white laborers would become foremen and directors.

Unfortunately, the utilization of Chinese laborers caused many problems. Sometimes the racial characteristics previously assigned to African Americans were given to the Chinese Americans. Chinese laborers were often described as heathen, morally inferior, savage, and lustful. They were also thought to be a threat to European-American laborers, thus creating a condition for racial strife.

References: Irving Stone, *Men to Match My Mountain* (Garden City, NY: Doubleday, 1956); Ronald Takaki, *A Different Mirror: A History of Multicultural America* (Boston: Little, Brown, 1993).

CROW TRIBE, a group of Native Americans of Siouan ancestry, were hunters and gatherers who occupied the present-day areas of Montana and Wyoming. The tribe was cooperative with European-American settlers and even served as scouts for the U.S. Army. The Crows referred to themselves as *Absaroka* or children of the long-beaked bird.

When European Americans commenced to encroach on their territory in the 1820s, the Crow people were introduced to metal tools and hunting rifles. Unfortunately, they were also introduced to diseases such as smallpox that reduced the Crow population to about 3,000 persons from an original population of more than 16,000 people. Today's population is 8,588, according to U.S. Census figures.

In 1851, the Crows and other Plains tribes were brought together by the U.S. government to delineate their "Indian Homelands." However, in 1868 they had almost 30 million acres taken away from the original homeland grant. They were placed under control of Indian agents who purported to prepare them for "civilized" life. By 1904, the Crow Reservation was further reduced to the 3 million acres that still exist. An understanding of the similarities and differences of Native American tribes must be part of any good multicultural educational program.

From 1880 to 1920, the Bureau of Indian Affairs tried diligently to force the Crow people to adapt to the dominant European-American macroculture, to force the Crows to remain on the reservation, become converted to Christianity, follow mainstream marriage traditions, and earn a livelihood through farming and/or ranching. Children were forced to attend boarding schools, which attempted to transform the students into "mainstream Americans." By the early 1990s, about one third of the Crow reservation residents were non-Indians, and about 20 percent of the Crow people lived off of the reservation.

References: Coe Smith Hayne, *Red Men on the Bighorn* (Philadelphia, PA: Judson Press, 1929); Frederick E. Hoxie, *The Crow Indians of North America*, Ed. Frank W. Porter III (New York: Chelsea House, 1989); Robert H. Lowie, *The Crow Indians* (New York:

Holt, Rinehart and Winston, 1956); Fred W. Voget, *The Shoshone—Crow Sun Dance* (Norman: University of Oklahoma Press, 1984).

CULTURAL AWARENESS refers to a level of sophistication about the various microcultures that reside around the world. The theory is that as people become more knowledgeable about and more familiar with persons who are different from themselves, they become more comfortable with persons who have different language patterns, values, and racial characteristics.

One useful model for developing cultural awareness is James Banks' six-stage model of ethnicity: Stage One is Ethnic Psychological Captivity; Stage Two is Ethnic Encapsulation, Stage Three is Ethnic Identity Clarification; Stage Four is Ethnicity, and the top two stages, five is entitled Multiethnicity and Reflective Nationalism, and Six is Globalism and Global Competency. As a person is able to move up through the various stages, they become more culturally aware. Teachers should help all students move up to higher stages.

Reference: James A. Banks, *Teaching Strategies for Ethnic Studies*, 6th ed. (Boston: Allyn and Bacon, 1997).

CULTURAL CONFLICTS are occurrences between specific groups of people who have differing beliefs, attitudes, and values. The cognitive belief systems might result in either overt or covert racial discrimination against a microculture because of its cultural belief system. For example, one person might believe that African Americans are immoral, sexually promiscuous, dirty, lazy, loud, prone to violence, less intelligent, and different. Such beliefs can directly affect the multicultural awareness levels of that individual.

The second person may believe that European Americans are stupid about life, intellectually superior, prejudiced against African Americans, intent on keeping African Americans in their place, born with highly undeserved advantages he or she does not have, and are emotionless and colorless. When two persons sharing such values come into contact with each other, cultural conflicts are almost certain to occur. *See also* CULTURAL ENCAPSULATION.

Reference: Christine I. Bennett, *Comprehensive Multicultural Education: Theory and Practice*, 3d ed. (Boston: Allyn and Bacon, 1995).

CULTURAL ENCAPSULATION is a necessary step that some people must take after they have rejected their own microculture when it represents something they do not wish to accept. Often, feelings of inferiority accompany this first stage, which James Banks refers to as ethnic, psychological captivity. If people are able to get past this stage of cultural rejection, they usually find a way to accept their own microculture.

This acceptance often results in a phenomenon called cultural encapsulation, where people acquire a great deal of information about their own microculture and decide that they like it so much that they may become highly ethnocentric and acquire a feeling of intense pride. While this stage is highly condemned by some, it may be a necessary stepping-stone on the way to an increased level of racial and ethnic openness. *See also* CULTURAL CONFLICTS.

References: James A. Banks, *Teaching Strategies for Ethnic Studies*, 6th ed. (Boston: Allyn and Bacon, 1997); Bruce M. Mitchell, et al., *The Dynamic Classroom*, 5th ed. (Dubuque, IA: Kendall/Hunt, 1995).

CULTURAL LITERACY refers to the extent of knowledge a person may exhibit about a given microculture or macroculture. It requires knowledge of the literature, language, history, artwork, customs and traditions of a given group. Consequently, if a person is culturally literate in several microcultures, communication of a significant nature could occur.

Over the years, many arguments have occurred over a definition of a given culture. For example, the American arguments about the merits of a Eurocentric approach to the curriculum used in the schools, have raged since the American Civil Rights Movement. Allen Bloom's book, *The Closing of the American Mind*, has attempted to argue the pre-eminence of Western civilization.

While conservatives have tended to opt for a Eurocentric point of view, others have argued for a more multicultural approach to the schooling of American students. The debate has tended to persist wherever cultural pluralism exists.

References: James A. Banks, *Teaching Strategies for Ethnic Studies*, 6th ed. (Boston: Allyn and Bacon, 1997); Allan Bloom, *The Closing of the American Mind* (New York: Vintage Books, 1987); E. D. Hirsch, Jr., *Cultural Literacy: What Every American Should Know* (New York: Vintage Books, 1987).

CULTURAL RELATIVISM is a term related to the ability to set aside an individual's microcultural values and analyze other microcultures from their own perspective. However, some have euphemistically referred to the concept as "anything goes." For example, some parents who have school-age children envision multicultural education as an educational strategy that demands their children accept social axioms violently contradictory to their own views.

While the notion of multicultural education was popularized during the American Civil Rights Movement and viewed as a strategy which resulted in greater cross-cultural understanding, the philosophy was viewed negatively by some conservative organizations during the 1980s and 1990s. In fact, concepts such as "politically correct"—referring to more acceptable terms relating to multicultural issues—became a source of irritation among conservative groups. However, most multicultural education advocates tend to refer to the issue of using appropriate terms that are not objectionable to certain microcultures as being "multiculturally sensitive."

The concept of cultural relativism does not require people to accept the practices of other cultural groups if they violate the integrity of their own beliefs. But a study of another culture might lead people to the realization that, had they been raised in a different culture, they might accept the values of the other group.

References: Christine I. Bennett, *Comprehensive Multicultural Education: Theory and Practice*, 3d ed. (Boston: Allyn and Bacon, 1995); Joan Thrower Timm, *Four Perspectives in Multicultural Education* (Belmont, CA: Wadsworth, 1996).

CULTURALLY DISADVANTAGED/DEPRIVED is a concept that first surfaced during the 1960s to explain why poverty students in the schools fared so poorly. The notion was that certain non-European–American students were raised in inferior microcultures. This automatically resulted in poorer school performance among African Americans, Latinos, and children of all low-income or poverty parents. It was felt that the inferiority of such homes caused the educational difficulties of students.

Gradually, the term "culturally disadvantaged" or "culturally deprived" disappeared from use due to the complaints of persons from such microcultural backgrounds. Writers sought euphemisms that would paint youth in a more favorable light. Consequently, the term of preference became "at risk." It was felt that this phrase did not castigate a culture for its particular value system.

Reference: Herbert Grossman, *Teaching in a Diverse Society* (Boston: Allyn and Bacon, 1995).

CULTURE refers to the patterns acquired and transmitted by groups of human beings. Many social scientists define "culture" as a pattern for survival that is created when groups of people attempt to satisfy their survival needs. Social scientists also view artifacts and material objects as a part of culture. These values and mores distinguish one group of people from another.

The macroculture usually refers to a large dominant culture, such as "United States citizens." On the other hand, "microcultures" are comprised of smaller numbers of persons with similar language patterns, values, feelings, mores, music, literature, artwork, religion, and the like. Typically, macrocultures are composed of many microcultures which may exhibit only slight differences or sometimes major differences.

Multicultural education addresses issues of education concerned with creating new environments in which people, from varying microcultural backgrounds, are entitled to educational equality. Educational equity ensures that the children from all microcultures are entitled to equal educational opportunities, as guaranteed by the American Constitution. In addition, the concept refers to the acquisition of positive understandings about microcultural differences to promote understanding and defuse racist and sexist misconceptions about people who are different.

References: James A. Banks, *Multiethnic Education: Theory and Practice*, 3d ed. (Boston: Allyn and Bacon, 1994); Alfred Kroeber and Clyde Kluckhohn, *Culture: A Critical Review of Concepts and Definitions* (New York: Vintage, 1952).

CULTURE-FREE TESTS refers to evaluation instruments that do not contain a cultural bias. The issue of cultural bias in tests first emerged during the American Civil Rights era. The concern was that since some students of color tended to score lower on various standardized tests and intelligence tests, they contained a middle-class, European-American bias. Consequently, test construction experts commenced to create "culture-free" alternative evaluation instruments, that is, they reflected no cultural bias in the language and/or construction of the questions.

This issue also relates to the concept of test validity. The crucial question in all test construction is whether a measurement instrument actually measures what it is supposed to measure. Consequently, if a student has a language deficiency or has not been exposed to the vocabulary and concepts detailed in the test questions, the test score may not reflect the true levels of intelligence, attitude or achievement of that student. Moreover, some pioneers have harbored erroneous views about the intelligence of different groups of people. For example, Sir Francis Galton was convinced that the most intelligent races on the planet were the light-skinned groups. Galton was considered by some as a major pioneer in the development of intelligence testing. Many educators feel that these biases have resulted in the development of tests which were not culture-fair.

As a result, many attempts were made to create "culture-free" or "culture-fair" tests. The basic notion is that children from all microcultures would have an equal chance of answering the questions, regardless of the racial and/or ethnic upbringing. Some of the "culture-free" or "culture-fair" intelligence tests are the Culture Intelligence Test by Catell and Catell and the DeAvila Cartoon Conservation Series. The creation of such instruments occurred during the late 1960s, 1970s, and early 1980s.

References: Arthur Bertram and Joseph Cebula, *Tests, Measurement, and Development, a Developmental Approach* (Reading, MA: Addison-Wesley, 1980); L. R. Gay, *Educational Research* (New York: Macmillan, 1992); Bruce M. Mitchell, et al., *The Dynamic Classroom*, 5th ed. (Dubuque, IA: Kendall/Hunt, 1995).

D

DACHAU, one of the German concentration camps during World War II, became a major participant in the extermination of about 6 million European Jews. Among the American military personnel who helped liberate the prison camp were African-American and Japanese-American troops. Paul Parks, an African-American soldier, observed he could understand why the Jewish prisoners were killed because of their ethnicity since, in the United States, African Americans suffered from similar actions.

Teaching about ethnic atrocities as drastic as the Holocaust can serve to illustrate what can happen in a country when citizens do not demand equal treatment of all groups regardless of race, religion, or national origin.

Reference: Ronald Takaki, *A Different Mirror: A History of Multicultural America* (Boston: Little, Brown, 1993).

DANCING RABBIT CREEK, TREATY OF was the first treaty signed after the Removal Act of 1830; it was enacted on September 27, 1830. After the War of 1812, the Choctaw tribe came under heavy pressure when settlers moved into their lands in Mississippi. Due to pressure by President Andrew Jackson, the Choctaws gave up 10 million acres of their land in return for new lands west of the Mississippi River. They received $20,000 in a 20-year annuity.

The Choctaws became the first Native American tribe to be moved west of the Mississippi under the Removal Act of 1830. A few Choctaws were allowed to stay in Mississippi. Even though Pushmataha, the Choctaw chief, remained loyal to the United States during the War of 1812, federal negotiators persuaded the Choctaws to sign the Treaty of Dancing Rabbit Creek and move to western Arkansas. Between 1830 and 1834, 4,000 of the 13,000 Choctaws died on the way to Arkansas. About 7,000 managed to circumvent the emigration orders. They remained in Mississippi and ultimately became citizens of that state.

From a multicultural education perspective, it is recommended that when teaching U.S. history, teachers divide such studies into two distinct segments: pre-and post-Columbian education. In the past, the accomplishments of Native Americans have been almost non-existent in textbooks. Thus, some children have acquired extremely distorted views of Native Americans.

Reference: Harvey Markowitz (Ed.), *American Indians* (Pasadena, CA: Salem Press, 1995).

DAVIS, BENJAMIN (1912–), one of the first five graduates of the Tuskegee Flying School in 1942 flew with the 99th Pursuit Squadron during World War II. Just twelve years later, Davis became the first African-American general in the United States Air Force.

Reference: Sharon Harley, *The Timetables of African-American History* (New York: Simon and Schuster, 1995).

DAWES SEVERALTY ACT OF 1887 (General Allotment Act) was a major reform effort relating to Indian policy. As a result of this act, the President of the United States was able to order the allotment of Indian reservations in severalty or among individual tribal members. The head of a family could receive 160 acres, while orphans and persons over 18 would receive 80 acres. Other single persons would receive 40 acres. After the land was allotted, excess land could be made available for European-American settlers.

The Act stipulated that the government should hold the title to allotments for 25 years. The land could not be sold during that period of time. Native Americans receiving the allotments were granted American citizenship. By the time the Dawes Act was terminated in 1934, 86 million acres were taken away from the Native American people.

References: Alvin M. Josephy, Jr., *Five Hundred Nations* (New York: Alfred A. Knopf, 1994); Harvey Markowitz (Ed.), *American Indians* (Pasadena, CA: Salem Press, 1995).

DE FACTO SEGREGATION, a Latin phrase referring to "how things are," describes the type of segregation that exists in the United States as a result of race, age, ethnicity, gender, and economic circumstances. The term does not relate to legal segregation of the type that existed during South Africa's apartheid days or the segregation of schools by race in the United States.

The term "de facto segregation" also has been used in referring to the socioeconomic factors of residential choice. As a result of economic circumstances, many Americans have experienced limited choices for determining where they can live. Poverty persons have been forced to live in inner-city areas or *barrios*, which have lower housing costs and consist of large numbers of African Americans and Latinos. Wealthier Americans have tended to opt for suburban living, which results in disproportionate percentages of European-American residents. Older Americans have frequently chosen gated communities, which traditionally have often housed large proportions of older European Americans.

However, it should be emphasized that "de facto segregation" refers only to the choices that human beings make in determining where they live. These choices often result in the creation of neighborhoods which experience "de facto segregation."

References: Bruce M. Mitchell, et al., *The Dynamic Classroom*, 5th ed. (Dubuque, IA: Kendall/Hunt, 1995); Ronald Takaki, *A Different Mirror: A History of Multicultural America* (Boston: Little, Brown, 1993); Joan Thrower Timm, *Four Perspectives in Multicultural Education* (Belmont, CA: Wadsworth, 1996).

DE JURE SEGREGATION is a phrase that refers to any kind of racial segregation occurring by legal means. Probably the most well-known example took place in the southern states during the Reconstruction Period following the termination of slavery in the United States. Virtually all human institutions were segregated by race, including schools, rest rooms, hotels, railway cars, busses, drinking fountains, and so on. In addition, some communities established "sundown" laws, which made it illegal for African Americans to be in certain communities after the sun went down.

Undoubtedly, the best example of "de jure segregation" occurred in the nation's public schools. Southern schools adapted a funding procedure similar to school financing formulas which occurred in South Africa before apartheid. Schools for African-American students received about 50 percent of the funding, which went to schools with European-American students. Throughout the country, segregated schools were also created for Latino and Asian students.

Despite the fact that the 1954 *Brown v. Board of Education* decision declared racially segregated schools to be unconstitutional, they still exist all over the land. In fact, racially segregated schools have increased in the 1980s and 1990s, partly due to the proliferation of private religious schools.

References: Bruce M. Mitchell, et al., *The Dynamic Classroom*, 5th ed. (Dubuque, IA: Kendall/Hunt, 1995); Joan Thrower Timm, *Four Perspectives in Multicultural Education* (Belmont, CA: Wadsworth, 1996); Ronald Takaki, *A Different Mirror: A History of Multicultural America* (Boston: Little, Brown, 1993).

DE KLERK, FREDERIK WILLEM (1936–), the last white South African president, served in that office from 1989 to 1994. In 1993, he was awarded the Nobel Peace Prize. Born in Johannesburg in 1936, he graduated from the University of Potchefstroom in 1958 and soon after began practicing law. In 1973, he was appointed as a member of parliament. Starting in 1978, he held a number of cabinet ministries, including internal affairs. In 1989, when Peter W. Botha suffered a stroke, de Klerk became the leader of the National Party, assuming the presidency after Botha's resignation.

In 1990, he released Nelson Mandela from prison and legalized the African National Congress and the South African Communist Party. In 1991, the basic elements of South African apartheid were revoked and de Klerk and Mandela discussed a new democratic constitution. They also convened a multiracial, multiparty conference for the creation of a new constitution. By February 1993, de Klerk and Mandela reached a decision for a transitional government, which resulted in a partnership between the African National Congress and the National Party. The two entities would be partners beginning in 1994.

In 1992, de Klerk dismissed 23 military officers for fomenting violence in the black townships. He made a trip to Nigeria in 1992. It was the first state visit by a white South African leader. In 1993, he toured the United States with Nelson Mandela. Both de Klerk and Mandela were awarded Nobel Peace Prizes in 1993. The first South African elections were held in 1994, and de Klerk was elected second deputy president by the National Assembly. Of interest to educators the world over, the old funding formulas for public education were revised so that the same amounts of money are now spent on all children, regardless of race or ethnicity.

Reference: Nelson Mandela, *Long Walk to Freedom* (Boston: Little, Brown, 1994).

DEES, MORRIS (1936–), chief trial council for the Southern Poverty Law Center in Montgomery, Alabama, won the organization's largest legal settlement in 1987 with a 7 million dollar award against the United Klans of America for the 1981 lynching of a 19-year-old Mobile man. In addition to other significant victories against hate-crime criminals, he instituted a successful program for monitoring hate groups in America. His primary strategy was to bankrupt hate groups through legal litigation. Another major victory was a 1990 civil victory against the White Aryan Resistance Group for its 1988 murder of a Portland exchange student from Africa.

An important education function of the Southern Poverty Law Center is the Teaching Tolerance Program. The Center established the program in an attempt to provide teachers with materials for promoting racial and religious tolerance. One of the organization's first publications was a video titled, *A Time for Justice*, with accompanying lessons and a teacher's guide for teaching about the history of America's Civil Rights Movement.

References: Sara Bullard (Ed.), *Free at Last: A History of the Civil Rights Movement and Those Who Died in the Struggle* (Montgomery, AL: Southern Poverty Law Center, 1989).

DELORIA, VINE, JR. (1933–), a member of the Yankton or Standing Rock Sioux tribe and one of America's most prolific Native American protest writers, has been a strong advocate for improving the education of Native American peoples. His writing style has consisted of well-written, biting satire. Two of the best examples of his writing style can be found in his first book, *Custer Died for Your Sins: An Indian Manifesto*. In his book, *We Talk, You Listen: New Tribes, New Turf*, he has also written extensively about the relationships between European Americans and Native Americans.

Deloria studied for a ministerial career, receiving a M.Th. degree from the Lutheran School of Theology in Illinois. Prior to that time, he received his B.S. degree from Iowa State University and later earned a J.D. degree from the University of Colorado.

In addition to his many writings, Deloria has been the executive director of the Congress of American Indians and a professor at the University of Colorado, teaching courses in sociology and Native American studies. An educator himself, his works have great value for teachers wishing to explore multicultural studies in social science and literature classes. Teachers can use his books as references when their students are studying the morality of Native American–European-American incidents throughout the history of the country.

References: James A. Banks, *Teaching Strategies for Ethnic Studies*, 6th ed. (Boston: Allyn and Bacon, 1997); Harvey Markowitz (Ed.), *American Indians* (Pasadena, CA: Salem Press, 1995); James C. Stone and Donald P. Nevi (Eds.), *Teaching Multicultural Populations* (New York: D. Van Nostrand, 1981).

DESEGREGATION PLANS, put into place as a result of the 1954 *Brown v. the Board of Education* Supreme Court decision, were designed to terminate racial segregation that existed in American schools throughout the history of the nation. Since the *Brown* decision required schools to desegregate with all deliberate speed, it was necessary to have specific strategies approved. The most common procedures utilized by the schools were as follows. *Central School Plans* referred to the practice of re-organizing elementary schools into single grades. For example, all of the kindergarten children residing in a given district would attend one or two schools. *Clustering* involved redistributing the students of three or more schools, while *Pairing* used the same procedure for desegregating two schools that were formerly segregated. These practices often resulted in ugly demonstrations such as the confrontations by parents in Flint, Michigan. *Educational Complexes* were schools that were restructured to offer especially strong programs in math/science, English and creative writing, the social sciences, the arts, and so on. Most of these practices were carried out in high schools.

Metropolitan Plans attempted to enlarge inner-city school districts so that the suburban areas were also included. These attempts were mostly unsuccessful.

Educational Parks were new educational facilities that would be able to accommodate thousands of students. Controversial and costly, they seldom materialized. *School Closings* referred to the practice of shutting down old, dilapidated schools, which often were located in highly segregated sections of inner cities. The children would be sent to surrounding schools in an attempt to establish integrated school populations.

Reference: Bruce M. Mitchell, et al., *The Dynamic Classroom*, 5th ed. (Dubuque, IA: Kendall/Hunt, 1995).

DISCRIMINATION, a term that essentially refers to the capacity to make distinctions, is an important concept in the multicultural education lexicon. It has been used in referring to the acting out of negative attitudes toward different groups of people and also individuals. The concept can refer to legal, economic, political, and social practices, which tend to denigrate persons of a specific racial, ethnic, religious, or language group.

Discrimination can be both overt and covert in nature. For example, members of the Ku Klux Klan openly discriminate against Jews and African Americans because of their basic beliefs. However, many persons practice subtle forms of discrimination because of beliefs that may not even be known to them.

Reference: Joan Thrower Timm, *Four Perspectives in Multicultural Education* (Belmont, CA: Wadsworth, 1996).

DIVERSITY, a term that refers to the differences in human beings, has been used by multicultural education writers in referring to the great number of different racial, ethnic, and religious groups in the United States. Moreover, the term has been used in referring to individuals whose ethnic heritage originates in another country or who may have special educational and other needs.

For a pluralistic society, such as the United States, this term conveys far-reaching implications. Diverse student groups can include young persons from the culture of poverty, different ethnic and/or racial backgrounds, and students who have special needs due to problems of gender, class and religion, extreme poverty, drug dependency, and language factors.

References: K. Cushner, A. McClelland, and P. Safford, *Human Diversity in Education* (New York: McGraw-Hill, 1992); Carl A. Grant (Ed.), *Educating for Diversity: An Anthology of Multicultural Voices* (Boston: Allyn and Bacon, 1995); Joan Thrower Timm, *Four Perspectives in Multicultural Education* (Belmont, CA: Wadsworth, 1996).

DOMESTIC DEPENDENT NATION refers to a U.S. Supreme Court decision passed in 1831. The landmark decision had a profound affect on multicultural education issues since it stipulated that the Native American lands and the persons who resided on them were "domestic dependent nations." In 1932, the

U.S. Supreme Court ruled in another case that these "domestic dependent nations" had a right to govern themselves.

These high court decisions helped develop the concept of "a nation within a nation." This notion became a legal right, the law of the land. It precipitated an ongoing controversy as to issues such as fishing rights, tax-exempt status, etc.

Reference: Bruce M. Mitchell, et al., *The Dynamic Classroom*, 5th ed. (Dubuque, IA: Kendall/Hunt, 1995).

DOUGLAS, FREDERICK (1817–1895), an African-American reformer and abolitionist, was born in Maryland in 1817. After escaping slavery in 1838, he settled in Massachusetts and commenced delivering anti-slavery lectures in the east. However, his life became endangered when he published *The Narrative of the Life of Frederick Douglas*. He was forced to flee to England because of his exposure of his ex-master. While Douglas was in England, friendly liberals bought his freedom from his ex-master.

Returning to the United States in 1847, he commenced publishing an abolitionist newspaper, the *North Star*. In addition to the newspaper's anti-slavery stance, it also supported women's rights. Known as an excellent orator, he used his lecture fees to aid runaway slaves and was the director of the underground railroad station in Rochester. Although Douglas was opposed to the Harper's Ferry raid in 1859, he was forced to flee to Canada since he had helped his friend, John Brown. During the Civil War, he recruited African Americans for the Union Army. From 1889 to 1891, he was the American Ambassador to Haiti.

References: Melvin Drimmer (Ed.), *Black History* (Garden City, NY: Doubleday, 1968); John Hope Franklin, *From Slavery to Freedom* (New York: Alfred P. Knopf, 1988); P. S. Foner (Ed.), *Frederick T. Douglass, Life and Writings* (New York: International, 1975); Nathan Irvin Hugguns, *Slave and Citizen: The Life of Frederick Douglas* (Boston: Little, Brown, 1980).

DU BOIS, W.E.B. (1868–1963), ironically died on the same day that Martin Luther King delivered his "I have a dream" speech. His achievements were many. He was the first African American to receive a Ph.D. from Harvard University after receiving his B.A. degree from Fisk University. His birthday was declared a national holiday in Japan, and he authored sixteen books on socialism, history, politics, and race relations. The founder of the Niagara Movement, his organization eventually became the National Association for the Advancement for Colored People (NAACP).

Du Bois believed strongly in the liberal arts education of young African-American students. He had major disagreements with Booker T. Washington, founder of the Tuskegee Institute, a vocational school for African Americans.

He believed that a liberal arts education would lead to empowerment in the political arena and in the area of civil rights. He felt that the concept of vocational education for African Americans was demeaning and reinforced the notion of European Americans that Blacks were intellectually inferior. Washington argued that his school was a practical solution for meeting the problems of high unemployment among African Americans.

Perhaps his most important accomplishment was his advocacy of civil rights for African Americans well before the civil rights movement developed. His pioneering efforts helped pave the way for Martin Luther King's efforts. He felt that education was the primary vehicle for achieving racial equality and that a well-educated mind was the best weapon for Blacks in their endless struggle against prejudice and discrimination. *See also* WASHINGTON, BOOKER T.

References: ''W.E.B. Du Bois,'' in P. Foner (Ed.), *W.E.B. Du Bois Speaks (1899–1919)* (New York: Pathfinder Press, 1970); C. G. Woodson, *The Miseducation of the Negro* (Washington, DC: Associated Press, 1933).

DYER ANTI-LYNCHING BILL was the culmination of a long campaign by the National Association for the Advancement of Colored People (NAACP). In 1919, the NAACP spearheaded the creation of a national program against bigotry and injustice in America. One of the key 1919 meetings was an anti-lynching forum for which the main speaker was Charles Evans Hughes.

During the same year, the NAACP decided to launch a major anti-lynching campaign. The organization persuaded Representative L. C. Dyer of Missouri to sponsor anti-lynching legislation. His House Bill sought to ''assure to persons within the jurisdiction of every state the equal protection of the laws, and to punish the crime of lynching.'' The measure passed the House by a vote of 230–119. However, despite the urging of 24 governors, 39 mayors, and support by numerous intellectuals, a filibuster led by Senators Underwood of Alabama and Harrison of Mississippi was successful in preventing a vote in the United States Senate. The Republicans had a lack of interest in the issue and voted to abandon it.

Reference: John Hope Franklin, *From Slavery to Freedom: A History of Negro Americans* (New York: Alfred A. Knopf, 1985).

E

EBONICS, a term combining the words "ebony" and "phonics," has been coined to describe an English dialect that is often utilized by inner-city, African-American children. During 1996, the Oakland School District agreed to recognize "Ebonics" as a distinct language pattern, which can be used to assist African-American youth to become more effective learners. The philosophy is similar to that of bilingual educational programs that utilize the native language of students in an attempt to ensure that they are learning basic concepts in their native language.

However, like all bilingual programs, the primary goal of "Ebonics" is to teach students standard English in order for them to be competent in the major language of communication and commerce of the United States. Many other countries have adopted similar bilingual educational programs to help students acquire understandings of learning concepts in their native language and to prevent them from falling behind academically. The over-riding characteristic of bilingual education programs in the United States is to help students acquire sufficient competency in the basic language of this country so that the need for bilingual instruction will disappear. This is also true of "Ebonics."

References: James Crawford, *Bilingual Education: History, Politics, Theory and Practice* (Trenton, NJ: Crane, 1989); Ricardo Garcia, *Learning in Two Languages* (Bloomington, IN: Phi Delta Kappa Education Foundation, 1976); Judy Pasternak, "Linguists Praise Plan to Use Ebonics," *Los Angeles Times*, January 1, 1997, A14; Bertha Perez and Maria E. Torres-Guzman, *Learning in Two Worlds: An Integrated Spanish-English Biliteracy Approach* (New York: Longman, 1992).

EINSTEIN, ALBERT (1879–1955), a Jew living in an era of genocide, was born in 1879 in the city of Ulm, situated on the left bank of the Danube at the base of the Swabian Alps. While his early education took place in a Catholic elementary school, he enrolled at the Luitpold Gymnasium at the age of 10. However, he was at odds with the system at Luitpold, because he felt the teachers were too rigid. Einstein was developing his ideas about the importance of imagination in the learning process.

Because of his imaginative approach to the sciences, he often found himself in opposition to his Jewish faith, and eventually he became rather disillusioned with his largely Catholic education and the Jewish traditions with which he grew up. His work in developing his famous theory of relativity catapulted him into a position of enormous prominence among mathematicians and scientists.

Because of political and economic problems in Germany, Einstein accepted an appointment to the California Institute of Technology in Pasadena, California, in 1930. After returning to Europe, he was persuaded to return to the United States to accept a position at the Institute of Advanced Studies at Princeton.

His work as a physicist and mathematician and his contributions to the math/science curriculum in the United States, Europe, and the rest of the world are well known. His notion of the use of imagination in the learning process has influenced educators concerned with the development of creative thinking potential. From a multicultural educational perspective, his accomplishments as a Jewish American help to articulate the value of pluralistic influences in the American mosaic.

References: Antonia Vallentin, *Einstein: A Biography* (London: Eidenfeld and Nicholson, 1954); Michael White and John Gribbin, *Einstein: A Life in Science* (New York: Dutton, 1993).

EL GRITO DE DOLORES, a concept that is very important not only to Mexicans but Mexican Americans as well, refers to the famous rallying cry of Miguel Hidalgo y Castillo that precipitated the Mexican Revolution against Spain. From a multicultural perspective, it is important for American children to understand something of the history of the United States' second largest ethnic minority, the Mexican Americans.

On September 16, 1810, Hidalgo began a move for independence against Spain. By the ringing of church bells, Mexican people joined him in a successful attempt for independence from the Spaniards. Finally, in 1821, the Treaty of Cordoba was signed, granting Mexico its independence. A provisional government was created, along with a new independent congress. About eight years later, under the leadership of Santa Anna, the remaining Spanish troops returned to Spain.

Students need to learn about the significance of these episodes to acquire a more comprehensive view of modern, multicultural America. For example, the reason that Mexico is a Spanish-speaking country is due to the colonization of the country by Spain.

References: Francois Chevalier, *Land and Society in Colonial Mexico: The Great Hacienda* (Berkeley: University of California Press, 1963); Michael Meyer and William Sherman, *The Course of Mexican History*, 2d ed. (New York: Oxford University Press, 1983); James Rudolph, *Mexico: A Country Study* (Washington, DC: Department of the Army, 1985).

EMANCIPATION PROCLAMATION was a document issued by President Abraham Lincoln stipulating that all slaves residing in the rebellious Confederacy states were free as of January 1, 1863. The final proclamation stipulated the specific states and districts that were affected and invited ex-slaves to join the Federal forces. The Thirteenth Amendment to the U.S. Constitution, specifically prohibiting slavery or involuntary servitude, was enacted into law on December 18, 1865.

The Emancipation Proclamation was a highly significant event in the country's multicultural history. A great majority of the African-American slaves had been kept illiterate through actual legal edicts and the actions of plantation owners. Educational efforts for African Americans during Reconstruction were woefully inadequate and did not change significantly until after 1954, the year of the *Brown v. Topeka Board of Education* Supreme Court decision.

References: David Herbert Donald, *Lincoln* (London: Jonathan Cape, 1995); Mark E. Neely, Jr., *The Abraham Lincoln Encyclopedia* (New York: McGraw-Hill, 1982); Allan Nevins, *The War for the Union* (New York: Charles Scribner's Sons, 1960); Ida M. Tarbell, *The Life of Abraham Lincoln* (New York: Doubleday, Page, 1909).

EMPOWERMENT is a multicultural, educational term that refers to helping children from oppressed racial and ethnic groups gain access to the economic and political systems of the United States though education. The premise is that the better the education, the greater the odds that all American children, particularly those from historically low-income backgrounds, will be able to become successful in the country's capitalistic system.

From a multicultural, educational perspective, this involves not only the acquisition of necessary academic skills and talents, but the creation of a more comprehensive understanding of themselves, their community, the nation, and the world. It also necessitates an understanding of the causes and consequences of racism and sexism and an understanding and appreciation of racial, ethnic, religious, and linguistic diversity.

References: Christine E. Sleeter, *Empowerment Through Multicultural Education* (Albany: State University of New York Press, 1991); P. McLaren, *Life in Schools* (New York: Longman, 1989).

ENCULTURATION refers to the understanding of language, traditions, values, and mores of a given culture. Normally, this level of understanding occurs when a person actually grows up in a given culture so that the characteristics are acquired through being involved from infancy.

However, some models have suggested that persons are able to progress through a number of stages of ethnicity. Some young people seem trapped at a stage of ethnic psychological captivity in which they grow up in a given culture but internalize negative attitudes about their ethnic group. However, an individual person may progress to the second stage characterized by a belief that his or her ethnic group is superior to all others.

Eventually, persons may develop positive attitudes about the ethnic group through a clarification of personal attitudes and ethnic identity. Through self-acceptance, persons are able to respond positively to others. Eventually, people may acquire the skills to participate in another culture in addition to their own. This occurs through the development of a healthy sense of ethnic identity. At this stage, the person desires to function in two cultures.

The next step sees the person becoming able to function within several ethnic microcultures. In this stage, the individual is able to lead a more enjoyable and fulfilling life. But the final stage of sophistication enables the person to seek out significant ethnic relationships on a more global basis, understanding that all microcultures on the planet have something to offer. Obviously, the goal of the committed multicultural educator is to help all students move through these stages. The more enculturated the person becomes, the greater the openness to pluralistic peoples, regardless of what microculture they represent.

References: James A. Banks, *Multiethnic Education*, 3d ed. (Boston: Allyn and Bacon, 1994); Ashley Montagu, *Man's Most Dangerous Myth: The Fallacy of Race* New York: Oxford University Press, 1974); Douglas L. Oliver, *An Invitation to Anthropology: A Guide to Basic Concepts* (Garden City, NY: The National History Press, 1964); Joan Thrower Timm, *Four Perspectives in Multicultural Education* (Belmont, CA: Wadsworth, 1996).

ENGEL v. VITALE, a landmark Supreme Court decision related to the legality of formal prayer in America's public schools, has helped to define legally the concept of church and state separation as it applies to the public sector in the United States of America. The Supreme Court decision centered around a New York state law that ordered a short, non-denominational prayer to be said aloud in each classroom in the presence of the teacher. The mandated prayers were given at the start of the school day.

The objection, brought by parents, challenged the constitutionality of the action because of the First Amendment's prohibition of a state-established religion. The holding was that regular recitations of school-sponsored prayer in the public schools is unconstitutional and therefore, illegal.

Since this 1962 case, many school districts around the country have attempted to initiate prayers in various forms. When legal actions were undertaken to prevent them, the practices were overturned on the basis of *Engel v. Vitale*. In recent years, the religious right has put pressure on lawmakers to overturn *Engel v. Vitale*, To date, all such attempts have failed. It should be emphasized that the *Engel v. Vitale* decision in no way restricts students from praying whenever and wherever they wish, as long as the prayers are not mandated by a school, school district, city, county or state.

References: Kern Alexander and M. David Alexander, *American Public School Law* (Belmont, CA: Wadsworth, 1998); Louis Fischer, David Schimmel and Cynthia Kelly, *Teachers and the Law* (White Plains, NY: Longman, 1995); Robert C. O'Reilly and Edward T. Green, *School Law for the 1990s* (Westport, CT: Greenwood Press, 1992); Perry A. Zirkel and Sharon Nalbone Richardson, *A Digest of Supreme Court Decisions Affecting Education* (Bloomington, IN: Phi Delta Kappa Educational Foundation, 1988).

ENGLISH AS A SECOND LANGUAGE (ESL) refers to instructional programs in English for persons who are not native English speakers. Such programs have been put into place as a result of the 1974 *Lau v. Nichols* Supreme Court decision. The decision required that the schools establish special preparation sequences for pupils who had Limited English Proficiency (LEP) to provide them with constitutionally guaranteed equal educational opportunities.

While the Lau decision did not mandate bilingual education programs, many school districts instituted them to assist the student to learn concepts in their native language, whenever that would provide the greatest educational benefit. Along with the bilingual, educational program, the student would also be provided with instruction in English through the ESL program. The ultimate goal of such efforts was to assist the student to become bilingual, enabling them to use both languages with equal proficiency. *See also LAU v. NICHOLS.*

References: James A. Banks, *Multiethnic Education: Theory and Practice*, 3d ed. (Boston: Allyn and Bacon, 1994); Christine I. Bennett: *Multicultural Education: Theory and Practice*, 3d ed. (Boston: Allyn and Bacon, 1995); Donna M. Gollnick and Philip C. Chinn, *Multicultural Education in a Pluralistic Society* (Columbus, OH: Merrill, 1990); M. Lee Manning and Leroy G. Baruth, *Multicultural Education of Children and Adolescents* (Boston: Allyn and Bacon, 1996).

ENGLISH ONLY, a concept used to reflect a notion that only English should be used as the official language of communication in the United States, has become a volatile issue throughout the country during the 1980s and 1990s. As the term implies, proponents of this movement have argued that since English is the ''official'' language of the country, no other language should be utilized.

However, the United States of America has no ''official'' language. In fact, in the U.S. Constitution there is nothing that gives English preference over any other language in spite of the fact that several states have passed ''English-only'' laws. And regardless of the fact that the country has never established a ''legal language,'' English is still the primary language of commerce, trade, and communication. Indeed, persons who are not fluent in English have a difficult time competing successfully in American society.

The argument over the use of English is not new. When the Europeans arrived in the United States, they were met by people who had no understanding of this new language. Likewise, in analyzing world history, it is clear that the language of the land invariably becomes the language of the conquerors. For example, Brazil is a Portuguese-speaking country simply because the Portuguese captured the land and imposed their language during the period of colonization.

The pro-official language movement has argued that a nation is limited in the amount of diversity that can be tolerated. Moreover, some of the pro-official language adherents have argued that it is actually ''un-American'' to speak a language other than English. However, it should be noted that this has sometimes been viewed to be an extreme position of the radical right with racist overtones. But as the argument goes, language assimilation (into English) would occur more quickly if speaking the English language were to be mandated by law.

Conversely, opponents of the English-only movement have maintained that to enforce persons to communicate in English only is not only unconstitutional but racist as well. Interestingly, the research tends to show that immigrants are now learning the language of their new country at about the same rate as immigrants in years past. Second-generation immigrants seem more apt to become bilingual, while third-generation immigrants have a strong tendency to become fluent in the use of English, while retaining very little knowledge of their native language.

References: Dennis Barron, *The English-Only Question* (New Haven, CT: Yale University Press, 1990); Bee Gallegos, *English: Our Official Language?* (New York: H. W. Wilson, 1994); Paul Lang, *The English Language Debate: One Nation, One Language?* (Springfield, NJ: Enslow, 1995).

EQUAL EDUCATION OPPORTUNITY has been a constitutional guarantee for all American school children regardless of race, gender, ethnicity, or socioeconomic status. The principle has been upheld in U.S. Supreme Court decisions such as *Brown v. Topeka Board of Education* (1954), *Lau v. Nichols* (1974), and several others.

Applying the principle in actual practice has been difficult. For example, throughout history, the funding for educating poor students has been inadequate when compared to the funding for more affluent students. The funding for African-American students during the Reconstruction Period of American history was about 50 percent of the amount spent on European-American children.

Equal education opportunities for American school children are guaranteed under the Fourteenth Amendment of the U.S. Constitution, which requires that a strict test of any state law be applied when such laws function to the disadvantage of a particular group of students or interferes with their explicit and implicit rights.

During 1972, Congress approved the Equal Education Opportunities Act, which stipulated that none of the states could deny equal education opportunities to any individual by virtue of the failure of a state or school district to take appropriate actions to overcome language barriers that might prevent a student from achieving normal educational success. So the concept has related to all phases of education such as funding, language, poverty problems, etc. Consequently, school districts have created compensatory educational programs to meet the needs of students with such deficiencies.

References: Herbert Grossman, *Teaching in a Diverse Society* (Boston: Allyn and Bacon, 1995); Perry A. Zirkel and Sharon Nalbone Richardson, *A Digest of Supreme Court Decisions Affecting Education* (Bloomington, IN: Phi Delta Kappa Educational Foundation, 1988).

EQUAL EMPLOYMENT OPPORTUNITY is a concept that has been designed to provide equal access to the American workplace regardless of race, religion, gender, and national origin. However, throughout the nation's history, unequal employment opportunities have sometimes been granted to European-American males. To compensate for such transgressions, a number of practices have been put in place.

For example, quota systems have been employed as a means of equalizing the historical preferences for white male hiring. The Bakke Supreme Court Decision of 1978 has stipulated a number of specific requirements for utilizing such procedures. In addition to initial hiring policies, the concept also relates to such issues as promotions and employment termination. The United States has established the Equal Employment Opportunities Commission, which is responsible for addressing equal employment issues.

Teachers are also entitled to such equal employment guarantees. For example, male and female teachers are entitled to the same pay for the same level of work. In the past, law suits have been filed for denial of promotion on grounds of race and/or gender and the failure to compensate men and women equally for equal services rendered.

References: Louis Fischer, David Schimmel, and Cynthia Kelly, *Teachers and the Law* (White Plains, NY: Longman, 1995); Bruce M. Mitchell, et al., *The Dynamic Classroom*, 5th ed. (Dubuque, IA: Kendall/Hunt, 1995); Perry A. Zirkel and Sharon Nalbone Richardson, *A Digest of Supreme Court Decisions Affecting Education* (Bloomington, IN: Phi Delta Kappa Foundation, 1988).

EQUAL PROTECTION CLAUSE is that portion of the U.S. Constitution that guarantees to all American citizens equal protection of the laws regardless of race, ethnicity, gender, socioeconomic status, or religion. This clause has sometimes provided the basis for court cases where equal education opportunities have been denied to students on the basis of race, etc. It is also the Due Process Clause of the Fifth Amendment pertaining to the Federal Government. The U.S. Supreme Court has interpreted this clause as providing equal protection.

References: Samuel Memin, *Law and the Legal System: An Introduction* (Boston: Little, Brown, 1982); Arval A. Morris, *The Constitution and American Education* (St. Paul, MN: West, 1980); LeRoy J. Peterson, Richard A. Rossmiller, and Martin M. Volz, *The Law and the Public School Operation* (New York: Harper and Row, 1978).

EQUAL RIGHTS AMENDMENTS have been put into place by many states. These are constitutional amendments, which sometimes have rather hazy legal meanings. While these amendments have related to a variety of subjects, one of the topics addressed is the issue of high school athletics. The state of Washington has ruled that girls can try out for football teams on an equal footing with boys, and Pennsylvania's courts have ruled that girls and boys can try out for all sports equally, including contact sports. Schools must fund girls and boys sports equally. These are but a few of the examples of equality issues addressed under the Equal Rights Amendments (ERAs).

Reference: Louis Fischer, David Schimmel, and Cynthia Kelly, *Teachers and the Law* (White Plains, NY: Longman, 1995).

ETHNIC CLEANSING, a term used in both the scholarly and popular literature during the 1980s and 1990s, refers to the practice of purging racial, ethnic, and/or religious groups to insure just one microculture within a given set of boundaries. The word is a euphemism for violent purges initiated against specific groups. Throughout the history of humans, the practice has persisted. Perhaps the best recent example occurred with the breakup of Yugoslavia.

After the Vatican recognized the two new nations of Slovenia and Croatia, Muslims in Bosnia-Herzegovina voted for independence. Bosnian Serbs argued that Islamic Fundamentalists were planning a male-dominated society similar to those in other Islamic parts of the world. Serbian President Slobidan Milosevic called for the ethnic cleansing of Bosnia, which meant the eradication of Muslims and Catholics. Eventually Croatia joined the conflict, supporting the Muslims for a period of time. Croats attempted to destroy Orthodox churches, while the Serbs destroyed Catholic churches. Orthodox troops attacked the Muslims.

After a period as allies, Muslim and Croat troops attacked each other. Catholic troops attacked Muslim towns, while Muslim soldiers attacked the Croats. Then, in 1994, the Muslims and Croats declared a truce. After the first year of fighting, the estimated number of deaths was about 200,000. Some 3 million people were forced to become refugees.

Another example of possible ethnic cleansing could occur in the United

States. The Aryan Republican Army (ARA) is a network of anti-government, white supremacist groups. Spiritual descendants of the Order, these well-armed, revolutionary groups have as their goal the ethnic cleansing of America, which would eventually result in a country consisting of European-American "Christians." All of the ethnic cleansing efforts are based on racial, religious, and ethnic hatred.

These examples serve to verify the drastic need for multicultural, educational programs throughout the schools. Hopefully, if teachers are able to craft successful multicultural, educational curricula, future generations will learn that ideological differences can and must be tolerated if the planet is to survive.

References: Yossef Bodansky, *Target America; Terrorism in the U.S. Today* (New York: S. P. I., 1993); James A. Haught, *Holy Hatred: Religious Conflicts of the '90s* (Amherst, NY: Prometheus, 1995); Robert D. Kaplan, *Balkan Ghosts: A Journey Through History* (New York: St. Martin's Press, 1993); *Los Angeles Times*, January 15, 1997, A1, A10, A11.

ETHNICITY is a multicultural term that has its roots in the Greek work *ethnos*, meaning "nation." In the literature on multicultural education, it is used when referring to the language, religion, socioeconomic status, and value structure of a group of people. It may or may not also include race, since key anthropologists agree that over the years, strict racial classification has become nearly impossible due to the inter-breeding of humans.

The degree to which a specific group of people subscribe to ethnic patterns often changes rather drastically throughout history. For example, prior to the arrival of the Europeans, the present African countries consisted of peoples with thousands of different languages and dialects. Now, many have lost their original language or have become English or French speakers. Also, with the coming of the Europeans, the Christian religions sometimes replaced the original tribal religious practices. As a general rule, the ethnicity of a people is constantly evolving. In teaching multicultural, educational concepts, teachers can help students identify their own ethnicity and emphasize the importance of helping pupils learn to value the similarities and differences in ethnicity.

References: James A. Banks, *Multicultural Education: Theory and Practice*, 3d ed. (Boston: Allyn and Bacon, 1994): Joan Thrower Timm, *Four Perspectives in Multicultural Education* (Belmont, CA: Wadsworth, 1996); Ronald Takaki, *Strangers from a Different Shore* (Boston: Little, Brown, 1989).

ETHNOCENTRISM refers to the judging of another person's culture by comparing the mores and values of the second group with their own. Ethnocentric people believe that their microculture is superior to others due to some form of biological inferiority in the other group. Two of the most important issues affecting ethnocentrism pertain to language and religion. Many ethnocentric persons are intolerant of other languages and religions.

The concept can be viewed as an attitude that has served historically as a rationalization for exploitation. For example, the notion of manifest destiny, which some European adventurers carried with them to the United States, Africa, Mexico, South America, and other parts of the world, was an idea based on an assumption of the biological inferiority of certain groups of people. The feeling was that since their own microcultures were superior to those of the persons with whom they came into contact, it was acceptable to exploit and occupy the land, take the minerals, and terrorize the people because of their biological inferiority.

When teaching history and/or biology, the educator can point out examples of various types of exploitation based on these mis-assumptions. Hopefully, such an approach will help students to realize the inherent dangers of ethnocentric beliefs and actions.

References: Peter T. Bauer, *Equality, the Third World, and Economic Delusion* (Cambridge, MA: Harvard University Press, 1982); Thomas Sowell, *The Economics and Politics of Race: An International Perspective* (New York: William Morrow, 1983).

EUROCENTRISM, a term which appeared in the lexicon of multicultural education during the 1970s, 1980s, and 1990s, refers to a perceived emphasis on European accomplishments and points of view in the school curriculum. Some multicultural, educational advocates have argued that the concept relates to the manner in which history and social studies texts have described the development of the United States as a history of Europeans crossing the Atlantic, shaping a nation in their image, promising freedom for all people, and making the country a world power.

The major argument is that the contributions of African Americans, Latinos, Chinese Americans and other non-European groups are scarcely discussed in the history books. Moreover, there is little mention of the pre-Columbian history of Native Americans and a lack of attention to the exploitation of non-European groups throughout the country's history.

Proponents of a more pluralistic approach to the curriculum have argued for a more multicultural approach to the discussions of history in the curriculum. Such groups would like to see an emphasis on the contributions of the non-European groups. For example, many of the names of special places in the United States were derived from the exploits of Europeans such as Christopher Columbus, who often has received credit for "discovering" America. But the Arawaks were the original inhabitants of the islands where Columbus originally landed.

References: James A. Banks, *Multiethnic Education: Theory and Practice*, 3d ed. (Boston: Allyn and Bacon, 1994); Christine I. Bennett, *Comprehensive Multicultural Education: Theory and Practice*, 3d ed. (Boston: Allyn and Bacon, 1995); Christine

Sleeter (Ed.), *Empowerment Through Multicultural Education* (Albany: State University of New York Press, 1991).

EUROPEAN AMERICANS, including many separate ethnic groups, are the largest body of people populating the United States. The term is generic in nature and provides little information as to specific ethnic characteristics of the people who are part of that macroculture. European Americans have assumed a position of dominance politically and economically since the end of the American Revolution. In fact, more than 90 percent of the chief executive officers of the nation's Fortune-500 corporations are European-American males. However, population projections indicate that about half way through the twenty-first century, European Americans will no longer be the dominant cultural group numerically.

References: Herbert Grossman, *Teaching in a Diverse Society* (Boston: Allyn and Bacon, 1995); M. Lee Manning and Leroy G. Baruth, *Education, Children and Adolescents* (Boston: Allyn and Bacon, 1996).

EVERS, MEDGAR (1925–1963), a Field Secretary for the National Association for the Advancement of Colored People (NAACP), was a central figure during the American Civil Rights Movement. Since the Civil Rights Movement is a basic prerequisite for the utilization of a multicultural, educational approach to teaching and learning, teachers and students need to understand the significance of his accomplishments and the reasons for his tragic death at an early age.

During his tenure in the NAACP, he played an important role in the Emmett Till case. Dressed as a sharecropper, he investigated Till's murder by visiting plantations, making contact with local people, and working with the press. He was a friend of James Meredith, the first African American to attend and graduate from the University of Mississippi. He monitored Meredith's situation for the NAACP.

He was also instrumental in organizing the civil rights movement in the state of Mississippi, launching a major campaign in Jackson. He had a running argument with Mayor Allen C. Thompson over a number of segregation issues. However, his speeches against segregation in Jackson and throughout Mississippi led to tragedy. His house was bombed with a Molotov cocktail, and he lodged a formal complaint with the U.S. Justice Department. His actions infuriated the Ku Klux Klan and other white supremacists in Mississippi.

An avowed racist, Byron de la Beckwith was particularly incensed. A member of the Ku Klux Klan and later the Christian Identity Movement, he believed that the Bible was not written for Jews, African Americans, and liberal European Americans. Moreover, he was consumed with hatred for Jews and African Americans. He also had a special hatred of President John Kennedy because of his Catholic religion and his advocacy of Civil Rights.

On June 11, 1963, Beckwith laid in wait for Evers and murdered him with a shot to the back. He was arrested because of a matched fingerprint on the scope of his rifle. However, his first and second trials, held in 1964, resulted in mistrials. The juries in both cases consisted of European-American males. However, 30 years later, Assistant District Attorney Bobby de Laughter was successful in his prosecution during Beckwith's third trial for murder. This time, the jury consisted of eight African Americans and four European Americans.

References: Medgar Evers, "Why I Live in Mississippi," *Ebony* (September 1963); Adam Nossiter, *Of Long Memory: Mississippi and the Murder of Medgar Evers* (New York: Addison-Wesley, 1994); Reed Massengill, *Portrait of the Man Who Killed Medgar Evers?* (New York: St. Martin's Press, 1994); Maryann Vollers, *Ghosts of Medgar Evers, the Trial of Byron de la Beckwith, and the Haunting of the New South* (Boston: Little, Brown, 1995).

EXECUTIVE ORDER #9066 was one of the most significant presidential orders in American history. Issued in 1942 by President Franklin Roosevelt, the action resulted in Japanese-American citizens being sent to assembly centers, many of them race tracks such as Santa Anita. Eventually, they were assigned to ten relocation centers throughout the United States. Two-thirds of the Japanese Americans who were sent to these camps were U.S. citizens.

Two of these camps (Tule Lake and Manzanar) were located in California. Minidoko was situated in Idaho, Topaz in Utah, Poston and Gila River in Arizona, Heart Mountain in Wyoming, Granada in Colorado, and Rohwer and Jerome in Arkansas. The Japanese-American prisoners were guarded by armed soldiers. During their incarceration, many prisoners' land and belongings were taken and sometimes never returned.

The justification for incarcerating the Japanese Americans was that they needed protection from other Americans because of the war. Being Japanese Americans, they were physically visible and from the same racial/ethnic group that the United States was fighting in the Pacific theatre. However, the United States was also fighting against Germany and other countries. None of these European Americans were interned in relocation centers.

Since a Japanese-American unit became the most decorated U.S. military unit in the European theatre, teachers can use this episode of the loyalty of American citizens who do not have European roots.

References: Harry H. L. Kitano, *Japanese Americans: The Evolution of a Sub-Culture* (Englewood Cliffs, NJ: Prentice-Hall, 1976); Takao U. Nakano and Leatrice Takano Nakano, *Within the Barbed Wire Fence: A Japanese Man's Account of his Internment* (Seattle: University of Washington Press, 1980); William Peterson, *Japanese Americans* (New York: Random House, 1971); John Tateishi, *And Justice for All: An Oral History of the Japanese-American Detention Camps* (New York: Random House, 1984).

F

FARMER, JAMES (1920–), one of the key African-American figures of the American Civil Rights Movement, was the director of the Congress of Racial Equality (CORE). He espoused an integrationist/interracial posture, something for which he was often criticized by his more militant followers. Farmer received a theology degree from Howard University and was instrumental in founding CORE in 1942.

During the American Civil Rights Movement, Farmer led a group of Freedom Riders who were arrested in Jackson, Mississippi. As director of CORE, Farmer was convinced that the federal government did not have the will to enforce the new civil rights laws enacted during the Kennedy Administration. So he organized the "Freedom Rides" to test the waters. During these episodes, Farmer and his followers adopted such strategies as having European-American sympathizers ride in the back of busses while African-American riders would ride in the front. At the rest stops, African Americans would frequent "Whites-Only" rest rooms.

Educators who are studying the American Civil Rights Movement may wish to hold debates on the wisdom of Farmer's non-violent strategies. Students might argue the wisdom of his non-violent position in terms of the zeitgeist (spirit of the times) and in terms of the present racial climate in the United States.

References: John Hope Franklin, *Race and History* (Baton Rouge: Louisiana State University Press, 1989); Sharon Harley, *The Timetables of African-American History* (New York: Simon and Schuster, 1995); Juan Williams, *Eyes on the Prize: America's Civil Rights Years, 1954–1965* (New York: Viking Press, 1987).

FARRAKHAN, LOUIS (LOUIS EUGENE WALCOTT) (1933–), head of the Nation of Islam, formed that organization in 1977. As a minister in the World Community of Islam, Farrakhan decided to leave the World Community of Islam in favor of starting a similar organization in the United States. Under his leadership, the Nation of Islam was based in the tradition of Elijah Muhammad's Black Muslim Mission. Critics of the organization have argued that the group is militant, anti-white, and anti-Jewish. In 1996, Farrakhan visited Libya's Muammar el-Qadaffi in hopes of securing additional funding for his group.

Farrakhan has been given credit for his efforts to aid African-American inner-city youth and the initiation of the largest civil rights demonstration to date. This occurred on October 16, 1995, when over 850,000 African-American men responded to the Nation of Islam's promotion of a mass meeting on the mall outside the U.S. Congress. The purpose of the gathering was to urge African-American men to become better fathers, husbands, and members of their communities. According to a *Washington Post* poll, only about 5 percent came because of any particular loyalty to Farrakhan. Most of them attended to show unity and to create a more positive image of African-American men.

References: George M. Fredrickson, *Black Liberation* (New York: Oxford University Press, 1995); Sharon Harley, *The Timetables of African American History* (New York: Simon and Schuster, 1995); Jeffrey C. Stewart, *One Thousand One Things You Wanted to Know About African-American History* (New York: Doubleday, 1996).

FIFTEENTH AMENDMENT, passed by Congress in 1870, prohibited the federal government and all states from denying voting privileges to any U.S. citizen on account of race, color, or previous condition of servitude. Teachers can discuss how this amendment also made it possible for Congress to enforce the article through the enactment of appropriate legislation.

To thwart the intent of this Constitutional Amendment, Southern states established poll taxes and literacy laws that effectively prevented many African Americans from voting. This condition did not change substantially until the passing of the Voter Rights Act of 1964.

References: Arval A. Morris, *The Constitution and Public Education* (St. Paul, MN: West, 1980); *Dictionary of American History* (New York: Charles Scribner's Sons, 1984); Perry A. Zirkel and Sharon Nalbone Richardson, *A Digest of Supreme Court Decisions Affecting Education* (Bloomington, IN: Phi Delta Kappa Foundation, 1988).

FILIPINO AMERICANS have become recognized as one of the United States' most effective participants in the nation's agricultural industry. From a multicultural, educational standpoint, history teachers who have emphasized the pluralistic nature of America's history have characterized Filipino Americans as key participants in America's agricultural industry. Moreover, they fought bravely with the United States at Bataan and other World War II battle sites.

Ever since the Philippine Islands were ceded to the United States in the 1898 Treaty of Paris, Filipinos have migrated to Hawaii, California, Washington, and Oregon in large numbers. By 1980, Filipino Americans had become the second largest Asian ethnic group in the United States.

Filipino Americans have been victimized because of their race and ethnicity. Since they were sometimes seen as competing for agricultural jobs held by European Americans, they have been the target of overt racism. For example, during 1928 in the Yakima Valley, 60 Filipino Americans were stopped by 200 European-American farm workers. An angry mob forced them to leave the city. They were told never to come back.

References: James A. Banks, *Teaching Strategies for Ethnic Studies*, 6th ed. (Boston: Allyn and Bacon, 1997); Edna Bonacick, ''A Theory of Ethnic Antagonism: The Split Labor Market,'' *American Sociological Review* 37(5) (October 1972); Hyung-Chan Kim and Cynthia C. Mejia, *The Filipinos in America, 1898–1974* (New York: Oceana, 1974): Ronald Takaki, *Strangers from Different Shores* (Boston: Little, Brown, 1989).

FONG, HIRAM LEONG (1906–), a Hawaiian-born, Chinese-American elected a U.S. senator when Hawaii first achieved statehood in 1959, became one of the very first Asian Americans elected to Congress. Prior to that time, he served in the Hawaiian Territorial House from 1938 until 1949, when he became Speaker of that organization.

References: Suchen Chan, *Asian-Americans: An Independent History* (Boston: Twayne Publishers, 1991); George Cooper and Gavan Daws, *Land and Power in Hawaii* (Honolulu: Benchmark Books, 1985); Bill Hosokawa, *Nisei—The Quiet Story of a People* (New York: William Morrow, 1969).

FOURTEENTH AMENDMENT, passed in 1967 by an act of Congress, stipulated that ''All persons born or naturalized in the United States, and subject to the jurisdiction thereof, are citizens of the United States and of the State wherein they reside. No State shall make or enforce any law which shall abridge the privileges or immunities of citizens of the United States; nor shall any State deprive any person of life, liberty, or property, without due process of law; nor deny to any person within its jurisdiction the equal protection of the laws.''

While the Fourteenth Amendment made civil rights legislation the law of the land, African Americans were still deemed to be ''second-class citizens'' by many Americans. In order for any state to be readmitted to the Union, it was necessary for their legislatures to first ratify the Fourteenth Amendment.

Teachers who are studying the U.S. Constitution with their students can examine a number of Supreme Court decisions that are based on interpretations of the Fourteenth Amendment.

References: James C. Curtis and Lewis L. Gould, *The Black Experience in America* (Austin: University of Texas Press, 1970); Louis Fischer, David Schimmel, and Cynthia Kelly, *Teachers and the Law* (White Plains, NY: Longman, 1995); John Hope Franklin, *Race and History: Selected Essays, 1938–1988* (Baton Rouge: Louisiana State University Press, 1989); Arval A. Morris, *The Constitution and American Education* (St. Paul, MN: West, 1980).

FREEDMEN'S BUREAU, established in 1865, had the responsibility for facilitating the reconstruction of the South after the Civil War. It provided emergency food and shelter to persons who were dislocated after the conflict. Originally, it was commissioned for one year, but subsequent Congressional actions sustained the Bureau until 1874. Major General Oliver Otis Howard was in charge of the organization during its period of operation. Howard University was named after him.

In addition to providing food and shelter for displaced persons, the Bureau also attempted to help newly freed slaves adjust to freedom. The Bureau provided medical care through army doctors and hospitals, improved sanitary conditions in the homes of freed slaves, and even helped negotiate labor contracts with employers and aided in the administration of justice to freed slaves. It was bitterly opposed in the South, and its agents were even attacked by the Ku Klux Klan.

The topic is not often addressed in American history books, and it is important for teachers to draw parallels between the Freedmen's Bureau and other modern-day attempts to address the special needs of Americans who make up the country's culture of poverty.

References: *Dictionary of American History* (New York: Charles Scribner's Sons, 1984); Jeffrey C. Stewart, *One Thousand One Things You Wanted to Know About African-American History* (New York: Doubleday, 1996).

FREEDOM RIDERS, beginning May 4, 1961, constitute an important segment of the curriculum concerning the American Civil Rights Movement. Thirteen young civil rights advocates, consisting of both European Americans and African Americans, embarked on a bus trip through the South to protest and challenge segregated bus facilities. Organized by the Congress of Racial Equality (CORE), the strategy was also intended to challenge not only the segregated seating on busses but the segregation of waiting rooms, rest rooms, etc.

In studying this aspect of the civil rights era, teachers can discuss the similarities and differences in the bombing of the Freedom Riders' bus near Amiston, Alabama, with the brutal bombing of the Federal Building in Oklahoma.

Eventually, the Freedom Riders were arrested in Mississippi, after being twice attacked in Birmingham and Montgomery. However, CORE was successful in convincing the U.S. Supreme Court to order a refund of their bond money.

Attorney General Robert Kennedy successfully persuaded the Interstate Commerce Department to issue a directive ending bus segregation in the South.

References: John Hope Franklin, *From Slavery to Freedom: A History of Negro Americans*, 3d ed. (New York: Vintage Books, 1967); Arthur Schlesinger, Jr., *Robert Kennedy and His Times* (Boston: Houghton, Mifflin, 1978); Juan Williams, *Eyes on the Prize: America's Civil Rights Years, 1954–1965* (New York: Viking Press, 1987).

FRENCH AND INDIAN WAR, a conflict in North America, was fought between 1754 and 1763. It was a series of battles between France, its Canadian colonies, and its Native-American allies against Britain and their American colonies. It was a struggle for the control of North America.

Beginning in 1754, when French Canadians constructed Fort Duquesne at the forks of the Ohio River, the Virginia colony sent a force under the command of George Washington, a 22-year-old lieutenant colonel at the time. However, his attempt to evict the Canadians failed. But, by 1763, the tide had turned in favor of the British, and the war was terminated through the Treaty of Paris agreement. Thus, the United States became an English-speaking nation, since the French relinquished most of their rights in North America.

Native Americans suffered enormous casualties during the conflicts. They also lost an important ally in France. Many of them would be moved west of the Mississippi less than 60 years later as a result of the Removal Act of 1830. Their guerrilla tactics had a profound affect on the nature of the future American wars.

References: Thomas Forsyth, "The French, British, and Spanish Way of Treating Indians," *Ethnohistory* 4(2) (Spring 1957); Frederick E. Hoxie (Ed.), *Indians in American History* (Arlington Heights, IL: Harlan Davidson, 1988); Edward H. Spicer, *A Short History of the Indians of North America* (New York: Van Nostrand Reinhold, 1968); Jack Weatherford, *Native Roots: How the Indians Enriched America* (New York: Crown, 1991).

FUGITIVE SLAVE LAWS were enacted to protect the property rights of slave owners in the American colonies and states prior to the Civil War. Extreme penalties were imposed on both the runaway slaves and anyone who aided them in their escape. Some of the laws were actually imposed during colonial times against white indentured servants, as well as African-American slaves.

Following the American Revolution, the Fugitive Slave Act of 1793 was passed. This gave legal support to masters attempting to retrieve their runaways. By that time, slavery had been abolished in most of the northern states. Northern states passed personal liberty laws intended to protect their citizens against slave catchers.

The sentiment in the North against slavery was intensifying during the first half of the nineteenth century due to the anti-slavery stances taken by Protestant religious denominations and the Amistad Case, which ruled in favor of African slaves. The Dred Scott Supreme Court decision of 1857 intensified the anti-slavery rhetoric when the Court ruled that slaves were not free, even when they moved to free states. Moreover, the decision stipulated that African slaves were not and could never become U.S. citizens. The North/South antagonisms intensified, moving the nation closer to the Civil War hostilities. These concepts can be included in educators' attempts to paint a true, multicultural picture of American history. The Fugitive Slave Act can also be used to illustrate the blatant racist attitudes of those times.

References: Bruce M. Mitchell, et al., *The Dynamic Classroom*, 5th ed. (Dubuque, IA: Kendall/Hunt, 1995); Ray Noel, *Witnessing America* (New York: Penguin Books, 1996); Jeffrey C. Stewart, *One Thousand and One Things Everyone Wanted to Know About African-American History* (New York: Doubleday, 1996).

G

GALARZA, ERNESTO (1905–1984), an activist and author during the Civil Rights movement, wrote his famous book *Barrio Boy*, which can be used to teach the concept of acculturation in middle school and high school. In *Barrio Boy*, Galarza has discussed the problems of Mexican people as they migrated north from Mexico. He has described the *barrio* as a place where Mexican immigrants were able to acquire a bed and something to eat until they were able to acquire employment and become self-sufficient. The *barrio* was also a microculture that contained many of the cultural traditions of Mexico.

Some of the typical *barrio* activities described by Galarza were such things as Mexican plays and traveling sideshows. In Mexican cafes people can purchase frijoles, tortillas, menudo, and dulces made from Mexican sugar (piloncillo). Galarza, in his writings, has described the *barrio* as a kind of cultural cooperative where people look out for one another.

In addition to his scholarly writing and educational accomplishments, he was also a labor organizer in the 1930s. He worked as a harvest hand, laborer, and cannery employee in the central valley of California. Born in Tepic, Mexico, Galarza received his Ph.D. from Columbia University.

References: Ernesto Galarza, *Barrio Boy* (South Bend, IN: University of Notre Dame Press, 1971); Ernesto Galarza, *Spiders in the House and Workers in the Field* (South Bend, IN: University of Notre Dame Press, 1970); Ernesto Galarza, *Merchants of Labor: The Mexican Bracero Story* (Santa Barbara, CA: McNally and Loftin, 1964); Ronald Takaki, *A Different Mirror: A History of Multicultural America* (Boston: Little, Brown, 1993).

GANDHI, MAHATMA (MOHANDA KARAMCHAND) (1869–1948), leader of the Indian Nationalist movement, was known during his later life as

Mahatma, which meant *great soul.* He became famous throughout the world for his notions of non-violent demonstrations against the British, as he attempted to gain his country's independence. Gandhi's ideas of non-violent, civil disobedience became the strategies of many great civil rights leaders around the world, including Martin Luther King and Caesar Chavez in the United States.

While his father was a chief minister for the maharaja of Porbander, the family came from a rather traditional caste of Indians, including grocers and money lenders. In fact, *Gandhi* means *"grocer."* Many of his non-violent ideas came from his mother, who was a follower of Jainism, a religion that placed great importance on non-violence and vegetarianism.

After studying law in England and passing the bar, he practiced law in Bombay, later working for an Indian firm in South Africa from 1893 to 1914. He first experienced racism in South Africa, which was directed at both the Indian community and black South Africans. After his return to India, he became involved in labor organizing.

Gandhi organized protest marches and boycotts against the British for unpopular British actions, such as the salt tax of 1930. For these actions he was repeatedly imprisoned and resorted to hunger strikes, which all became part of his civil disobedience strategies. In addition to his struggle for independence from the British, Gandhi fought to improve the status of India's Untouchables, and he attempted to terminate the hostilities between the Hindus and Muslims and prevent them from forming a separate state, Pakistan. He was assassinated in 1948 by a Hindu fanatic.

Studying the life of Gandhi can assist classroom teachers in helping students to understand the employment of non-violent strategies during the American Civil Rights Movement. His commitment to non-violence and his accomplishments through such strategies can provide valuable lessons for students of all ages.

References: Geoffrey Ashe, *Ghandi* (New York: Stein and Day, 1968); Erik Ericson, *Gandhi's Truths* (New York: W. W. Norton, 1969); Mahatma Gandhi, *All Men Are Brothers*, Ed. Krishna Kripalani (Ahmadabad, India: Navajivan Press, 1960); Ved Mehta, *Mahatma and His Apostles* (New York: Viking Press, 1976); March Shepard, *Gandhi Today* (Washington, DC: Seven Locks Press, 1987).

GARVEY, MARCUS (1887–1940), an African-Jamaican, founded the Universal Negro Improvement Association (UNIA) in 1914 and moved it to New York City in 1916. The goals of the organization were to create unity and improve the lives of African Jamaicans and African Americans. By 1919 the organization had acquired a membership of about 2 million people, and branches of the organization were established in several American cities.

In his weekly newspaper, *Negro World*, he argued that African Americans had a proud past and a great future. He maintained that it was necessary to abandon their feelings of inferiority and create their own unique culture. He also felt that it was important for African Americans to return to their homeland. To do this, he started a back-to-Africa movement, and created the Black Star Line, a steamship line that attempted to establish trade routes among Black areas of the world. He was successful in helping many African Americans return to Liberia. However, many of them returned to the United States when they discovered that they often had little in common with native Liberians. The Black Star Line ran into immediate financial difficulties and only lasted about a year.

During the sale of the Black Star Line, Garvey was convicted of mail fraud. Then, under pressure from Britain and France, the Liberian government abandoned the UNIA's colonization and development program in Africa. After serving four years of his mail fraud sentence, Garvey was deported to Jamaica in 1927. He moved to London in 1934, where he resided for six years until his death.

References: E. David Cronon, *Black Moses: The Story of Marcus Garvey and the Universal Negro Improvement Association* (Madison: University of Wisconsin Press, 1969); John Hope Franklin (Ed.), *Color and Race* (Boston: Houghton Mifflin, 1968); Amy J. Garvey (Ed.), *Philosophy and Opinions of Marcus Garvey* (Dover, MA: Majority Press, 1986).

GENDER EQUITY in multicultural, educational circles refers to nonsexist education and socio/political issues that affect American life in general. The multicultural, educational literature makes a strong point of exposing students to the contributions of both women and men, while required readings include the works of renown contemporary female authors such as Barbara Kinsolver and Ursula Hegi. This example can also be carried out in other areas of the curriculum, including science, math, music, art, and the like.

In the social sciences, students can explore such issues as the dearth of women in the *Fortune* 500 CEO positions or the problems relating to Title IX of the 1972 Education Amendments. These and other topics should be addressed regularly in the social studies curriculum as an integral part of the economic and historical life of the nation.

Expanding on these topics, teachers might also do studies of comparative modern-day cultures to investigate the role of religion in gender roles and expectations for women. Also, gender issues can be investigated through women's studies, approaches that analyze the concepts of consciousness-raising, along with the examination of special needs, accomplishments, and achievements of a specific group.

References: Donna M. Gollnick and Philip C. Chinn, *Multicultural Education in a Pluralistic Society* (Columbus, OH: Merrill, 1990); Herbert Grossman, *Teaching in a Diverse Society* (Boston: Allyn and Bacon, 1995); M. Lee Manning and Leroy G. Baruth, *Multicultural Education of Children and Adolescents* (Boston: Allyn and Bacon, 1996).

GENOCIDE, an English word having its roots in the Greek word *genos*, which means race, and the Latin word *cide*, which means killing, has been used in the multicultural, educational literature to represent systematic attempts to kill members of specific ethnic groups. Coined by a Polish-American scholar named Raphel Lempkin, genocide was practiced by the Russians against the Jews and by the German Nazis.

Normally, genocide occurs when one ethnic group is concerned about the rising power of another specific ethnic group. World War II examples of genocide include the murders of ethnic Jews, Poles, and Gypsies by German Nazis. After World War II, various tribal groups in Africa were slaughtered by Edi Amin Dada, former president of Uganda.

The General Assembly of the United Nations declared that genocide was a crime and a matter of international concern that could result in major punishments inflicted through the offices of the United Nations. Nations ratifying this 1958 measure agreed that genocide was a matter of international concern, even though it might be committed by a government against its own peoples. An example of such a situation would be the assault on the Iraqi Kurds by Iraqi President Saddam Hussein.

The U.S. Senate, with a historical preference for not subjecting U.S. citizens to the jurisdictions of international tribunals, finally ratified this measure in 1986.

References: Irving Horowitz, *Taking Lives: Genocide and State Power*, 3d ed. (New Brunswick, NJ: Transaction Books, 1980); Isador Wallman and Michael Dobkowski, *Genocide and the Modern Age* (Westport, CT: Greenwood Press, 1987).

GERONIMO (1829–1909), a leader of the Chiricahua Apaches, conducted a series of raids against American and Mexican settlements in the Southwest. His Apache name was Goyathlay ''one who yawns.'' Studies of multicultural America can address the concept that the original residents of the United States represented a plethora of microcultures, each with their unique ways of life. Geronimo can be used as an example of an Apache leader who offered fierce resistance against the European notion of manifest destiny, which provided a rationalization for their encroachment on Native American territories.

Geronimo was not a chief in the typical sense. Rather, he was a shaman to whom chiefs would often turn for guidance. His skill in guerrilla tactics made him one of the most successful defenders against the European-American invasions of Apache lands. In fact, after the death of such notable chiefs as Cochise, Mangss Coloradus, and Victorio, he held out for five years.

Finally, General Nelson A. Miles, who had aspirations of becoming President of the United States and was a renowned Indian fighter, subdued Geronimo through the use of deceitful tactics in 1886. After being united with his wife in Florida, Geronimo was returned to Fort Sill, Oklahoma, where he died and was buried in 1909.

References: Alexander B. Adams, *Geronimo: A Biography* (New York: G. P. Putnam's Sons, 1971); John Bigelow, *On the Bloody Trail of Geronimo* (Los Angeles: Westernlore Press, 1968) Angie Debo, *Geronimo: The Man, His Time, His Place* (Norman: University of Oklahoma Press, 1976); M. M. Quaife (Ed.), *The Truth About Geronimo* (New Haven, CT: Yale University Press, 1969); John Edward Weems, *Death Song: The Last of the Indian Wars* (Garden City, NY: Doubleday, 1976).

GHETTO was used originally in referring to areas of European and Middle-Eastern cities that became Jewish communities. Starting in the twelfth century, Jews were often required by law to live apart from Christians in their own ethnic enclaves. However, the term acquired a new meaning after the termination of World War II when it was used to describe areas of confinement or voluntary residences of minority populations. Some of these areas were residences for persons because of ''sundown laws,'' which made it impossible for certain racial and/or ethnic groups to stay in certain cities or sections of cities after the sun went down. Other ghettos were created because of redlining tactics of realtors who only sold houses to minority persons in designated sections of cities.

Ghettos are often associated with poverty, high crime rates, drug sales, prostitution, poor school performance by children, and people from the same or similar racial and/or ethnic backgrounds. For many people, there has been a perception that you are confined to these areas, but often the goal has been to become upwardly mobile economically to break away from poverty. However, for others, the racial and/or ethnic characteristics have provided a comfort zone, which has negated any desire to move away.

Probably the most famous African-American ghetto in the United States has been Harlem, New York. Other famous ghettos are the south side of Chicago and Watts in Los Angeles. In spite of the poverty that has plagued such areas, ghettos have motivated some of America's most significant accomplishments in the arts. For example, the Apollo Theater in Harlem provided a performance site for some of the country's most gifted and talented musicians who were often denied access to ''Whites-only'' performance sites.

From this description, the multicultural implications for teachers are obvious. Sociologically and historically, studying the ghetto is mandatory if students are to understand the effects of poverty on America's microcultures. Artistically, it is necessary to investigate life in the ghetto to understand the nuances of the various American art forms.

References: Kenneth Clark, *Dark Ghetto: Dilemmas of Social Power* (New York: Harper and Row, 1965); Robert C. Smith and Richard Seltzer, *Race, Class, and Culture* (Albany: State University of New York Press, 1992); James C. Stone and Donald P. DeNevi (Eds.), *Teaching Multicultural Populations* (New York: D. Van Nostrand, 1971); William Julius Wilson, *The Truly Disadvantaged, The Inner City, The Underclass, and Public Policy* (Chicago: University of Chicago Press, 1987).

GHOST DANCE, referring to a messianic movement that developed during the last three decades of the nineteenth century, expressed a longing for the restoration of the past. The Ghost Dance, based on the vision experienced by a Paiute Indian named Wovoka, called for a return to a life free of hunger and disease and free of the encroachments of European Americans. The vision also precipitated ideas such as the resurrection of tribal members who had died, the restoration of game animals, and a flood that would destroy only the European-American settlers.

During the Battle of Wounded Knee, which cost the lives of about 200 Sioux warriors, women, and children, many of the Native American participants wore "ghost shirts" adorned with eagle, buffalo, and morning-star decorations. The belief was that such symbols of powerful spirits would protect them from the European-American bullets. The defeat at Wounded Knee was instrumental in putting an end to much of the Ghost Dance lore.

References: Paul Bailey, *Wovoka: The Indian Messiah* (Los Angeles: Westernlore Press, 1957); James Mooney, "The Ghost Dance Religion and the Sioux Outbreak of 1890," *Annual Report of the Bureau of American Ethnology*, Vol. 14 (Washington, DC: U.S. Government Printing Office, 1986); Thomas Overhold, *Channels of Prophecy: The Social Dynamics of Prophetic Activity* (Minneapolis, MN: Fortress Press, 1989); Bryan R. Wilson, *Magic and the Millennium* (New York: Harper & Row, 1973).

GONG LUM v. RICE, a key Supreme Court Decision leading up to the *Brown v. Board of Education* decision related to a Chinese-American student in Mississippi, who was forced to attend a segregated school for African-American students. Believing that their daughter was not receiving an adequate education in the segregated Black school, the parents petitioned the school district to reassign her to the segregated school for European Americans. The school district, backed by the Mississippi Superintendent of Schools, ruled that she must attend the segregated school for African-American children, based on the state Constitution that stipulated that "separate schools shall be maintained for children of the White and colored races."

In a 9–0 decision, the Supreme Court ruled that the rights of the Chinese-American student were not violated by including her with African-American children for educational purposes. The Court stipulated that states could regulate the manner in which education is provided at public expense.

References: *Gong Lum v. Rice*, 275 U.S. 78, 1927; Perry A. Zirkel and Sharon Nalbone Richardson, *A Digest of Supreme Court Decisions Affecting Education* (Bloomington, IN: Phi Delta Kappa Education Foundation, 1988).

GONZALES, CORKY (1928–), an ex-boxer known as the "Denver Battler," first became known as a civil rights leader during the American Civil Rights Movement in the 1960s. He founded the Crusade for Justice, one of the first organizations that promoted the rights of Chicanos. He started a school (Escuela Tlatelolco) that taught the history of the southwestern United States from a Latino perspective. The school achieved a population of about 350 during its peak years.

Gonzales was influential in persuading boards of education to revise their Eurocentric curricula in favor or a more multicultural approach to better help students appreciate the cultural and racial diversity of the United States. He also argued that the contributions of Latinos must be part of the teaching curriculum along with bilingual/bicultural programs in the schools. Eventually, Gonzales' school declined in enrollment, but he was always firm in his convictions about the importance of developing pride in culture among Latino peoples.

References: *Denver Post*, March 3, December 10, 1985; Lester D. Langley, *MexAmerica: Two Countries, One Future* (New York: Crown Publishers, 1988); Matt Meier and Feliciano Rivera, *The Chicanos: A History of Mexican Americans* (New York: Hill and Wang, 1972).

GOODMAN, BENNY (1909–1986), known as the king of swing, led one of America's finest swing bands when that musical art form was popular during the 1940s and 1950s. A Jewish American, Goodman became known for his prowess on the clarinet and because he was one of the first major American jazz figures to integrate his groups racially with the addition of Teddy Wilson (piano), Charlie Christian (guitar), and Lionel Hampton (vibraphone).

One of the most important groups in the evolution of American jazz was the Benny Goodman Trio, including Goodman (clarinet), Gene Krupa (drums), and Teddy Wilson (piano). After 1945, he usually played with small groups, but he also performed as a soloist with classical orchestras. Viewed as one of the key figures in American jazz, he is an essential exponent of the racial integration of this important American art form.

References: James Lincoln Collier, *Benny Goodman and the Swing Era* (New York: Oxford University Press, 1989); Stanley Dance, *The World of Swing* (New York: Scribner, 1974); Ross Firestone, *Swing, Swing, Swing: The Life and Times of Benny Goodman* (New York: Norton, 1993).

GREEK ORTHODOX CHURCH, one of the Eastern Rite Christian churches, has several Orthodox churches in the United States with ties to the old-world churches. In Greece, aside from a few Muslims, most people are members of the Greek Orthodox Church. The term "Greek Church" has been used somewhat generically and usually refers to the patriarchate of Constantinople, the Church of Greece, and religious bodies using the Byzantine rite with the liturgy in Greek. The Greek Orthodox Church is the church of choice for many Greek Americans.

GREGORY, DICK (1932–), one of the first African-American comedians to use topical, nonstereotyped material, became a highly successful performer during the 1960s when his satirical wit brought him wide fame in college concerts, nightclubs, and on television. Known as a civil rights activist, his comedy routines espoused an anti-Vietnam War posture. He was particularly prominent in promoting better health care and nutrition for American persons from the culture of poverty.

In 1968, he was the presidential candidate for the Peace and Freedom Party. His writings include *From the Back of the Bus* (1962), *Write Me In* (1968), *Dick Gregory's Political Primer* (1971), and *The Murder of Dr. Martin Luther King Jr.* (1977).

References: Dick Gregory, *Nigger: An Autobiography* (New York: Dutton, 1964); Dick Gregory, *No More Lies: The Myth and Reality of American History* (New York: Harper and Row, 1971).

GYPSIES, a distinct ethnic group originating in north central India, were a migratory group known for their singing and dancing. They have been known for their nomadic lifestyle and now live all over the world, maintaining their distinctive language and folk culture. Today (1997) there are an estimated 8 to 10 million Gypsies living in some 40 countries. About 1 million reside in North America.

The first Gypsies arrived in North America from England. There is a 1695 court record in Henrico County, Virginia, of their presence in North America. Between 1801 and 1803, Napoleon transported hundreds of Gypsies to Louisiana, Spain, and Portugal. However, most of the Gypsies residing in the United States descend from immigrants of the Eastern European diaspora of the 1880s, 1890s, and 1900s. North American Gypsies work and live in extended families, preferring to be self-employed.

Many women are fortune tellers, while a large number of the men prefer occupations in buying and selling automobiles and trucks. Some are involved in real estate transactions. American Gypsies have their own legal system and legal disagreements are adjudicated by the *kris*, a tribunal of elders.

References: Bart McDowell, *Gypsies: Wanderers of the World* (Washington, DC: National Geographic Society, 1970); Walter Fitz Starkie, *In Sara's Tents* (New York: E. P. Dutton, 1953); John Hornby, *Gypsies* (New York: H. Z. Walck, 1967); Jean Paul Clebert, *The Gypsies* (London: Vista Books, 1963); Bernice Kohn, *The Gypsies* (Indianapolis, IN: Bobbs & Merrill, 1972).

H

HALEY, ALEX (1921–1992) was an African-American author who became famous for his 1976 book, *Roots: The Saga of an American Family.* Spending about twelve years researching the project, the story depicts life as he imagined it for his ancestors in Gambia as they were abducted and sold into slavery. Haley's ancestor, Kunta Kinte, was kidnapped in 1767 and taken to America on a slave ship. The story traces the exploits of the family as they were sold into servitude and later became free people.

The resulting television dramatization attracted one of the largest audiences in television history. Born in Ithaca, New York, Haley grew up in several southern communities. When his famous book came out in 1977, it was seen by one of the largest television audiences in American history. Haley got his start writing while he served in the U.S. Coast Guard from 1939 to 1959.

Roots sold more than 1.6 million copies just six months after it was first published. It was printed in 22 languages, and Haley received a special Pulitzer prize for the book, which has been successfully used by teachers as a piece of classic American literature about the history of slavery in the United States.

However, Haley is also noted for his other works of literature, including a biography of Malcolm X. Literature teachers can use Haley as a classic example of the many contributions of African-American writers in the field of literature. *Roots* can also become a useful work when discussing the colonization of Africa and the slave trade that was carried on by Europeans and Americans.

References: Alex Haley, *Roots: The Saga of an American Family* (Boston: G. K. Hall, 1979); Alex Haley, *Autobiography of Malcolm X* (New York: Ballantine Books, 1992); Alex Haley and David Stevens, *Queen: The Story of an American Family* (New York: Avon, 1994); Sharon Harley, *The Timetables of African-American History* (New York: Simon and Schuster, 1995).

HAMILTON, VIRGINIA (1936–) has become known as an important author of multicultural reading materials for children. The great-granddaughter of an African-American slave, she has received the Hans Christian Anderson Medal, the National Book Award, the John Newberry Medal, the Coretta Scott King Award, the Boston Globe-Horn Book Award, the Edgar Allen Poe Award, and the Regina Medal. In 1995, she received the Laura Ingalls Wilder Medal for her many contributions to children's literature. She lives in the same Ohio community where her grandmother resided after escaping from slavery. In recognition of her many contributions to the field of children's literature, she received an honorary doctorate from Ohio State University.

Reference: Virginia Hamilton, *Her Stories: African American Folktales, Fairy Tales, and True Tales* (New York: The Blue Sky Press, 1995).

HARDIN, LILLIAN (1898–1971), the second wife of Louis Armstrong, was one of the African-American women who helped in the early development of American jazz. While playing at the Dreamland Cafe in South Chicago with Ollie Powers' Band, she met Louis Armstrong, who had been called to Chicago to become the second cornet for Joe ''King'' Oliver's Band. She and Armstrong married at Chicago's City Hall on February 5, 1924.

Although Hardin had begged her husband to start his own group, he spent about a year in New York with the Fletcher Henderson Band. Lil remained in Chicago, performing at the *Dreamland* with her own group. In 1925, she played piano in the Hot Five, which made some of the finest New Orleans jazz recordings of all time. The group included Kid Ory (trombone), Johnny St. Cyr (banjo), and Johnny Dodds (clarinet), in addition to Lil and Louis.

While Hardin has sometimes been characterized as a rather mediocre piano player, she is important to the development of jazz because of her gender. In the early days of jazz, it was a man's world; Lil Hardin must be remembered because she was a musician who played jazz with the famous African-American males of that era. Thus, she can be used as an important example of the courageous American women who broke into male-dominated professions.

References: Dave Dexter, Jr., *The Jazz Story: From the '90s to the '60s* (Englewood Cliffs, NJ: Prentice-Hall, 1964); Gunther Schuller, *Early Jazz: Its Roots and Musical Development* (New York: Oxford University Press, 1968).

HARLEM, located on Manhattan Island in New York, was primarily a European-American residential area of New York City until about 1910. However, African Americans had resided there since the seventeenth century. During slavery, they constructed the original wagon road on Manhattan Island and also worked on estates and farms in New Amsterdam. By 1790, about one third of the residents in present-day Harlem were of African-American descent. However, by 1890, Harlem was composed of predominantly European-American residents.

During the last decade of the 1800s, African Americans commenced to settle in Harlem. And while Harlem was still composed of many European Americans during 1910, by 1914, about 50,000 African Americans resided there. Between 1920 and 1930, approximately 119,000 European Americans left the Harlem area. The Temple of Israel in Harlem became the Mount Olive Baptist Church. Harlem became home to more than 60 percent of all the African-American people living in Manhattan.

Harlem had become a place where African Americans felt that they could pursue the American dream. During the 1920s, 1930s and 1940s, Harlem became known as an African-American cultural center, which helped promote the development of American jazz, drama, and other art forms as well. Many of the residents worked as barbers, waiters, and skilled craftspersons.

References: Gilbert Osofsky, *Harlem: The Making of a Ghetto, Negro New York, 1890–1930* (New York: Harper and Row, 1966); Thomas Sowell, *Ethnic America: A History* (New York: Basic Books, 1981); Ronald Takaki, *A Different Mirror: A History of Multicultural America* (Boston: Little, Brown, 1993).

HARLEM RENAISSANCE, a phenomenon that emphasized the accomplishments of African Americans, helped to establish an African-American microculture in the arts. It occurred during the great African-American migrations from the South during the first quarter of the twentieth century. Writer Langston Hughes reportedly wanted to see Harlem become "the greatest Negro city in the world."

Harlem was said to provide hope for the new wave of middle-class African Americans. They were sometimes referred to as the "New Negro." This "New Negro" would be an important factor in the creation of a new heterogeneous American civilization. Notable proponents of the Harlem Renaissance and the "New Negro" movement included such writers as Langston Hughes and Claude McKay and social philosophers like W.E.B. Du Bois.

Multicultural education components should make use of this historical era as a means of understanding the development of today's African-American macroculture. Teachers can utilize the works of such writers as Langston Hughes and include curriculum sequences that help students appreciate the early influences on microcultural America through the works of such early jazz musicians as Louis Armstrong, Fats Waller, and Eubie Blake.

References: Gilbert Osofsky, *Harlem: The Making of a Ghetto, Negro New York, 1890–1930* (New York: Harper and Row, 1966); Ronald Takaki, *A Different Mirror: A History of Multicultural America* (Boston: Little, Brown, 1993).

HARPER'S FERRY, the site of John Brown's raid on October 16, 1859, was a federal arsenal in Virginia. With a band of 21 followers, including five African

Americans, Brown seized the facility but was soon defeated in a counter-attack by federal forces. He and his band were taken prisoner and Brown was subsequently executed on December 2, 1859.

While Brown's raid on Harper's Ferry caused him to be perceived as a martyr by anti-slavery sympathizers, Southerners and even many Northerners condemned his actions, feeling that the raid was outside the law. This battle was one of the first confrontations in which African Americans and European Americans fought together for a common cause. *See also* BROWN, JOHN.

References: David Herbert Donald, *Lincoln* (London: Jonathan Cape, 1995); Homer Cary Hockett and Arthur Meier Schlesinger, *Land of the Free* (New York: Macmillan, 1944).

HART–CELLAR ACT, a piece of legislation enacted in 1965, constituted a major change in the immigration policies of the United States. Since the country has been called a nation of immigrants, this measure essentially limited ethnic origin as a basis for admittance to the United States. It was specifically designed to end the immigration barriers against Asians. From the time of its enactment until 1985, approximately 3 million Asian people migrated to the United States.

This major change in immigration laws helped end the mistaken stereotype that America was primarily a European American "White" nation. It is also an event that should be included in the multicultural, educational curriculum to help all students understand and appreciate the many contributions of Asian Americans throughout the history of the country.

References: James A. Banks, *Teaching Strategies for Ethnic Studies*, 6th ed. (Boston: Allyn and Bacon, 1997); Leonard Dinnerstein, et al., *Natives and Strangers* (New York: Oxford University Press, 1990); David Reimer, *Still the Golden Door: The Third World Comes to America* (New York: Columbia University Press, 1985); Ronald Takaki, *A Different Mirror: A History of Multicultural America* (Boston: Little, Brown, 1993).

HAWAIIAN AMERICANS, a polyglot of ethnic microcultures, are unique since all residents of the state at the time of statehood can be considered Native Americans. Ethnically, only about 1 percent of the state's inhabitants are pure-blooded Hawaiians. When Captain Cook became one of the first Europeans to visit the islands, he estimated that there were approximately 300,000 native Hawaiians living there. However, since that time, there have been a number of immigration periods, creating a state of extraordinary ethnic diversity.

For example, the Japanese contract laborers arrived in Hawaii in 1848, becoming the first Japanese people to emigrate to the present U.S. boundaries. Korean-Hawaiian Americans originally came to work in the sugar cane and pineapple fields. Filipinos and Chinese immigrants also became part of the Hawaiian work force, along with people from virtually every part of the earth. The concept of Aloha Aina, meaning "love for the land," has served to underscore Hawaiian Americans' concern with the preservation of the environment. There are many restrictions to prevent developments that might compromise the island's fragile environment.

References: A. Grove Day, *Hawaii and Its People* (New York: Monthly Review Press, 1983); Noel J. Kent, *Hawaii: Islands Under the Influence* (New York: Monthly Review Press, 1983); Andrew Lind, *Hawaii's People* (Honolulu: The University Press of Hawaii, 1980); Ronald Takaki, *Pau Hana: Plantation Life and Labor in Hawaii* (Honolulu: The University Press of Hawaii, 1983).

HIGH YELLER, a concept that originated during the Reconstruction Period of American history, referred to the skin color of African Americans. During this time, it was beneficial if an African-American person could "pass" (pass for White). The derivation of the term had to do with the color charts in paint stores. These paint charts usually started with the color black being at the bottom. As a customer looked at the various colors, it could be seen that they became lighter toward the top of the paint chart until the color white was perched at the top. The color just underneath white was a very pale yellow. Thus, if African-American persons had very light skin, they might be able to "pass" for being a European American.

During the days of segregation, this entitled the person to all kinds of special privileges. If African-American passengers were riding on a train and they could "pass," it meant that they could ride on the racially segregated car for European Americans. The same concept held true for other types of segregated facilities such as restrooms, drinking fountains, and hotels. The slang term used for a person who could "pass," was often "high yeller." The term was also quite prominent during the developmental years of American jazz, particularly in the blues lyrics.

HILL, ANITA (1956–), an African-American attorney, was involved in the U.S. Senate hearings for the confirmation of Clarence Thomas. Thomas was nominated by President George Bush as a replacement on the U.S. Supreme Court to take the seat of the Honorable Thurgood Marshall, the first African American to be appointed a member of the U.S. Supreme Court.

President Bush was searching for a Republican African American to replace Marshall. During the hearings, Hill testified against the appointment of Thomas. She charged him with sexual harassment occurring during their tenure with the Equal Employment Opportunities Commission. The hearings were volatile and politically focused. Republican senators, such as Orrin Hatch from Utah, argued in favor of Thomas and attempted to denigrate the character of Hill. Thomas was appointed by Bush in an attempt to create a more right-leaning Supreme Court.

References: David Brock, *The Real Anita Hill* (New York: The Free Press, 1993); Albert R. Hunt, "Tales of Ignominy: Beyond Thomas and Hill," *Wall Street Journal*, October

28, 1991; Toni Morrison, *Race-ing, Justice, and Engendering Power* (New York: Pantheon, 1992); William Raspberry, ''Southern Conservatives Change Their Stripes,'' *The Oregonian*, October 18, 1991.

HIPPIES, often characterized as persons from the ''beat generation,'' were generally viewed as anti-establishment persons who were questioning the morality of many American institutions. Hippies were prominent in San Francisco during the middle 1960s, residing in several parts of the city. Often referred to as the ''counter culture,'' Hippies sought a world based on peace and the love of humanity. Many of them tended to live in quasi-communes. They sometimes were called the ''flower children,'' because they often used flowers to communicate their interest in love and gentleness.

Hippies had a tendency to question most parts of the American macroculture. Many protested the United States involvement in the Vietnam War, claiming it to be immoral and unjustified. They were a thorn in the side of corporate America, questioning the morality of the capitalistic system in general. They often staged protests in colleges and universities and even in some high schools. In general, they were asking for student rights, which they felt had not been taken into consideration in the American educational system.

The term ''hippie'' comes from the word ''hip,'' which means to be ''tuned in'' to art forms, ideologies, and so on. For example, one of the earliest uses of the language occurred through the development of American jazz when ''hip'' musicians were those who understood and empathized with that particular art form.

Hippies often attempted to ''make a statement'' by wearing clothes that might shock the American establishment. They rejected the standard wearing apparel of the business and professional community and turned to clothing they hoped would be shocking. A large number of Hippies used drugs such as marijuana and LSD and were fond of such musical groups as the Grateful Dead, the Beatles, Joan Baez, Jimmie Hendrix, and Jefferson Airplane. Some of their favorite authors included poet Alan Ginsberg and novelist Ken Kesey.

Reference: Nicholas von Hoffman, *We Are the People Our Parents Warned Us Against* (Chicago: Quadrangle, 1968).

HISPANIC AMERICANS are one of the nation's fastest-growing minority populations. This term refers to Americans whose roots are from Spain, Central, and South America, and whose ancestry stems from any of the Spanish-speaking nations. The largest number of Hispanic Americans are of Mexican descent, who live in the present boundaries of the United States established when parts of Mexico became part of the United States after the Treaty of Guadalupe Hidalgo in 1848.

Hispanic groups consist of a number of different ethnic backgrounds. For example, some Hispanic Americans include persons from Mexican and/or Caribbean areas whose ancestors come from Mexican, African, Spanish, and other backgrounds. The term is extremely generic in nature and has been used in referring to any person whose native language is Spanish.

In the United States, Hispanic Americans historically have been involved in agricultural pursuits. Linguistically, they are the largest minority group in the United States. Many Hispanics prefer to be called Cuban Americans, Mexican Americans, Puerto Rican Americans, and so on.

Based on statistical data of 1993, 22.5 million Hispanic Americans lived in the United States, constituting about 9 percent of the total United States population. The increasing numbers of Hispanic children, who are finding their way into schools, has created new problems and opportunities for American educators. The language issue has resulted in the addition of numerous efforts toward developing English as a Second Language (ESL) programs to improve school performance. However, many Hispanic children also come from poverty backgrounds, which contribute to a proliferation of low test scores and poor school performance.

The term itself is difficult to define. Often, writers use the term ''Latino'' instead of ''Hispanic American.'' Some people do not like the term ''Hispanic'' since it is used by the U.S. government for classification purposes. Also, some Hispanics do not consider themselves to be ''Chicanos,'' a term initiated during the American Civil Rights Movement, which implies that the person comes from a Spanish-speaking background and is involved in improving the welfare of Latino people.

All groups of Hispanic Americans have a number of common characteristics such as common language patterns (Spanish) and a common religion (Catholic).

References: David T. Ablaze, *Latinos in the United States: The Sacred and the Political* (Notre Dame, IN: University of Notre Dame Press, 1986); James Crawford, *Bilingual Education: History, Politics, Theory, and Practice* (Trenton, NJ: Crane, 1989); Joan W. Moore and Harry Pachon, *Hispanics in the United States* (Englewood Cliffs, NJ: Prentice-Hall, 1985); Earl Shorris, *Latinos: A Biography of the People* (New York: W. W. Norton, 1992); Maurilio E. Vigil, *Hispanics in American Politics: The Search for Political Power* (Lanham, MD: University of Maryland Press, 1987).

HITLER, ADOLF (1889–1945), the ruler of Germany from 1933 to 1945, created an enormous military nation and started World War II in 1938 with a bloodless invasion of Austria, his native land. Before the final demise of Germany in 1945, his forces had defeated and occupied most of Europe. While he ordered the death of tens of thousands, he particularly hated Jews. According to the best available evidence, he had about 6 million European Jews murdered, approximately 4 million of them executed in concentration camps.

Born in Austria in 1889, he was the fourth child in the third marriage of Alois Hitler, a customs official. A good student in elementary school, he struggled in high school, inciting the ire of his father. Seeking to become an art student in Vienna, he failed the entry examination and later moved to Munich, Germany.

After failing his physical examination for the Austrian army, he ended up in the German army.

He came to admire the political structure of the Social Democratic party in Vienna and became strongly nationalistic. After the beginning of World War I in 1914, Hitler volunteered to be a messenger. He was wounded once and cited twice for bravery. He was extremely distraught over the armistice, believing that he must try and save Germany.

After recovering from wartime injuries caused by mustard gas, Hitler joined the National Socialist German Workers' Party, later referred to as the Nazi Party. In an attempt to help Germany become great again, he organized a small army of storm troopers. But by 1923, Germany was beset with enormous economic problems when France and Belgium sent troops to occupy the Ruhr District. German workers went on strike, precipitating the terrible economic circumstances that devastated the nation economically.

By 1932, the Nazis had become Germany's strongest political party, and a year later they controlled the country, outlawing labor unions, the free press, and all political parties except for the Nazis. Hitler set up organizations for Nazi youth to condition German children to military discipline and establish their loyalty to the Nazi government.

In 1938, Germany invaded Austria, which became part of the German nation. By March 1939, Hitler had captured Czechoslovakia, and in 1939 Poland fell to the Nazis. In the spring of 1940, Denmark, Norway, the Netherlands, Belgium, and Luxemburg also fell. But after Hitler lost 300,000 men in the Battle of Stalingrad, the tide commenced to turn against him. After the Allies marched into Germany in 1945, Hitler committed suicide and Germany surrendered seven days later.

The rise and fall of Hitler is an example of how hatred itself can destroy human beings. Teachers who incorporate instructional strategies for teaching tolerance can help students to tolerate and, hopefully, celebrate the differences in human beings the world over. *See also* AUSCHWITZ; HOLOCAUST.

References: Alan Bullock, *Hitler: A Study in Tyranny* (New York: Harper and Row, 1964); Joachim C. Fest, *Hitler* (New York: Random House, 1975); Sebastian Haffner, *The Meaning of Hitler* (Cambridge, MA: Harvard University Press, 1983); John Toland, *Adolf Hitler* (New York: Ballantine, 1986).

HOLOCAUST, a term referring to wide-scale destruction by fire or nuclear warfare, also has been used in the literature to describe the systematic murder of European Jews by the German Nazis during World War II. As part of Hitler's plan to conquer the world, he attempted to eradicate the Jewish population. At the war's end in 1945, the Nazis had executed approximately 6 million Jewish men, women, and children in Europe. In addition, they killed many members of other ethnic groups, particularly Poles, Gypsies, and Slavs. Some historians estimate that the total number of murders could have been as high as 11 million.

On the evening of November 9, 1938, the Nazis murdered scores of Jews and destroyed about 7,500 Jewish-owned businesses. That evening was referred to as Kristallnacht (Crystal Night) or the night of broken glass. Along with the German invasion of the Soviet Union in 1941 began the Nazi reign of terror against the Jews in all of their occupied countries.

The Germans attempted to keep their actions as secret as possible during the Holocaust, finding numerous ways to deceive their victims who were killed with poison gas. Others were worked to death or died because of starvation or disease. Still others were involved in cruel experiments. When word of the atrocities commenced to leak out, there were instances in which Jews attempted to fight back, even though they were terribly outnumbered and usually unarmed.

References: Lucy S. Davidowicz, *The War Against the Jews, 1933–1945* (New York: Holt, Rinehart, and Winston, 1975); Helen Fein, *Accounting for Genocide* (New York: Macmillan, 1979); Peter G. J. Pulzer, *The Rise of Political Anti-Semitism in Germany and Austria* (New York: Wiley, 1964); Gordon Zah, *German Catholics and Hitler's Wars: A Study in Social Control* (New York: Sheed and Ward, 1962).

HORSESHOE BEND, TREATY OF had the effect of eliminating any chance of establishing an effective alliance by the Creeks against U.S. expansion. This 1814 treaty made it possible to remove the Creeks to "Indian Territory" under the presidency of Andrew Jackson. When Jackson was a general, he defeated the Red Stick faction of the Creeks at Horseshoe Bend. As a result of the negotiated peace treaty, Jackson received 22 million acres of Creek land in south Georgia and central Alabama. This was about one half of the Creeks' land.

When Jackson presented this land to the U.S. government, Creek political power decreased. Only one Red Stick actually signed the document. The rest were Creek allies of Jackson. Ironically, they lost much of their land. However, each of the Creek allies could keep one acre of their land as long as they continued to use it. Under the treaty terms, the United States could build roads, trading posts, and forts on the land. This treaty provides a useful illustration for students to understand the historical issues relating to the loss of Native American lands.

References: Michael D. Green, *The Politics of Indian Removal: Creek Government and Society in Crisis* (Lincoln: University of Nebraska Press, 1982); Charles Hudson, *The Southeastern Indians* (Knoxville: University of Tennessee Press, 1976); Daniel F. Littlefield, Jr., *Africans and Creeks: From the Colonial Period to the Civil War* (Westport, CT: Greenwood Press, 1979); Frank L. Owsley, Jr., *Struggle for the Gulf Borderlands: The Creek War and the Battle of New Orleans, 1812–1815* (Gainesville: University Presses of Florida, 1981).

HUGHES, LANGSTON (1902–1967), an African-American writer, was considered to be one of the first African-American writers to portray African-

American people in a realistic light. Born in Joplin, Missouri, in 1902, Hughes grew up in several midwestern cities and went to Mexico to teach English. While working as a busboy in Washington, DC, he met Vachel Lindsay, who helped him publish *Weary Blues* in 1926. Returning to college, he graduated from Lincoln University in 1926. His graduating classmates included: Kwame Nkrumah, who became the first Ghanaian president after the end of colonialism; Nelson Mandela of South Africa; and Thurgood Marshall, who became a U.S. Supreme Court justice.

In addition to his poetry, Hughes also published novels, an autobiography, short stories, and drama. His poems expressed the frustration and misery that African-American citizens were forced to endure. Teachers can use the works of Langston Hughes in literature classes to illustrate the many contributions of African-American writers.

Reference: Langston Hughes, *The Langston Hughes Reader* (New York: George Braziller, 1958).

I

IDEOLOGY, a system of ideas, beliefs, traditions, principles and myths held by a given microculture, is instrumental in determining patterns of behavior in social, political, and economic pursuits. These behavior patterns are often used by the dominant culture in defending its actions and behaviors and legitimizing its control over other subordinate microcultures.

Advocates of assimilationist ideology argue that pluralism exaggerates the degree of cultural differences in a given macroculture. There is a tendency for assimilationists to feel that the ethnic/racial differences will disappear as a result of technological advances and modernization. Insofar as education is concerned, assimilationists tend to believe that the differences in cognitive learning styles are rather universal across different cultures.

Proponents of a pluralist ideology describe the importance of racial and ethnic identities. In the United States and other societies, competing ethnic groups champion their own causes in the areas of politics and economics. Pluralists argue the importance of remaining loyal to their particular microculture, particularly if it suffers from being oppressed by the dominant culture. The cultural pluralist makes use of the research on learning style differences of children from differing microcultures and attempts to alter educational programs so that they are consistent with their cognitive learning styles.

The multicultural ideology feels that both the assimilationists and pluralists have unrealistic views of the socialization process. In the view of multicultural theorists, individuals must belong both to their microculture and to the macroculture. Not only should they function within their own group, but in the larger group as well. Advocates of this group believe that students from the various microcultures within a given society have unique learning styles, but they also share numerous learning characteristics with students from other microcultures.

References: James A. Banks, *Teaching Strategies for Ethnic Studies*, 6th ed. (Boston: Allyn and Bacon, 1997); B. Bullivant, *The Ethnic Encounter in the Secondary School* (London: The Farmer Press, 1987); Arthur R. Jensen, "How Much Can We Boost IQ and Scholastic Achievement?" *Harvard Educational Review* (Winter, 1969); R. Ramirez and M. Castaneda, *Cultural Democracy, Bicognitive Development and Education* (New York: Academic Press, 1974); W. Shockley, "Dysgenics, Geneticity, Raceology: Challenges to the Intellectual Responsibility of Educators," *Phi Delta Kappan* 5 (1973); B. A. Sizemore, "A Reality Approach to Inclusion?" in R. L. Green (Ed.), *Racial Crisis in American Education* (Chicago: Follett Educational Corporation, 1969).

ILLINOIS* EX REL. *McCOLLUM v. BOARD OF EDUCATION related to the decision by an Illinois board of education that allowed fourth through ninth grade students to participate in religion classes taught by representatives of several different religious organizations. These classes were held in the school building during school hours and required permission cards signed by the parents. Students involved were excused from their regular classes during the time the classes were held. The constitutionality of the practice was challenged by a taxpayer.

The U.S. Supreme Court declared the practice to be unconstitutional based on the First Amendment of the U.S. Constitution that prohibits the establishment of a state religion and mandates the separation of church and state. Providing state support for the religious programs and utilizing state buildings for the classes fails to maintain the Constitutional separation of church and state mandate.

Reference: Perry A. Zirkel and Sharon Nalbone Richardson, *A Digest of Supreme Court Decisions Affecting Education* (Bloomington, IN: Phi Delta Kappa Foundation, 1988).

IMBALANCE, a term used in multicultural writings, has related to the percentage of persons from differing racial and ethnic groups as they are represented in various occupations, areas of responsibility, school programs, clubs and organizations, and other public and private institutions. The "imbalance" has related to the under-representation or over-representation of persons from different minority groups.

For example, an ethnic imbalance of persons in gifted/talented educational programs has consistently occurred in the United States due to the under-representation of African Americans, Latinos, and Native Americans. On the other hand, a similar imbalance of persons among the chief executive officers (CEOs) in the *Fortune* 500 corporations in America exists due to the huge preponderance of European-American males.

To correct imbalances, it is necessary to approximate the proportions of people according to age, gender, race, ethnicity, and socioeconomic status in a given community, regardless of the size of that community. This has been a primary concept of affirmative action programs throughout the western world. For example, in the United States, to correct an imbalance in the number of school superintendents, about half of those administrators should be females. By the same token, about 10 percent of the CEOs of American corporations should be African Americans. Likewise, to correct the imbalance in U.S. prisons, only about ten percent of the prison population should include African-American men and women.

IMMERSION, a term related to language instruction, refers to the instructional technique of forcing the learner to communicate in the new language only. Rather than being instructed in the mother tongue, the student is immersed in English-only instruction. Two North American examples are the French immersion program in Quebec and the Chinese language immersion program in Indiana. Enrichment immersion programs are sometimes used when students wish to acquire the second language. However, research seems to show that motivation to learn the new language is the key factor in successful second language acquisition.

Immersion programs should not be confused with bilingual, educational programs, which are designed for students who come from families utilizing languages other than standard English.

Bilingual programs tend to use a transitional approach that attempts to transition students into English-only classes as quickly as possible. Maintenance or developmental procedures help children acquire cognitive skills in their native language and standard English, as well. In most bilingual, educational programs, instruction in the student's mother tongue is provided whenever needed. Another approach is the English as a Second Language (ESL) approach that provides students with instruction in standard English while the students become assimilated into the regular instructional program as quickly as possible. The ESL component does not usually contain a bilingual instruction approach. *See also* BILINGUAL EDUCATION.

Reference: Christine I. Bennett, *Comprehensive Multicultural Education: Theory and Practice*, 3d ed. (Boston: Allyn and Bacon, 1995).

IMMIGRANTS, a term used to designate persons who settle in a foreign country, have affected virtually every nation in the world. Perhaps no country has been impacted more by immigrants than the United States. When students study the patterns of immigration to the United States, it is useful for them to analyze the real or probable reasons for the various groups of immigrants throughout American history. For example, it is important to point out that the only group of immigrants brought to the United States against their will were African Americans. Chinese Americans were brought to the nation to provide a cheap labor force for constructing the railroads and the mining of minerals. Hmong Americans were allowed to immigrate to the United States because of their loyalty to the United States during the Vietnamese war. Other groups, particularly from Europe, came voluntarily in hopes of improving their economic circumstances, while still others came to find religious freedom.

An important learning concept relates to the notion that Native Americans are the only Americans whose ancestors are not immigrants. Without the plethora of microcultures that immigrated to the United States, the nation would be totally different. Also, it is useful to discuss the enormous problems suffered by the Native Americans due to the immigration of the Europeans and their attitudes of manifest destiny.

Multicultural, educational programs can focus on the contributions of the various groups of immigrants to help students acquire more positive attitudes about the great cultural diversity within the country. One technique some teachers use is the multicultural calendar. Each day the accomplishments of individuals from differing racial/ethnic groups are discussed with the students. A study of American immigrants can help students appreciate how the nation's ethnic/racial diversity is the country's greatest national resource.

Reference: Leonard Dinnerstein, et al., *Natives and Strangers* (New York: Oxford University Press, 1990).

INDENTURED SERVITUDE, a common practice for acquiring cheap labor during America's colonial period, was carried out by requiring immigrants to work for a specified period of time. Many indentured servants were poor Europeans who sometimes would be given a plot of land and their freedom after completing their period of indentureship. In some cases, Europeans who were convicted in the courts, would be given the option of prison terms or indentureships in the colonies.

During the formative years of the Virginia colony, most of the European colonists came as indentured servants. The European indentured servants came mostly from England, but immigrants from Germany and Ireland helped comprise the population of indentured servants, along with a relatively small population of Africans.

According to historians, the Europeans who became indentured represented the downtrodden element of European society. They have been characterized in the literature as "rogues, vagabonds, whores, cheats, and sometimes as the 'surplus inhabitants of England.' " Most of the indentured servants came to the new colonies without families. While they were not strictly regarded as chattels, their lives in Virginia and the other colonies closely resembled the life of slaves in servitude.

References: Kerby A. Miller, *Emigrants and Exiles: Ireland and the Irish Exile to North America* (New York: Oxford University Press, 1987); Abbot Emerson Smith, *Colonists in Bondage: White Servitude and Convict Labor in America, 1607–1776* (Magnolia, ME: Peter Smith, 1965); Thomas Sowell, *Ethnic America* (New York: Basic Books, 1981);

Ronald Takaki, *A Different Mirror: A History of Multicultural America* (Boston: Little, Brown, 1993).

INDIAN CITIZENSHIP ACT, also referred to as the Snyder Act, was a piece of legislation enacted in 1924 that granted citizenship to all Native Americans. Until the enactment of this legislation Native Americans were unable to become United States citizens if they were members of tribes or nations which negotiated settlements with the U.S. government through the treaty process. The act permitted dual U.S. citizenship and tribal citizenship. The legislation was initiated by Homer P. Snyder of New York in the form of House Resolution 6355, authorizing the Secretary of the Interior to grant citizenship to all Native Americans. Signed into law by President Calvin Coolidge, the acquisition of citizenship had little affect on the actions of the BIA, which continued to treat Native Americans as wards of the government. Moreover, some Native Americans were still disenfranchised until the 1960s.

Reference: Harvey Markowitz (Ed.), *American Indians* (Pasadena, CA: Salem Press, 1995).

INDIAN EDUCATION has constituted a major problem since the middle of the sixteenth century when specific programs for Native Americans commenced. Attempts to provide an education for Native American children were initiated and carried out by public school districts, the federal government, and Christian religious groups. The first known school established by European Americans for Native American students was founded in Havana, Florida, in 1868.

Many of the schools, particularly the religious ones, tended to be quite paternalistic. Some Native Americans have complained that the attempts to provide educational services to Native American students have had tragic results from some tribes. Often, Native American students were told by their teachers that their microcultural mores were wrong or improper.

The first Indian boarding schools were established during the presidency of Ulysses S. Grant. Grant believed that the way to solve the "Indian problem" was to establish schools away from their homes. In these schools, it would be possible to "civilize" the youngsters. The feeling was that the only way for Native Americans to prosper in the United States was to teach them to feel at home in the European-American world.

The Bureau of Indian Affairs (BIA) has always assumed an active role in the education of Native Americans. By 1902, the BIA operated 25 boarding schools located in 15 states. However, the complaints against the BIA schools were vigorous and numerous because of the perceived inadequacy of such educational efforts. The complaints, particularly on the part of Native Americans, eventually culminated in attempts to reform Indian education from 1924 to 1944. The Committee of One Hundred Citizens recommended better school facilities, better trained personnel, and an increase in the number of Native American children in the public schools. Also, it was recommended that there be more money available for Native Americans to become involved in higher education.

During the 1960s and 1970s, special career-ladder teacher preparation programs were initiated in schools to improve the education of Indian children through the use of Native American teachers. It was postulated that properly trained Native American teachers could provide Indian children with a good education that could be tailored to meet the unique needs of Native American students. During this period of time, the Indian Education Act was passed (1972). The act provided funding for special programs in urban and reservation schools.

References: Edgar S. Cahn and David W. Hearne, *Our Brother's Keeper: The Indian in White America* (New York: New American Library, 1975); Theodore Fischbacher, *A Study of the Federal Government in the Education of the American Indian* (San Francisco: R. & E. Research Associates, 1974); Estelle Fuchs and Robert Havighurst, ''Boarding Schools,'' in *To Live on This Earth* (Garden City, NY: Doubleday, 1972.

INDIAN REMOVAL ACT, ostensibly an action designed to protect Native Americans from the encroachments of Europeans, affected all tribes east of the Mississippi. This 1830 legislation made it possible for the federal government to resettle Native Americans in lands west of the Mississippi River. The Removal Act was consummated through the efforts of President Andrew Jackson, who was attempting to defuse the conflicts between states and the federal government over issues of state sovereignty. The concept was originally articulated by President James Monroe, who recommended that all Native Americans be resettled west of the Mississippi River.

One of the significant issues precipitating the enactment centered around the discovery of gold in Georgia and the encroachment of European-American settlers on Cherokee lands. Moreover, the European Americans were in need of new lands in Georgia for cotton production. Consequently, the Georgia Legislature enacted laws nullifying Cherokee land claims and extending state law over the Cherokee Nation.

The Removal Act was responsible for one of the more tragic sagas in American history, the Cherokee Trail of Tears. After losing a protest to the U.S. Congress, the Cherokees were forcibly removed from their lands in Georgia and relocated west of the Mississippi. Those who remained behind were victimized by speculators and squatters.

Teachers who expect students to acquire accurate concepts of the microcultural history of America can discuss the differing circumstances that have led to modern-day conditions. The Indian Removal Act was about power and how human beings use it. In this case, the powerful European-American settlers used their power to acquire the land they wanted.

References: Russel Barsh and James Y. Henderson, *The Road: Indian Tribes and Political Liberty* (Berkeley: University of California Press, 1980); Dee Brown, *Bury My Heart at Wounded Knee: An Indian History of the West* (New York: Holt, 1971); William T. Hagan, *American Indians* (Chicago: University of Chicago Press, 1961); Alvin M. Josephy, Jr., *The Indian Heritage of America* (New York: Bantam Books, 1969); Edward H. Spicer, *A Short History of the Indians in the United States* (New York: Van Nostrand Reinhold, 1969).

INDIAN REORGANIZATION ACT OF 1934, perhaps the most radical change in Indian policy in the history of the country, shifted the federal policy away from attempting to assimilate Native Americans in the dominant European-American macroculture toward the preservation and fortification of existing Native American tribes and cultures.

Crafted by John Collier, one of the most popular Commissioners of Indian Affairs, the Indian Reorganization Act attempted to implement the recommendations of the 1928 Meriam Report, which was extremely critical of the various policies orchestrated by the Bureau of Indian Affairs (BIA). Although the language of the Act was toned down and modified greatly in comparison to Collier's original version, the Act was generally considered to be quite radical for that time.

Collier, appointed to the position during the Franklin Roosevelt administration, was considered to be a well-informed expert on Native American matters and a champion of civil rights for Native Americans. He deeply cared for Native American people and made it a point to initiate policies accepted by pantribal groups. He had a great deal of understanding about Native American cultures and admired the traditional Native American religions. His legislation was sometimes referred to as The New Deal for Native Americans. While 172 tribes and Native American communities agreed to adhere to the tenets of the 1934 Indian Reorganization legislation, 63 others refused. Many Native American groups were too distrustful of the U.S. government to participate.

Helping students to acquire something other than erroneous, popular concepts of Native Americans is a primary goal of the multicultural, educational educator. Some sociologists have been distressed over the misperceptions about Native Americans that have prevailed in the past. The study of key pieces of legislation can help students develop more accurate impressions of past, present, and future issues pertaining to the original residents of the United States.

References: Harvey Markowitz (Ed.), *American Indians* (Pasadena, CA: Salem Press, Inc., 1995); Ronald Takaki, *A Different Mirror; A History of Multicultural America* (Boston: Little, Brown, 1993); Jennings C. Wise, *The Red Man in the New World Drama* (New York: Macmillan, 1971).

INSTITUTIONAL RACISM is a concept referring to racist practices that are pervasive throughout an entire institution. Racism, per se, is based on the assumption that the physical characteristics of a human being determine the behavioral characteristics of that group. Moreover, racism relates to the conviction that because of the overt physical characteristics, a microculture is automatically inferior intellectually, psychologically, and/or morally. When institutional racism occurs, the characteristic is pervasive, rather than a belief held by only one person.

One example of institutional racism cited in some writing is the Florida judicial system. The state is one of the national leaders in the number of per-capita executions of African Americans for the murder of European Americans. Another example of institutional racism occurs right in the public schools, where the education of African-American children has been and still is inferior to the education for European Americans insofar as the amount spent per child, preparation of teachers, adequacy of building maintenance, and the provision of supplies are concerned.

References: Christine I. Bennett, *Comprehensive Multicultural Education: Theory and Practice*, 3d ed. (Boston: Allyn and Bacon, 1995); M. Lee Manning and Leroy G. Baruth, *Multicultural Education of Children and Adolescents* (Boston: Allyn and Bacon, 1996).

INTEGRATED SCHOOLS, still a law of the land based on the 1954 *Brown v. Board of Education* Supreme Court decision, must not have a preponderance of students from one particular racial and/or ethnic group as a result of either de jure or de facto segregation policies. Following the 1954 *Brown v. Board of Education* Supreme Court decision, segregated schools in the United States were ordered to become desegregated "with all deliberate speed."

As a result of this Supreme Court action, a number of desegregation plans were used to comply with this 9–0 Supreme Court mandate. One such plan was referred to as the grade-level plan, whereby a school district would designate one or more elementary schools to house all the kindergartners, one or more others to accommodate all of the first graders, and so on. In this manner, all the children in a given school district would automatically become desegregated.

Pairing or cluster refers to a procedure where either two or more schools transfer students by lot to achieve racial balance. Pairing was a common practice in communities such as Athens, Georgia, which had two segregated high schools. Pairing has also been carried on in elementary schools when three or more previously segregated schools transfer students to achieve racial balance.

Some school districts, such as St. Paul, Minnesota, closed a number of older schools in the inner-city and transferred students to other schools to become desegregated. This was done at the elementary school level. In some large communities, high schools were desegregated by providing special programs that would attract students with special skills and talents. For example, one high school might specialize in math/science, attracting students from all over the city.

However, since the initial efforts in school desegregation following the 1954

Brown v. Board of Education Supreme Court decision, many American schools have gradually become re-segregated racially. Supreme Court decisions sometimes must be supported by the Justice Department, which is subject to the political preferences of the administration in power; during the past few years, desegregated schools have not been a high priority of the various administrations in office. Moreover, the phenomenon of ''white flight'' (European Americans moving to more segregated suburbs) and a proliferation of private schools for more affluent students has made it more difficult to maintain racially balanced schools throughout the United States. *See also BROWN v. BOARD OF EDUCATION.*

References: James A. Banks, *Multicultural Education: Theory and Practice*, 6th ed. (Boston: Allyn and Bacon, 1997); Bruce M. Mitchell, et al., *The Dynamic Classroom*, 5th ed. (Dubuque, IA: Kendall/Hunt, 1995); James C. Stone and Donald P. DeNevi (Eds.), *Teaching Multicultural Populations* (New York: Litton Educational Publications, 1971).

INTEGRATION, a multicultural term relating to the removal of barriers that segregate human beings, has been a difficult concept to define. For some writers, integration can only happen when tolerance in the form of mutual respect and acceptance occurs on the part of racially and ethnically different groups of human beings.

Teachers interested in multicultural education have searched for teaching strategies that would help students become more integrated in term of their ethnic, gender, and/or racial preferences. This also requires an acceptance and understanding of persons from racial and ethnic backgrounds which differ from their own. In the classroom, this requires teachers to place heavy emphasis on helping students recognize the value of students interacting in a pluralistic society.

References: James A. Banks, *Multiethnic Education: Theory and Practice*, 3d ed. (Boston: Allyn and Bacon, 1994); L. Barton and S. Walker, *Race, Class, and Education* (London: Croom Helm, 1983); H. Higham, ''Integration v. Pluralism: Another American Dilemma,'' *The Center Magazine* 7 (1974); Asa Hilliard, et al., *Infusion of African and African-American Content in the Curriculum* (Morristown, NJ: Aaron Press, 1990); G. K. Verma (Ed.), *Education for All: A Landmark in Pluralism* (London: The Falmer Press, 1989).

INVISIBLE EMPIRE is part of the entire title for the Ku Klux Klan. In 1960, Calvin Craig, the Grand Dragon of Georgia, defected from the dominant U.S. klans. He formed a new group called the Invisible Empire, United Klans of America that was chartered in Fulton County, Georgia, in 1961. Subsequently, a number of southern splinter groups merged into a new organization called the United Klans of America (UKA). The ''Invisible Empire'' has been used as a pseudonym and as part of the title of the Ku Klux Klan throughout the years.

Throughout its history, the Invisible Empire has espoused a philosophy of hatred against African Americans and Jews. The organization began in 1865 when six Confederate army officers sought a way to alleviate their boredom on Christmas Eve, about eight months following the termination of the Civil War. After numerous lynchings of African Americans, the Klan was dissolved in 1869 when northern carpetbaggers left the South and southern European Americans regained control of their lands. However, it resurfaced in 1915 when a southerner named William Joseph Simmons recruited 15 friends. Scaling Stone Mountain in Georgia, they lit a cross and re-established the Invisible Empire. After its numbers swelled to about 5 million members, including senators and congressmen, it waned during the great depression. During the 1950s, it became popular among southern racists who were upset over federal attempts to desegregate public schools. Failing to stop these changes by legal means, the Klan then resorted to bombing and murdering African Americans. The Invisible Empire also professes to be a ''Christian'' organization that has added gays to their list of microcultures they have chosen to hate.

Multicultural education has an enormous responsibility if it is to help students learn to value diversity rather than despise it. Teaching tolerance may provide one means of counter-balancing the messages of hate some children learn at home. *See also* KU KLUX KLAN.

References: Tyler Bridges, *The Rise of David Duke* (Jackson: The University of Mississippi Press, 1994); Wyn Craig Wade, *The Fiery Cross: The Ku Klux Klan in America* (New York: Simon and Schuster, 1987); Michael Zatarain, *David Duke* (Gretna, LA: Pelican, 1990).

IRISH AMERICANS, one of the largest ethnic groups comprising the European-American macroculture, became one of the first American ethnic minorities to populate the country's urban cities. Usually beginning their employment career at the bottom of the socioeconomic ladder, most of the men performed some sort of manual labor, while the women often were maids. Their arrival commenced in the 1820s and numerous persons of Irish descent arrived during the rest of the nineteenth century and beyond.

During their early years in America, they were stereotyped as drunkards, brawlers, and incompetents because of the housing conditions in which they were forced to live. These residences often contributed to the development of social problems such as violence, alcoholism, and crime. Because of their poverty, they were more susceptible to disease. During their early years in America, the average life expectancy was only about 40 years.

Agricultural problems in Ireland were largely responsible for their immigration to America. Beginning in 1830, Ireland was beset with crop failures and famines. In 1845, an international potato blight afflicted the land, resulting in several disastrous years for the country. An estimated 1 million Irish people died of starvation or starvation-related diseases. The resulting emigrations caused a depletion in the population that was so dramatic by 1914 the country had only one-half the population it experienced in the 1840s.

Gradually, Irish Americans commenced to improve their lot in the United States through great determination and hard work. They acquired positions as policemen, firemen, clerks, schoolteachers, and other jobs in city government. By 1855, nearly 40 percent of the New York police force were immigrants and about 40 percent of these immigrants were Irish.

Teachers wishing to help students acquire valid concepts about pluralistic America can talk about the accomplishments of Irish Americans and use them as an example of the many contributions of the European-American macroculture. The Kennedy family can be used as an example of how Irish Americans have overcome severe anti-Irish attitudes to assume important roles in politics and other positions of prominence.

References: Oscar Handlin, *Boston's Immigrants* (New York: Atheneum, 1970); Oliver MacDonagh, *The Irish Famine Emigration to the United States* (New York: Pantheon, 1974); Maire and Conor Cruise O'Brien, *A Concise History of Ireland* (New York: Beckman, 1972); George Potter, *To the Golden Door: The Story of the Irish in Ireland and America* (Westport, CT: Greenwood Press, 1973).

IROQUOIS LEAGUE was a coalition of eastern Native American tribes, consisting of the Seneca (The Great Hill People) the Cayuga (People of the Mucky Land), Onondaga (People on the Hills), Oneida (People of the Standing Stone), and the Kenienghagas or Mohawks (Keepers of the Flint). Founded long before the arrival of European settlers, the League was created to deal with the constant strife between the tribes of the Northeast. The Tuscarora became a member of the League in 1722.

Still another name for this confederacy was "Haudenosaunee" (People of the Longhouse). The Haudenosaunee created a constitution, which was passed down from generation to generation. When Colonial delegates were sent to Albany to learn from the Iroquois, they were urged to form assemblies to discuss common problems. In 1749, Benjamin Franklin reportedly wondered, "If Iroquois savages could govern themselves with such skill, how much better would the civilized English colonists do?"

The foundation of the Iroquois League was the fireplace, composed of a mother and her children. Each hearth was part of a larger "owachira," an extended family, traced through the mother in keeping with the matrilineal nature of the clans. Chiefs were selected by the clan mothers, who could also remove chiefs for unethical or immoral actions. The power of the Iroquois members increased up until the American Revolution. At this time in history, the tribes became divided, some siding with the British and others with the Americans.

Studies of Native Americans need to address these historical developments. The colonists were quite impressed with the Iroquois League and thought that type of representation should be incorporated into the U.S. Constitution.

Through such studies, students can begin to understand the significant contributions of Native Americans throughout the country's history.

References: Alvin M. Josephy Jr. (Ed.), *The American Heritage Book of Indians* (New York: Simon and Schuster, 1961); Alvin M. Josephy, *The Indian Heritage of America* (New York: Alfred A. Knopf, 1968); Robert F. Spencer, Jess D. Jennings, et al., *The Native Americans* (New York: Harper and Row, 1977); Colin F. Taylor (Ed.), *The Native Americans: The Indigenous People of North America* (New York: Smithmark, 1991).

J

JACKSON, ANDREW (1767–1845) was able to accomplish what Thomas Jefferson and James Monroe advocated, the removal of eastern Native Americans to lands west of the Mississippi River. Nicknamed "Old Hickory," Jackson first became a national hero because of his victory in the 1815 Battle of New Orleans. His ultimate political and economic successes were related to what occurred in the lives of Native Americans.

Practicing law in Nashville, where he moved from North Carolina, he engaged in the speculation of land belonging to Native Americans. He led U.S. troops against the Creeks in Mississippi, referring to them as "savage bloodhounds" and "bloodthirsty barbarians." At the Battle of Horse Shoe Bend in 1814, Jackson surrounded about 800 Creeks, killing most of them. Prior to the conflict, he referred to the enemy as "savage dogs."

He became famous as the quintessential hero of Indian wars, which helped vault him into the presidency. As President, he backed the efforts of Georgia and Mississippi in their attempts to abolish Native American tribal units and extend state authority over the Native Americans. However, he also argued that he favored humane and just treatment of Native Americans and wanted to protect them from the mercenary interests of European-American males. Thus, he proposed moving them west of the Mississippi. During his administration, the Choctaws and Cherokees were forcefully removed.

References: Michael Paul Rogin, *Fathers and Children: Andrew Jackson and the Subjugation of the American Indian* (New York: Knopf, 1975); Ronald Takaki, *A Different Mirror: A History of Multicultural America* (Boston: Little, Brown, 1993); Jennings C. Wise, *The Red Man in the New World Drama* (New York: Collier-Macmillan, 1971).

JACKSON, JESSE (1941–) is an American civil rights activist, political leader and spokesperson for the poverty powerless, whose charisma, leadership skills, and oratorical brilliance have made him the most commanding African-American leader since Martin Luther King. Born to a poor teenager, he survived the inferior segregated schools of South Carolina and matriculated at North Carolina Agricultural and Technical College in Greensboro, North Carolina. He was the quarterback on the football team and also demonstrated extraordinary oratorical talent and leadership skills during the civil rights era of the 1960s.

In 1967, he was made the head of Operation Breadbasket, a project of the Southern Christian Leadership Conference (SCLC). Jackson was a member of Martin Luther King's party in Memphis when King was assassinated by James Earl Ray. During that same year, Jackson became an ordained Baptist minister and founded People United to Save Humanity (PUSH) to assist persons of color improve their workplace skills and start businesses. Through his efforts, many corporations with big operations in African-American communities initiated affirmative action programs, hired more African-American supervisors and executives, and purchased more supplies from African-American distributors.

His interest and belief in education prompted the founding of PUSH-EXCEL, which was instrumental in improving the acquisition of basic educational skills for low-income, inner-city children. During 1983, he launched a massive voter registration drive to counter the policies of the Reagan Administration, which were devastating to low-income African Americans. This launched him into the political arena where he became an unsuccessful candidate for the presidential nomination in the Democratic Party.

After his 1984 defeat for the presidential nomination, Jackson turned his energies to his Rainbow Coalition. He felt that the Republican victory by Ronald Reagan was primarily due to the timidity of the Democratic Party. While he argued against the Reagan attempts to aid the wealthy at the expense of the poor, he attempted to register many members of his Rainbow Coalition so that they might become more politically active. His last unsuccessful bid for the presidency occurred in 1988. He railed against all those who were victims of economic violence, such as indebted farmers, gays and lesbians who fought against discrimination.

References: Tom Cavenaugh and Lorn S. Foster, *Jesse Jackson's Campaign: The Primaries and the Caucuses* (Washington, DC: Joint Center for Political Election Studies '84, Report #2, 1984); Ken Denglinger, "Running Comes Naturally to Jackson," *Washington Post*, May 13, 1984; David Farrell, "A Winning Jackson," *Boston Globe*, December 16, 1984; Bob Faw and Nancy Skelton, *Thunder in America* (Austin: Texas Monthly Press, 1986).

JAPANESE-AMERICAN CITIZENS LEAGUE was formed by a group of prominent west coast *Nisei* in the summer of 1930. The goals of the organization were to improve the lives of Japanese Americans and to verify the importance they placed on American citizenship. The *Niesi* organizers agreed on a national organization with no local chapters. Delegates in subsequent annual conventions came from the three west coast states and from as far away as Illinois.

By 1936 the organization initiated the Second Generation Development Program, which created the following goals for Japanese Americans: (1) contribute to the social life of the nation, living with other citizens in a common community of interests and activities to promote the national welfare; (2) contribute to the economic welfare of the nation by taking key roles in agriculture, industry, and commerce; and (3) contribute to the civic welfare as intelligent voters and public-spirited citizens.

However, the organization had a difficult time establishing itself as an organization that would be taken seriously by the American macroculture. The 1930s were difficult times for Japanese Americans because anti-Asian sentiment on the part of the European-American community was great, due to the problems created by the great economic depression. Moreover, Japan's aggressive foreign policies did not play well in the United States. Nonetheless, the organization was effective insofar as it helped Japanese Americans develop a spirit of camaraderie and pride.

Reference: Bill Hosokawa, *Nisei: The Quiet Americans* (New York: William Morrow, 1969).

JAPANESE AMERICANS, first recruited as contract laborers in Hawaii, migrated to Hawaii and the United States between 1885 and 1924. During that time, about 200,000 men went to Hawaii and some 180,000 made their home on the U.S. mainland. The motivating factor was the economic hardships suffered by Japanese agricultural workers as a result of new policies initiated by the Meiji emperor following Commodore Perry's famous visit to the country in 1853.

Because of Japan's economic plight, young Japanese men were anxious to set out for Hawaii where wages for agricultural laborers were reportedly six times greater than in Japan. While mostly men immigrated to the United States during this period, "picture brides" soon followed. By 1920, about 46 percent of the Japanese-Hawaiian population consisted of women, while women comprised 35 percent of the Japanese-American population in California.

To leave the country, Japanese Americans were required to apply through their government. They were subjected to a rather thorough screening process to make sure they were healthy and literate to represent the country well. The fact that education in Japan had been viewed with reverence for centuries meant that the Japanese people who migrated to the United States tended to be relatively well-educated and carried the time-honored respect for education with them. Throughout the years, Japanese students have excelled in American schools.

In spite of a number of strikes by Japanese-Hawaiian/American agricultural laborers, they became known for their keen knowledge of agriculture and their excellent work ethic. However, their success often inspired deep racial animosity from white laborers who sometimes felt they were losing jobs that were rightfully theirs. Sometimes they were not allowed to integrate swimming pools and other public and private organizations. And with the beginning of World War II, Japanese Americans would suffer from overt racial hatred as severe as the actions against any of America's microcultures. Presidential Order #90667 authorized the United States Army to exclude them for their own protection. Consequently, ten relocation centers were established in the western region of the United States and in Rohwer and Jerome, Arkansas. The western sites included Manzanar and Tule Lake, California; Minidek, Idaho; Topaz, Utah; Heart Mountain, Wyoming; Ameche, Colorado; and Poston and Gila, Arizona. Educational programs were established for the children in the centers, and the teachers were often adult volunteers. One of the difficulties related to the very nature of the curriculum itself. While the social studies content was supposed to stress democracy, many of the incarcerated Japanese people and the students felt that the approach was highly hypocritical, given the fact that they were given no choice in their assignments to the ten centers.

During World War II, many Japanese-American men volunteered for the armed services. The 442nd Regimental Combat Team became the most highly decorated military unit in the country's history. It was comprised entirely of Japanese Americans. Shortly after the death of President Franklin Roosevelt, who issued the executive order, President Harry Truman ordered the armed forces to become desegregated.

Since World War II, Japanese Americans have continued to achieve at an extraordinarily high rate in America's schools. Gradually, they have tended to move away from their agricultural pursuits into the various professions. Students have become famous for high test scores and their matriculation into the country's most prestigious universities in large numbers.

References: William K. Hosokawa, *Nisei: The Quiet Americans* (New York: William Morrow, 1969); Yuji Ichioka, *The Issei: The World of the First Generation Japanese Immigrants, 1885–1924* (London: The Free Press, 1988); Ivan H. Light, *Ethnic Enterprise in America: Business and Welfare Among Chinese, Japanese, and Blacks* (Berkeley and Los Angeles: University of California Press, 1972); Alan T. Moriyama, *Imingaisha: Japanese Emigration Companies and Hawaii* (Honolulu: University of Hawaii Press, 1985); Edward K. Strong, *Japanese in California* (Stanford: Stanford University Press, 1933).

JAZZ, a musical concept related to the American art form that surfaced around the turn of the century, has often been referred to as the only pure American art form. However, even though it was born in America, it is an excellent example of the power of pluralism in that so many microcultures contributed to its development. Many of the melodic influences came from Europe. The rhythmic patterns and the blues influences are West African. And newer jazz styles have evolved with the Latino influences form Mexico and South America, along with the Brazilian Portuguese contributions.

First played in the early twentieth century, the music capitalized on the work chants, ring shouts, field hollers, spirituals and other folk music of African Americans. The earliest jazz musicians also relied on marches, arias, operas, popular songs, ragtime, and blues.

Early in its development, jazz relied on the cornet, clarinet, trombone, piano, string bass, drums, banjo and piano. However, through the years, with the advent of modern jazz, other instruments have been substituted such as the saxophone, violin, tuba, flute, and many others.

Musically, jazz is an improvised art form with little or no written music used. The cornet or trumpet plays the melody while the clarinet weaves another melody around the main musical theme. The string bass and drums provide much of the rhythm. Originally, it was played by African Americans and later copied by European Americans.

Jazz went through a number of stages. Following its original appearance in New Orleans, jazz evolved into the swing era of the 1930s and 1940s, the bebop era of the 1950s, and large dance bands during the 1950s and 1960s. The original New Orleans jazz style has never died, and in the 1990s, the traditional jazz festivals have occurred all over the land. In fact, many bands from other countries became quite popular during the 1990s. One example is the excellent Grand Dominion Jazz Band from Canada.

Some of the early pioneers were cornetist Buddy Bolden from New Orleans, along with King Oliver and Jelly Roll Morton, also from the Crescent City. America's appetite for jazz became enormous in other parts of the country as well, so many of the New Orleans musicians headed north to New York and Chicago where the art form flourished.

Teachers have a remarkable opportunity to use jazz as a theme for teaching tolerance and helping students learn to value cultural diversity. If the United States did not have the enormous cultural and racial diversity, it is doubtful that jazz would ever have become so popular. The fact musicians from differing racial and/ethnic groups listened to each other and sometimes played together was partly responsible for the development and nurturing of this truly remarkable American art form.

References: Dave Dexter, Jr., *The Jazz Story: From the '90s to the '60s* (Englewood Cliffs, NJ: Prentice-Hall, 1964); Gunther Schuller, *Early Jazz: Its Roots and Musical Development* (New York: Oxford University Press, 1968).

JEWISH AMERICANS have lived within the present-day boundaries of the United States from the earliest days of the arrival of Europeans. In 1655, a contingent of European Jews arrived in New Amsterdam. Russian Jews began their migration to the United States in the 1880s. A persecuted minority in

Russia, they were often viewed as political refugees. The Russian government was able to characterize the Jewish ethnic minority as the problem and in that manner, they were successful in saving the throne from revolutionary upheaval. The Czar was able to convince the peasants that the Jews were to blame for the country's ills, and the government encouraged acts of violence against them. They were forced to reside in the Pale of Settlement, a region between the Baltic and the Black Sea.

By the beginning of World War I, almost one third of all the Jews in Russia and the rest of Europe had emigrated, most of them going to the United States. Many Jewish immigrants settled in New York City's Lower East Side. By 1905, the Jewish population in New York City had swelled to nearly one-half million people.

Historically, the Jewish microculture had placed great emphasis on education. Also, Jews possessed a powerful work ethic. Consequently, Jewish Americans tended to become highly educated citizens. Many went to college and received their degrees, enabling them to excel in the professional and business world. To meet their labor needs, Jewish-American entrepreneurs created a network to hire immigrant Jews in the garment industry. Since that time, Jews have been visible in all American walks of life. Not only have Jewish Americans become outstanding scientists, writers, and doctors, but they have also excelled in less traditional professions like comedy.

Historically, the Jewish-American population has suffered enormous racial hatred. Ultra conservative ''Christian'' and neo-Nazi factions have persecuted Jewish Americans for their religious beliefs. These same groups have also published anti-Jewish hate literature, and the Ku Klux Klan has adopted a strong anti-Jewish posture.

Multicultural educators have numerous examples of successful Jewish Americans, such as Jacob Riis or Israel Zangwill, who can become role models for students. Since this microculture is represented in all elements of American society, there are ample opportunities for teachers to discuss the strong sense of accomplishment and the many successes that provide a powerful message—oppressed persons are able to excel in spite of having to overcome enormous obstacles.

References: Jerold S. Auerbach, *Rabbis and Lawyers: The Journey from Torah to Constitution* (Bloomington: University of Indiana Press, 1990); Howard M. Sachar, *A History of Jews in America* (New York: Alfred A. Knopf, 1992); Ronald Takaki, *A Different Mirror: A History of Multicultural America* (Boston: Little, Brown, 1993).

JIM CROW LAWS relate to the de jure and de facto segregation laws throughout the South after the termination of the Civil War. The term came from Thomas ''Daddy'' Rice, an early impersonator of African Americans, who performed at New York City's Bowery Theatre, singing the lyrics of an American song, which became a great hit. The lyrics were: ''Weel a-bout and turn a-bout and do just so; Every time I weel a-bout I jump Jim Crow.'' The name

"Jim Crow" was first heard in 1832. Rice's portrayal of an African American was the portrayal of a lame man. By the middle of the century, the name Jim Crow became synonymous with the racist attitudes of European Americans who thought African Americans had a comical way of life.

During 1881, the state of Tennessee passed a law requiring the racial segregation of railway cars. This concept of segregation spread to the other southern states where segregation became a way of life. Drinking fountains, rest rooms, schools, restaurants, hotels, neighborhoods, theatres and busses would become segregated racially. In Florida, the schools even had separate textbooks for African-American and European-American mill workers, who were not allowed to look out the same window. All of these practices were referred to as the Jim Crow laws.

In 1896, the *Plessy v. Ferguson* Supreme Court decision upheld the notion of racial segregation through the "separate but equal" doctrine. However, that decision was overturned in 1954 when the Supreme Court ruled that segregated schools were inherently unequal. Schools were ordered to de-segregate "with all deliberate speed." Even though the case related to the segregation of schools, the effects were far reaching and legal segregation of all institutions became illegal.

References: Sharon Harley, *The Timetables of African-American History* (New York: Simon and Schuster, 1995); Milton Meltzer, *The Black Americans: A History in Their Own Words* (New York: Thomas V. Crowell, 1984); Juan Williams, *Eyes on the Prize: America's Civil Rights Years, 1954–1965* (New York: Viking Press, 1989).

JIVE, a term originally used in referring to the be-bop branch of modern jazz, later became used in describing the language of the art form. Phrases such as "hep to the jive" meant that someone understood not only the music itself, but the total environment in which it took place.

Since many of the musicians who were involved in the be-bop revolution were African Americans, the term gradually acquired other implications. Eventually, the term was used to describe a type of "Black English," which was used in inner-city, African-American communities. Originally, terms such as "flipped out" referred to musicians who invented musical passages that caused the listener to become ecstatic over what they heard. Eventually, phrases such as "slide over to my crib and catch some sides" (come on over to my place and listen to some jazz) or "what's happening, brother" (what's going on my friend) became part of the ever-changing lexicon.

JOHNSON, JACK (1878–1946), heavyweight boxing champion from 1907 to 1915, became champion with his defeat of Tommy Burns in a 1907 bout during the fourteenth round. Prior to this time, African Americans were not allowed to compete in the heavyweight division. In 1910 he fought Jim Jeffries, who had retired from the heavyweight championship a few years before. The outcome of this bout caused European-American fight fans to riot, resulting in the deaths of several African Americans. Congress even banned the distribution of film clips of the fight across state lines for profit.

In 1913 Jack Johnson fought Jim Johnson in the world's first heavyweight bout between two fighters of African descent. This London bout ended in a draw. Johnson was subsequently knocked out by Jess Willard in the twenty-sixth round to lose the heavyweight championship in 1915. Later, he confessed to throwing the fight to receive money from Willard's manager.

Johnson became champion when racial segregation in the United States was still highly evident. His prominence in the boxing world contributed to the racial hostilities, and his ascension in the boxing world helped other African-American pugilists to participate and earn decent money for their efforts.

Reference: Sharon Harley, *The Timetables of African-American History* (New York: Simon and Schuster, 1995).

JOHNSON, JAMES WELDON (1871–1938), a leading figure of the Harlem Renaissance, was one of the prominent African-American writers who described this exciting time in American history. In his classic work, *Black Manhattan*, he describes the accomplishments of such African-Americans as W.E.B. Du Bois, Langston Hughes, Countee Cullen, Zora Neale Hurston, and many more.

Born into a supportive, secure family in 1871, Johnson was somewhat isolated from low-income, African Americans and learned about that segment of his microculture when he taught summer school in rural Georgia after completing his freshman year at Atlanta University. This experience caused him to become vitally interested in learning more about the cultural heritage of African Americans. Following his graduation in 1894, he became principal of the Station School in Jacksonville, Florida; he went on to found the first three high schools for African Americans in that state.

Johnson later became the first African American to pass the Florida bar exam, and in 1900, he wrote the lyrics to *Lift Every Voice and Sing*, the Black National Anthem. During the summers, he collaborated with his brother, J. Rosamond Johnson, and vaudevillian Bob Cole to produce over 200 popular songs. Two of the more successful ones were *Under the Bamboo Tree* and *Ain't That Scandalous*.

After avoiding a near lynching in Jacksonville, he decided that he would move to New York, which had a more intellectual climate. Continuing his studies at Columbia University, he became interested in politics and became president of the New York Colored Republican Club. These activities eventually led to an appointment as United States Consul to Venezuela in 1906. President Theodore Roosevelt then transferred him to Nicaragua. During his tenure in Nicaragua, he wrote his only novel, *The Autobiography of an Ex-Colored Man*. After returning to New York, he joined the staff of the *New York Age*, the oldest African-American paper in the city. After writing a column on lynching, employment discrimination in the Federal Government, and the problems of African-American armed servicemen, he became involved with the NAACP, spending fourteen years with that organization.

In 1930, he moved to Nashville, Tennessee, to become the Adam K. Spence Professor of Creative Literature at Fisk University. His literary works include: *Fifty Years and Other Poems; The Book of American Negro Poetry; The Book of American Negro Spirituals; God's Trombones: Seven Negro Sermons in Verse*; and *Along This Way: Negro-Americans, What Now*? He held the NYU position until his death in 1938.

Teachers can use James Weldon Johnson as an example of a true ''Renaissance Man.'' As a writer, song lyricist, lawyer, diplomat, political activist and college professor, he surmounted many racist obstacles to accomplish his goals. He can serve as a positive role model for all students, particularly African Americans.

Reference: James Weldon Johnson, *Black Manhattan* (New York: De Capo Press, 1930).

JOHNSON, RAFER (1934–), an outstanding African-American decathlete from the University of California at Los Angeles (UCLA), became an Olympic Games gold medal winner. However, in spite of his athletic prowess, this outstanding UCLA student athlete became known later for his brave attempt in helping professional football player Roosevelt Grier wrest the gun out of the grasp of Sirhan B. Sirhan after he assassinated Attorney General Robert Kennedy.

JOHNSON–O'MALLY FUNDS, designated for Native American assistance programs, became available in 1934 during the Roosevelt Administration. These funds can be used for the education, medical attention, agricultural assistance, and social welfare of Native Americans. The Johnson–O'Malley Act authorized the Secretary of the Interior to enter into contracts with the states. However, due to disputes between the Bureau of Indian Affairs, the states, and school districts, Indian groups eventually were given the authority to negotiate contracts. Consequently, Johnson–O'Mally funds comprise an important funding source for the education of Native Americans.

References: Chapter 174, *Statutes of the United States of America (Part One)* (Washington, DC: U.S. Government Printing Office, 1934); N.A.A.C.P. Legal Defense and Educational Fund, Inc., *An Even Chance* (New York: The Fund, 1971); Margaret C. Szasz, *Education and the American Indian: The Road to Self Determination Since 1978* (Albuquerque: University of New Mexico Press, 1977).

JOPLIN, SCOTT (1868–1917) was one of the key persons in the evolution of American jazz through his contributions to the development of ragtime. His

creation of *The Entertainer*, first published in 1899, became the most famous ragtime number in American history and was the Academy-award winning score for the movie, *The Sting*.

Born in Texarkana, Arkansas, in 1868, he studied piano near his childhood home and traveled through the Midwest playing piano at Chicago's Columbian Exposition in 1893. Two years later, he studied music at the George R. Smith College in Sedalia, Missouri. The Scott Joplin Ragtime Festival is now an annual event in Sedalia.

His first extensive published work was a 1902 ballet suite in which he used all of the rhythmic patterns of ragtime. Moving to New York City in 1907, he wrote an instruction book for ragtime. The work outlined his syncopation and breaks, complex bass patterns, and harmonic ideas. He produced an opera, *Treemonisha*, in 1915, which combined all of his musical ideas into a conventional, three-act opera. However, the creation of this work took a toll on his health, and he was institutionalized with a nervous breakdown in 1916. He died on April 1, 1917.

The study of ragtime as an American art form cannot be undertaken without analyzing the incredible contributions of Scott Joplin. Teachers using jazz as a multicultural learning device can incorporate ragtime into the curriculum and use it as a major ingredient in the generic definition of the art form. Contributions such as Joplin's serve to illustrate the value of multicultural interaction in a pluralistic society.

References: Dave Dexter, Jr., *The Jazz Story: From the '90s to the '60s* (Englewood Cliffs, NJ: Prentice-Hall, 1954); Gunther Schuller, *Early Jazz: Its Roots and Musical Development* (New York: Oxford University Press, 1968).

JOSEPH, CHIEF (1835–1904), leader of the Nez Perce Indian tribe in the Pacific Northwest, was instrumental in leading his people to an amazing saga of resistance against the European Americans' attempts to take over their lands. Joseph was born in the Wallowa Valley of the Oregon Territory about 1840. The tribe was ordered to move to the Lapwai Reservation in Idaho. Initially, Joseph agreed, but after an event in which three of his braves killed a group of European-American settlers, he attempted to escape into Canada.

Joseph and his followers traveled more than 1,600 miles through Oregon, Washington, Idaho, and Montana. The pursuing U.S. Army suffered a number of defeats, but the Nez Perce finally surrendered on October 5, 1877. After being forced to resettle in Indian Territory in present-day Oklahoma, Chief Joseph returned to Washington and Idaho. He died in 1904 on the Colville Reservation in Washington, where he was buried.

References: Alan Axelrod, *Chronicle of the Indian Wars: From Colonial Times to Wounded Knee* (New York: Prentice-Hall, 1993); Merril D. Beal, *I Will Fight No More Forever: Chief Joseph and the Nez Perce War* (Seattle: University of Washington Press, 1963); E. Jane Gay, *With the Nez Perces: Alice Fletcher in the Field*, Eds. Frederick E.

Hoxie and Joan T. Mark (Lincoln: University of Nebraska Press, 1981); Helen Addison Howard, *Saga of Chief Joseph* (Caldwell, ID: Caxton, 1965); Alvin M. Josephy, Jr., *The Nez Perce Indians and the Opening of the Northwest* (New Haven, CT: Yale University Press, 1965); David S. Lavender, *Let Me Be Free: The Nez Perce Tragedy* (New York: HarperCollins, 1992).

K

KAMEHAMEHA (1758–1819), King of Hawaii, first took control of the islands in 1795 under the leadership of Kamehameha I, uniting the people for the very first time. Prior to his death in 1819, Kamehameha was successful in getting Europeans to invest and participate in the islands' economic pursuits. He was considered to be instrumental in establishing the concept of one nation by unifying the people on all the islands and subjecting them to a single ruler.

Kamehameha was succeeded by his son, Liholiho (Kamehameha II), who abolished the ancient *tabu* system in 1819. It has been argued that the elimination of the *tabu* system of taboos began a major decline of the Native Hawaiian culture. The *tabu* system had prevented women from engaging in such activities as eating bananas. During his tenure, the European-American missionaries commenced to visit the islands from New England to bring Christianity to the Hawaiians. Many of the missionaries were successful in acquiring land for commercial purposes.

Under the rule of Kamehameha III, the land of the Hawaiian Islands was redistributed so that 60 percent was allocated to the crown. Eventually, because of this action, Hawaii's economy came to rely on plantation farming.

Sometimes, children from the mainland states fail to realize that the state of Hawaii is also a part of the American macroculture. A study of the island's history can help young students to acquire a more realistic understanding of the nation's pluralistic society.

References: James A. Banks, *Teaching Strategies for Ethnic Studies*, 6th ed. (Boston: Allyn and Bacon, 1997); Clifford Gessler, *Hawaii, Isles of Enchantment* (New York: D. Appleton–Century, 1937); Paul Jacobs and Saul Landau, *To Serve the Devil, Vol. 2: Colonials and Sojourners* (New York: Vintage, 1971).

KENYATTA, JOMO (1890–1978) became Kenya's first president after the country became an independent nation in 1964. He served until his death in 1978. As president, his greatest task was the unification of the African, Arab, Asian, and European factions of the new independent African country. He also worked hard to develop a stable economy. Born near Nairobi in 1890, he was educated by Church of Scotland missionaries. Between 1931 and 1946, he lived in Europe, spending most of his time in England.

Since the late 1920s Kenyatta had been considered one of the leaders in the crusade for African Nationalism. Prior to assuming the country's presidency, he was convicted of leading the Mau Mau Movement even though he vigorously denied the charge. After his conviction, he was imprisoned in a remote area of Kenya until 1961.

The fact that he became an important Kenyan leader in the early days of independence and was committed to unifying the different pluralistic factions within his country can be used by teachers to illustrate the benefits of national leadership that promotes tolerance among diverse groups. Also, the fact that Kenya's economy is one of the more stable economies in sub-Saharan Africa further illustrates the advantages of such a leadership style.

References: Jomo Kenyatta, *Facing Mt. Kenya* (New York: Vintage Books, 1965); Harold D. Nelson (Ed.), *Kenya: A Country Study* (Washington, DC: The American University, 1984).

KING, MARTIN LUTHER, JR. (1929–1968), American clergyman and Nobel Peace Prize winner, was the primary leader of the American Civil Rights Movement during the 1950s and 1960s.

Born in Atlanta, Georgia, in 1919, he was the son and grandson of Baptist ministers. After graduating from Morehouse College, he earned a bachelor of divinity degree from Crozer Theological Seminary. In 1955, he received his Ph.D. at Boston University, just one year after Rosa Parks' refusal to relinquish her seat to a European-American man.

While working on his theological degree at Crozer, King acquired a deep respect for Mahatma Gandhi, who had led India in passive resistance against the United Kingdom. In 1954, he accepted a ministerial position at the Dexter Avenue Baptist Church in Montgomery, Alabama. The next year he became president of the Montgomery Improvement Association, which organized a city-wide effort to boycott the city transit system due to its racist segregation policies. He adopted a strong non-violence philosophy in the various demonstrations which were carried out.

The boycott was concluded in one year when the city of Montgomery agreed to integrate its public transportation system. King then assumed the pastorship of the Ebeneezer Baptist Church along with his father. He also organized the Southern Christian Leadership Conference (SCLC) to broaden the civil rights movement he had initiated in Montgomery. Over the next few years, King organized many non-violent protest demonstrations and became a role model for other civil rights leaders such as Cesar Chavez.

However, even though he preached a non-violent position, some of the demonstrations got out of hand. In Birmingham, the police used dogs and fire hoses to get rid of African-American demonstrators, who were attempting to desegregate department stores, hotels, and restaurants. An African-American church was bombed, killing four little girls attending Sunday School. King was arrested, along with several of his associates. While in jail, he wrote *Letter from Birmingham Jail,* which provided a framework for his moral philosophy.

In 1963, he organized a massive march on Washington, DC in which about 250,000 people from all religious faiths and racial groups participated in a massive show of support for racial equality. Two years later, King, Rabbi Abraham Heschel of the Jewish Theological Seminary, and Ralph J. Bunche, Undersecretary of the United Nations, participated in a 54-mile march from Selma to Montgomery, protesting racial oppression and stating the case for African-American voters rights. President Johnson federalized 1,800 Alabama National Guard members and dispatched 2,000 U.S. Army troops, 100 F.B.I. agents and 100 Federal marshals to guarantee the safety of some 25,000 marchers who represented many races and religious groups.

While King still held to his non-violent philosophy, younger and more militant leaders began to participate in the civil rights movement. He attempted to organize a poor people's campaign to illustrate the fact that people from all racial groups were suffering from poverty. During discussions to finalize the plans in Memphis, Tennessee, he was assassinated. James Earl Ray was convicted of the crime and sentenced to serve 99 years in prison.

Perhaps no American figure is used so much in multicultural education programs as Martin Luther King, Jr. On his birthday, many students do activities that help them understand his contributions. Perhaps King's most important message was that his peaceful, non-violent philosophy proved to be successful. In a country where violence is a way of life, this message of passive resistance is truly a critical piece of the multicultural education mosaic.

References: James H. Cone, *Martin & Malcolm & America: A Dream or a Nightmare* (Maryknoll, NY: Orbis Books, 1991); David J. Garrow, *Bearing the Cross: Martin Luther King, Jr. and the Southern Christian Leadership Conference, 1955–1968* (New York: William Morrow, 1986); C. Eric Lincoln, *Martin Luther King Jr.: Dreams for a Nation* (New York: Fawcett Books, 1989); Flip Schulke and Penelope O. McPhee, *King Remembered* (New York: W. W. Norton, 1986); Ira G. Zepp, Jr., *The Social Vision of Martin Luther King Jr.* (New York: Carlson, 1989).

KINGSOLVER, BARBARA, an outstanding Native American author, specialized in the complicated social issues that affect Native Americans. Her first novel, *The Bean Trees,* addresses the problem of adoption of Native American children by non-Native Americans. Other novels by Kingsolver include *Pigs in*

Heaven and *Animal Dreams*. Her writing style is biting and fast-paced, and she is able to weave a believable story around the theme.

One of the dilemmas for classroom teachers is the lack of suitable literature pertaining to the key issues affecting Native Americans. Barbara Kingsolver's work provides teachers with extraordinary literature that illuminates the problems faced by Native American people in the United States. Her work is well suited to high school literature classes.

Reference: Barbara Kingsolver, *The Bean Trees* (New York: Harper and Row, 1988).

KINTE, KUNTA, the protagonist in the classic work *Roots* by Alex Haley, has become an icon for the slave trade strategies responsible for rounding up West Africans and forcing them into bondage. Haley's excellent book provides students with a view of slavery, articulating the atrocities and cruelties that occurred. The story of Kunta Kinte is the tale of savage exploitation of human beings and the courage exemplified by the victims of the slave era.

Helping young students come to grips with the concept of slavery can be difficult because of the time factor. The novel *Roots* can help because of the excellent manner in which the book conveys the terrible trauma that persons suffered when they were unwilling participants in the slave trade. The fact that Kunta Kinte is a believable character in the drama casts the episode in a highly realistic light.

References: James A. Banks, *Teaching Strategies for Ethnic Studies*, 6th ed. (Boston: Allyn and Bacon, 1997); Alex Haley, *Roots: The Saga of an American Family* (Garden City, NY: Doubleday, 1976).

KOREAN AMERICANS, although ethnically different from other Asian microcultures, have the same strong work ethic, high value for education, and a profound faith in the opportunities that other Asian Americans have brought with them to the United States. However, Asian-American students have experienced the same sort of culture shock that has been a problem for other microcultures coming to America.

Large populations of Korean Americans reside in New York, Chicago, San Francisco, Los Angeles, and Washington, DC. The 1990 census revealed a population of nearly 800,000, and estimates are that presently (1998) the population of Korean Americans has topped 1 million residents.

The first Korean people to migrate to the United States came to Hawaii in the early 1900s, becoming agricultural laborers on the plantations. However, many of them went on to the west coast regions of the United States in search of higher wages. About 1,000 Koreans came to San Francisco from Hawaii between 1904 and 1907 and then moved up and down the coast. Most of them remained in California.

Korean philosophical and value systems were formulated by combining the roots of the indigenous belief systems, Chinese Confucianism and Mahayama Buddhism, which surfaced in India and later were imported to Korea through China. To truly understand the Korean philosophical macroculture, it is useful to have some knowledge of these three thought systems and to understand the impact and interaction of all three.

One of the biggest problems for educators who instruct Korean-American children has centered around the issue of biculturality. For example, Korean parents often trust teachers not only with the academic education of their children but also with their social development. Korean people often view teachers with a type of reverence. American teachers play an important role in helping Korean children adjust to the new American macroculture. Korean-American students need teachers who can help them preserve their Korean heritage while also learning to become a part of this new pluralistic macroculture. To do this, teachers must become acquainted with the visible characteristics of the Korean microculture, such as the religious institutions, cultural characteristics, and the like.

References: Suchen Chan, *Asian Americans: An Interpretive History* (Boston: Twayne, 1991); Bong Youn Choy, *Koreans in America* (New York: Nelson-Hall, 1979); John K. Fairbank, *East Asia: Tradition and Transformation* (Boston: Houghton Mifflin, 1978); Tae Hung Ha, *Korea: Forty-Three Centuries* (Seoul: Yonse University Press, 1962); Philip R. Harris and Robert T. Moham, *Managing Cultural Differences*, (Houston, TX: Gulf, 1987); Hyung-Chan Kim and W. Patterson, *The Koreans in America; 1882–1974* (Dobbs Ferry, NY: Oceana Publications, 1974); Ronald Takaki, *Strangers from a Different Shore: A History of Asian Americans* (Boston: Little, Brown, 1989).

KU KLUX KLAN. *See* INVISIBLE EMPIRE.

KURDS, the fourth largest ethnic group in the Middle East, rank behind the Arabs, Iranians, and Turks in size. The vast majority of Kurds are concentrated in southeastern Turkey, northern Iraq, northwestern Iran, and northeastern Syria. This region is referred to as Kurdistan, meaning land of the Kurds. Originally a nomadic people, they have become more urban during recent years.

The Treaty of Sevres in 1920 partitioned the Ottoman Empire after the termination of World War I. It provided for the creation of a Kurdish state that never materialized, due to a lack of support by several European states. Since that time, the Kurds have endured great suffering, particularly from 1975 to 1988. In 1991 the Kurds attempted to overthrow the regime of Saddam Hussein in Iraq. The overthrow attempt failed, and the Kurds were once again subjected to great persecution.

Studying the Kurds can provide students with valuable concepts about the manner in which certain ethnic minorities have been persecuted throughout history all over the world. Parallels can be drawn to the treatment of the Kurds by

Saddam Hussein in Iraq and the treatment of the Native Americans in the United States.

References: Nader Entessar, *Kurdish Ethnonationalism* (New York: Lynne Reinner, 1992); Michael Gunter, *The Kurds of Iraq: Tragedy and Hope* (New York: St. Martin's Press, 1992); Martin VanBruinessen, *Agha, Shaikh and State: The Social and Political Structures of Kurdistan* (New York: Zed Books, 1992).

KWANZAA, an African-American holiday based on the traditional African celebration for the first crops harvest, begins on December 26 and lasts for seven days. The word comes from the East African Swahili language and the literal translation means *first fruits*. The holiday was initiated by Maulana Karenga, a professor of Pan-African studies. It is a combination of traditional African practices and African-American interests.

The holiday related to seven principles of black culture (*Nguzo Saba*) that were created by Karenga. These seven principles include unity (*Umoja*), self-determination (*Kujichagulia*), collective work and responsibility (*Ujima*), co-operative economics (*Ujamaa*), purpose (*Nia*), creativity (*Kuumba*), and faith (*Imani*). During each day of the holidays, members of a family light one of the seven candles in a candleholder (*kinara*) and discuss the significance of each day's focus.

Toward the end of the holiday, people in the community come together for a feast (*karamu*). The festivities also include music and dancing, along with assessments of the year passed and special ceremonies that pay homage to the ancestors. Kwanzaa has become a significant segment of year-long multicultural, educational programs.

L

LA GUARDIA, FIORELLO (1882–1947), an Italian-American Congressman from the Upper East Side of Manhattan, became mayor of New York City in the 1933 election. A Republican, he had lost his congressional seat in the 1932 Roosevelt landslide. Previously, he had run for the office in 1929, losing to Jimmie Walker. He was considered to be capable and uncorruptible.

His nickname, Little Flower, comes from his first name. His father was Italian and his mother Jewish. A second nickname, The Hat, stemmed from the broad-brim black stetson hat that he always wore. He spent his early years mostly in Arizona, even though he was born in lower Manhattan in 1882. His father, a military bandmaster, became ill when Fiorello was in his teens. The family moved to Trieste, Italy, and lived with his maternal grandparents. He returned to New York in 1906, working at Ellis Island as an interpreter. He was fluent in Italian, German, Croatian, Yiddish, French, and Spanish.

Graduating from law school at New York University, La Guardia established a legal practice, representing men's clothing workers during the 1913 and 1914 strikes. He was only five feet tall, but he made up for his lack of size with intelligence and stubbornness. It has been said that he had a difficult time taking criticism, and he had a rather volatile temper. He disliked both industrialists and capitalists, and he loathed Tammany Hall.

La Guardia also had a flair for the dramatic. He loved humor and used it extensively in his public sessions. He even read the funnies to children during a newspaper strike in 1945. He had a slightly smaller margin of victory in his bid for a third term in 1941, partly due to some negative remarks he made to Governor Herbert Lehman.

During his tenure as mayor, New York enjoyed enormous progress. New and rehabilitated parks and other recreational facilities were created because of his appointment of Robert Moses as parks commissioner. Some of the first public housing in the nation occurred under his leadership in Harlem, Williamsburg, and the lower east side. Central Park was refurbished and its zoo remodeled. During this time period, 17 outdoor swimming pools were constructed, along with 200 tennis courts and a number of new golf courses. In addition to these additions, many new roadways were constructed, including the Henry Hudson Parkway.

In addition to the remarkable building projects, La Guardia carried on a relentless attack on crime, particularly against gangsters such as Frank Costello and Dutch Schultz. But the most noteworthy achievement during La Guardia's Administration was the apprehension of Lucky Luciano. He initiated a war on slot machines and cleaned up the New York Police Department. He appointed Thomas E. Dewey as a special state prosecutor to investigate organized crime in New York County. This catapulted Dewey into the national limelight and ultimately to the presidential candidacy. For classroom teachers, La Guardia's accomplishments can be used to illustrate the many contributions of Italian Americans throughout the history of the country.

References: Oliver E. Allen, *New York, New York* (New York: Atheneum Press, 1990); Edward R. Ellis, *The Epic of New York City* (New York: Coward-McCann, 1966); Ernest Cuneo, *Life with Fiorello* (New York: Macmillan, 1955); Charles Garrett, *The La Guardia Years, Machine and Reform Politics in New York City* (New Brunswick, NJ: Rutgers University Press, 1961).

LA OPINION, a Spanish newspaper published in Los Angeles, is one of the largest Spanish-language newspapers in the United States. Originally, the paper was read mostly by the Latino macroculture in East Los Angeles. However, the circulation grew as the population demographics changed and Latino people moved into surrounding cities such as Montebello, Downey, and Whittier. During the 1980s and 1990s, the circulation continued to increase as Latino people commenced to populate other portions of California, including the south-central portion of Los Angeles.

La Opinion can be used by classroom teachers to help students understand more about the Latino macroculture. Foreign language instructors can use it to improve the Spanish proficiency of their students. One of the most important multicultural, educational goals for teachers is to help students acquire an appreciation of different languages to raise the tolerance levels for the appreciation of ethnic diversity. Foreign language newspapers such as *La Opinion* can be valuable to teachers who are involved in such endeavors.

LA RAZA UNIDA, meaning The United Race, was formed in hopes of electing more Latinos to public office and providing a pressure group to help pass legislation that would benefit Latinos. It was viewed as an alternative to the Democratic and Republican Parties that many Latinos felt had little interest in promoting the welfare of Latino people.

La Raza Unida was first organized in Texas in 1969. Colorado followed in 1970, Arizona in 1971, and New Mexico in 1972. The preamble of La Raza Unida's manifesto states that "the decision of the people of La Raza to reject the existing political parties of our oppressor and take it upon ourselves to form La Raza Party which will serve as a unifying force in our struggle for self-determination." The early leaders of the party envisioned it as an ethnic institution that would organize community groups, launch massive voter registration drives, and provide draft counseling services and economic expertise to Latino chambers of commerce.

Teachers can use La Raza Unida as an example of the political efforts of American racial and/or ethnic groups to create special political bodies to establish a more aggressive political voice.

References: Elizabeth Sutherland Martinez and Enrique Longeaux y Vasquez, *Viva La Raza* (Garden City, NY: Doubleday, 1971); Matt S. Meier and Feliciano Rivera, *The Chicanos: A History of Mexican Americans* (New York: Hill and Wang, 1972).

LATINO, a generic term used when referring to groups of Spanish-speaking people, is often used as a synonym for "Chicanos," the term used by the federal government for census purposes. Perhaps no issue is more controversial than the terms relating to different macrocultures and microcultures, when it is necessary to identify certain groups for communication purposes. It has been argued that the term "Latino" or "Latina" is preferred in Chicago and California, and some people believe that the term "Latino" implies a political position which is to the left of center. The *Los Angeles Times* uses the term "Latino."

Sixty percent of all Latino people in the United States are of Mexican descent. Some are descendants of the original southwest settlers who resided in the 1 million square miles the United States acquired through the Treaty of Guadalupe Hidalgo in 1848. Hence, these Latino people are often considered to be Native Americans.

A second group of Mexican Americans are the descendants of persons who migrated to the United States after the termination of the Mexican-American War. Many of them came to the United States to work as unskilled laborers in the fields. Most recently, many Mexicans have moved north to the United States to become united with their families.

The other 40 percent of the Latino population consists of people from Puerto Rico, Cuba, Central America, South America, and Spain. Between 1980 and 1990, the Latino population grew about seven times faster than the rest of the nation. These increases were due to the high birth rate of Latinos and the accelerated migrations of persons from Mexico, South America, Central America, the Caribbean, and South America. Nine out of ten Latino people reside in ten states (California, Texas, New York, Florida, Illinois, New Jersey, Arizona, New Mexico, Colorado, and Massachusetts).

Multicultural education efforts should help students understand the ethnic characteristics of different microcultures. One portion of such investigations must relate to the names persons wish to be used when referring to specific groups. To make certain that teachers are using appropriate names, it is necessary to listen and determine which names the people prefer. In addition, students need to understand the various language, religious, and cultural characteristics of America's microcultures.

References: V. Yans McLaughlin (Ed.), *Immigration Reconsidered: History, Sociology, and Politics* (New York: Oxford University Press, 1990); M. Lee Manning and Leroy G. Baruth, *Multicultural Education of Children and Adolescents* (Boston: Allyn and Bacon, 1996); Joan Thrower Timm, *Four Perspectives in Multicultural Education* (Belmont, CA: Wadsworth, 1996).

LAU v. NICHOLS, a landmark Supreme Court decision affecting multicultural education, related to the use of mother tongue languages to ensure that American students receive equal educational opportunities, a guarantee of the United States Constitution. The U.S. Supreme Court ruled that the San Francisco Unified School District was denying Lau, a native Mandarin-Chinese speaker, a meaningful opportunity to participate in the public education program.

This ruling by the high court established a legal basis for compensatory programs that would assist students for whom English was a second language. Special programs in bilingual education and English as a Second Language were established as a result of this high court ruling.

The Supreme Court determined that because California required that English was the basic language of instruction in the schools, students with no understanding of English were prevented from receiving a meaningful education. The inability to understand the language of instruction excluded language-different students from meaningful participation in the educational process. Therefore, school districts are required to take positive steps to rectify the language deficiency.

References: Kern Alexander and M. David Alexander, *American Public School Law* (Belmont, CA: Wadsworth, 1998); Philip C. Chinn, *Multicultural Education in a Pluralistic Society* (Columbus, OH: Merrill, 1990); *Lau v. Nichols*, 414 U.S. 563; Joan Thrower Timm, *Four Perspectives in Multicultural Education* (Belmont, CA: Wadsworth, 1996).

LEWIS, GEORGE (1900–1968), an African-American clarinet player from New Orleans, was a key figure in the early development of American jazz. Born in New Orleans in 1900, he became a prominent member in the Black Eagles, the Pacific Brass Band, the Olympia Band, and the Eureka Brass Band. A deeply religious man, Lewis played in over 500 funeral processions during his lifetime. New Orleans funeral processions were an important part of jazz development. Musicians played hymns on the way to the cemetery and jazz on the way back.

Lewis was instrumental in the resurgence of traditional New Orleans jazz after World War II. He brought his band from New Orleans to New York and California. He was also active in the creation of the Preservation Hall in New Orleans, where he performed frequently until his death.

Since jazz provides an extraordinary means of illustrating the value of pluralistic interaction, teachers can use Lewis as an example of the African-American influence on the art form. The fact that Lewis recorded many religious works can provide further insights about the religious influences in the development of American jazz.

Reference: William Carter, *Preservation Hall* (New York: W. W. Norton, 1991).

LIBERAL, from a multicultural education standpoint, has been used to refer to persons who favor a more pluralistic approach to American education as opposed to a conservative position, which has often promoted a Eurocentric philosophy. The "liberal" has tended to support approaches that recognize the accomplishments of women and persons of color.

During the American Civil Rights Movement of the 1950s and 1960s, "liberals" were often viewed in a favorable light while "conservatives" were sometimes thought to be "obstructionists." However, starting in the 1980s, "liberals" were often characterized as being fiscally irresponsible, favoring higher rates of government spending and higher taxes. It even became politically dangerous for politicians to say they were "liberal."

However, semantics experts have tended to define the word "liberal" as a term that means persons who are broad minded and not narrow in their views. Another definition has referred to the capacity to tolerate a wide disparity of viewpoints as well as favoring progress and reforms. Consequently, the "liberal/conservative" dichotomy is a less than accurate means of defining the concept.

LINCOLN, ABRAHAM (1809–1865), elected in 1860, came to office as the winning candidate of the new Republican Party. He inherited a nation divided as the result of the Dred Scott Decision, a 1857 Supreme Court ruling rendered by the Taney Court. Chief Justice John Taney, a wealthy 80-year-old son of a slave-holding family, wrote the majority opinion, which said that Scott had no right to bring suit since he was an African-American. The ruling stipulated that African Americans were of an inferior class and were not and never could be citizens.

The ruling helped lead to the Civil War, and Lincoln refused to allow the southern states to secede from the Union. The resulting war ended slavery in the United States, but the bloody conflicts caused 600,000 deaths. During the war in 1863, President Lincoln signed the Emancipation Proclamation that stipulated the slave population residing in the Confederate states would be "forever free."

References: Roy P. Balser (Ed.), *Lincoln, Collected Works* (Piscataway, NJ: Rutgers University Press, 1953); Eric Foner, *Reconstruction: America's Unfinished Revolution, 1863–1977* (New York: Harper, 1988); *Dred Scott v. Sandford,* 60 U.S. 393, 1857.

LINGUISTIC BIAS, also known as linguistic chauvinism, refers to educational measurement procedures that utilize instruments written in a language (usually English) in which the student is not proficient. If the student has limited English proficiency, any assessment must be conducted in the student's native language to secure valid results. If an assessment instrument contains linguistic bias, it means that the results will probably be invalid.

Providing students with linguistically appropriate measurement materials is difficult because in the United States and around the world, children bring a huge variety of language backgrounds to the schoolroom. In the United States, children utilize more than 100 mother tongues other than English. Consequently, it is often difficult to obtain appropriate materials for children representing so many different language groups.

However, the matter is further complicated by several other issues. First is the problem of translation. There is a difference between the student's native language and the student's preferred language. Utilizing assessment instruments in the student's native language, if the preferred language is English, will not improve the validity of the results. Also, poor translations that are not sensitive to culturally specific terms and concepts create validity problems as do translations that fail to address the issue of linguistic competency in the native language.

Reference: Herbert Grossman, *Teaching in a Diverse Society* (Boston: Allyn and Bacon, 1995).

LITERACY TESTS. Following the termination of the American Civil War in 1865, the question of voting rights for freed slaves became a crucial issue. The Thirteenth Amendment to the U.S. Constitution terminated slavery in the United States, while the Fourteenth Amendment granted citizenship to all freed slaves. However, it was the Fifteenth Amendment that allowed African-American males the right to vote. No American women had voting privileges.

Following this action, southern states felt it necessary to initiate strategies to prevent freed slaves from voting. The poll tax and the literacy tests were utilized to disenfranchise freed male slaves. Literacy tests were used to prevent African Americans from voting. Since literacy was essentially forbidden during the slavery era, many African Americans were unable to read. However, those who were literate were thwarted from passing the tests. Voting registration offices were usually open for only two days a month and most African Americans "failed" the literacy tests. Illiterate European Americans were not required to take the tests.

Eventually, the Voters Rights Act of 1964 banned literacy tests as a prerequisite for voting in presidential elections, as long as residency was established at least one month prior to the election day.

References: James MacGregor Burns and Stewart Burns, *A People's Charter: The Pursuits of Rights in America* (New York: Alfred P. Knopf, 1991); Sharon Harley, *Timetables of African-American History* (New York: Simon and Schuster, 1995); Juan Williams, *Eyes on the Prize: America's Civil Rights Years, 1954–1965* (New York: Viking Press, 1987).

LITTLE ROCK HIGH SCHOOL, in Little Rock, Arkansas, was the scene of the nation's first instance of military intervention to enforce the decision of the U.S. Supreme Court in the 1954 *Brown v. Board of Education* case. Arkansas Governor Orville Faubus refused to allow the Little Rock schools to become integrated. He ordered the State's National Guard to prevent the integration of the high school. His argument was that as governor, he was required to back the will of Arkansas citizens who were against racial integration in the schools.

However, in this 1957 incident, President Dwight Eisenhower reminded Governor Faubus that he would be expected to comply with the Supreme Court decision and adhere to the wishes of the U.S. District Court. Eventually, it was necessary for President Eisenhower to order more than 1,000 members of the 101st Airborne Division to ensure the safety of the nine African-American students who were the first to integrate high school. The incident served notice throughout the land that the *Brown v. Board of Education* decision would be the law of the land. Each of the nine students was provided with a personal bodyguard, a member of the 101st Airborne Division. However, after the school was racially integrated, Faubus, who was re-elected to a third term for his anti-integration stance, closed all of Little Rock's public schools. However, they were re-opened in August 1959, coming into compliance with the federal mandates.

Educators can order *America's Civil Rights Movement*, a video tape and corresponding teaching materials that address the history of the American Civil Rights Movement. The materials provide an excellent account of the Little Rock High School incident with quotes from participating students.

References: Sara Bullard (Ed.), *Teaching Tolerance, America's Civil Rights Movement* (Montgomery, AL: Teaching Tolerance, 1991); Juan Williams, *Eyes on the Prize: America's Civil Rights Years, 1954–1965* (New York: Viking Press, 1987).

LYNCHINGS have proven to be one of the more embarrassing occurrences throughout American history. Sometimes motivated by mob action and other times by hate groups, such as the Ku Klux Klan, lynchings of African Americans and other Americans reached crisis proportions between the 46 years from 1882 to 1927 when nearly 5,000 Americans were lynched. Of this number, more than 3,500 were African Americans. During this time period, Mississippi and Georgia lynched more than 1,000 African Americans.

More than 4,100 of the lynchings occurred in the states of Mississippi, Georgia, Texas, Louisiana, Alabama, Arkansas, Florida, Tennessee, Kentucky, South Carolina, Oklahoma, Missouri, Virginia, and North Carolina. Notable crusaders against lynching have included journalist Ida B. Wells and Walter White, an Assistant Secretary of the National Association for the Advancement of Colored People.

References: National Association for the Advancement of Colored People, *Thirty Years of Lynching* (Washington, DC: NAACP, 1918); Walter White, *Rope and Faggot* (Salem, NH: Ayer, 1992).

M

MACROCULTURE, a sociological term, refers to any predominant culture. In the United States, it developed from western European traditions and values that determined the language, social values, and religion. While there is no legally recognized national language in the United States, the common language is the standard dialect of English, even though many other tongues are also prominent. Thus, in defining macroculture, it is necessary to identify the parameters of the group. So the macroculture of the United States or any other country refers to the predominant characteristics of the total group. Thus, in the United States, the macroculture can be defined as Anglo-Western European. The reason for this is that throughout the country's history, the English language has prevailed and curriculum materials have been written from a Eurocentric perspective until the American Civil Rights Movement.

Complicating the definition even further, other groups have their own macroculture. For example, the macroculture of Latino Americans can be characterized by the Spanish language, the Catholic religion, relatively large families, industriousness, strong support for the extended family, and predominant influences from Spain that suppressed the language, religion, and values of the indigenous populations.

Reference: Christine I. Bennett, *Comprehensive Multicultural Education: Theory and Practice*, 3d ed. (Boston: Allyn and Bacon, 1995).

MAGNET SCHOOLS, usually found in public school districts, have been established to entice students with special aptitudes. They have also been established to help desegregate school districts racially. For example, a school may become designated as a math/science school. That would mean that students from all over a given school district's attendance area might opt to participate in this excellent math/science school.

The "magnet school" attempt at school desegregation has been one of the more successful models. If educators can create exceptionally strong programs in math/science, fine arts, literature/English, and the like, they tend to have solid arguments regarding the general quality of education in the school district. These "beefed-up" programs can lure students from around the attendance areas and desegregate schools in the process. The most successful magnet school programs have provided transportation for students when needed.

To create a magnet school environment, school districts have recruited the "cream of the crop" teachers and have created programs that offer courses not found in typical school programs. Most magnet schools have been established as middle schools and high schools.

MAINTENANCE BILINGUAL EDUCATION, one of several usage models, emphasizes the continuation and improvement of the child's mother tongue while learning the second language. The instruction is carried on in the student's native language until an acceptable proficiency level in English has been acquired. This usually takes four or five years, depending on the linguistic history of the student. For example, the acquisition of English fluency usually occurs more rapidly with children who have a good syntactical understanding of their native language.

The advantage of this approach is that children are able to keep up with other children in subjects such as social studies, math, and science. The ultimate goal is to have students reach the point where they are equally literate in both languages. Excellent examples of this approach can be found in East Los Angeles, California, and Rock Point, Arizona, on the Navajo reservation.

References: L. H. Gann and Peter J. Duignan, *The Hispanics in the United States: A History* (Boulder, CO: Westview Press, 1986); Manuel H. Guerra, "Bilingualism and Biculturalism: Assets for Chicanos," in Arnulfo D. Trejo (Ed.), *The Chicanos as We See Ourselves* (Tucson: University of Arizona Press, 1980); Judith Harlan, *Bilingualism in the United States: Conflict and Controversy* (New York: Franklin Watts, 1991).

MANDELA, NELSON (1918–), kept a prisoner in apartheid South African prisons, was finally freed in February of 1990. The South African policy of apartheid denied basic human rights to about 87 percent of the South-African population. The funding formula for the public schools provided two-thirds of the money allotted to "Whites" for "Colored" students (Indians and mixed-race students) and only one-half of the money for black Africans.

Mandela was a member of the Tembu ruling family in the Transkei. In his younger days, he was a sheep herder and helped his family with the plowing. He wanted to become a lawyer, but after attending a Methodist school he went on to University College of Fort Hare in South Africa, where he was suspended for his involvements in political activism. He returned home but moved to Johannesburg, South Africa. Mandela joined the African National Congress in 1944 and soon after was elected General Secretary. He was one of twenty African leaders who were arrested in 1952 for their involvement in the organization of the Defiance Campaign. He received a nine-month suspended sentence.

He established a law practice with Oliver Tambo in Johannesburg. They handled legal cases for persons who had been victimized by apartheid and the Urban Areas Act. Tambo described Mandela as passionate, impatient, and fearless. These qualities were exemplified in his many speeches.

His first marriage was to Nomzano Winnie Madikizela, a social worker who had moved from the Transkei to Johannesburg. They both made substantial contributions to the liberation struggle of South Africa. In 1962, he was imprisoned and sentenced to five years hard labor for his involvement in the anti-apartheid struggle in the country of South Africa. While he was imprisoned in Pretoria, he wrote his final papers for his London University law degree. Later, he was sentenced to life imprisonment for sabotage in connection with his struggle for equality of black Africans.

In 1990, under relentless world pressure, Pretoria's ban on the African National Congress was ended, and Mandela was freed after his 27 years of incarceration. In the subsequent election, the African National Congress Party received 62 percent of the vote, defeating the racist Nationalist Party, which received 20 percent. He was inaugurated president of South Africa, while F. W. de Klerk became the Second Deputy. Thabo Mbeki was named the First Deputy.

References: Nelson Mandela, *Nelson Mandela Speaks* (New York: Pathfinder, 1993); Nelson Mandela, *The Struggle Is My Life* (London: Canon Collins House, 1986); Greg McCartan (Ed.), *Nelson Mandela Speeches* (New York: Pathfinder Press, 1990); Allister Sparks, *Tomorrow Is Another Country* (New York: Hill and Wang, 1995).

MANZANAR, created as a result of President Franklin Roosevelt's Executive Order #9066, was one of ten relocation centers for Japanese Americans during World War II. The executive order authorized the U.S. Army to exclude specific populations when deemed necessary for security reasons. The other nine sites were located in the states of California, Arizona, Idaho, Utah, Colorado, and Arkansas.

Located about 200 miles northeast of Los Angeles, Manzanar was arguably situated in the most majestic location at the base of Mount Whitney, the highest peak in the "lower forty-eight." Until Manzanar and the other sites were constructed, Japanese Americans were housed in the stables at race tracks such as Santa Anita and Tanforan.

Decisions to intern Japanese Americans were based on irrational war hysteria, often spurred by irresponsible newspaper stories. Moreover, many growers in California's Central Valley were anxious to get rid of their Japanese-American competitors. Education programs at Manzanar were difficult due to disagreements over the curriculum and a lack of experienced teachers. Most of the Manzanar residents lost their homes and other personal belongings during their incarceration.

References: Roger Daniels, *Concentration Camps: North American Japanese in the United States and Canada During World War II* (Malabar, FL: Krieger, 1981); Gary Okihiro, *Whispered Silences: Japanese-Americans During World War II* (Seattle: University of Washington Press, 1996); Ronald Takaki, *A Different Mirror: A History of Multicultural America* (Boston: Little, Brown, 1993).

MARSHALL, THURGOOD (1908–1993), the first African American to become a member of the U.S. Supreme Court, was appointed by President Lyndon Johnson in 1967. He served until 1991, when he resigned from the Court because of poor health. He was replaced by Clarence Thomas, a conservative Republican appointed by President George Bush. The Court swung strongly to the right with Thomas' appointment.

Marshall, a graduate of Howard University Law School, became a key lawyer for the National Association for the Advancement of Colored People (NAACP) at the request of Charles Houston, the NAACP's chief legal counsel. He became one of the key attorneys in *Sweatt v. Painter, McLaurin v. Oklahoma*, and finally, *Brown v. Board of Education*, key NAACP-sponsored Supreme Court decisions that resulted in racial segregation in U.S. schools becoming unconstitutional.

During his 27-year tenure on the U.S. Supreme Court, Marshall was known for his liberal positions on Supreme Court decisions. But with the Supreme Court appointments during the Reagan/Bush years, the Court began a decided swing to the right. When Justice William Brennan, the other consistent liberal, tendered his resignation in 1990, Marshall was the only remaining liberal. When he learned that the Rehnquist Court wished to strengthen the death penalty, he resigned.

References: Henry J. Abraham, *Justices and Presidents: A Political History of Appointments to the Supreme Court* (New York: Oxford University Press, 1974); Laurence Baum, *The Supreme Court* (Washington, DC: CQ Press, 1985); Richard Kluger, *The History of Brown v. Board of Education and Black America's Struggle for Equality* (New York: Alfred A. Knopf, 1976); Jane Mayer and Jill Abramson, *Strange Justice: The Selling of Clarence Thomas* (Boston: Houghton Mifflin, 1994); Juan Williams, *Eyes on the Prize: America's Civil Rights Years, 1954–1965* (New York: Viking Press, 1987).

McCARRAN–WALTER ACT, passed by Congress in 1952, provided limited immigration rights to Asians. The earlier Immigration Act of 1924 had resulted in the total exclusion of Asians for a period of 28 years. The McCarran–Walter Act terminated the racial restriction of the 1790 Naturalization Law. But in spite of lifting the restrictions on Asians, there were still limitations. For example, only 185 Japanese people were allowed to immigrate each year.

However, it was not until the passage of the Immigration Act of 1965 that quota restrictions against Asians were terminated. This act liberalized immigration to the United States by eliminating the quotas based on national origins. This 1965 Act caused a dramatic change in previous immigration laws that had created a society of European immigrants, along with African slaves and Native Americans.

References: James A. Banks, *Teaching Strategies for Ethnic Studies*, 6th ed. (Boston: Allyn and Bacon, 1997); Leonard Dinnerstein, et al., *Natives and Strangers* (New York: Oxford University Press, 1990); Thomas Sowell, *Ethnic America: A History* (New York: Basic Books, 1981); Ronald Takaki, *A Different Mirror: A History of Multicultural American* (Boston: Little, Brown, 1993).

MELTING POT THEORY, a conceptual metaphor dating clear back to the early days of European immigration to the United States, stipulated that new immigrants should jump into the crucible, get rid of their mother tongue and other cultural traditions, and adapt the cultural mores of the dominant macroculture (English-speaking European Americans). The notion resurfaced as a result of Israel Zangwill's play, *The Melting Pot*, performed in New York City in 1908.

During the American Civil Rights Movement in the 1960s, the melting pot theory came under attack from a number of American microcultures. New phrases commenced to surface. One was the "stew theory," which proclaimed that the American mosaic was analogous to a stew. Each ingredient served a purpose. Take away the carrots, and the essence of the total product suffered. Take away the meat, and the same thing would happen. So at this time in history, the "melting pot" notion was replaced by the "stew" or the "salad" theory. The metaphor meant that each ingredient provided a special and important dimension of the American mosaic that retains its own unique identity.

The message for teachers is clear. It is important to encourage students to maintain their microcultural traditions, including their language. However, it is also crucial that teachers expose students to the macrocultural traditions of the United States. This should be done overtly in the structure of curricular offerings and covertly with the positive relationships teachers have with individual pupils.

References: James A. Banks, *Teaching Strategies for Ethnic Studies*, 6th ed. (Boston: Allyn and Bacon, 1997); Bruce M. Mitchell, et al., *The Dynamic Classroom*, 5th ed. (Dubuque, IA: Kendall/Hunt, 1995); Pamela Tiedt and Iris M. Tiedt, *Multicultural Teaching: A Handbook of Activities, Information, and Resources* (Boston: Allyn and Bacon, 1995).

MENOMINEE TRIBE, members of the Algonquians, occupied the Great Lakes regions for many years before the arrival of the Europeans. Travelers and traders, they were noted for transporting themselves in birch bark canoes. The Menominees championed the notion of individual rights for all people, including children. Religiously, they believed in several different gods who subscribed to humor and also violence.

During the War of 1812, the Menominees sided with the British after some prior involvement with the French. The tribe signed a treaty with the United States in 1856, receiving 235,000 acres of land on which they were allowed to reside. However, during the Eisenhower Administration, the Menominee Termination Act was signed into law in 1954 and their reservation was dissolved. Subsequently, the Menominee Restoration Act of 1973 re-established federal recognition of the tribe. By 1992, the reconstituted Menominee Reservation had a population of 3,182 Native Americans.

References: Patricia K. Ourada, *The Menominee Indians: A History* (Norman: University of Oklahoma Press, 1979); Nicholas C. Peroff, *Menominee Drums: Tribal Termination and Restoration, 1954–1974* (Norman: University of Oklahoma Press, 1982).

MESTIZOS, a term referring to persons of mixed racial blood, commonly pertains to people who were products of interbreeding between the Spaniards and the various Native American populations with whom they came into contact. Few *Mestizos* were landowners and many of them became involved as craftsmen, laborers, and soldiers. Most were Spanish speaking and Roman Catholics.

References: L. H. Gann and Peter J. Duignan, *The Hispanics in the United States: A History* (Boulder, CO: Westview Press, 1986); Himilce Novas, *Everything You Need to Know About Latino History* (New York: Penguin, 1994).

MEXICAN AMERICANS, persons who migrated to the present boundaries of the United States from the past or present boundaries of Mexico, have become the nation's fastest-growing microculture. Mexican Americans were in the regions comprising U.S. boundaries before the arrival of the Europeans. About 60 percent of America's Latino population are Mexican Americans.

Geographically, one group of Mexican Americans resides in the southwest portion of the United States. These Americans are the descendants of the original residents of the regions. The major cities in the area have Spanish names such as El Paso, San Diego, Los Angeles, and San Antonio. The Treaty of Guadalupe Hidalgo ended the war with Mexico and in 1848, the United States received over 1 million square miles of new territory, including all or part of the existing states of California, Arizona, New Mexico, Texas, Utah, Nevada, and Colorado. However, European Americans moved to these areas in great numbers during the second half of the nineteenth century, so that by 1990, Mexican Americans comprised only about 10 percent of the population.

The second group of Mexican Americans are the descendants of people who entered the United States after the end of the United States war with Mexico, extending to the end of World War II. Many of these persons were recruited as a source of cheap labor to meet the nation's growing labor needs in the southwestern United States. Many of these unskilled workers became part of the burgeoning agricultural industry. Both groups tended to use Spanish as their native language and were Roman Catholics.

The third group of Mexican Americans consists of the more recent residents who have migrated to the United States during the second half of the twenty-first century. Many of these immigrants came to the United States to become unified with family members who were already in the United States. Many were undocumented, and the great majority of the third group were also unskilled laborers who toiled in the agricultural industry. The children of many migrant farm laborers struggled in school because of their frequent relocation as they were forced to follow the crops. These laborers had the same ethnic characteristics as the first two groups and made it possible for the southwestern agricultural industry to prosper. *See also* CHICANOS; LATINOS.

References: Laurence A. Cardoso, *Mexican Emigration to the United States, 1897–1931: Socioeconomic Patterns* (Tucson: University of Arizona Press, 1980); Virginia Yans-McLaughlin (Ed.), *Immigration Reconsidered: History, Sociology, and Politics* (New York: Oxford University Press, 1990); Carey McWilliams, *North from Mexico: The Spanish-Speaking People of the United States* (Westport, CT: Greenwood Press, 1990); Julian Samora and Patricia Vandel Simon, *A History of the Mexican-American People* (Notre Dame, IN: University of Notre Dame Press, 1977); Ronald Takaki, *A Different Mirror: A History of Multicultural America* (Boston: Little, Brown, 1993).

MIGRANT EDUCATION in the United States relates to the efforts of educators to provide an equal education for children whose parents are in the "migrant stream" and must move from place to place, necessitating their children to endure many interruptions in their schooling. With the population increases in the southwest and the corresponding increase in available irrigation water, a need for more cheap agricultural labor came into existence. Water projects such as California's Colorado and Feather River projects created vast new agricultural areas.

Documented and undocumented workers from Mexico crossed the border, some of them bringing their entire families. As they moved from place to place, children were enrolled in schools that were often racially segregated until after the 1954 *Brown v. Board of Education* case. Children with limited English-speaking proficiency often struggled in the schools when they encountered teachers who had little understanding of Spanish and little experience working with Latino children from low-income backgrounds.

During the American Civil Rights Movement, special funding for migrant education programs became available through federally funded programs. These inservice educational programs attempted to help educators better understand the socioeconomic conditions encountered by children in the migrant stream. In addition, teachers were provided instruction in Spanish to communicate more effectively with students and parents. Computerized tracking systems were also established to cut down on the time it took to acquire the cumulative records of migrant children who were forced to move from school-to-school throughout the year.

References: Rodolfo Acuna, *Occupied America: A History of Chicanos* (New York: Harper and Row, 1980); Livie Isauro Duran and Russell H. Bernard (Eds.), *Introduction to Chicano Studies* (New York: Macmillan, 1982); Eugene E. Garcia, *Early Childhood Bilingualism with Special Reference to the Mexican-American Child* (Albuquerque: University of New Mexico Press, 1983); Thomas Sowell, *Ethnic America: A History* (New York: Basic Books, 1990).

MILITIA MOVEMENT, UNITED STATES. Throughout American history, militia groups have existed in the socio/political environment. However, during the 1980s and 1990s, such organizations have surfaced in large numbers. The militia members are usually disaffected European-American males who are convinced that they must become armed and organized to achieve what they perceive to be "justice."

During the 1980s and 1990s, militia organizations became connected with right-wing causes such as anti-taxation, "white separatism," Constitutional interpretations, suspicions of government and the like. Some organizations have even argued that the secession of entire states is legal. Militia groups have had substantial numbers of people, while others have acted alone or in pairs. However, others, such as the Aryan Republican Army, have a white-power network in many parts of the United States.

Some militias have been intent in overthrowing the government, while others also have a racist agenda and want to purge the country of Jews and African Americans. Using Biblical phrases taken out of context is a favorite tactic of some militia organizations that claim to have a "Christian" identity. While many of the identified militia organizations have been located in such states as Michigan, Montana, and Idaho, now they can be found in virtually every part of the nation. However, there is a tendency for them to be located in portions of the country where there is a high proportion of European-American residents.

Militia members are mostly European-American males, many of whom are convinced that their constitutional rights have been violated. Much of this attitude can be traced to affirmative action programs, which have been especially irritating to European-American males who historically have benefited economically and professionally because of their race and gender. Many of the militia members have also struggled in school and been relatively unsuccessful in the economic and job markets.

Since a number of militia members have been unemployed, the organizations have often resorted to criminal activities to support themselves and to acquire the arms and ammunition they feel are necessary. Bank robberies have been a common method utilized for the procurement of such armaments. Also common have been thefts of dynamite, fuel oil, fertilizer, and the like. These items are necessary for the creation of bombs, such as the explosive devices used in the obliteration of the government building in Oklahoma City.

For teachers, there are a number of issues that need to be addressed. Perhaps the most important issue is that students need to be well-educated, successful, and well-informed to help prevent their involvement in such organizations. Studies of the U.S. Constitution need to be stressed, as do multicultural education studies that emphasize the value of American pluralism.

References: "Letter Suggests McVeigh Was Moving Beyond Talk," *Spokesman-Review*, Friday, May 9, 1997; "McVeigh Pointed to as Ryder Truck Renter," *Spokesman-Review*, May 10, 1997; "A Bank Robbing Army of the Right Is Left in Tatters," *Los Angeles Times*, January 15, 1997; "Siege Suspect Has Ties to Region," *Spokesman-Review*, May 8, 1997.

MILLIKIN v. BRADLEY, a U.S. Supreme Court decision rendered in 1974, pertained to busing programs for desegregating schools to comply with the 1954 *Brown v. Board of Education* Supreme Court decision. The desegregation strategy in question was proposed for the Detroit public schools. This landmark case involved the desegregation of the Detroit schools through the implementation of an inter-district busing plan.

The *Milliken v. Bradley* decision ruled there was a lack of evidence that school districts adjacent to Detroit were racially segregated or did any of their actions affect segregation in other districts. Therefore, they could not be involved in Detroit's desegregation plan. The Court decreed that segregation that existed in one school district could not be remedied by plans involving inter-district solutions.

The implications for educators are clear. Desegregation plans that involve several school districts collectively are quite likely to be declared unconstitutional.

Reference: Kern Alexander and M. David Alexander, *American Public School Law* (Belmont, CA: Wadsworth, 1998); *Milliken v. Bradley*, 418 U.S. 717, 94 S.Ct. 311, 41 L.Ed.2d 1069 (1974).

MISSOURI v. GAINES, a key Supreme Court decision leading up to the *Brown v. Board of Education* case, was a critical test case relating to the constitutionality of the "separate but equal" principle established in the 1896 *Plessy v. Ferguson* Supreme Court decision. In 1936, Lloyd Lionel Gaines, a 25-year-old African American, attempted to gain entrance to the University of Missouri's racially segregated law school. However, since he was an African American, the state of Missouri offered to provide him with tuition expenses for attending a law school in a neighboring state and promised to create a law school for African Americans that he could attend.

Charles Houston, the NAACP lawyer who pleaded Gaines' case, argued that in order for the "separate but equal" doctrine to apply, any school for African Americans clearly had to be equal in quality to the school for European Americans. In this 1938 case, the Supreme Court ruled against the state of Missouri, and Gaines was allowed to attend the University of Missouri Law School. The significance of the decision was far reaching, because it sent a clear message that all states must provide an equal education for all students.

References: Kern Alexander and M. David Alexander, *American Public School Law* (Belmont, CA: Wadsworth, 1998); Juan Williams, *Eyes on the Prize: America's Civil Rights Years, 1954–1965* (New York: Viking Press, 1987).

MOJADOS, a Spanish word meaning "the wet ones" refers to Mexicans who crossed the Rio Grande River into the United States. *Mojados* have been an object of ridicule because large numbers of these Mexicans, including many "undocumented" laborers, came into the United States illegally. Another source of American cheap labor, *mojados* were particularly welcome in Texas since that state did not acknowledge the new bracero program designed to help Mexican laborers work in the United States. However, they could be found in every agricultural region in the Southwest.

After the termination of the first Bracero Program in 1947, a dramatic increase in *mojados* occurred because the United States relied on Mexican Americans in the nation's agricultural industry. Throughout American history, many *mojados* were able to elude the immigration authorities, in spite of the fact that between 1947 and 1955, over 4 million undocumented workers were deported to Mexico.

The immigration of *mojados* still occurs on a regular basis. Because of Mexico's poverty problems, many *mojados* still continue to enter the United States and provide a large, cheap, labor force that has become a vital element of the nation's agricultural industry. Many *mojados* are smuggled in by people called coyotes who earn a profit by helping Mexican nationals get across the border. However, others literally risk their lives to find economic improvement by seeking employment in agricultural occupations in the United States. Teachers with Latino students need to know the history of this American microculture to craft successful education programs in the schools.

References: Edna Acosta-Belen and Barbara R. Sjostrom (Eds.), *The Hispanic Experience in the United States: Contemporary Issues and Perspectives* (New York: Praeger, 1988); George J. Borjas, *Friends or Strangers: The Impact of Immigrants on the United States Economy* (New York: Basic Books, 1990); Joan W. Moore and Harry Pachon, *Hispanics in the United States* (Englewood Cliffs, NJ: Prentice-Hall, 1985); Himilce Novas, *Everything You Need to Know About Latino History* (New York: Penguin Books, 1991).

MOMADAY, N. SCOTT (1934–), a Nobel Prize winning author and professor of literature and Native-American Studies, is the child of a Cherokee mother and a Kiowa father. Receiving his Ph.D. at Stanford University in American literature, Momaday established a noted career as a professor and author. His 1968 novel, *House Made of Dawn*, resulted in a Pulitzer Prize. He was also the narrator in a classic film, *More Than Bows and Arrows*, which depicts the accomplishments of Native Americans throughout American history.

Momaday was one of the early Native American writers to address the oral traditions of Native Americans through his writings. His experimentation with prose, poetry, photography, and sketches have made him an extraordinary role model for young writers. Teachers can use his excellent work as an example of the fine accomplishments of Native American writers in the field of literature.

Reference: Harvey Markowitz (Ed.), *American Indians* (Pasadena, CA: Salem Press, 1995).

MONOCULTURAL, an adjective relating to sociological descriptions of human groups, pertains to persons who possess similar ethnic/racial characteristics. Monocultural societies consist of persons who have the same or similar religions, language patterns, levels of education, moral values, and ways of viewing and interpreting the environments with which they come into contact.

The term can describe either large or small groups of people. For example, Japanese people consist of a rather large number of human beings whose native language is Japanese and who maintain a certain number of basic values and traditions. But it must be remembered that smaller groups of people can also be considered to be "monocultural." For example, the term could also relate to the *Fortune* 500 Chief Executive Officers, since they are mostly English-speaking, business oriented, European-American males.

MONTAGU, ASHLEY (1905–), a noted physical anthropologist who studied the racial characteristics of human groups, classified humankind into four major groups. Negroid people were mostly from sub-Saharan Africa. Australoid (Archaic White) people comprised the second group. The other two groups were the Caucasoids and Mongoloids, the largest group of all.

While Montagu spent much of his early career in the development of these classification schemes, he later decided that classifying human beings by race was unproductive due to the historical inter-breeding of people. He went on to question the validity of the concept of race, since the overlapping of physical traits was the general rule.

Teachers can make good use of Montagu's work in helping students develop more realistic understandings of race as a factor that defines human beings. Racist groups, such as the Ku Klux Klan, place extreme importance on racial definitions. Teachers can help students acquire more sophisticated views of race through studies of his later work.

Reference: Ashley Montagu, *Man's Most Dangerous Myth: The Fallacy of Race* (New York: Oxford University Press, 1974).

MORTON, JELLY ROLL (1885–1941), one of the key figures in the development of New Orleans jazz, was raised by his aunt, Eulalie Echo. His grandfather was a member of the Louisiana Constitutional Convention of 1868, and his father was a small businessman. Ferdinand Morton was a laborer in a barrel factory before he went to Storyville, the red light district in New Orleans, to play the piano. While his Creole grandmother disowned him, Morton commenced to earn good money, and his familiarity with light classical music and European technique enabled him to contribute many new ideas to the new art form, jazz.

While Morton played the blues, he tended to argue that they were crude and unpolished. But his extraordinary piano style became a model for many other New Orleans piano players. In addition to his genius on the piano, Morton was also an accomplished arranger. His gifted Red Hot Peppers Jazz Band became known for Morton's orchestrated compositions. In fact, he actually broke tradition when he wrote out the clarinet and cornet parts for several tunes, including "Doctor Jazz" and "Black Bottom Stomp."

His musical accomplishments are well known, and he was interviewed about his knowledge of the early development of jazz for the Library of Congress. He became a musical icon for many musicians who were attempting to recapture the original New Orleans jazz genre in traditional New Orleans jazz bands all over the country. Teachers can use his musical accomplishments and his influence in American jazz development to illustrate the value of pluralistic involvement in the creation of this American art form.

References: Robert Goffin, *Jazz from the Congo to the Metropolitan* (Garden City, NY: Doubleday, 1944); Gunther Schuller, *Early Jazz: Its Roots and Early Development* (New York: Macmillan, 1946).

MOTHER TONGUE, a term pertaining to the native language of a child, is a phrase which is commonly used as a synonym for "native language." It is the language that is first acquired by young children, and consequently becomes a crucial part of their ethnic value system. Obviously, it is easier for young learners to study basic concepts in reading and language development in their mother tongue or native language. Therefore, educators have grappled with the issue of how to provide the best education possible for students coming to American schools whose native language is something other than English.

The topic is also a concern in other countries. While the phrase "mother tongue" is not commonly used in the United States, it is used in other countries throughout the world. For example, the Norwegian school system has been concerned about the issue of "mother tongue" instruction. Norwegian educators fall into two groups. One faction believes in "total immersion," while the other group believes in using bilingual education programs that utilize the student's mother tongue. In those circumstances, students would also be involved in Norwegian as a second language (NSL) programs. The same issue exists in other countries such as Brazil and Australia.

Reference: Bruce M. Mitchell and Robert E. Salsbury, *Multicultural Education: An International Guide to Research, Policies, and Programs* (Westport, CT: Greenwood Press, 1996).

MULTICULTURAL EDUCATION, sometimes referred to as *multiethnic education, anti-racist education*, or *multiracial education*, has been used by countries all over the world in referring to educational efforts that have attempted to inculcate more positive values about human pluralism and improve the learning potential for all students. Throughout the literature, four basic premises regarding multicultural education can be identified: for the mature, sensitive teacher, culture is the unit of analysis; education in a democratic society requires teachers to respect the rights of students to be culturally different; education for cultural pluralism requires the rejection of assimilationist theory as an anecdote to racism; and multicultural education strategies require the maintenance of native languages and cultures.

Moreover, five dimensions of multicultural education can be identified: content integration requires teachers to use examples from a variety of microcultures in illustrating basic educational concepts; the knowledge construction process refers to the analysis of the manner in which biases and frames of reference within a discipline influences how its basic concepts and generalizations are constituted; an equity emphasis will help facilitate the academic achievement of students from a variety of socioeconomic backgrounds through the use of teaching styles, which are effective for learners with varying cultural characteristics; racism reduction deals with the racial attitudes students bring to the schoolroom and the various teaching strategies and multicultural understandings, which can be instrumental in developing higher levels of tolerance; and empowering school and social structures, which are designed to help students and teachers cross racial and ethnic boundaries, will help students function more effectively as a total school population.

References: James A. Banks, *Multicultural Education: Theory and Practice*, 6th ed. (Boston: Allyn and Bacon, 1997); Bruce M. Mitchell, et al., *The Dynamic Classroom*, 5th ed. (Dubuque, IA: Kendall/Hunt, 1995).

N

NATION OF ISLAM, founded by Wallace D. Fard in 1930, is based on Islamic religious doctrines but is influenced by African and African-American traditions, as well. The Nation of Islam taught its followers to take pride in their African roots rather than attempting to hide from them. After Fard disappeared in 1933, one of his assistants, Elijah (Poole) Muhammad, assumed the leadership of the organization. At that time, the Nation of Islam commenced to declare the racial superiority of persons with African blood. Muhammad also claimed that Fard was Allah.

Muhammad's ideology was prominent until his death in 1975. His son, Wallace D. Muhammad, became the head of the Nation of Islam. After three years of an ill-fated attempt to move the organization into an orthodox Islamic group, the leadership shifted into the hands of Louis Abdul Farrakhan, who sought to move the Nation of Islam back to the philosophical traditions of Elijah Muhammad.

Much of the Nation of Islam's growth occurred because of the evangelistic efforts of Malcom X (born Malcolm Little) who advocated African-American separatism. He interpreted the original Islamic theology as a theology that advocated Black supremacy. Presently, under Louis Farrakhan's leadership, the Nation of Islam has argued for a more cohesive African-American community through the development of social action programs, such as child-care centers, drug clinics, and protective services.

References: Joseph D. Eure and M. Jerome (Eds.), *Back Where We Belong: Selected Speeches by Minister Louis Farrakhan* (New York: International Press, 1990); C. Eric Lincoln, *The Black Muslims in America* (New York: Eerdmans, 1994); C. E. Marsh, *From Black Muslims to Muslims: The Resurrection, Transformation, and Change of the Lost-Found Nation of Islam in America, 1930–1995* (New York: Scarecrow Press, 1996).

NATION WITHIN A NATION is a phrase that some writers have used to define the reservation system in the United States. As the phrase implies, a "nation within a nation" is a political settlement for Native American people. The nation within a nation, or "reservation," is governed by laws that are not always the same pieces of legislation governing the nation's cities, counties, states, and federal government.

The reservation movement in the United States began in earnest during the presidency of Ulysses S. Grant at the end of the Civil War. Massive encroachments on Native American territories led to the establishment of reservations for Native American tribes. These new nations within a nation were affected by such pieces of legislation as the Indian Appropriation Act of 1871, the General Allotment Act of 1887, and the American Indian Religious Freedom Act of 1978. In addition, treaties have affected reservation policies, although many treaties between the U.S. government and Native American tribes have been broken.

In 1975, the U.S. Congress passed the Indian Self-Determination and Education Assistance Act, which gave the tribes more local control. While some of these measures are similar to pieces of legislation affecting non-Indians, there were many Congressional Acts affecting Native Americans only. Other Congressional Acts have provided special educational funds for Native American children.

The largest "Nations Within a Nation" are the Navaho Reservation (143,405), Pine Ridge (11,182), and Fort Apache (9,825).

References: William Brandon, *The Indian in American Culture* (New York: Harper and Row, 1974); Wilcomb E. Washburn (Ed.), "History of Indian–White Relations," Vol. 4 in *Handbook of North American Indians* (Washington, DC: Smithsonian Institution Press, 1988).

NATIONAL ASSOCIATION FOR THE ADVANCEMENT OF COLORED PEOPLE (NAACP), originally an organization for combating the growing violence against African Americans, was first established in 1909 by W.E.B. Du Bois and a group of African Americans and European Americans. The group is an outgrowth of the Niagara Movement, founded by Du Bois in 1905. Du Bois finally resigned from the NAACP in 1934 over a dispute involving policies that he thought did not represent the best interests of the great majority of African Americans.

While the organization is well known and has been quite influential throughout its history, it is perhaps best known for its aggressive involvement in the fight to end school segregation. The organization assumed an active role in the *Brown v. Board of Education* Supreme Court Decision of 1954, overturning the *Plessy v. Ferguson* decision of 1896. Thurgood Marshall, a young NAACP attorney, argued on behalf of the plaintiff, Brown.

Throughout its history, the NAACP has sponsored a legal defense fund. These monies have been used to provide legal services for African-American clients whose civil rights have been violated. In its battles to end school segregation, the NAACP also took an active role in arguing for the termination of racial segregation in the armed forces. The U.S. military was finally desegregated during the administration of President Harry Truman.

Reference: Sharon Harley, *The Timetables of American History* (New York: Simon and Schuster, 1995).

NATIONAL FARM WORKERS OF AMERICA (NFWA), an organization that represented Latino agricultural workers, was started through the efforts of Cesar Chavez. Initially, the NFWA was created in the southern portion of the Sacramento Valley, the first union of its type to represent farm workers, most of whom are Latinos. Chavez tried to use the non-violent tactics of Martin Luther King and Ghandi in his initial attempts to organize grape pickers in 1962.

In 1966, the NFWA merged with the Filipino-dominated United Farm Workers Organizing Committee (UFWOC) after both unions had been on strike against California grape growers since 1965. After the merger, the newly constituted UFWOC won an agreement with California's wine grape growers, becoming the bargaining agent for the grape pickers. However, the table-grape growers refused to enter into a similar agreement, and the UFWOC initiated a boycott until 1970, when many table-grape growers entered into an agreement with the UFWOC.

During the 1970s, the UFWOC, which became the United Farm Workers of America (UFW) in 1973, turned its efforts to working conditions for farm workers. In 1975, about 3,000 marchers walked from Union Square in San Francisco to Modesto to call attention to the problems of California farm workers. By this time, California had a governor (Jerry Brown) who was much more sympathetic to their cause than Ronald Reagan, the previous governor of the state.

During the 1990s, the UFW fell on hard times when only about 100 contracts were negotiated. Also, the practice of agricultural interests, using undocumented workers, built up labor surpluses, making it more difficult for the UFW to organize laborers. As Cesar Chavez was forced to battle health problems, some of the leadership tactics of the UFW were called into question. Chavez died in 1993.

References: Lewis H. Gann, *The Hispanics in the United States: A History* (Boulder, CO: Westview Press, 1986); Jacques E. Levy, *Cesar Chavez: Autobiography of La Causa* (New York: Norton, 1975); Himilce Novas, *Everything You Wanted to Know About Latino History* (New York: Penguin Books, 1994); F. Arturo Rosales, *Chicanos: The History of the Mexican-American Civil Rights Movement* (Houston: Arte Publico Press, 1996).

NATIONAL ORGANIZATION OF WOMEN (NOW), one of the largest national groups dedicated to achieving full equality between women and men, was created in 1966 during the American Civil Rights Movement. One of its strongest and most controversial platforms has been the pro-choice stance on abortion. Also, NOW has fought for legislation leading to an Equal Rights Amendment that would require men and women be treated equally by law. The organization's first attempt narrowly failed because fewer than the necessary 38 states approved it by the 1982 deadline. Since that time, this constitutional amendment has been re-introduced into Congress several times without success.

Resistance to NOW's attempts to acquire equal rights for women has come from the Christian right, anti-choice abortion advocates, and the conservative wing of the Republican Party. These two groups have disagreed with NOW's stand on abortion rights and the organization's attempts to liberalize the roles of women in society.

When teachers attempt to incorporate America's sociopolitical issues into legitimate studies of multicultural education, they need to address the equal rights concerns addressed by NOW as they help students to understand the complex multicultural social problems relating to constitutional guarantees for women as citizens of the United States.

References: Rene Denfeld, *The New Victorians: A Young Woman's Challenge to the Old Feminist Order* (New York: Warner, 1995); Susan Faludi, *Backlash: The Undeclared War Against American Women* (New York: Crown, 1991); Sherrye Henry, *Why American Women Resist Equality* (New York: Macmillan, 1994); Jane J. Mansbridge, *Why We Lost the ERA* (Chicago: University of Chicago Press, 1986); Sidney Verba and Gary R. Orren, *Equality in America: A View from the Top* (Cambridge, MA: Harvard University Press, 1985).

NATIVE AMERICANS, a term referring to the original residents of the United States of America, includes all of the aboriginal tribes and bands that constitute the present boundaries of the country. Also, the word is sometimes used to refer to the aboriginal groups in the entire continent of North America. For many people, it is preferable to the term *Indian* originally used to characterize indigenous North American groups because of the Columbus expeditions to the Far East. Many social scientists have rejected the term, declaring it to be inaccurate, since the expeditions of Columbus failed to reach India. Believing that he had sailed to the East Indies in Asia, Columbus referred to the Arawakan-speaking people as *los indios*, or *the Indians*.

Some "Native Americans" reject the term because it fails to depict the linguistic and cultural uniqueness of individual tribes and bands that populated the United States and other portions of the North American continent long before the arrival of the Europeans. The Navajos in the Southwest and the Penoboscots in the Northeast are Native Americans, but both groups have distinct cultural/sociopolitical characteristics.

When teachers weave Native American topics into their curricula, it is necessary to convince the students that there were legitimate groups of people on the continent and within this country prior to the arrival of the Europeans.

References: Alvin M. Josephy, Jr., *Five Hundred Nations* (New York: Alfred A. Knopf, 1994); Joan Thrower Timm, *Four Perspectives in Multicultural Education* (Belmont, CA: Wadsworth, 1996); Jack Weatherford, *Native Roots: How the Indians Enriched America* (New York: Crown, 1991).

NATIVISM, a term relating to an extreme form of ethnocentrism and nationalism, has been used in the multicultural education lexicon by sociologists who attempted to describe the attempts of European Americans to prevent other immigrants from settling in the country. Some of the earlier nativistic attitudes were exhibited against German Americans in Pennsylvania in 1927. The Alien and Sedition Acts, passed by Congress, were intended to denigrate a strong base of the Republican Party's immigrant support.

Other nativistic actions included the 1924 Johnson–Reed Act, the Know Nothing Movement, the Chinese Exclusion Acts, and the Johnson Act of 1921, which established a quota system governing immigrations to the country. A literacy bill, which overcame the veto of President Woodrow Wilson, required that adult immigrants must be able to demonstrate reading competency before being allowed to enter the United States.

Teachers can create lessons examining the reasons why some Americans have sought to prevent the immigration of people from different parts of the country. Some of the reasons for nativism have been based on political considerations, while other reasons have pertained to economic factors. However, some of the nativism exhibited by Americans have been based on racism.

References: James A. Banks, *Teaching Strategies for Ethnic Studies*, 6th ed. (Boston: Allyn and Bacon, 1997); Joan Thrower Timm, *Four Perspectives in Multicultural Education* (Belmont, CA: Wadsworth, 1996).

NATURALIZATION ACT OF 1790, a racist act restricting the naturalization of persons of color, reserved citizenship for ''Whites only.'' This piece of legislation affirmed the young nation's commitment to restricting citizenship to ''useful men'' from Europe. Only those considered to be the ''worthy part of mankind'' would be able to acquire citizenship in the United States.

The federal government would screen out ''vagrants, paupers, and bad men.'' Applicants for citizenship were forced to reside in the United States for two years, and they were required to be Caucasians. Excluded from citizenship were Native Americans and persons of color. This piece of legislation was not overturned until the McCarran-Walter Act of 1952.

References: Leonard Dinnerstein, et al., *Natives and Strangers* (New York: Oxford University Press, 1990); Ronald Takaki, *A Different Mirror: A History of Multicultural America* (Boston: Little, Brown, 1993).

NAVA, JULIAN (1927–), a Harvard-educated professor of history, became the first Latino to become elected to the board of trustees in the Los Angeles Unified School District. His 1967 victory occurred at a time in history when Mexican-American groups in East Los Angeles were making demands for major changes in the city's school system. Among the demands given the board of the Los Angeles Unified School District were the requests for bilingual/bicultural education in the schools and the hiring of more Latino teachers.

The Educational Issues Coordinating Council (EICC) felt that the school board was acting too slowly on the demands, and students walked out of several East Los Angeles high schools with large percentages of Latino students. Nava's presence on the school board was invaluable, since most members had little understanding of the East Los Angles Latino/Chicano culture. His calm manner and excellent educational background was impressive to the other trustees. However, because of his position, he was viewed by some Mexican Americans as having "sold out" to the establishment.

Reference: F. Arturo Rosales, *Chicano: The History of the Mexican-American Civil Rights Movement* (Houston: Arte Publico Press, 1996).

NAVAJO TRIBE, located in the southwestern United States, is the second largest Native American tribe in the United States. Located in northeastern Arizona, the Navajos are part of the Athapaskan language group, the largest of several Navajo subgroups. The Navajo tribe has a population of 219,198 persons according to the 1990 census. This large hunting and gathering group is thought to have moved south from Alaska and northwestern Canada. Why they decided to move to the American Southwest is still a topic of discussion among Native American scholars.

Anthropologists believe that the Navajos were impressed by the Pueblo culture and felt somewhat intimidated by their cultural traditions that were perceived to be more advanced than their own. Their initial agricultural efforts were apparently motivated by the Pueblos. After the United States took possession of the Mexican territories in 1846, as a result of the Treaty of Guadalupe Hidalgo, General S. W. Kearney vowed to stop all of the raids by Native Americans. A treaty was signed by thirteen Navajo leaders. Believing that these "leaders" could speak for the entire Navajo nation, the U.S. authorities believed that the Navajos were not to be trusted, since the treaties were broken by some individual members and bands.

During the outbreak of the Civil War in the United States, the Navajos, along with the Apaches and other Native American groups, increased their raids on encroaching settlers. Kit Carson was dispatched to Navajo country and ordered the Navajos to surrender at Fort Defiance. Carson won his point by destroying the crops and livestock of the Navajos. Finally, in 1868, the Navajos were allowed to return to their homeland, a 3.5 million acre reservation within their original territory. This was accomplished through a treaty with the U.S. government.

During World War II, Navajos were active participants in the war against Germany and Japan. The Navajo code talkers created a code that was used effectively by the U.S. military. The code was never broken by the enemy. The war had the effect of exposing thousands of young Navajo men to the world outside the Reservation. The military actions also helped convince the Navajos that education and the development of economic enterprises were necessary for the tribe's survival.

The Navajo tribe has become well known for its excellence in pottery making and weaving. Recently, Navajo artists, such as Atsidi Sani, have become well known for their expertise in crafting silver jewelry and working with iron, copper, and brass. Also, their excellent work with silver has become an important trademark of the Navajo culture.

Teachers need to utilize the accomplishments of the Navajo people to help young students understand the valuable artistic contributions of this Native American microculture.

References: Clyde Kluckhohn and Dorothea Leighton, *The Navajo* (Cambridge, MA: Harvard University Press, 1974); Robert S. McPherson, *The Northern Navajo Frontier, 1860–1900: Expansion Through Adversity* (Albuquerque: University of New Mexico Press, 1988); Ruth M. Underhill, *The Navajos* (Norman: University of Oklahoma Press, 1967).

NEGRO, an anthropological term used to describe the ''Black'' race, was used by both European-American and African-American writers until the American Civil Rights Movement. Developed by anthropologists, the term ''Negro'' was one of Ashley Montagu's racial descriptions for categorizing human groups according to their physical characteristics.

Negros were described as persons with ebony-colored skin, black, curly hair, and fuller lips than those of Caucasians and Mongoloids (an anthropological term for Asian groups). The term was considered to be proper until the American Civil Rights Movement. Other synonyms for the term were ''colored'' and ''Negra,'' which were used primarily in the southern states. The term ''nigger'' was considered to be extremely detrimental and inflammatory. ''Negra'' was used mostly in the south and was usually considered to be a semi-polite word for ''nigger.''

However, during the American Civil Rights Movement, the term ''Negro'' was viewed as a condescending word used by European Americans. Some civil rights activists condemned the term, since it was originally crafted by European-American anthropologists and social scientists. At this time, the term ''Black'' became the word of choice among social science scholars. Later, the term of choice became ''African American'' as scholars attempted to refer to microcultures according to their original area of residence.

Educators need to research the terms of choice among people to determine the accepted terms and phrases among the microcultural groups with whom they will be coming into contact in the schoolroom. Innocent misuse of terms can have a detrimental effect on the levels of rapport necessary for optimum interaction between teachers and students.

References: Sharon Harley, *The Timetables of African-American History* (New York: Simon and Schuster, 1995); Donna M. Gollnick and Philip C. Chinn, *Multicultural Education in a Pluralistic Society* (Columbus, OH: Merrill, 1990); Ashley Montagu, *Statement on Race: An Annotated Elaboration and Exposition of the Four Statements on Race Issues by the United Nations Educational, Scientific, and Cultural Organization* (New York: Oxford University Press, 1972).

NEO-NAZIS, a term referring to any organization adapting the racist policies of Adolph Hitler's Nazi Party in Germany, relates to the activities of certain extremist groups in the United States and Europe. Neo-Nazis subscribe to concepts of white separatism and the inferiority of any persons with African blood. They also have been vocal in their chastisement of Jews.

Neo-Nazis strongly subscribe to notions of white supremacy and are closely allied to the Ku Klux Klan in philosophy. Their sponsorship of young ''skinhead'' organizations has resulted in numerous acts of violence. Believing in becoming heavily armed, many neo-Nazi groups have resorted to crime in the acquisition of both legal and illegal firearms.

Teachers need to help students understand how and why persons acquire such attitudes and the inherent problems in becoming allied with organizations that practice hatred and acts of violence against other human beings and the nation in general.

NEWTON, HUEY (1942–1989), was a cofounder of the Black Panther Party in the United States. Initiated in Oakland, California, with Bobby Seale, the organization sought to promote the civil rights of African Americans. Also, the Black Panther Party organized a number of community programs that were structured to provide free breakfasts for school children, along with free medical services, free clothing, and free legal advice. The Black Panther Party became known as a revolutionary organization that championed the rights of African Americans.

Newton eventually was arrested and convicted of manslaughter in the state of California. However, he was released after the courts discovered that there were a number of procedural errors in his trial. Newton died in 1989.

References: Sharon Harley, *The Timetables of African-American History* (New York: Simon and Schuster, 1995); Edward M. Keating, *Free Huey: The True Story of the Trial of Huey P. Newton for Murder* (New York: Ramparts Press, 1971).

NIAGARA MOVEMENT, the first national organization for promoting the civil rights of African Americans, was started in 1905 by W. E. B. Du Bois and a group of Black intellectuals as a result of their organizational efforts in Fort Erie, Canada. The group sought to acquire black freedom and growth through aggressive action. One year after its creation, about 100 men marched from Harper's Ferry, West Virginia, to the site of John Brown's raid. John Hope, the first African-American president of Morehouse College, became the only college president to become a member of the Niagara Movement. Du Bois served as the Niagara Movement's general secretary until 1909, when he helped create the National Association for the Advancement of Colored People (NAACP).

While the Niagara Movement was initiated long before the beginning of the American Civil Rights Movement, it is important for students to understand the motivation for the formation of groups that sought to secure civil rights for persons of color before it was popular to do so. Some African Americans, including Booker T. Washington, opposed the creation of programs appearing to be at all militant.

References: John Hope Franklin, *From Slavery to Freedom: A History of Negro-Americans* (New York: Vintage, 1980); Sharon Harley, *The Timetables of African-American History* (New York: Simon and Schuster, 1995).

NKRUMAH, KWAME (1909–   ), born in the village of Nkroful in the southwest portion of the Gold Coast, went to Lincoln University in Pennsylvania. Among his classmates were Thurgood Marshall and Langston Hughes. While at Lincoln University, he also taught and developed his revolutionary ideas that he brought back to Ghana. He became Ghana's first leader in 1957, when the nation received its independence from the British.

Among his objectives was the promotion of pan-Africanism. Consequently, he became instrumental in helping other African countries acquire their independence. In addition, he was instrumental in helping to form a pan-African union. However, the first few years of Ghanaian independence were turbulent, and after economic problems plagued the new nation, Nkrumah was overthrown by Ghanaian army officers. Throughout the country's recent history, Nkrumah has been viewed quite favorably, since he was the first national leader after independence.

Reference: Kwame Nkrumah, *Ghana: The Autobiography of Kwame Nkrumah* (New York: Thomas Nelson, 1957).

NON-VERBAL COMMUNICATION, a multicultural concept pertaining to communication patterns between human groups, is a critical segment of the teacher's education to help instructors become successful with all students. It has been viewed as a significant portion of a child's ethnicity and refers to ethnic characteristics that are formed during the child's developmental years through interactions with family, friends, neighbors, and others.

Five characteristics of ethnicity have been identified for helping teaches focus on potential communication problems among pluralistic classrooms. Understanding these communication differences can be equally important for teachers and students. Moreover, it is incumbent on teachers to convey the message that differing communication characteristics are neither good nor bad. Rather, they are merely the physical and psychological patterns of communication possessed by human beings.

These five ethnic communication aspects include: verbal communication related to sound, pitch, rhythm, tempo; non-verbal communication based on body language, distance, or eye contact; orientation modes related to body position, time modes and attention modes; social value patterns; and intellectual modes that affect learning styles. For teachers to interact effectively with students from a variety of ethnic and racial backgrounds, it is necessary for them to understand the similarities and differences in communication styles among the students with whom they work.

References: James A. Banks, *Multiethnic Education: Theory and Practice*, 3rd ed. (Boston: Allyn and Bacon, 1994); Christine I. Bennett, *Comprehensive Multicultural Education: Theory and Practice*, 3d ed. (Boston: Allyn and Bacon, 1995); Wilma S. Longstreet, *Aspects of Ethnicity: Understanding Differences in Pluralistic Classrooms* (New York: Teachers College Press, 1978).

NON-VIOLENT PROTEST, a term that came into prominent use during the American Civil Rights Movement, refers to the use of different protest strategies, which do not result in violent confrontations among groups. The principle is based on the philosophy of Mahatma Gandhi, who used such strategies when India was attempting to achieve its independence from England.

American civil rights leaders, such as Martin Luther King, Jr. and Cesar Chavez, adapted Gandhi's belief that the most effective change occurs when protest movements do not capitalize on the use of violence. Chavez advocated the use of boycotts, marches, and picketing as a means of creating change and acquiring equal employment opportunities and livable wages for Latino agricultural workers throughout America.

King also made effective use of non-violent protest strategies through the organization of sit-ins, strikes, marches and the like. Both men were strongly influenced by Gandhi and sometimes were severely criticized by members of their own party. Their critics believed that the non-violent protest philosophy was slow and cumbersome and did not attract adequate attention to their causes. Many of the critics felt that since life was so short, it was foolhardy to spend too much time in forcing the establishment to meet their demands.

Classroom teachers, who are discussing the American Civil Rights Movement, need to address the causes and consequences of the various protest actions used by different microcultures during that period of time. It is important for students to understand the desperate situations that motivated Americans to participate in such actions to achieve equality.

References: James H. Cone, *Martin & Malcolm & America: A Dream or a Nightmare* (Maryknoll, NY: Orbis, 1991); L. H. Gann and Peter Duignan, *The Hispanics in the United States: A History* (Boulder, CO: Westview Press, 1986); Earl Shorris, *Latinos: A Biography of the People* (New York: W. W. Norton, 1992); Ira G. Zepp, Jr., *The Social Vision of Martin Luther King Jr.* (New York: Carlson, 1989).

O

O'CONNOR, SANDRA DAY (1930–), the first woman to become a U.S. Supreme Court Justice, was appointed during the Reagan Administration in 1981. Prior to her confirmation, she was an Arizona Court of Appeals judge. She became a Supreme Court Justice because of the retirement of Justice Potter Stewart, who was appointed by President Dwight Eisenhower 23 years prior to his retirement.

O'Connor was considered to be a moderate Republican, and the Reagan appointment upset members of the Religious Right Movement, particularly Jerry Falwell, who was head of the Fundamentalist-Christian Moral Majority. Antichoice groups also criticized her for several pro-choice abortion votes. However, she received strong support from women's rights groups; Senators Udall and Kennedy were strongly supportive of O'Connor's nomination, as was Republican Senator Barry Goldwater from Arizona.

Given an unqualified endorsement by the American Bar Association Committee on Federal Judiciary, the ABA expressed concern over O'Connor's limited time as a judge and practicing attorney. Professor G. Edward White of the University of Virginia Law School opined that if she had been a male, she would likely not have received the nomination to the Bench. However, the U.S. Senate affirmed her by a vote of 99–0.

O'Connor graduated from high school at the age of sixteen, enrolled at Stanford University, and completed her law degree and her undergraduate degree in just five years. Unable to find a law firm that would hire her because of her gender, she became a deputy county attorney in San Mateo, California. After marrying John O'Connor, she spent three years in Frankfort, Germany and then returned to the United States where she became an assistant attorney general in Arizona.

For classroom teachers, O'Connor's story can be used to illustrate the gender inequities which have been addressed through affirmative action programs in the public and private sectors. The fact that it took more than 200 years to seat a woman on the U.S. Supreme Court can be used to illustrate the glaring gender inequities which have become quite controversial political issues. Multicultural, educational programs can help students analyze such situations as they attempt to make rational decisions about other similar inequities.

References: Henry J. Abraham, *Justices and Presidents, A Political History of Appointments to the Supreme Court* (New York: Oxford University Press, 1992); R. H. Lorraine Dusky, *Still Unequal* (New York: Crown, 1996); *Time* Magazine, ''Justice—At Last,'' July 20, 1981.

OFFICE OF CIVIL RIGHTS, consisting of several federal government divisions responsible for enforcing the various civil rights laws enacted by the U.S. Congress, is the formal term that relates to the collective federal efforts to monitor such activities. The Office of Civil Rights includes: the Office of Civil Rights in the Department of Health and Human Services; the Department of Justice's Civil Rights Division; the Equal Opportunity Office in the Department of Housing and Urban Development (HUD); and several others. In addition, the Office of Civil Rights in the Office of Education is responsible for enforcing any actions pertaining to discrimination because of race, religion, gender, or national origin. Several other federal offices of civil rights exist.

In addition to the federal Office of Civil Rights, similar departments exist throughout the 50 states and even at the local level. They, too, are responsible for enforcing local and state civil rights efforts. These relate to such issues as racial harassment, equal employment opportunities, fair housing guarantees, and any other actions that pertain to the maintenance of the civil rights of all Americans.

For teachers, understanding the role of the Office of Civil Rights is a basic necessity in order for students to acquire an understanding of the manner in which the local, state, and federal governments enforce the nation's civil rights laws. Since these laws are based on constitutional guarantees of equality, teachers can examine Supreme Court decisions and other pieces of legislation that relate to civil rights issues. For social science classes, the political issues surrounding the passage of the 1964 legislation could be used as a starting point. Backed wholeheartedly by President Lyndon Johnson, the legislation passed after vigorous partisan wrangling. Students should enjoy the wrestling match between South Carolina Senator Strom Thurmond and Texan Ralph Yarborough.

References: Joan M. Burke, *Civil Rights* (New York: Bowker, 1974); Bernard Schwark (Ed.), *Civil Rights* (New York: Chelsea House, 1980); Robert Weisbrot, *Freedom Bound: A History of America's Civil Rights Movement* (New York: W. W. Norton, 1990).

OFFICE OF ECONOMIC OPPORTUNITY (OEO), established as a result of the passage of the Economic Opportunity Act during the Johnson administration, was given the responsibility of monitoring federal programs designed to meet the needs of low income clients. Some of the OEO programs include Head Start, VISTA, Job Corps and Community Action Programs (CAPS). All of the OEO programs were part of the Johnson Administration War on Poverty.

While such programs as Head Start were highly successful, all of them were somewhat controversial, and the results were mixed. In general, the philosophy of the OEO programs was sound. Having low-income clients take the major responsibility for their own improvement is a noble goal. Unfortunately, sometimes low-income persons in a position of leadership had a difficult time creating viable programs because of their own lack of experience.

However, many programs were successful, and the philosophy of having low-income clients take responsibility for their own destiny is laudable. The VISTA program was unique in that it utilized volunteers in social service agencies to provide services to poverty clients. One segment of the VISTA program was the University Year for Action (UYA) that recruited college students who were interested in working at social service agencies, which met the needs of poverty clients in the community. Students served as volunteers who also took experiential-learning courses to help them make normal progress toward their college degrees. The Office of Economic Opportunity was dismantled by President Richard Nixon.

Teaching about the American culture of poverty is a crucial part of the total multicultural education commitment. It is necessary to aid students in analyzing the socioeconomic structure of American society to comprehend the cultures of poverty and help students who bring such backgrounds to the schoolroom. Teachers also need to examine the morality of sociopolitical decisions that have increased the gap between the "haves" and "have-nots" in the United States. *See also* UNITED STATES DEPARTMENT OF EDUCATION.

References: Doris Kearns, *Lyndon Johnson and the American Dream* (New York: Harper and Row, 1976); Sar A. Levitan, *The Great Society's Poor Law: A New Approach to Poverty* (Baltimore: Johns Hopkins University Press, 1969); Office of Economic Opportunity, Memorandum from the Director, *Involvement of the Poor in All OEO Programs*, September 9, 1966; Robert Weisbrot, *Freedom Bound: A History of America's Civil Rights Movement* (New York: W. W. Norton, 1990).

OFFICE OF EDUCATION (UNITED STATES DEPARTMENT OF EDUCATION), now a United States Cabinet position, is a federal organization that oversees the educational efforts within the 50 states. In the United States, education is a federal interest, a state responsibility, and a local function. Unlike most other countries throughout the world, the federal government takes no active role in ordering a national curriculum, uniform certification requirements for teachers, and the like.

The Office of Education does take an active role in enforcing federal actions affecting education. One example is the Elementary and Secondary Education Act of 1965, which established a number of title programs for the nation's schools. The role of the Office of Education is to monitor such programs and ensure that the guidelines and fiscal-management responsibilities are being met.

The Office of Education was established during the Carter administration, functioning for the first time in May 1980. Following the election of Ronald Reagan, Terrell H. Bell was appointed as the second Secretary of Education. However, Reagan did not believe that the Health, Education, and Welfare Department should be changed to Health and Welfare with a separate cabinet position for education. Nonetheless, Bell became convinced that it was a wise move to create the separate cabinet position, and the Office of Education has survived the attempts of Republican politicians to abolish it.

In addition to the enforcement of federally funded programs, the Office of Education is in charge of the Office of Educational Research and Improvement (OERI). While the Office of Education has no authority over the 50 state departments of education, it has served as an advisory body and provides research services as well as support and supervision of federal programs. Moreover, it has the responsibility for civil rights efforts, the National Institute of Education, the National Center for Education Statistics, and the Fund for the Improvement of Post-Secondary Education.

References: ''Secretary Hufstedler Sets Goals for New Department,'' *American Education*, November 1979; Skee Smith, ''The U.S. Department of Education,'' *American Education*, (November 1979); ''Why a Cabinet Post for Education?'' *NEA Reporter* (May/June 1979).

OFFICE OF MINORITY BUSINESS ENTERPRISE (OMBE), established by executive orders issued by Richard Nixon in 1969 and 1970, was housed in the Small Business Administration (SBA), created during the Nixon administration. Fortunately for this program, it had strong support in the United States Congress. However, the program was heavily criticized by European-American businessmen who argued that small minority businesses enjoyed an unfair advantage over them. Moreover, they argued that many of the businesses had only token black representation.

As a result of the criticisms, the OMBE was abolished in 1977 and replaced by the Minority Business Development Administration (MBDA). Participants were provided with technical assistance and management services. A law passed in 1980 required the Small Business Administration to create a program for terminating successful minority business enterprises from special assistance. However, Congress refused to allow the Reagan administration to ''graduate'' large numbers of minority enterprises.

Reference: Gerald David Jaynes and Robin M. Williams, Jr. (Eds.), *A Common Destiny: Blacks and American Society* (Washington, DC: National Academy Press, 1989).

OKLAHOMA CITY BOMBING, occurring at the Alfred P. Murrah Federal Building on April 19, 1995, was orchestrated by Timothy McVeigh, an angry, antigovernment individual, allegedly in retaliation against federal agency involvement in the Branch Davidian compound fire in Waco, Texas, two years earlier. McVeigh's activities resulted in the deaths of 168 persons and injuries to more than 500 others. Many of the victims were small children. These casualties made the event the worst act of domestic terrorism in American history.

McVeigh, a bronze star recipient during the "Desert Storm" military operation, rented a Ryder truck and constructed a bomb out of racing fuel and fertilizer. McVeigh was arrested 90 minutes after the blast. His alleged accomplice, Terry Nichols, was also arrested in connection with his possible involvement in the episode. Government prosecutors contended that McVeigh became livid with rage against the U.S. government's involvement in the Waco incident, as well as its activities at Ruby Ridge, Idaho, during the F.B.I. engagement with a white separatist, Randy Weaver.

During the trial, prosecutors argued that McVeigh was highly influenced by the *Turner Diaries*, an antiSemitic, racist writing that has become a bible for many antigovernment terrorist groups in the United States. These antigovernment hatreds seem to be reaching an all-time high with the advent of numerous paramilitary and militia groups located in all 50 states.

References: Peter Annin, "After a Brisk Trial in the Case of the Deadliest Act of Terrorism in U.S. History, the Oklahoma City Bombing Goes to the Jury," *Newsweek*, June 9, 1997; Anthony Lewis, "Abroad at Home," *New York Times*, September 6, 1996; Karen Matthews, "The Terrorist Next Door," *New York Times*, June 1, 1997.

OLD BOY NETWORK, a term first used during the American Civil Rights Movement, refers to the situation where European Americans have enjoyed an enormous advantage in many areas of employment and appointments to prestigious positions. Consequently, males of color in the United States have been under-represented in many educational programs and occupational areas. As the phrase implies, it suggests that instead of interviewing candidates for employment and appointments on an equal footing, European-American males have received employment, placement in university programs, and the like, simply because of their race or ethnicity.

To counteract these advantages, a number of Affirmative Action programs have been put into place to ensure that persons other than European-American males had an equal chance at employment, securing admission to college and university programs, and the like. However, due to Republican-sponsored legislation during 1997, many Affirmative Action programs were terminated.

It is an important term in the multicultural, educational lexicon, since it pertains to issues of equality in American society. Studies of constitutional guarantees in regard to equal rights are of particular concern to the multicultural, educational curriculum.

Reference: Bruce M. Mitchell, et al., *The Dynamic Classroom*, 5th ed. (Dubuque, IA: Kendall/Hunt, 1995).

OLIVER, JOE (KING) (1885–1938), a New Orleans cornet player during the early development of American jazz, was one of the key figures in the formative years of this American art form. Born in 1885, Oliver started his professional career in 1910 as a member of the Eagle Brass Band in New Orleans. He received $1.25 a night for his efforts. The next year he replaced the legendary Freddie Keppard at Pete Lala's Cafe in New Orleans, where he played with clarinetist Sidney Bechet. By 1916 he led a band at Pete Lala's after playing with legendary trombonist Kid Ory and clarinetist Johnny Dodds.

It was in Storyville, New Orleans, where Oliver earned his nickname (King). He felt slighted when two fellow musicians (Freddie Keppard and Manuel Perez) were being praised. As a result, he played so brilliantly that people came out from the surrounding establishments to hear him, and from that day forward he became known as "King" Oliver.

Oliver had a profound effect on Louis Armstrong, who looked upon him as a father figure. After Oliver moved to Chicago, he wrote for Louis Armstrong to come and play second cornet in the Creole Jazz Band, a premier musical group in the evolution of American jazz. The two-cornet breaks by Oliver and Armstrong became some of the most important developments in jazz history. However, Oliver's musical career declined, and he quit music altogether. He was a custodian when he died in 1938.

Oliver's contributions to American jazz are important for multicultural educators, since teachers can explore the socioeconomic issues that affected the development of American jazz. The fact that jazz declined in 1929 was due to the great American Economic Depression, which put many musicians out of work. Many of these jazz musicians were low-income African Americans. Economic problems, coupled with the racist attitudes of European Americans, made times particularly hard for Black musicians who found it difficult to locate other types of employment.

Reference: Al Rose, *Storyville, New Orleans* (Tuscaloosa: University of Alabama Press, 1974).

OPEN-HOUSING LAW, enacted in 1968, was a measure designed to assist persons of color in the acquisition of decent housing. For years, African Americans and other persons of color had been denied the opportunity to acquire adequate housing, often due to "redlining," which referred to the practice of realtors drawing red lines on real estate maps around the portions of the community in which houses could be sold to African Americans and other minorities. If persons who were not European Americans (particularly African Americans) wished to purchase a home, they were steered to the "redlined" segment of a community. Homes in the redlined areas were usually of inferior quality.

To counteract this practice, persons of color often resorted to a practice called "blockbusting." This meant that people of color would pool their resources and make it possible for prospective buyers to purchase a home at an inflated price. European-American homeowners would often panic and put their homes up for sale, many times at a lesser price than the market value. This would make it possible for other home buyers to take advantage of the falling rates, and all of the participants would benefit because of the decreased rates.

The Open-Housing Law was initiated by liberal Democrats in January 1968. President Johnson signed the Open-Housing Bill that prevented racial discrimination in approximately 80 percent of the rentals negotiated and in new house purchases. However, many of the bill's stipulations were far weaker than many people realized.

Reference: Robert Weisbrot, *Freedom Bound: A History of America's Civil Rights Movement* (New York: Norton, 1990).

OPERATION BREADBASKET was a civil rights era program designed to provide food and jobs for poor African Americans. It was one of several interrelated programs directed by the Reverend Jesse Jackson. At its inception, Jackson was a 25-year-old aide to Dr. Martin Luther King. He used a number of churches to negotiate with European-American firms and conduct selective buying campaigns. Among a number of economic issues addressed by Operation Breadbasket was the attempt to encourage European-American owned firms to employ more African Americans.

The program was sponsored by the Southern Christian Leadership Conference. Later, it became known as Operation PUSH (People United to Save Humanity), an organization devoted to economic improvement for African Americans. PUSH then became PUSH-Excel, which was devoted to the improvement of education for African-American people.

Operation PUSH provided important information for parents and educators through the organization's identification of the harmful influences that affected children so negatively in America's poverty enclaves. Jackson acknowledged that teachers and parents fought hard to provide a healthy environment, but Jackson perceived the necessity for a successful ''love triangle'' consisting of the school, home, and church.

References: Henry Hampton and Steve Fayer, *Voices of Freedom: An Oral History of the American Civil Rights Movement* (New York: Bantam, 1990); Gerald David Jaynes and Robin M. Williams (Eds.), *A Common Destiny: Blacks and American Society* (Washington, DC: National Academy Press, 1989); Daniel U. Levine and Robert J. Havighurst, *Society and Education* (Boston: Allyn and Bacon, 1992); Robert Weisbrot, *Freedom Bound: A History of America's Civil Rights Movement* (New York: W. W. Norton, 1990).

OPERATION HEAD START, one of America's most successful early-childhood programs for low-income children, provides for the developmental needs of children from poverty backgrounds. Beginning during the summer of

1965, the program was crafted as one of President Lyndon Johnson's compensatory programs in his war on poverty. Originally available for children below the poverty line, the program was made available to children above the poverty level, who paid according to their income level for the services.

In addition to providing instruction to improve reading and math-readiness skills, Head Start also serves healthy meals and makes nutritional instruction available to the parents. Medical and dental care are also provided. Families are able to take advantage of social service programs as a result of the family counseling efforts in the various local Head Start programs.

Research on Head Start has proven the program to be quite beneficial. The primary goals of enabling poverty children to improve the necessary readiness skills for successful performance in public schools have been achieved. Head Start was originally established by the Office of Economic Opportunity and makes use of parents who serve as tutors and quasi-teachers. The programs accommodates about 750,000 children each year.

References: Daniel U. Levine and Robert J. Havighurst, *Society and Education* (Boston: Allyn and Bacon, 1992); Sar A. Levitan, *The Great Society's Poor Law: A New Approach to Poverty* (Baltimore: Johns Hopkins University Press, 1969).

OPERATION PUSH. *See* OPERATION BREADBASKET.

ORAL HISTORY, a strategy being used increasingly by teachers interested in multicultural education, is especially helpful in assisting students from poverty backgrounds to acquire more information about their family units. Teachers working with such students have had great success in teaching students how to interview family members to acquire data for constructing family genealogies, which can be useful in helping such students acquire a higher degree of pride in their family ethnicity. Interviews can be conducted with parents, grandparents, aunts, uncles, etc. to create useful genealogies.

While such strategies are valuable for students from low-income backgrounds, they also can be beneficial for students from more affluent families as well. However, children from poverty backgrounds often struggle in school because of poor self-esteem. The use of oral history programs can help to change negative attitudes and to create a higher level of pride in the student's microculture, if that is a problem.

However, the use of oral history has other benefits as well. In the area of language development, the interview can become a meaningful vehicle for motivating the student in the improvement of writing skills. By transcribing the oral statements into written language, students can learn that writing is merely a way of putting people's ideas on paper so that other persons can learn about them. Thus, the use of oral history in the classroom can provide students with insights about the integrity of their own microculture, as well as the microcultural characteristics of students from different economic, racial, and ethnic backgrounds.

In addition to the valuable multicultural lessons that can be taught through the use of oral history, the student can also learn how historians write history and develop an increased level of interest in history themselves.

References: Jane McCracken (Ed.), *Oral History: Basic Techniques* (Manitoba, Canada; Manitoba Museum of Man and Nature, 1974); Bruce M. Mitchell, "Nurturing the Low-Income Child: Selected Vignettes from Project HUNCHES," *G/C/T* 9–1 (1986); Karen J. Winkler, "Oral History in the 1980s," *The Chronicle of Higher Education*, October 14, 1980.

ORDER, THE, also called the Silent Brotherhood (Bruders Schweigen), was organized in Metaline Falls, Washington, in 1983. The founder was Robert Mathews, an Arizona man, who had a history of involvement with a number of right-wing associations. One of The Order's subgroups was called the Zionist Occupation Government (ZOG), a paramilitary group whose goal was to initiate a campaign of guerrilla actions that would motivate a major uprising of America's European-Americans.

To carry out its goals, The Order needed large sums of money, and they successfully robbed a Brinks armored car in Ukiah, California, which netted the organization about 3.8 million dollars. These funds were spent in acquiring arms and supplying large donations to right-wing organizations. One of The Order's other major acts of violence was the murder of Denver talk show host Alan Berg. Mathews was eventually killed in a shoot-out with the F.B.I.

The philosophy of The Order came from the writings of the *Turner Diaries*, which has served as a "bible" for a number of right-wing militia organizations and other hate groups. Members of The Order were required to subscribe to an oath that they had no fear of death or their "enemies," and they would do whatever was necessary to bring total victory to the "Aryan Race." The oath was highly anti-Semitic.

Since the rising number of militia organizations have created a kind of militia-movement subculture, they have become a serious area of study in the multicultural, educational curriculum. Teachers need to help their students understand the various economic, social, religious, and political factors that motivate the types of human behaviors based on the hatred of specific groups.

Reference: Michael Barkun, *Religion and the Racist Right: The Origins of the Christian Identity Movement* (Chapel Hill: University of North Carolina Press, 1994).

ORIENTAL AMERICANS. *See* ASIAN AMERICANS.

OUTREACH PROGRAMS, referring to special attempts to meet the needs of low-income clients, have often been developed in American churches committed to helping persons from the culture of poverty. Outreach programs have been developed for homeless persons and others in need of various kinds of assistance. Some outreach programs are specifically designed to provide beds, food, and clothing for such people. Food and clothing banks make it possible for persons to acquire needed items. Other outreach programs might provide counseling services, employment assistance, tutoring services, free advice on the preparation of income tax forms, or even legal counseling.

While many of these services are sometimes provided by local, state, and federal agencies, outreach programs are usually offered by churches or other quasi-religious agencies. Volunteers are often in charge of activities that are created to help the clients.

OWENS, JESSE (1913–1980), one of America's most famous track and field athletes, has become an important figure in the history of multicultural involvement in the United States because of his successes during the 1936 Olympics in Berlin, Germany. His unparalleled victories in the 100 and 200 meters and the broad jump (now the long jump) were particularly irritating to Adolph Hitler, who wanted to use the 1936 Olympic Games as a means of demonstrating what he believed was the superiority of the ''Aryan Race.'' In the Olympic Games, Owens also was on the United States' winning relay team. He won a total of four gold medals, and Hitler left the stadium in a rage, refusing to hand out the medals, as was the custom at the time.

Owens set his first sprint record in Danville, Alabama, when he ran the 100-yard dash in 10.0 seconds as a student in Cleveland's Fairview Junior High School. After winning three interscholastic championships in high school, Owens equaled the world record in the 100-yard dash at 9.4 seconds, the 220-yard dash record at 20.3 seconds, the 220-yard low hurdles at 22.6 seconds, and the running broad jump at 26 feet 8 1/4 inches.

After terminating his track and field career at Ohio State University in 1937, Owens worked for a number of years for the Illinois Athletic Commission. In 1955, he made goodwill trips to the Far East and India for the U.S. State Department. He died in Phoenix in 1980.

Owens' incredible performances must be considered in accordance with the track and field situations that existed during the decade of the 1930s. The tracks on which he ran were far from the sophisticated composition tracks of today. Teachers can look at his outstanding performances to illustrate how all Americans have the potential to excel regardless of their gender, race, or ethnicity.

Reference: Sharon Harley, *The Timetables of African-American History* (New York: Simon and Schuster, 1995).

P

PACHUCO, a term referring to Mexican-American youth groups that were viewed by sociologists as a subculture, first appeared in El Paso during the late 1920s and early 1930s. Pachucos did not attract a lot of attention, since they were located primarily in barrios. However, during World War II, the Sleepy Lagoon incident of 1942 and the Zoot Suit riots of 1943 sparked an intensified degree of public concern.

Pachucos, also referred to as *cholos*, were characterized by dress and appearance. The dress often consisted of long coats with padded shoulders, pegged pants, thick-soled shoes, watch chains, and broad-brimmed hats. Pachucos were often tattooed with a pachuco cross between the thumb and forefinger. The Pachuco hairdo featured a duck-tailed comb with a vertical wedge down the middle.

The Zoot Suit riots involved a series of altercations between Mexican-American youth and servicemen stretching over a ten-day period in June 1943. One of the precipitating incidents occurred at the Aragon Ballroom in Venice, California. Later, sailors cruised Whittier Boulevard in East Los Angeles in cabs looking for Pachuco gang members. Military shore patrol units were forced to quell the riots, since the Los Angeles Police Department appeared unwilling or unable to deal with the violence. Inflammatory headlines in the *Los Angeles Daily News* and *Los Angeles Times* seemed to exacerbate the problem and help fan the flames of hatred against Mexican Americans in Los Angeles. Many Mexican Americans had their heads shaved and were often beaten by mobs. The Los Angeles Police Department, under the direction of Chief of Police C. B. Horrall, arrested many Pachucos, even though they were beaten up by mobs. Because of these actions, law-abiding Mexican Americans were sometimes vilified as being primitive and backward.

For teachers, the story of the Pachucos constitutes an important chapter in the Nation's problems with ensuring equality for all. Biased press and police departments created major problems for young Latino youth. Multicultural studies of the various episodes pertaining to anti-Latino bias can help students of all ages learn about the national damage that occurs when persons in positions of leadership have difficulty understanding America's microcultures.

References: Rodolfo Acuna, *Occupied America: A History of Chicanos* (New York: HarperCollins, 1988); David G. Gutierrez, *Walls and Mirrors* (Berkeley: University of California Press, 1995); Himilce Novas, *Everything You Need to Know About Latino History* (New York: Penguin Books, 1991); Carey McWilliams, *North from Mexico: The Spanish-Speaking People of the United States* (Westport, CT: Greenwood Press, 1990).

PARKS, ROSA (1913–), a seamstress in Montgomery, Alabama, was arrested in December 1955 for refusing to give up her seat on a city bus to a European-American man who was standing. The bus driver, James Blake, previously had evicted her from the bus for refusing to use the back door. This time, Parks was arrested and taken to jail in a police car.

After her arrest, Parks agreed to work with the NAACP to end segregated busing in the city of Montgomery. During her trial, she was convicted of violating Montgomery's segregation laws and was fined $10 plus $4 in court fees. Under the leadership of Dr. Martin Luther King, the 26-year-old president of the Montgomery Movement Association and Reverend of the Dexter Avenue Baptist Church, African Americans refused to ride the city buses because of the city's segregation policies.

One year later, December 1956, a U.S. Supreme Court decision terminated bus segregation. Because of her involvement, Rosa Parks became an important icon in the freedom movements during the American Civil Rights era. The City of Montgomery estimated that they had lost about 65 percent of their bus revenues during the boycott.

In studying the American Civil Rights Movement, the Montgomery Bus Boycott has been viewed as one of the major incidents that motivated many other episodes of civil disobedience. It was also an important lesson in the use of the U.S. legal system for achieving civil rights.

References: Henry Hampton and Steve Fayer, *Voices of Freedom: An Oral History of the Civil Rights Movement from the 1950s Through the 1980s* (New York: Bantam, 1990); Juan Williams, *Eyes on the Prize: America's Civil Rights Years 1954–1965* (New York: Viking Press, 1987).

PASSING (FOR WHITE), referred to a practice among some African-American persons who were able to pose as European Americans during the days of Reconstruction, before the advent of the *Brown v. Board of Education* Supreme Court decision. During that era, segregated facilities for African Americans and European Americans were legal, and the facilities for European Americans were vastly superior. Therefore, African-American persons with very little African lineage, often were able to utilize the facilities for ''Whites Only.'' This was referred to as ''passing'' or ''passing for White.''

Perhaps the best example of this practice occurred when Homer Plessy, a Louisiana man, chose to ride in a segregated railway car that was specifically for European Americans. When he was asked to move to the ''Blacks-only'' car, he refused on the grounds that since he was fifteen-sixteenths European American, he was entitled to ride on the ''Whites-Only'' cars. However, the U.S. Supreme Court ruled that if persons in the United States had any African blood, they were classified as ''Negro.''

Scholarly studies of the American Civil Rights Movement can include substantive discussions of U.S. Supreme Court decisions, such as this one. The legal description of ''Negro'' can serve to illustrate the pervasive racism that existed in the nation. *See also PLESSY v. FERGUSON.*

Reference: Juan Williams, *Eyes on the Prize: America's Civil Rights Years, 1954–1965* (New York: Viking Press, 1987).

PEOPLE OF COLOR, a phrase coming into existence during the late 1980s and utilized extensively throughout the 1990s, has been used in the multicultural, educational literature when referring to persons living in the United States who were not from European American backgrounds. Commonly, the term has referred to African Americans, Latinos, Asians, and indigenous populations in the United States. The phrase should not be confused with ''colored person'' or ''colored,'' which is often viewed as demeaning by many people.

For classroom teachers, such messages are clear. In order for teachers to be successful, it is vitally important that they know the terms of preference when it is necessary to specify certain microcultures, according to their race or ethnicity. In the past, some teachers have innocently used terms and phrases that were sometimes viewed as offensive. Such errors can easily destroy the levels of rapport between teachers and students.

Reference: Pamela L. Tiedt and Iris M. Tiedt, *Multicultural Teaching: A Handbook of Activities, Information, and Resources* (Boston: Allyn and Bacon, 1995).

PEOPLE UNITED TO SAVE HUMANITY. *See* OPERATION BREADBASKET.

PEQUOT TRIBE, located in Connecticut, is one of the American Indian tribes that was part of the Algonquian language group. The Pequots became famous for their involvement in the so-called Pequot War, which took place between 1636 and 1637. One of the reasons for the war stemmed from the fact that

Puritan settlers wanted the land. Hostilities between the Pequots and the Puritans reached their peak in 1637.

In 1633, a smallpox outbreak ravaged the tribe, reducing it to just over 3,000 members. The Pequots were primarily a horticultural group, subsisting primarily on corn. The men were hunters while the women, as well as the men, harvested large quantities of shellfish and fish. The Pequots were decimated by the Puritans who violated treaties and purchased land from individual Pequots. The Puritans believed that this smallpox epidemic had been sent by God to help them in their mission to establish new towns in the area.

Studying the problems of the Pequot Tribe constitutes an important segment of the early stages of post-Columbian history. The history of the United States needs to consist of these two important time segments in order for students to understand that, prior to the arrival of the Europeans, a rich history of the United States already existed.

References: Russell Bourne, *The Red King's Rebellion: Racial Politics in New England, 1675–1678* (New York: Antheneum, 1990); Francis Jennings, *The Invasion of America: Indians, Colonialism, and the Cant of Conquest* (New York: W. W. Norton, 1975); Neal Salisbury, *Manitou and Providence: Indians, Europeans, and the Making of New England, 1500–1643* (New York: Oxford University Press, 1982); Charles M. Segal and David C. Steinbeck, *Puritans, Indians, and Manifest Destiny* (New York: G. P. Putnam's Sons, 1977).

PICTURE BRIDES, the young women who married U.S. immigrants from Japan and other countries around the world, came to the United States to marry male immigrants who wished to stay in the United States and desired to get married. For the Japanese, arranged marriages such as these were common practice and worked quite well, since Japanese custom had not required romantic love to be a necessary ingredient for successful marriage. As a general rule, Japanese men were quite a bit older than the picture brides they acquired.

Reference: James A. Banks, *Teaching Strategies for Ethnic Studies*, 6th ed. (Boston: Allyn and Bacon, 1997).

PLANNING MULTICULTURAL LESSONS, an important issue for the serious teacher in the country's pluralistic society, must become a constant point of focus to help students celebrate the racial and ethnic diversity of the United States. Regardless of the curriculum content areas for which an individual teacher is responsible, there are ample opportunities for helping students to acquire a more realistic and positive perspective about the country's pluralistic composition. The age of the student is not an issue. In fact, it has been posited that students need to become exposed to multicultural education topics as soon as they enter the schoolroom.

Most states have persons or departments in the state superintendent's office for addressing various multicultural education issues. Many of these efforts commenced during the 1960s as a result of the American Civil Rights Movement. Educators throughout the 50 states sought ways of restructuring the curriculum to help students develop a more complete understanding of the nation's racial and ethnic diversity. As of 1995, 28 states had a person in charge of such enterprises. For example, the State of Michigan has required that the teacher certification process include instructional components to ensure that prospective teachers understand the cultures, communication styles, beliefs, and social conditions of various racial and ethnic groups, genders, and religious groups of the United States.

Another facet of multicultural education includes the selection of textbooks that are not gender and/or racially biased. About half of the states have a central procedure for ensuring that such materials are free of racial and sexist content. Some states, such as New Jersey, require prospective teachers to have at least 90 hours of pre-service instruction in the cultural/historical background of students with limited English proficiency. Specialized teaching techniques and experience in creating and evaluating curriculum, and specialized instructional content are also part of the teacher-preparation components.

Iowa believes it is important for all students to recognize the contributions and viewpoints of persons from all racial and ethnic groups. The state requires that all curriculum materials, textbooks, and curriculum guides incorporate the accomplishments of persons from both genders, representing all the racial and ethnic backgrounds found in the United States.

Planning models tend to stress the incorporation of multicultural, educational issues into all areas of the curriculum. For example, the study of American history and/or music history might include segments on the multicultural development of American jazz. The multicultural components of this American art form include the influences from the African-American churches and the European contributions of the French quadrille and "classical" music, while other African rhythmic patterns are well known. In addition to these are the Mexican and South American influences from south of the border, which became important factors in the 1960s and 1970s in the evolution of the art form. But perhaps most important was the involvement of musicians from different racial and ethnic backgrounds who sometimes played together after the end of racial segregation.

Strand or theme-planning models suggest the incorporation of multicultural elements into the curriculum content areas. Studies of American history could include both the political and economic contributions of Native Americans in addition to Native American music and art, which became part of the American macroculture. Other contributions in architecture can be included to provide students with important information regarding the contributions of all American microcultures in the creation of the macrocultural characteristics of the nation.

References: James A. Banks, *Multiethnic Education*, 3d ed. (Boston: Allyn and Bacon, 1994); Bruce M. Mitchell, et al., *The Dynamic Classroom*, 5th ed. (Dubuque, IA: Kendall/Hunt, 1995); Bruce M. Mitchell and Robert E. Salsbury, *Multicultural Education: An International Guide to Research, Policies and Programs* (Westport, CT: Greenwood Press, 1996).

PLESSY v. FERGUSON the landmark Supreme Court decision which legitimized racial segregation in the United States, was enacted in 1896 as a result of a case related to the segregation of public accommodations. The issue centered around a Louisiana law which required racial segregation in railway coaches. Homer Adolph Plessy, a Creole of color and New Orleans shoemaker, bought a first-class ticket from New Orleans to Covington, Louisiana. He decided to sit in the segregated coach for European Americans. Since Plessy was only one/sixteen African, he had been able to "pass for White." However, he was recognized as having African lineage and refused to leave the "Whites-Only" coach. He was arrested and imprisoned for violating the state of Louisiana's 1890 Segregation Act.

Plessy was judged guilty by John H. Ferguson, an Orleans Parish Criminal District Court judge. However, due to pressure exerted by the African-American community in New Orleans, the case was appealed, eventually reaching the U.S. Supreme Court. At issue was whether the Louisiana segregation law compromised the principle of equality as guaranteed by law. Also at issue was the matter of Plessy's race and the possibility that the "separate but equal" concept branded African Americans as being inferior. A final issue pertained to the definition of "Negro," since Plessy was fifteen/sixteen European American.

While the Supreme Court vote was 7–1 in favor of the state's segregation legislation, the dissenting vote of John Harlan was crucial. Harlan argued that the United States had no dominant ruling class, and no caste system. He said that the U.S. Constitution was "colorblind and knew no racial distinctions." However, the Supreme Court's 7–1 decision upheld the constitutionality of racial segregation and also defined "Negro" as any person with any African blood.

Harlan became a member of the U.S. Supreme Court in 1877, after serving as an attorney general for the state of Kentucky, receiving his appointment during the administration of President Rutherford B. Hayes. He had become a member of the Republican Party which, during that time, believed in civil rights for African Americans.

Harlan became known as the great dissenter, since he was the only negative vote in the *Plessy v. Ferguson* Supreme Court decision. He had previously owned several household slaves and did not free them until the enactment of the Thirteenth Amendment in 1865. He believed that the federal government should not have become involved in the issue of slavery.

References: James A. Banks, *Multicultural Education: Theory and Practice*, 6th ed. (Boston: Allyn and Bacon, 1997); Bruce M. Mitchell, et al., *The Dynamic Classroom*,

5th ed. (Dubuque, IA: Kendall/Hunt, 1995); Ronald Takaki, *A Different Mirror: A History of Multicultural America* (Boston: Little, Brown, 1993); Charles Thompson, ''Harlan's Great Dissent,'' *Kentucky Humanities*, No. 1 (1996).

PLURALISTIC SOCIETY, a multicultural term referring to the plethora of microcultures in the United States, has been used in the literature of multicultural education in referring to the different microcultures that comprise the macroculture in the United States. A pluralistic society refers to the different racial and ethnic groups that can be found in the country. In addition to such characteristics as race, religion, language patterns, and the like, it also can be used in referring to socioeconomic factors, as well as gender and age characteristics.

Researchers have become concerned with the pluralistic nature of the country in regard to the accuracy of research techniques as they relate to sampling procedures in the polling process. For example, it is possible to identify a microculture in regard to its language, religion, political preference, income level, personal preferences, etc. These characteristics can vary greatly from group to group. One of the great dangers in the identification of specific microcultures is the possibility of stereotyping. However, from a research standpoint, it is known that there is a high probability that persons from a given microculture will harbor the same attitudes and values. Thus, it is possible for researchers to gain crucial information about beliefs and attitudes by surveying small numbers of persons from a particular microculture.

Teachers can help students view America's pluralistic society as an extraordinary strength by studying the microcultures and investigating the values of human beings. The excitement of the pluralistic composition of the country has been viewed as a critical national resource by educators throughout the land.

References: Daniel Levine and Robert U. Havighurst, *Society and Education* (Boston: Allyn and Bacon, 1992); Ronald Takaki, *A Different Mirror: A History of Multicultural America* (Boston: Little, Brown, 1993).

POCHO, a multicultural term pertaining to Latino people, was used when referring to Latinos who became assimilated into the dominant European-American macroculture. The literal translation of the word means ''faded'' or ''bleached ones.'' The term has been used as a synonym for ''Mexican American'' or persons from Mexico who became American citizens.

The other group considered itself to be part of *Mexico de afuera* (Mexico outside Mexico). Such persons have considered themselves to be the true Mexicans, and they have viewed the Pochos as persons without a true culture. Also, they felt that the Pochos viewed them as second-class citizens.

These conditions have persisted throughout history, and a large population of ''Mexicans outside Mexico'' still resides in the Southwest. They are loyal to Mexico, maintain the Spanish language, and consider themselves to really be

Mexicans who are loyal to the original country. Teachers must be careful to be sensitive to the value structures of these two groups.

References: Manuel Gamio, *Mexican Immigration to the United States: A Study of Human Migration and Adjustment* (New York: Dover, 1971); David G. Gutierrez, *Walls and Mirrors: Mexican Americans, Mexican Immigrants, and the Politics of Ethnicity* (Berkeley: University of California Press, 1995).

POLITICALLY CORRECT, a common phrase in the multicultural lexicon, has been used frequently during the late 1980s and 1990s to describe the irritation that some people harbor to terms and phrases of preference for groups of people from different racial and ethnic backgrounds. The perception sometimes is that these ''politically-correct'' terms must be used to keep from getting into trouble. Often, people who object to the concept of ''political correctness'' feel they should be able to use whatever terms they wish when referring to persons from different microcultures.

The complaints about ''political correctness'' are countered by persons who argue that ''political correctness'' is merely a phrase relating to the courtesy of using terms that people prefer. Some have argued that ''politically correct'' simply means being multiculturally sensitive and calling people what they prefer to be called. For teachers, the message is clear. Being multiculturally sensitive is mandatory if teachers wish to maintain the highest levels of rapport with students.

PONCE DE LEON (1460–1521) was a Spanish explorer and soldier who gained fame for his fabled expeditions into present-day Florida in search of the Fountain of Youth. He had accompanied Christopher Columbus on his second voyage. In addition to his search for the Fountain of Youth, it was reported that he was searching for gold and was interested in finding another source of Native American slaves.

He first landed on the Atlantic Coast in the lands of the Timucuan and Ais, the Native American tribes. After a number of battles with the Calusas at San Carlos Bay, he withdrew even though he managed to capture nine warriors who he took with him to Puerto Rico. He named the area Pascua Florida, the Spanish word for ''flowery feast.''

His exploits in 1513, and later in 1521, constitute some of the earliest encounters between Europeans and Native Americans. During his return trip in 1621, he was wounded during an attack by Native Americans, and he was taken to Cuba where he died. He is buried in a San Juan, Puerto Rico cathedral. For teachers, his journeys are important, since they constitute some of the earliest acts of aggression by Europeans who came to the United States in search of a better life.

Reference: Alvin M. Josephy, Jr., *Five Hundred Nations* (New York: Alfred Knopf, 1994).

POOR PEOPLE'S CAMPAIGN, orchestrated by the Southern Christian Leadership Conference (SCLC), was an attempt to cast national attention to the poverty conditions of many Americans. Martin Luther King, Jr. pioneered the concept, and the 1968 march was led by Ralph Abernathy, head of the SCLC. Poor people walked, rode mules, and traveled by bus and automobile to reach Washington, DC.

Resurrection City, a tent community, was established at the Mall near the Lincoln Memorial. Ironically, the Poor People's Campaign occurred during the administration of Lyndon Johnson, who had earlier initiated his famous War on Poverty. Resurrection City was created to accommodate about 1,500 persons, but about 2,500 poor African Americans, Native Americans and Latinos lived in the facilities. During this week, Robert Kennedy was assassinated in California after his victory in the California Democratic presidential primary.

Reference: Henry Hampton and Steve Fayer, *Voices of Freedom: An Oral History of the Civil Rights Movement from the 1950s Through the 1980s* (New York: Bantam, 1990).

POST-COLUMBIAN HISTORY, a term created by some multicultural education professionals and revisionist historians, refers to the historical events in the United States that occurred after the arrival of the Europeans. For many years, American history books focused almost exclusively on the nation's history after the arrival of the Europeans. Classroom teachers sometimes need to supplement their textbooks and curriculum materials to present a valid depiction of both pre-and post-Columbian history.

POVERTY, perhaps the most nagging problem for public school educators in the United States, has experienced dramatic increases among children between the ages of six and seventeen during the 1980s. The poverty rates for Native American, African American, and Latino youth continue to be much higher than the rates for European Americans. During this time, the poverty rates for all other Americans increased only slightly. In fact, poverty rates for older Americans experienced a sharp decline. Due to the expanded benefits of Social Security, the decline in the number of elderly Americans in poverty has been dramatic, as has the increase in poverty among children. By the 1990s, the per capita federal expenditures for the elderly were ten times greater than the per capita expenditures for children under the age of seventeen.

Poverty in the United States has a devastating affect on the lives of school children. Children from poverty backgrounds have lower test scores, higher dropout rates, more aggressive behavior, far higher proportions of students classified as mentally retarded, lower career aspirations, and higher rates of aggressive behavior. The reasons for these behaviors are many. Some of the school problems may be caused by brain cell damage due to poor pre-natal care, fetal alcohol syndrome, the effects of crack cocaine, and physical and/or psychological abuse.

Other causes relate to sociopsychological problems, such as a lack of appropriate role models, parents who do not have the skills to help their children with their schoolwork, parental neglect, overcrowded homes, and an endless list of negative environmental living conditions. However, it is important to recognize that many children from poverty families do quite well in school, have caring parents who worry about their school performance, and work very hard to provide their children with a better life than they had.

It is imperative that teachers become educated about the microcultural characteristics of children from poverty backgrounds. This means listening for clues that will help them become more educated about social conditions, problems encountered by families, and the like. It also means that teachers must find ways for parents to become more effective in helping their children with schoolwork. Teachers, most of whom come from middle-class socioeconomic circumstances, may need to re-educate themselves to understand the subtle nuances of poverty issues and learn how to use alternative strategies in establishing appropriate levels of rapport with their students for optimum learning to occur.

References: R. D. Lamm, "Age Again Beats Youth," *New York Times*, December 2, 1990; Daniel U. Levine and Robert J. Havighurst, *Society and Education* (Boston: Allyn and Bacon, 1992).

POWHATAN (1550–1618), the more commonly used name for Wahunsonacock, ruled a small empire consisting of about 13,000 persons from 31 tribes located in the present-day State of Virginia. In 1607, a new colonizing expedition from England sailed into the lower Chesapeake Bay, creating a fort on the James River. Because of past experiences with English adventurers, Powhatan and his subchiefs did not greet this latest group of Europeans with open arms. About two weeks after the Europeans landed, Powhatan's warriors attacked them but were held off by the English muskets and cannons.

Historians disagree as to the reasons that Powhatan did not exterminate the small number of British colonists in the area. In fact, he even made a number of peaceful overtures, sometimes supplying the English with food. Moreover, he permitted his favorite daughter, Pocahontas, to visit the English settlement to facilitate trade relations with the Powhatan Confederacy. Eventually, after a meeting with John Smith, Powhatan realized that the English had not come for the purpose of trading but to possess their lands.

However, instead of attacking the invading Europeans, Powhatan chose to move his home further inland. Nonetheless, intermittent warfare between the Native Americans and English colonists existed for a period of five years from 1609 to 1614. Powhatan's daughter, Pocahontas, was captured in 1613 and held hostage. However, Powhatan refused to barter for her release, and she eventually joined the Anglican Church and married John Rolfe, an English planter.

References: Wesley F. Craven, *Red, White, and Black* (Charlottesville: University of Virginia Press, 1971); Anthony J. Paredes (Ed.), *Indians of the Southeastern United States in the Late Twentieth Century* (Tuscaloosa: University of Alabama Press, 1992); Helen C. Rountree, *Pocahontas's People: The Powhatan Indians of Virginia Through Four Centuries* (Norman: University of Oklahoma Press, 1990).

POWWOW, a term relating to the ancient and traditional tribal ceremonies of Native Americans, often had religious significance and involved various forms of music and dancing. Tribal ceremonies are still quite popular and held on North American reservations and other sites as well. They help Native Americans keep in touch with their cultural traditions. However, they also are sometimes performed primarily for tourists. Powwows usually include music, food, and dancing. On some occasions, they also involve dancing competition.

Prior to the arrival of the Europeans, most Native Americans had no understanding of the European concept of land ownership. However, there was almost always a strong tie to the earth. In addition, there was also a reverence for all life. Spirits resided in the animals, in the living trees, in the waters, and in the sky.

Actually, the term "powwow" is a derivative of an old Algonquian word relating to the work of shamans. Later, it was used in referring to various types of religious ceremonies and eventually broadened to large gatherings of people for a celebration of any type.

References: Norman Bancroft-Hung, *People of the Totem* (New York: G. P. Putnam's Sons, 1979); Charles Hudson, *The Southeastern Indians* (Knoxville: University of Tennessee Press, 1976); Gladys A. Reichard, *A Navajo Religion: A Study of Symbolism*, 2 vols. (Princeton, NJ: Princeton University Press, 1950); Robert F. Spencer and Jesse D. Jennings, et al., *The Native-Americans* (New York: Harper and Row, 1977).

PRE-COLUMBIAN HISTORY is a multicultural education term referring to the events that occurred in the United States prior to the arrival of the Europeans. Often the accomplishments were not included in the history books used in American classrooms. For example, the Pueblo Bonito ruins of Chaco Canyon, New Mexico, were once inhabited by an estimated 4,000 Anasazis, long before the arrival of the Europeans. Their structures were miracles of architecture with thick walls that made them warmer in the winter and cooler in the summer.

The Mogollon of the mountainous portions of southern New Mexico were the first Native Americans to develop the bow and arrow and cultivate corn. In the Northeast, the Iroquois Confederacy was a coalition of the Cayugas, Mohawks, Onondagas, Oneidas, Senecas, and Tuscaroras. Founded between 1400 and 1600, the Iroquois League reportedly provided the "founding fathers" with some of their ideas for the creation of the Articles of Confederation.

These and numerous other events and accomplishments constitute the history of the United States prior to the arrival of Europeans. However, since history books typically have been written by European Americans, many of the important pre-Columbian events have been excluded from the American history curriculum. Thus, it is often necessary for classroom teachers to supplement existing materials to craft cogent and realistic depictions of American history before the arrival of the Europeans. *See also* POST-COLUMBIAN HISTORY.

References: Lindea S. Cordell, *Prehistory of the Southwest* (Orlando, FL: Academic Press, 1984); Alvin M. Josephy Jr. (Ed.), *The American Heritage Book of Indians* (New York: Simon and Schuster, 1961); David Muench, *Anasazi, Ancient People of the Rock* (Palo Alto, CA: American West, 1975); Colin F. Taylor (Ed.), *The Native Americans: The Indigenous People of North America* (New York: Smithmark, 1991).

PREDOMINANTLY BLACK OR PREDOMINANTLY WHITE are terms used in different agencies for referring to American schools that have at least 75 percent African-American students (Black) or at least 75 percent European-American students (White).

Reference: Bruce M. Mitchell, et al., *The Dynamic Classroom*, 5th ed. (Dubuque, IA: Kendall/Hunt, 1995).

PREJUDICE, a term commonly used in the multicultural, educational lexicon, refers to a set of pre-determined attitudes that are seldom based on valid data. While the term is commonly used in discussing the racial, religious, and ethnic attitudes of people, it differs from "bias," because "prejudice" refers to ideas that are based on emotions rather than hard-core data. These pre-determined attitudes are rigid and often unfavorable. For example, the person who is prejudiced against Jews might argue that Jews are "pushy" and "loud," regardless of the number of Jewish individuals the person has known who are quiet and not pushy.

Prejudice leads to discrimination, but the words convey different meanings. While *prejudice* refers to a set of attitudes, *discrimination* occurs when people exhibit negative behaviors toward a person or persons because of the prejudices they happen to harbor. Often, prejudiced attitudes are passed on to children by their parents. This often happens at a very young age.

In addition to the acquisition of prejudiced attitudes from their parents, people can acquire attitudes of prejudice from a failure to understand the cultural value systems and history of persons who happen to be different from them. Prejudice can also occur when people judge others from their own microcultural perspective. This can result in a person, or groups of persons, learning to hate an entire group. For example, the Aryan Nations Church in North Idaho openly discriminates against Jews because they are *Jews*. A negative attitude perpetuated through prejudice produces attitudes of fear, anger, hatred, and mistrust.

Dealing with prejudice is an enormous problem for teachers who are interested in improving the attitudes of their students regarding race, ethnicity, and gender. Many of the educational programs have been developed at the Poverty Law Center in Montgomery, Alabama.

References: James A. Banks, *Teaching Strategies for Ethnic Studies*, 6th ed. (Boston: Allyn and Bacon, 1997); Morris Dees, *Teaching Tolerance* (Montgomery, AL: Southern Poverty Law Center, 1991); Donna M. Gollnick and Philip C. Chinn, *Multicultural Education in a Pluralistic Society* (Columbus, OH: Merrill, 1990).

PROTESTANT WORK ETHIC referred to a commitment by the "founding fathers" from Europe to support the "pure principles of Republicanism" and a determination to ensure that the "new" nation should be composed of "good and useful 'men.' " Only the most worthy should be able to settle in the New Republic. Screened out of the pool of participants would be "vagrants, paupers, and bad men." Applicants for citizenship were required to live in the United States for at least two years and demonstrate their good character and republican fitness.

Republicanism presented the new European transplants with a psychological attitude that would help fuel the economic expansion throughout the United States. The Protestant work ethic defined work as virtuous and requiring self-control; the acquisition of wealth was a sign of salvation. Moreover, the Protestant Work Ethic, viewed as a critical characteristic of republicanism, proclaimed worldly acquisitions as a sign or measure of virtuousness.

Successful Americans were persons who had toiled diligently and, through the labor of their physical pursuits, had been able to acquire substantial physical wealth as measured by the totality of their financial acquisitions. Thus, the Protestant Work Ethic was evaluated largely by tangible material wealth as measured in dollars and cents. Throughout the years, it has become a sociological concept related to the behavior of European-American males.

Reference: Ronald Takaki, *A Different Mirror: A History of Multicultural America* (Boston: Little, Brown, 1993).

PUEBLA, MEXICO, a city located inland from the Bay of Campeche, was the site of a victory of Mexican forces over the French forces. The victorious General Zaragosa was the commander of the Mexican army, which forced the French to retreat. The event became important in Mexican history, since it helped Mexico become a fully independent nation.

Since the Mexican victory on May 5, 1862, the event has acquired a high level of significance in Mexican history. While it seems to be celebrated more extensively in the United States than Mexico, the victory over the French has been viewed as an important step in Mexico's fight for independence. Zaragosa's victory has become an important time for Latinos in the United States.

In American schools, Cinco de Mayo is a time for celebrating the Latino culture. Consequently, this event has provided teachers with an opportunity to help children appreciate the many contributions of Mexican Americans. Fun-filled fiestas include pinata parties, parades, dancing and other delightful activities. It has become a time for the celebration of life by all American microcultures. However, it should be mentioned that even though May 5 (Cinco de Mayo) is an important event to commemorate, it is also important that teachers deal with the many accomplishments of Mexican-American people throughout the entire school year. *See also* CINCO DE MAYO.

Reference: Pamela L. Tiedt and Iris M. Tiedt, *Multicultural Teaching: A Handbook of Activities, Information, and Resources* (Boston: Allyn and Bacon, 1995).

PUEBLO TRIBE, a group of Native Americans residing in the southwestern United States, is considered by anthropologists to be part of the desert culture. The tribes constituting the Pueblos consist of the Zuni, Laguna, Acoma, and Hopi. They are believed to have been in the area at least 10,000 years ago. While the cultural patterns of the Pueblos have remained intact over the years, the changes that occurred did so after they came into contact with the Europeans, specifically the Spaniards.

Among the most disruptive influences on the Pueblo Indians were the western European beliefs brought to this country. These religious attitudes, as a general rule, seemed to be incapable of tolerating the spiritual/religious beliefs of the indigenous populations with whom they came into contact. By the middle of the seventeenth century, the Pueblos revolted against the religious influences of the Spaniards. This Pueblo Revolt of 1680 resulted in a siege on Santa Fe, the Spanish capital. The purpose of the siege was to obliterate any reminders of the Spanish culture.

Anthropologists believe that the Hopi and Zuni are the descendants of the Anasazi culture. While there are great similarities between the four Pueblo Tribe groups, a number of interesting differences also exist. The Acoma and Laguna Pueblos have the same native language patterns. Both of these sites are close to Albuquerque. Acoma and Laguna Puebloans have a matrilineal clan structure in which men go to live with their wives. One of their major art forms is the creation of beautiful pottery decorated with designs of leaves, geometrical designs, flowers, and birds. Potters are held in very high regard in both the Acoma and Laguna cultures.

Hopi society tends to be rather complex, and the people are affiliated with one of thirteen different villages. Floors of the clan kivas consist of sand paintings based on the cultural traditions of the different clans. Since the Hopi macroculture is also matrilineal, the women own the houses and are in charge of the economy. However, the men are most prominent in the various tribal ceremonies. The governmental structure is based on a board of directors.

The Zunis now have their own school system, which was created during the 1980s. This public school system attempts to perpetuate a better understanding of the culture. Six Zuni villages have constituted the present Zuni Pueblo for several centuries. It has been posited that the fabled "Seven Cities of Cibola" may have been the six Zuni villages. However, when Coronado visited the area, he found that what was actually worshipped seemed to be water, not gold. While the Zuni language tends to be the primary language of communication, most Zunis are also fluent in English.

References: Edward P. Dozier, *The Pueblo Indians of North America* (New York: Holt, Rinehart, and Winston, 1970); Alan M. Josephy, Jr., *Five Hundred Nations* (New York: Alfred A. Knopt, 1994); Vincent Sculley, *Pueblo: Mountain Village Dance*, 2d ed. (Chicago: University of Chicago Press, 1989).

PUERTO RICAN AMERICANS, the second largest Latino group in the United States, commenced migrating to the United States following the Treaty of Paris agreements of 1898. This treaty formally ended the Spanish-American War. Prior to that time, Puerto Rico was under control of Spain after the voyages of Christopher Columbus. Juan Ponce de Leon was governor of Puerto Rico, commencing in 1508. The Spaniards brought African slaves to the country in 1513 to work their plantations in Puerto Rico. Consequently, the three racial and ethnic heritages of the Puerto Rican Americans consist of Arawak Indians (the native inhabitants), Spaniards, and Africans.

By 1910, the U.S. Census reported that 1,513 native Puerto Ricans were living in the United States. Puerto Rican immigrants were required to pass an English literacy test in New York State, where many of the early immigrants resided. They worked as cigar makers and in the city's garment industry. This literacy test was terminated as a result of the Civil Rights Act of 1965. Puerto Ricans have been able to become American citizens since 1917, due to the passage of the Jones Act.

Most of the early Puerto Rican immigrants have settled in New York City. In 1940, 88 percent of all the Puerto Rican Americans lived there. However, since that time, more Puerto Ricans have settled in other parts of the United States, as well. However, throughout their history, Puerto Ricans have been victimized by racism occurring partly because they were viewed as competitors for unskilled and semi-skilled jobs by other microcultures.

When classroom teachers are studying the problems encountered by immigrants to this country, the conflicts and problems addressed by this microculture can be compared and contrasted to the cultural conflict, racial problems, and colonialism issues that have affected the lives of other groups of non-Native Americans who came to the United States from various parts of the world.

References: James A. Banks, *Teaching Strategies for Ethnic Studies*, 6th ed. (Boston: Allyn and Bacon, 1997); Leonard Dinnerstein, Roger L. Nichols, and David Reimers, *Natives and Strangers* (New York: Oxford University Press, 1990).

Q

QUADROONS, persons with mixed-blood ancestry, is a term that sometimes has been used when referring to persons who had one mulatto parent (the offspring of parents with African and Caucasian blood) and one Caucasian parent. The term actually is used to designate the percentage of African blood (25 percent) of a particular individual.

During the Reconstruction Period, some quadroons were able to ''pass for White,'' which sometimes made it possible for an individual who had African blood to use the ''Whites-Only'' facilities in the South. However, being a quadroon sometimes carried some disadvantages. For example, a Louisiana ordinance was passed in 1785 that restricted the activities of quadroon women. The new law prevented quadroon women from wearing jewels and feathers. It also prevented them from going to balls and forced them to wear their hair in a kerchief. During that time in history, people who were the products of mixed-race relationships were sometimes chastised.

Reference: Sharon Harley, *The Timetables of African-American History* (New York: Simon and Schuster, 1995).

QUECHAN TRIBE, often referred to as the Yuma Tribe, is one of the very few Native American tribes that was never forced to leave its original place of residence. According to the 1990 census, there were nearly 2,000 tribal members. Most Quechans live on the 25,000 acres given to them in 1978 by the U.S. government. A great deal of their original reservation land had to be sold to survive. Working on this land as craftspersons, artisans, farmers, and laborers, they continue to commemorate many of their tribal traditions.

Throughout their history, the Quechan were sometimes involved in hostilities with the Pima, Maricopa, and Cocopa. During the 1770s, Europeans and Mexicans attempted to control the area in the vicinity of the Gila and Colorado River confluence. Eventually, the Quechan ran them out of the area, tiring of their attempts to inflict new cultural values on the people. Fort Yuma was established in 1852 on a cliff overlooking the Colorado and Gila Rivers. The Quechans were given their original reservation lands in 1912 by the U.S. government.

For teachers, the story of the Quechan can be used to illustrate the problems faced by Native Americans from the Southwest. Not only were they forced to deal with incursions from Mexico but with European settlers as well. Moreover, the arid Southwest created great difficulties for farmers. The fact that the Quechan were forced to sell their land to survive can be used by teachers to address the economic problems that emerged as a result of the European-American encroachments.

Reference: Harvey Markowitz (Ed.), *American Indians* (Pasadena, CA: Salem Press, 1995).

QUEEN OF THE VOODOOS (1796–1881), Marie Laveau, was born in New Orleans in 1796. Actually, the Queen of the Voodoos was two or more women who succeeded each other, but in the minds of many New Orleaneans, it was just one person. The last Laveau died early in the twentieth century, but many people refused to believe that the Voodoo Queen was gone. Her mortal remains are said to be buried in St. Louis Cemetery No. 1 at the downtown end of Basin Street.

Perhaps no other city in the United States has more unique microcultures than New Orleans, and the voodoo microculture is one of them. While conducting the various voodoo ceremonies, the first Marie (nee Glapion) remained a devout Catholic, and her voodoo ceremonies were not interfered with by the New Orleans Catholic Church. She was a highly skilled hairdresser and among her clientele were some of the most fashionable European-American women of New Orleans.

Voodoo has been considered by some to be the true religion of Storyville, the red-light district of New Orleans where jazz was born. This religion was practiced by Protestants, Jews, Catholics, and Moslems. The ceremonies were thought to keep evil spirits away. For example, one practice for accomplishing this was sprinkling the doorstep with red brick dust.

While multicultural educators may be reluctant to pursue the topic of voodoo, due to its connection with prostitution in New Orleans' Storyville, the voodoo mythology of New Orleans constituted a fascinating and significant microculture and can be used to illustrate the great diversity of racial, religious, ethnic, and racial microcultures in the United States.

Reference: Al Rose, *Storyville, New Orleans* (Tuscaloosa: University of Alabama Press, 1974).

QUILLWORK, a form of decoration used across the northeastern United States and Canada, was one of the main forms of art utilized by Native Americans. The practice was also carried on in the western slopes of the Rockies and throughout the Central Plains. These regions were inhabited by large populations of porcupines, native to those locales.

Porcupines supplied the tribes with quills that could be used to adorn moccasins, shirts, gloves, hats, leggins, bandoliers, jackets, dresses, and robes. The quills were dyed and plaited together in geometric designs and pictorial representations. While the quills were tubular shaped, some tribes flattened them by pulling them through their teeth. After the Europeans moved into these Indian territories, much of the quillwork was replaced with beadwork.

Reference: Harvey Markowitz (Ed.), *American Indians* (Pasadena, CA: Salem Press, 1995).

QUINAULT TRIBE, one of the members of the Salishan language group, is located on the mouth of the Quinault River in Washington State. The Quinault belong to the southwestern coastal Salish group. Quinaults traditionally have been fishers and hunters, and to some extent, gatherers. Known for their ability to construct ocean-going canoes, they were also able whale hunters.

Spiritual worship was prominent in the lives of the Quinault, and guardian spirits were important in their daily lives. The religion was also based on mythical spirits such as Misp, considered to be the creator and caretaker of the world, and a trickster spirit named Xwoni Xwoni. The salmon always has been of critical significance in the lore of the Quinault tribe.

Living in large houses, the Quinaults traded with neighboring tribes and a great deal of intermarriage took place. While the primary economy of the reservation has been based on fishing and government jobs, there has not been enough work to go around in recent years, so many members of the Quinault tribe have left the reservation to seek employment in Seattle and other urban locations.

Reference: Harvey Markowitz (Ed.), *American Indians* (Pasadena, CA: Salem Press, 1995).

QUOTA SYSTEMS are programs that set aside percentages of applicants for jobs and admission to colleges and universities. They came into existence as a result of legislation enacted during the American Civil Rights Movement. Quota systems were put into place as a means of evening the playing field for women and minorities, who had been kept out of certain professions because of a history of racist and sexist acts which disallowed them from participating in occupations and professional endeavors. For example, eighteen years after *Brown v. Board of Education*, minority groups were dramatically underrepresented in the University of Washington Law School. The same problem exists in law schools, medical schools, and other professional programs throughout the country.

The key Supreme Court decision pertaining to the use of quota systems took place at the University of California at Davis (*University of California Regents v. Bakke*). Bakke, after being turned down at several other medical schools, applied at the University of California, Davis. Several African-American applicants were granted admission to the program ahead of Bakke. According to Bakke, they were less qualified than he was. He appealed the university's decision on the grounds that the quota system resulted in reverse discrimination against him for being a European-American male.

The decision, in Bakke's favor, only pertained to the manner in which the quota system was carried out. Bakke was not allowed to petition for the quota slots because of his race. However, the decision did not outlaw quota systems, as long as all the applicants who had been rejected were allowed to re-apply for one of the quota slots. Since that time, a series of legislative actions at the state and federal levels have ended many affirmative action programs and quota systems. In the states that have terminated such programs, the number of minority participants has diminished dramatically.

Reference: Daniel Selakovich, *Schooling in America* (New York: Longman, 1984).

R

RACE, a term referring to the physical characteristics of human beings, has been greatly misunderstood. It refers to physical characteristics such as skin color and facial features and does not relate directly to religion, values, and language. One of the leading anthropologists, Ashley Montagu, has classified human beings into four racial sub-groups: Negroid, Archaic White (Australoid types), Caucasoid (the mis-named ''White'' race), and Mongoloid. Montagu then questioned the entire validity of ''pure race.'' Late in his career he argued that human beings from different racial backgrounds had been inter-breeding throughout history and it was almost impossible to determine specific racial groups.

Another anthropologist (Oliver), identified seven major racial groups: early Mongoloid, late Mongoloid, Negro, Bushman, Australian, Pygmy Negroid, and White. The Encyclopedia Britannia has identified fifteen different racial groups. Montagu has described race as man's ''most dangerous myth'' and argued that the concept had been one of the most destructive factors throughout the history of humankind.

Regardless of the plethora of racial classification schemes developed by anthropologists, and despite the arguments against classifying people by race, teachers are deeply affected by the issue of race in numerous ways. The most obvious issue throughout American history has been school segregation. African-American children and other children of color were sometimes forced to attend segregated schools, which were decidedly inferior. Due to this factor and a history of forced illiteracy during slavery, African-American children and other students of color have struggled in the schools compared to European-American students.

While educators would like to function in a ''color-blind'' instructional milieu, racial issues profoundly affect student's school performance in numerous ways. Multicultural, educational programs attempt to address the learning problems children encounter because of racial factors. Moreover, the multicultural educator is charged with the responsibility of helping students learn to celebrate the racial diversity of the nation.

To address the issues, it is important for teachers to learn that race per se has very little to do with the school performance of children. Factors such as poverty, dysfunctional families, poor role models, alcohol and drug abuse, violence, teenage pregnancy, parental ineptitude, poor ego strength, and the like, are the primary factors that determine school success. These problems can afflict all racial groups, and it is important that teachers prepare themselves to deal effectively with all their students, regardless of their racial backgrounds.

References: James A. Banks, *Teaching Strategies for Ethnic Studies*, 6th ed. (Boston: Allyn and Bacon, 1997); Daniel U. Levine and Robert Havighurst, *Society and Education* (Boston: Allyn and Bacon, 1992); Ashley Montagu, *Man's Most Dangerous Myth: The Fallacy of Race* (New York: Oxford University Press, 1974); Douglas L. Oliver, *An Invitation to Anthropology: A Guide to Basic Concepts* (Garden City, NY: The National History Press, 1964); William J. Wilson, *The Declining Significance of Race: Blacks and Changing American Institutions* (Chicago: University of Chicago Press, 1978).

RACIAL BALANCE, a concept often used in the creation of desegregation strategies for school districts, refers to the policies of many states demanding that the racial and ethnic groups of a given school must approximate the racial composition found in its school district or community area. Regardless of the desegregation strategy used, the individual schools must contain the same or a similar distribution of students racially and ethnically compared to the total community.

States such as New Jersey, require that attendance zones be drawn up so that schools segregated by race or ethnicity be integrated. For example, the composition of an individual school must not contain all upper-socioeconomic, European-American students nor can a school located in a city's *barrio* consist of only Latino students. Regardless of the desegregation plan employed, racial balance must exist in individual school attendance areas.

Reference: Office of Equal Educational Opportunity, *Guidelines for Education That Is Multicultural* (Trenton: New Jersey State Department of Education, 1993).

RACISM, directly related to the notion of race, refers to the presupposition that humans can be grouped according to their overt biological characteristics and postulates that members of individual racial groups automatically inherit such preordained characteristics as intelligence and a variety of cultural traits. Moreover, these and other attributes are believed to be superior or inferior to those possessed by members of other racial groups. One of the most common examples of racism is the idea that Caucasians are superior in intelligence to Africans and other dark-skinned groups. In fact, Sir Francis Galton even suggested that the lightest-skinned persons on the planet were superior in intelligence to all other people.

Racism extends beyond merely a set of values to which some people subscribe. It also refers to the discriminatory practices carried out against certain groups. The classic example in the United States and other countries is grounded in the history of oppression of African slaves. Even after slavery was terminated in the United States after the end of the civil War, African Americans were forced to attend segregated schools and other public and private institutions that were decidedly inferior. In fact, some experts have argued that racism is a rather recent phenomenon and did not really exist until the beginning of the seventeenth or eighteenth century.

Some anthropologists have argued that racism was carried out by a group of people who were bent on the exploitation of other groups. Due to a profit motive based on this exploitation, it was necessary to use racist practices to maintain the various advantages accrued through the exploitation of other groups. For example, the South defended slavery because of the profits generated by European Americans through the use of their chattels as a source of cheap labor.

Some sociologists have classified racism into three segments. *Institutional Racism* refers to racist actions that have been characteristic of an entire institution. For example, the State of Louisiana refused to allow African Americans to ride in rail cars with European-Americans, and some school districts in the southwestern United States created separate schools for Latino children. *Individual Racism* refers to the racist practices carried out by individual persons against other persons or groups deemed to be inferior. For example, the slogan, "A good Indian is a dead Indian" was a popular statement reflecting an attitude harbored by many individual settlers during the so-called westward expansion of the United States. *Cultural Racism* refers to the racist beliefs carried by individuals or groups against an entire culture. For example, Adolph Hitler had extremely negative attitudes against the Jews; so much so that he felt justified in exterminating millions of Jewish persons during World War II. They were killed because of their cultural and/or racial characteristics and values.

Racism is one of the most severe problems addressed by educators who are trying to create viable classroom programs that attempt to address the issues of racism and ethnocentrism. Organizations such as the Poverty Law Center in Montgomery, Alabama, have created valuable classroom materials for creating positive racial attitudes among young servicemen.

References: Ashley Montagu, *Man's Most Dangerous Myth: The Fallacy of Race* (New York: Oxford University Press, 1974); Douglas L. Oliver, *An Invitation to Anthropology: A Guide to Basic Concepts* (Garden City, NY: The National History Press, 1964); Peter I. Rose, *They and We: Racial and Ethnic Relations in the United States* (New York:

Random House, 1974); Pierre L. van den Berghe, *Race and Racism: A Comparative Perspective* (New York: John Wiley, 1978).

RAINBOW COALITION, a term coined by the Reverend Jesse Jackson, referred to a lobbying effort which he organized after his unsuccessful attempt at the U.S. presidency in 1984. As the term implies, the organization sought to unite the forces of a wide variety of ethnic and racial groups who felt victimized by administrative practices during the conservative Reagan Administration. Politically, the Rainbow Coalition sought to influence lawmakers to pass appropriate civil rights legislation.

Reference: Gerald David Jaynes and Robin M. Williams (Eds.), *A Common Destiny: Blacks and American Society* (Washington, DC: National Academy Press, 1989).

RECONSTRUCTION, from a multicultural perspective, can be used to teach about an important era of American history. It constituted a time in American history when the role of African-American persons began a major change, moving from a time of the total oppression of slavery to a period during which new forms of anti-African discrimination assumed different directions. Some sociologists have argued that this time period extended roughly from 1865 (the end of slavery) to 1954 and the *Brown v. Board of Education* Supreme Court decision. This era persisted for nearly 90 years.

While the name itself refers to the attempts to rebuild the South after the tremendous devastation during the U.S. Civil War, it is sometimes used to characterize a period of time when the United States adjusted to the desegregation of African Americans and the termination of slavery. In doing so, virtually all American institutions experienced segregation in some form. Segregation practices were used on various forms of public transportation, in housing, rest rooms, transportation stations, drinking fountains, restaurants, hotels, and perhaps most significantly, schools. Most of the racial segregation that came into effect at the termination of the Civil War was between African Americans and European Americans.

School segregation was one of the key areas of racial segregation; this issue eventually resulted in the termination of racially segregated schools which became illegal in 1954. During the Reconstruction Period, less than adequate schools were constructed for African-American children, most of whom never had attended formal school in the United States.

Due to the poverty-stricken southern communities economically devastated by the Civil War, the southern educational systems suffered harsh consequences. When Robert E. Lee surrendered at Appomatox, many private academies and colleges were closed, and the public education system was in shambles. Moreover, most European Americans were illiterate, as were most freed slaves who had been forbidden the right to learn how to read by various pieces of legislation and edicts by individual plantation owners.

Consequently, when southern states turned to the arduous task of recreating their school systems, adequate funding was not available. This created enormous hardships on African-American students, who had been denied a formal education during the days of slavery. During the Reconstruction Period, it was easy for southern states to create a two-tiered educational system segregated for African-American and European-American students.

The funding formulas for these segregated school systems were similar to those found in South Africa prior to the termination of the apartheid era. Records show that for every dollar spent on the education of European-American children, just 50 cents was spent on the education of African Americans. Consequently, it was very difficult to close the huge gap in academic performance between the two groups.

During Reconstruction, southern European Americans were forced to deal with two issues that had a dramatic effect on their social structure: the total devastation of their land and a large population of freed slaves. Many of the returning southern Civil War veterans viewed slaves as intellectually and socially inferior. And the minimal economic resources for the recreation of southern institutions was a major problem well into the twentieth century. Moreover, the enactment of ''Jim Crow'' laws and the brutal tactics of the Ku Klux Klan put freed slaves in a position that was not much better than the days of slavery.

References: S. Alexander Rippa, *Education in a Free Society; An American History* (New York: Longman, 1988); Ronald Takaki, *A Different Mirror: A History of Multicultural America* (Boston: Little, Brown, 1993); C. Vann Woodward, *The Strange Career of Jim Crow* (New York: Oxford University Press, 1974).

REDLINING refers to the pre–Civil Rights practice of realtors who drew red lines around city maps, thus designating sections of communities in which houses could be sold to persons of color. For European Americans, realtors would show houses in any part of a given city. However, if the person happened to be an African American or belonged to a non-European-American group, it was likely that purchasing a home outside of a ''redlined'' area would be impossible. Moreover, ''Restrictive Covenants'' were sometimes written into the bylaws of housing developments. Sometimes these covenants were worded as follows: ''No race or nationality other than the White race shall use or occupy any building on any lot, except that this covenant shall not prevent occupancy by domestic servants of a different race or nationality employed by an owner or tenant.''

One strategy used to circumvent this practice was called ''blockbusting.'' This involved several people who wished to upgrade their homes in a redlined area located in more affluent parts of the community. People would pool their money, making it possible for one minority family to purchase a home for an inflated price in a previously segregated neighborhood. Then when ''White Flight'' occurred, resulting in many homes going for sale, often the prices would drop, making it possible for the other members of the coalition to purchase homes at a reduced rate.

While the practice became illegal as a result of legal actions carried out during the American Civil Rights era, often more subtle means have been taken to accomplish the same goal. The red lines disappear and the salespersons steer potential buyers of color away from certain parts of a given community.

References: Scott Finnie, *African-American History in the Northwest* (Spokane, WA: A Community Congress on Race Relations, 1997); Bruce M. Mitchell, et al., *The Dynamic Classroom*, 5th ed (Dubuque, IA: Kendall/Hunt, 1995).

RELIGIOUS FREEDOM, a controversial issue for American schools, has been guaranteed through the Establishment Clause of the U.S. Constitution. Throughout the years, a plethora of court cases have pertained to the issue of separation of church and state. Supreme Court decisions in cases such as *McCollum v. Board of Education* and *Abington School District v. Schempp* have ruled against such controversial topics as organized prayer and Bible reading.

The Schempp decision, which rules that prayer and Bible reading were not constitutional, did not rule against the schools' capacity to study about the contemporary religions of the world. However, the ruling did stipulate that it was unconstitutional to advocate the merits of any religion. However, the decision had the effect of declaring that educators could teach about the religion, art, religious exercises, rituals, and celebrations of a given religion as part of the school's curriculum. Thus, ''religion'' is not constitutionally excluded from the school curriculum; but, attempts to advocate a particular religious persuasion, are clearly unconstitutional.

Moreover, students are even allowed the freedom to receive religious indoctrination during school hours, as long as it is conducted away from the school. The *Lemon Test* has been used for determining whether student-led religious programs are constitutional: (1) Does the policy or practice have a secular purpose? (2) Is the primary effect of the policy or practice one that neither advances or inhibits religion? (3) Does the policy or practice avoid an excessive entanglement with religion? To be constitutionally acceptable, the answer must be ''yes'' to all three questions.

In addition to such well known religious issues as instruction about gay and lesbian issues, issues of abortion, moral education, and saluting the flag have become embroiled in constitutional court challenges. And, the arguments over the initiation of voucher systems relating to ''school choice'' have split communities. The issue in this case has been whether public monies can be spent for educating children in private religious schools. Throughout the history of public education in the United States, such attempts have been declared constitutionally illegal.

References: Louis A. Fischer, David Schimmel, and Cynthia Kelly, *Teachers and the Law* (White Plains, NY: Longman, 1995); David L. Kirp and Mark D. Yudof, *Educa-*

tional Policy and the Law, Cases and Materials (Berkeley, CA: McCutchan, 1974); David Tavel, *Church-State Issues in Education*, PDK Fastback No. 123, (Bloomington, IN: Phi Delta Kappa Educational Foundation, 1979); Daniel Selakovich, *Schooling in America* (New York: Longman, 1984).

REMOVAL ACT OF 1830. See INDIAN REMOVAL ACT.

REPATRIATION refers to effort to coax immigrants to return to their native country. For example, Marcus Garvey attempted to persuade African Americans to repatriate to Liberia. A Repatriation Act, passed by Congress during the administration of President Franklin Roosevelt, not only made it difficult for Filipinos to immigrate to the United States, but it provided free transportation for Filipino Americans to return to the Philippines. The provisions of the legislation disallowed any of the repatriated Filipinos to return to the United States About 2,000 Filipino Americans returned to their native islands.

Reference: James A. Banks, *Teaching Strategies for Ethnic Studies*, 6th ed. (Boston: Allyn and Bacon, 1997).

REPUBLICAN RIGHT, an ultra-conservative coalition of the Republican party, is a political body that has shaped American politics, particularly in recent years. It is incumbent on classroom teachers to help students investigate the political efforts of this group to understand the important nuances of American politics. For teachers in America's public schools, the conservative Republican elements have often had direct effects on a number of public school practices.

For example, the Republican Right has consistently fought for prayer in schools, Bible reading, and school choice (voucher systems), which have been declared unconstitutional in a number of supreme Court decisions. While the right wing of the Republican Party has been a political entity for decades, it attracted unusual attention with the election of Ronald Reagan in 1980.

Reagan's election solidified the Republican right faction that became stronger than ever due to the amazing rhetorical skills of Reagan. After his election in 1980, Reagan became one of the most popular presidents in American history. Campaigning on a platform of reduction in government, and blessed with an amazing sense of humor, the newly elected president captured the imagination of the American people. When Congress voted to create an Office of Education during the early years of his administration, the president appointed Terrell Bell as the first Secretary, in an attempt to subvert this new cabinet position.

However, much to the newly elected president's chagrin, Bell decided that the newly constituted position was an important one and that it should not return to its former placement as a segment of the Office of Health, Education, and Welfare. The issue was over the continuing controversy of whether the country should have a strong nationally focused educational system or 50 separate educational entities housed in each state.

References: Chip Berlet (Ed.), *Eyes Right! Challenging the Right Wing Backlash* (Boston: South End Press, 1995); David W. Reinhard, *The Republican Right Since 1945* (Lexington: The University Press of Kentucky, 1983).

RESEGREGATION, a concept in the multicultural education lexicon, refers to a sociological concept suggesting that after the *Brown v. Board of Education* Supreme Court decision that declared racial segregation to be unconstitutional, new patterns of racial segregation commenced to resurface throughout the United States.

Since the historic *Brown v. Board of Education* decision, many European-American families sought ways in which they could distance themselves from African Americans. The two critical issues related to housing and education. In the housing market, many European Americans were willing to sell their homes for less than the market rate to move away from African-American persons. To do this, a procedure called "white flight" referred to the practice of European Americans leaving their homes to distance themselves from African-American families.

One phenomenon, which led to racially-segregated living environments, was caused by the movement of European Americans away from racially integrated neighborhoods to suburban neighborhoods that were located away from inner-city areas. Such locales were havens for European Americans who became concerned about high crime rates and a number of issues related to the schooling of their children.

Another factor entering into the resegregation equation pertained to the public attitude toward American schools. As the population of America's public school system commenced to consist of larger numbers of low-income children, the perception was that public schools were deteriorating in quality. Consequently, many affluent families commenced to place their children in private schools. Since the private schools required the payment of tuition expenses and persons of color sometimes had a difficult time affording such tuition payments, the population of the private schools tended to become skewed with large proportions of European-American children.

Thus, the resegregation of American society, particularly in educational and residential circles, occurred in spite of the *Brown v. Board of Education* Supreme Court decision and increased in intensity during the decade of the 1990s.

Reference: Daniel U. Levine and Robert J. Havighurst, *Society and Education* (Boston: Allyn and Bacon, 1992).

RESERVATION SYSTEM FOR U.S. NATIVE AMERICANS was developed as a result of the increasing number of Europeans who migrated into the lands that had long been the homeland for the original residents of the United States. Educational programs for Native American children have been provided by public school districts, such as the Toppenish School District in south-central Washington, by Bureau of Indian Affairs schools throughout the United States, or by private schools, such as the St. Labre Indian School in Ashland, Montana.

During the administration of President Ulysses S. Grant, following the termination of the Civil War, the United States commenced to create large numbers of Indian Reservations. Since the American Revolution and extending to 1830, Native Americans were treated as if they resided in foreign nations within the United States As the Europeans moved westward and as the need for land became exacerbated, the physical conflicts between the two groups escalated dramatically.

Most of the newly established reservations were developed within the Plains States. Treaties were established with tribes, such as the Cherokee, who had been removed from the South. By the start of the reservation movement, Native Americans had negotiated treaties between the European Americans and the Native Americans. The new European groups did not challenge the Reservation lands, because they believed that the lands were too arid to grow crops. Originally, it was felt that the new reservations had to be large enough to grow crops.

In 1887, the General Allotment Act (also known as the Dawes Severalty Act) was passed to treat Native Americans as individuals, rather than as members of tribes. The legislation also provided for the end of the Reservation system. The Menominee tribe was one group that voted to terminate its tribal status as a result of this legislation.

One of the problems with Reservations that were administered by the Bureau of Indian Affairs (BIA) was that the BIA sometimes seemed reluctant to help Native Americans maintain their original cultural value systems. However, John Collier, appointed as head of the BIA by President Franklin Roosevelt in 1933, helped President Roosevelt pass the Indian Reorganization Act of 1934. This law gave Native Americans control of their lands.

References: William Brandon, *The Indian in American Culture* (New York: Harper and Row, 1974); Henry E. Fritz, *The Movement for Indian Assimilation* (Philadelphia: The University of Pennsylvania Press, 1963); Benson Priest, *Uncle Sam's Stepchildren: The Reformation of Unites States Indian Policy, 1885–1887* (New Brunswick, NJ: Rutgers University Press, 1942); Wilcomb E. Washburn, *The Indian in America* (New York: Harper and Row, 1975).

REVERSE DISCRIMINATION is a term referring to practices that are used in connection with quota systems and policies to set aside jobs and entrance to specific academic programs on the basis of a person's race. For example, prior to 1978, the University of California, Davis, set aside 60 of its 100 admission slots to medical school for persons who were not European Americans. Opponents of such practices declared them to constitute "reverse discrimination" against European Americans.

While the U.S. Supreme Court declared that such practices were not unconstitutional, they ordered the University to admit Bakke to its medical school on the grounds that his civil rights had been violated and he was not allowed to apply for the quota slots.

The quota systems were one practice carried on under the rubric of "Affirmative Action," which attempts to allow more persons of color to be represented in the various professions and in the higher echelons of business and commerce. Reverse discrimination accusations have been initiated by European-American males, who often become convinced that their non-selection to various jobs and/or school programs has occurred solely because of their race and gender. The rancor has peaked during the decade of the 1990s as several states have passed legislation prohibiting the utilization of any affirmative action programs. For example, California passed an anti-affirmative action measure that terminated all admission quotas in university programs. Passage of the measure resulted in fewer persons of color being admitted to law schools, medical schools, etc. *See also* AFFIRMATIVE ACTION; BAKKE, ALLAN; QUOTA SYSTEMS.

References: James A. Banks, *Teaching Strategies for Ethnic Studies*, 6th ed. (Boston: Allyn and Bacon, 1997); James A. Johnson, et al., *Introduction to the Foundations of American Education* (Boston: Allyn and Bacon, 1996); Bruce M. Mitchell, et al., *The Dynamic Classroom*, 5th ed. (Dubuque IA: Kendall/Hunt, 1995).

RITES OF PASSAGE are the various activities of Native American tribes used in religious, social, and funeral ceremonies to ease grief and to perpetuate the leadership behaviors of the various tribes. The four primary events associated with rites of passage are birth, naming, marriage, and death. These rites of passage are associated with the movement from one phase of life to another.

Childbirth has been viewed as a crisis time for Native American people because of the high infant mortality rate. The notion of life existing in the body of a woman was viewed with the utmost reverence, since the entire process of childbirth was thought to be an act of the Creator. The Creator was implored to provide safety for the mother and infant alike.

Until Native American children were named, they were considered to be powerless. The belief was that they would acquire some status when the spirits recognized them after they had become named. Persons could have several names during their lives. The first name occurred at birth, another one as a young child, while still another name could be utilized during an important event in one's life.

Marriage was treated differently by different tribes. Some tribes had no actual marriage ceremonies and people were considered to be married when the first child was born. Cherokee marriages were celebrated with separate feasting by the bride and groom with their relatives and after that a community ceremony took place. Hopi brides were required to grind corn for several days, and later the same procedure was carried out at the groom's house for three days.

Navajos feared death and the ceremonies were brief. The deceased were placed in crevices and covered with stones after the body was bathed and dressed in fine clothing and jewelry. In the Great Basin, burials often took place in caves, while in California, cremation was common. The Hurons held a feast for the dead every ten to twelve years.

Teachers who attempt to portray accurate pictures of Native Americans can create curriculum sequences that include accurate portrayals of Native American microcultures to counteract the inaccurate pictures portrayed by Hollywood movie productions. In addition to teaching about traditional Native American cultural values, it is also important to help students acquire accurate depictions of Native Americans in modern times.

References: Paula Gunn Allen, *The Sacred Hoop: Recovering the Feminine in American Indian Traditions* (Boston: Beacon Press, 1992); Marwyn S. Gabarino, *Native-American Heritage* (Boston: Little, Brown, 1976); Victor W. Turner, *The Ritual Process: Structure and Anti-Structure* (Chicago: Aldine, 1969).

RIVERA, DIEGO (1886–1957), a talented Mexican-American muralist, is a fine example of a Mexican-American artist who can be used by classroom teachers to illustrate the numerous contributions of Latinos in the United States. Politically controversial because of his leftist leanings, Rivera's murals frequently depicted the plight of the working poor. He was often commissioned to paint murals in post offices and other public buildings. One of his best efforts was a mural that he painted in the Burbank, California, Post Office during the 1940s.

Reference: Marilyn P. Davis, *Mexican Voices, Mexican Dreams* (New York: Henry Holt, 1990).

ROBESON, PAUL (1898–1976), an outstanding student athlete at Rutgers University and an important African-American singer, made his major entertainment debut in *Body and Soul*, a film by Oscar Micheaux. In 1933, he became the first African-American performer to play in a starring role with European Americans, who were in less important roles. *Emperor Jones* was Robeson's first movie in which he was the star. He became the first African-American actor to play the title role in *Othello* on Broadway.

In 1946, Robeson founded the Progressive Party, which lobbied for the passage of more progressive political legislation. At the start of the Korean War, he criticized the U.S. Government for its treatment of African Americans and questioned the morality of asking African-American soldiers to fight against the Communist forces in North Korea. He received an award for his political efforts from the National Church of Nigeria, which declared Robeson to be the ''Champion of African Freedom.'' In 1952, he became the first American to receive the International Stalin Peace Prize.

Because of his visits to the Soviet Union, he was required to testify before Senator Joseph McCarthy's House Committee on Un-American Activities. In 1958, Robeson and his wife moved to the Soviet Union to escape the racial discrimination that existed in the United States. They returned to the United States in 1963. In 1960, he received the German Peace Medal for bringing attention to the appalling conditions under which the Australian aborigines were forced to live.

Reference: Sharon Harley, *The Timetables of African-American History* (New York: Simon and Schuster, 1995).

ROBINSON, JACKIE (1919–1972), one of baseball's legendary greats, was also famous for becoming the first African American to play in the major leagues in the United States. Born in Cairo, Georgia, in 1919, he was raised in Pasadena, California, and attended Pasadena Junior College, where he became well known for his extraordinary athletic prowess. Later he enrolled at UCLA where he excelled in baseball, football, track, and basketball.

After spending three years in the U.S. Army during World War II, he received a medical discharge in 1945 and spent a year playing baseball for the Kansas City Monarchs in the Negro National League. By that time, baseball owners recognized the enormous talent pool in the Negro Leagues, and Branch Rickey, president of the Brooklyn Dodgers (now the Los Angeles Dodgers), picked him to become the first African American to break the color line in baseball.

After playing for the Montreal Royals, a Brooklyn Dodger farm team, Rickey brought him up to the Brooklyn Dodgers. During his first year with the Dodgers in 1947, he batted .297, scored 125 runs, and stole 29 bases to lead the league. He was named Rookie of the Year. In 1949, he was named the most valuable player in the National League, batting .342, stealing 37 bases, scoring 122 runs, batting in 124 runs and getting 203 hits. Moreover, he led the league three years in fielding.

While Robinson's baseball talents are well known, perhaps his most important accomplishment was his ability to deal with the racism that occurred as a result of breaking the color barrier. Robinson's successes, both on and off the field, paved the way for other African-American athletes. He also became the first African-American athlete to have his picture placed on the cover of *Life Magazine*.

While Robinson's accomplishments occurred prior to the beginning of the American Civil Rights Movement, classroom teachers can look upon his breakthrough, along with Truman's order to desegregate the armed forces, as key events leading to the *Brown v. Board of Education* Supreme Court decision and other critical events that helped to usher in the Civil Rights era.

References: Sharon Harley, *The Timetables of African-American History* (New York: Simon and Schuster, 1995); Gerald David Jaynes and Robin M. Williams (Eds.), *A*

Common Destiny: Blacks and American Society (Washington, DC: National Academy Press, 1989).

ROGERS, WILL (1879–1935), a Cherokee, became one of the first Native Americans to gain fame as a movie actor. Rogers became famous for his subtle humor, which he used in poking fun at the racism existing in the United States. In the film, *More than Bows and Arrows*, narrated by prize-winning author Scott Momaday, a Kiowa, he deadpanned the famous line, "Well I wasn't one of those Americans who come [*sic*] over on the Mayflower, but we met 'em at the boat when they landed."

Born in 1879, he acquired a deep pride in his Cherokee heritage and exhibited his unique skills in an outstanding career as an entertainer. Rogers was well known for his generosity and his sense of humility. He died in a plane crash in 1935. Rogers can provide teachers with an excellent example of the numerous contributions made by Native Americans in the entertainment field.

Reference: Harvey Markowitz (Ed.), *American Indians* (Pasadena, CA: Salem Press, 1995).

ROOSEVELT, FRANKLIN DELANO (1882–1945) was born at Hyde Park, New York, the son of English and Dutch parents. His early life was quite sheltered, as he was educated by governesses and his life was deeply affected by the family estate in a rural section of Dutchess County. His childhood hobbies were swimming, stamp and bird collecting, and boating. His education at Groton School in Massachusetts helped him to acquire a strong sense of social responsibility.

He married a distant cousin, Anna Eleanor Roosevelt, whose uncle was President Theodore Roosevelt. The Roosevelts were active in social circles but were also sensitive to the problems encountered by persons in poverty circumstances. He became Assistant Secretary of the Navy after he backed candidate Woodrow Wilson at the 1912 Democratic National Convention. By this time, he was becoming known as a leading progressive figure in the Democratic Party, and in 1920, he was the vice-presidential candidate with newspaper publisher, Governor James Cox of Ohio. However, Warren Harding won the election handily, campaigning on a promise to "return the country to normalcy." Roosevelt defended Wilson's advocacy of U.S. membership in the League of Nations.

While vacationing at his Campobello Island home, Roosevelt suffered from Poliomyelitis during the summer of 1921. After his recuperation, he retired to Hyde Park but was encouraged by his wife, Eleanor, to return to politics, which he did. He was persuaded by losing candidate Al Smith to run for the New York governorship, which resulted in a narrow victory. The stock market crash of 1929, and the resulting economic depression, led to his easy victory over Herbert Hoover in 1932.

His New Deal legislation resulted in numerous social programs, such as the

Works Projects Administration (WPA), that were designed to help unemployed persons get back to work. He became known as the "golden-tongued orator," and he was able to stir the passions of Americans throughout the country. His re-election campaign against Republican Alfred M. Landon resulted in the greatest electoral sweep in the nation's history.

However, much of his New Deal legislation was declared to be unconstitutional by the conservative U.S. Supreme Court. He was rebuffed in his attempt to increase the size of the Court with younger, more liberal members. By 1932, World War II had begun in Europe and Roosevelt attempted to keep the United States away from any direct involvement. However, when the Japanese bombed Pearl Harbor in 1941, Roosevelt asked the Congress to declare war against the Axis powers. Soon after, he ordered Japanese Americans to be incarcerated in ten relocation centers, mostly in the West. During the war, the armed forces were still racially segregated.

However, the pressures of war and the enormous pressures of his three terms in office took their toll. After the Yalta Conference, Roosevelt traveled to Warm Springs, Georgia, to rest after he was totally exhausted from overwork. On April 12, 1945, he died from a cerebral hemorrhage.

Few other presidencies have been more controversial. The first president to opt for a third and fourth term, Roosevelt was forced to take decisive actions to preserve the country's capitalistic economic system. He backed the western forces during World War II to help preserve the democratic institutions of the Western world. He was also effective in addressing the nagging needs of America's working poor. From a multicultural perspective, he was able to attract the presidential support of the poverty powerless and persons of color from urban areas.

References: Dean Acheson, *Present at the Creation* (New York: W. W. Norton, 1969); James MacGregor Burns, *Roosevelt: The Lion and the Fox* (New York: Harcourt, Brace, 1956); Max Freedman, *Roosevelt and Frankfurter: Their Correspondence, 1928–1945* (Boston: Little, Brown, 1967); Willard Range, *Franklin D. Roosevelt's World Order* (Athens: University of Georgia Press, 1959).

S

SALAD BOWL THEORY, a phrase that surfaced during the Civil Rights Movement of the 1960s, refers to the notion that American pluralism has been the concept that made the country great. The ''melting-pot theory,'' which originally was articulated in New York City as the result of a turn of the century play by Israel Zangwill, became viewed by some as a racist concept implying that persons who were not English-speaking European Americans should attempt to acquire the language and value structure of the dominant culture, which was that of English-speaking Europeans.

The ''melting-pot theory'' suggested that an assimilationist practice was what should occur. Immigrants should reject their ethnicity and adapt the value structure of the English-speaking Europeans. However, the ''salad-bowl theory'' relied on the analogy that each ingredient of a succulent salad was important to the total taste. Eliminate the croutons, tomatoes, or lettuce and some of the original flavor disappeared. Take away the mushrooms, peppers or salad dressing and the same thing would happen.

Likewise, the analogy pertains to a similar situation with human beings. The excitement of the United States rests in its cultural diversity. Human diversity is what makes the United States unique. So while obviously there is a great need for a set of macrocultural values, the microcultures in the land are what provides the nation with its marvelous flavors. *See also* STEW THEORY.

Reference: George E. Pozzetta (Ed.), *Assimilation, Acculturation, and Social Mobility* (New York: Garland, 1991).

SAND CREEK MASSACRE, occurring in Colorado in 1864, involved the Arapaho and Cheyenne tribes, who were attacked by the Colorado Calvary. An

1851 treaty gave the Cheyenne and Arapaho an area of land bounded by the Arkansas and North Platte rivers on the north and a line stretching from Dodge City, Kansas, to North Platte, Nebraska, on the east and west. As was true in other parts of the west at that time, the discovery of gold resulted in an incursion of European Americans into that part of the country. A failed treaty involving the Cheyenne and Arapaho led to attempted negotiations between the Native Americans and a European-American contingency, led by territorial governor John Evans in 1863.

However, the Native American factions disdained Evans' attempts at negotiation. As a result, the First Colorado Cavalry and Third Colorado Cavalry, under the command of Colonel John M. Chivington, raided a small group of Cheyenne and Arapahoe Indians who were camped at Sand Creek. Chivington's forces attacked about 500 Native American women and children, resulting in several hundred deaths. There were about 47 trooper casualties, including nine fatalities.

The massacre precipitated a large uprising among the tribes of the plains, including the Cheyenne and Arapahoe. Finally, in 1869, the Battle of Summitt Springs put an end to most of the hostilities between the Native Americans and the European-American settlers.

References: Reginald S. Craig, *The Fighting Parson: The Biography of Colonel John M. Chivington* (Los Angeles: Westernlore Press, 1959); William R. Dunn, *I Stand by Sand Creek: A Defense of Colonel John F. Chivington and the Third Colorado Cavalry* (Ft. Collins, CO: Old Animal Press, 1985); Stan Hoig, *The Sand Creek Massacre* (Norman: University of Oklahoma Press, 1961); Michael A. Sievers, "Sands of Sand Creek Historiography," *Colorado Magazine* 49 (Spring 1972); David Svaldi, *Sand Creek and the Rhetoric of Extermination: A Case Study in Indian-White Relations* (Lanham, MD: University Press of America, 1989).

SANTA ANNA, ANTONIO LOPEZ DE (1797–1874), a Mexican General during the Mexican War was a dominant leader for 30 years, leading his nation against the forces of the United States. Between 1824 and 1845, Santa Anna shifted his loyalties to different Mexican political groups. In 1829, he won an important battle against the Spanish at Tampico, which helped him become President of Mexico in 1833.

Born in 1797, Santa Anna became a cadet in the Spanish army, fighting against Native Mexicans in the northern part of the country. He joined an independence movement led by Agustin de Iturbide but eventually decided not to back him, and Iturbide was overthrown.

During his period of leadership commencing in 1833, Santa Anna faced a series of rebellions but led the successful campaign against Texas rebels at the Alamo in 1836. However, in 1847 he was defeated and captured by the Americans at San Jacinto, leading up to the Treaty of Guadalupe Hidalgo that ended the Mexican War and gave the United States all or part of the existing states of

California, Arizona, New Mexico, Texas, Utah, Nevada, and Colorado. After going into exile, he returned to Mexico in 1853, assuming the leadership of the country until he was overthrown in 1855. After living in Cuba until 1874, Santa Anna returned to Mexico where he died during that year. Santa Anna provides teachers with a key figure, who had important implications in the development of multicultural America. This story of the American Southwest is part of the history of the Mexican people and provides historians with important insights about the Mexican-American macroculture.

References: Carey McWilliams, *North from Mexico: The Spanish-Speaking People of the United States* (Westport, CT: Greenwood Press, 1990); Ronald Takaki, *A Different Mirror: A History of Multicultural America* (Boston: Little, Brown, 1993).

SCHOOL PROGRAMS FOR INTERCULTURAL COMMUNITY EXPLORATION (SPICE), funded through Title IV of the Elementary/Secondary Education Act, allowed grant recipients to develop desegregation centers that provided needed services for school districts and social services agencies. The services addressed various problems stemming from racial matters. One of the more successful programs was housed at Eastern Washington University and served the Region Ten area of the Pacific Northwest.

The SPICE Cadre for Action Training (SPICECATS) worked with school districts and social service agencies to help develop more positive attitudes about racial diversity and to solve a variety of problems related in some way to racial desegregation occurring during the 1960s as a result of the historic *Brown v. Board of Education* Supreme Court decision of 1954.

One such program centered around racial confrontations occurring at a Pacific Northwest high school. A specific incident related to a brief scuffle between an African-American and a European-American student in the school cafeteria. The local newspaper described the incident as a ''race riot.'' The SPICE consultants helped school district participation teams identify the problem, which was the manner in which the local newspaper reported such issues. They then created a plan of action designed to help the local newspaper make appropriate changes in their reporting practices.

A second example of their activities related to the 1974 International Exposition in Spokane, Washington. The Spokane Police Department participated in a series of workshops designed to assist the officers in working effectively with visitors from all over the United States and throughout the world. Since Spokane is an isolated small city with a 95 percent European-American population, the concern was that officers might not be able to deal with possible problems occurring due to the array of cultural differences among the 5 million visitors.

Reference: Dr. Edward Dodson, Director, Operation SPICE, 36946 Madrona Blvd., N.E., Hansville, WA 98340.

SCOTT, DRED v. SANDFORD was a landmark Supreme Court decision resulting in the declaration that an African-American slave could not become a citizen under the U.S. Constitution. Scott was owned by John Emerson, who took him to Illinois, a free state, as a result of the Northwest Ordinance of 1787. After being returned to Missouri, he sued the state for his freedom by virtue of his residence in Illinois. Losing the case, he then brought federal suit after Scott became the property of Emerson's wife's brother, John F. A. Sandford.

Eventually reaching the United States Supreme Court, the case was heard in 1857. By a vote of 7–2 the Supreme Court ruled that Scott was not a citizen and, therefore, had no right to sue in the courts. Chief Justice Roger B. Taney, in his majority opinion, wrote that neither free nor enslaved African Americans could ever be considered citizens according to the U.S. Constitution. Scott had not become "free" because of his residence in a free territory. Whatever his temporary status in Illinois, he eventually returned to Missouri where his status pertained to Missouri law. The case was one of the most controversial in American history and seemed to be a major factor in leading to the beginning of the Civil War.

The case provides educators with an important focus on one of the key issues of the Civil War—the morality of slavery. It also provides teachers with the opportunity to examine the issues that can be addressed by the Supreme Court and the manner in which it functions.

References: Kern Alexander and M. David Alexander, *American Public School Law* (Belmont, CA: Wadsworth, 1998); Sharon Harley, *The Timetables of African-American History* (New York: Simon and Schuster, 1995).

SEMINOLE TRIBE, located in Florida and Oklahoma, includes groups of Native Americans from Georgia and Alabama, moved into northern Florida. The name comes from a Muskogee word, *seminola*, meaning "wild." The Seminoles are members of the Muskogean language group, and the population is about 13,797, according to the 1990 Census.

Following the American Revolution, conflicts evolved between the European settlers and the Seminoles. Seminoles sought protection from Britain due to the attacks by European settlers who complained that the Seminoles helped to hide runaway slaves. After being involved in the Creek War of 1813–1814, General Andrew Jackson invaded Florida and destroyed the Seminole towns in the northern portion of the state.

After Florida was ceded to the United States in 1819, the Seminoles realized that they were in territories occupied by their old enemies. By 1823 they gave up their claim to Northern Florida and the U.S. government pressured them to leave the area completely. In 1832, a few Seminoles signed the Treaty of Payne's Landing. However, the treaty was not honored. When the federal government attempted to remove them in 1835, the second Seminole War broke out.

Approximately 3,000 Seminole people were removed to the Indian Territory but about 500 Seminoles fled to the Everglades, where they make their home. The Seminoles were given land in Oklahoma, but in 1906, the Seminole government was terminated and the land was allotted to Seminole members in 120-acre plots. Some of the Seminoles became wealthy because of the oil discoveries in the area. By 1930 a majority of Florida Seminoles resided on reservation lands.

References: James H. Howard and Willie Lena, *Oklahoma Seminoles* (Norman: University of Oklahoma Press, 1984); Daniel F. Littlefield, *Africans and Seminoles: From Removal to Emancipation* (Westport, CT: Greenwood Press, 1977); Edwyn C. McReynolds, *The Seminoles* (Norman: University of Oklahoma Press, 1957).

SEPARATE BUT EQUAL DOCTRINE, a concept emerging as a result of the 1896 *Plessy v. Ferguson* Supreme Court decision, established a constitutionally defensible rationale for segregated facilities in the United States. Prior to that time the "Separate But Equal" concept was assumed to be a legal practice that had been occurring during the Reconstruction Period, particularly in the southern states. For America's schools, it meant the perpetuation of a two-tiered education system for African-American and European-American children. The practice resulted in a decidedly inferior system of education for African-American students.

The *Plessy v. Ferguson* Supreme Court decision provided a legal justification for the Separate But Equal Doctrine. The principle was not rejected until the *Brown v. Board of Education* Supreme Court decision of 1954 that made racial segregation unconstitutional and illegal.

References: S. Alexander Rippa, *Education in a Free Society: An American History* (New York: Longman, 1988); Ronald Takaki, *A Different Mirror: A History of Multicultural America* (Boston: Little, Brown, 1993); Charles Thompson, "Harlan's Great Dissent," *Kentucky Humanities*, No. 1 (1996).

SEPARATISM is a term referring to non-European-American groups of people who attempt to distance themselves from the European-American majority. This occurs when the minority group decides that it is difficult to participate with members of the majority culture due to racist actions that make it impossible for the minority group to participate successfully in the macroculture. Separatist actions also include a heightened sense of racial and/or ethnic pride.

In the case of African Americans, for example, separatism existed since the days of slavery when separatism was forced. Even through the days of reconstruction, separatism was forced through the segregation of schools, drinking fountains, restaurants, hotels, and the like. Following the American Civil Rights Movement, when many institutions were integrated, African Americans continued to suffer from the more subtle racist actions of European Americans, resulting in new separatist actions.

Sometimes separatist tendencies among Latinos appear to be stronger than those of African Americans. In this case, the retention of the Spanish language seems to be a powerful motivational factor for the separatist philosophy, thus constituting a movement away from assimilation. On the other hand, the attainment of English proficiency may help the Spanish-speaking American to function well in both cultures and lessen the drive for separatism.

For teachers, the concept of separatism is important for students to understand. Curriculum units can examine the separatist movements of leaders such as Marcus Garvey, Louis Farrakhan, and others to learn why groups of people felt that separatism was important for their well-being. Classroom debates might argue the merits or disadvantages of eastern Canada's bilingual issues as they relate to separatism.

References: James A. Banks, *Teaching Strategies for Ethnic Studies*, 6th ed. (Boston: Allyn and Bacon, 1996); Daniel Levine and Robert J. Havighurst, *Society and Education* (Boston: Allyn and Bacon, 1992); A. Portes and R. G. Rumbaut, *Immigrant America* (Berkeley, CA: University of California Press, 1990).

SEXISM relates to stereotypical attitudes toward human beings because of their gender. It is an issue that has deeply affected the schools throughout the history of American education. Sexual stereotypes have frequently occurred in the literature and curriculum materials used in the schools. Perhaps the most blatant example of sexism in written materials has been the persistent use of the masculine pronoun (he) when referring to both genders.

One major problem for female students has been the messages they get from the written materials. Consistently, children's story books have portrayed masculine protagonists as being adventuresome, risk takers, able to pursue numerous challenging occupations, creative, good in math/science and aggressive, while female protagonists have seldom exhibited such traits.

Reviews of the literature have revealed that sex-biased language distorts students' perceptions of reality and that many popular instructional materials are gender-biased. On the other hand, gender-equitable instructional materials have been found to enhance students' sex-role behaviors and heighten learning motivation. Good gender-equitable materials can influence the behaviors of children.

References: Christine I. Bennett, *Comprehensive Multicultural Education: Theory and Practice*, 3d ed. (Boston: Allyn and Bacon, 1995); Daniel U. Levine and Robert J. Havighurst, *Society and Education* (Boston: Allyn and Bacon, 1992); Kathryn Scott and Candace Schau, "Sex Equity and Sex Bias in Instructional Materials," in Susan S. Klein (Ed.), *Handbook for Achieving Sex Equity Through Education* (Baltimore: Johns Hopkins University Press, 1985).

SHARECROPPERS, a group of low-income farmers from the southern states, do not normally own any farmland, but work for landowners for a share of the crops. They receive a proportion of the profits in return for doing the work of raising crops on a given piece of land.

Many American sharecroppers have been the descendants of African slaves who chose to stay on the plantations or farms after the end of the Civil War. Due to their vulnerable position, many people were forced to remain in the south, and sharecropping actually provided many freed slaves and their offspring with a livelihood.

Sharecroppers have included large numbers of African Americans. Many of them suffered severe problems when the farmowners had their land subsidized by the Federal government. This meant that sometimes there were no arable acres on which the sharecroppers could raise crops, necessitating them to rely on welfare to survive. Thus, many African Americans in sections of the rural south became part of the poverty-powerless microculture in the United States.

SILENT MAJORITY, a reference to the surging conservative Republican faction that surfaced during the campaign of Ronald Reagan in the 1980 presidential campaign, was a concept invented by William Safire. Safire, a former Nixon speechwriter turned conservative columnist, penned the phrase in one of his columns for the *New York Times*. As the phrase implied, the conservative voters in the United States had been silent since the 1928 election of Herbert Hoover.

However, in 1980, the Republican Party took a strong turn to the right and the "Silent Majority" commenced to become much more vocal, when it became acceptable to do so. During the 1980 election, Ronald Reagan won an impressive victory over President Jimmie Carter, the Democratic candidate. Even though a third-party candidate, John Anderson siphoned off nearly 8 percent of the popular vote that might have gone to Jimmie Carter, Reagan still was victorious.

Thus, conservative Republicans re-surfaced as a commanding force in American politics, being dubbed the Silent Majority. A large proportion of the Silent Majority consisted of the religious right, which adamantly backed such concepts as prayer in schools, voucher programs, the abolishment of the income tax, larger expenditures for the military forces, and the termination of abortion.

The Silent Majority was also successful in terminating the illustrious careers of Senators Birch Bayh of Indiana, Frank Church of Idaho, George McGovern of South Dakota, and John Culver of Iowa. Their defeat helped the Republicans gain control of the U.S. Senate in 1982. The Silent Majority, officially referred to as the National Conservative Political Action Committee (NCPAC), targeted Senator Ted Kennedy and Republican Senators Robert T. Stafford of Vermont, John Chafee of Rhode Island, and Lowell Weickert of Connecticut in 1982. This action virtually destroyed the moderate/liberal wing of the Republican Party.

From that time on, it became dominated by the "Silent Majority" and the ultra-conservative "Moral Majority" of Jerry Falwell.

For educators, it is necessary to examine the constitutionality of several basic principles espoused in the platform of the Silent Majority. Two of the more obvious notions are the issues of prayer in schools and voucher systems. Supreme Court decisions such as *Wallace v. Jaffree* in 1985, *Steele v. Van Buren* in 1988, and *Doe v. Duncanville Independent School District* in 1993 have declared school prayer to be unconstitutional. In a like manner, the funding of private schools with public funds has also been declared to be unconstitutional in *Lemon v. Kurtzman* in 1971, *Levitt v. Committee for Public Education and Religious Liberty* in 1973, and *Meek v. Pittenger* in 1975. Nonetheless, the Silent Majority still lobbies for these and other practices in America's public schools.

References: *The 1994 Deskbook Encyclopedia of American School Law* (Rosemount, MN: Data Research, 1994); David W. Reinhard, *The Republican Right Since 1945* (Lexington: University of Kentucky Press, 1983).

SIOUX TRIBE, with a population of better than 100,000 persons, is one of the largest Native American tribes in the United States. Part of the Siouan language group, the Sioux are concentrated in South Dakota, Montana, North Dakota, Minnesota, Nebraska, Manitoba, and Saskatchewan. The term "Sioux" actually referred to a complex web of bands and tribes that were located in the forested areas of the northern Mississippi. Sioux who spoke any dialect of Dakota considered themselves to be allies, while those who spoke other tongues were considered enemies unless they had negotiated a treaty.

Socially, the core of traditional Sioux society was the extended family, which consisted of relatives living together in a spirit of cooperation. Social units at the next larger level were considered to be Tiyospaye or "lodge groups." The Tiyospaye provided a mechanism for establishing and maintaining social order.

Beginning in the early 1800s, the Sioux in both the United States and Canada negotiated a number of treaties, many of which were broken. European-American encroachments into Sioux lands, along with numerous broken promises, resulted in a number of conflicts that culminated in direct wars with the United States in 1862 and 1877. These Sioux Wars include the Minnesota Uprising of 1862, the War for the Bozeman Trail from 1866–1868, and the famous Battle of the Little Bighorn in 1876. The Teton Sioux were considered to be the most aggressive faction of Sioux in attempting to prevent the European-American encroachments of their lands.

By 1877, most Sioux were on reservations, resulting in the demise of living standards and the development of severe health problems by 1889. At this time, they were severely disturbed over the loss of millions of acres of their reservation lands. Before being forced into reservation status, the Sioux enjoyed excellent buffalo herds, an ample supply of horses, and good health.

As a result of the deplorable conditions on the Sioux reservation, many tribal members participated in the Ghost Dance, which created an atmosphere of hostility between the U.S. government and the Sioux. A major conflict resulted in the Wounded Knee Massacre in which approximately 300 Sioux men, women, and children were killed by the Seventh Cavalry.

By the mid-1930s, the Federal government attempted to get out of the business of tribal government, encouraging tribes such as the Sioux to establish constitutional forms of government and create elected tribal councils to conduct their business and govern the people. The passage of the Indian Reorganization Act (IRA) of 1934 made this possible.

At the present time, the population of the Sioux people is increasing with the majority of the people residing on six reservations in South Dakota. However, large numbers of Sioux also live in such locales as Rapid City, South Dakota, Denver, the San Francisco Bay area, and Los Angeles. All of the tribal reservations are fighting to maintain the original cultural values.

References: Thomas Biolsi, *Organizing the Lakota: The Political Economy of the New Deal on the Pine Ridge and Rosebud Reservations* (Tucson: University of Arizona Press, 1992); Joseph Epes Brown (Ed.), *The Sacred Pipe: Black Elk's Account of the Seven Rites of the Oglala Sioux* (Norman: University of Oklahoma Press, 1953); Frances Densmore, *Teton Sioux Music and Culture* (Lincoln: University of Nebraska Press, 1992); George E. Hyde, *Red Cloud's Folk: A History of the Oglala Sioux Indians* (Norman: University of Oklahoma Press, 1937); James Mooney, *The Ghost Dance Religion and the Sioux Outbreak of 1890*, Annual Report of the Bureau of American Ethnology, 14 (Washington, DC: U.S. Government Printing Office, 1896).

SIRHAN SIRHAN (1943–), a Jordanian immigrant, assassinated Robert F. Kennedy in California during Kennedy's candidacy for the Democratic presidential nomination. After the fatal shooting in the kitchen of the Ambassador Hotel, Sirhan Sirhan was wrestled to the ground by Rafer Johnson and Roosevelt Grier, who were campaigning with Kennedy. Johnson and Grier were part of a coalition of enthusiastic supporters including young people, African Americans, professionals, and blue-collar workers. Also shot were Paul Schrade, Ira Goldstein, Irwin Stroll, and Elizabeth Evans. Sirhan Sirhan, who resided in Pasadena, was convicted and sentenced to life imprisonment. The incident occurred toward the end of the American Civil Rights Movement and brought national attention to the increasing incidents of gun violence throughout the country.

Reference: Robert Blair Kaiser, *R.F.K. Must Die! A History of the Robert Kennedy Assassination and its Aftermath* (New York: E. P. Dutton, 1970).

SIT-INS, occurring during the American Civil Rights Movement, were carried out by protest groups interested in making changes in practices deemed to be unfair and even unconstitutional. One of the first sit-ins occurred in Chicago during the 1940s. It was relatively unsuccessful. However, in 1958, branches of the National Association for the Advancement of Colored People (NAACP) enjoyed moderate successes with their sit-ins in Kansas and Oklahoma.

Perhaps the most publicized sit-in occurred in 1960 in Greensboro, North Carolina, when four African-American students from North Carolina A & T College staged a sit-in at a Woolworth's lunch counter. When they were denied service and refused to leave, they were harassed by angry groups of European Americans. This and other incidents attracted attention nationally and helped pave the way for the integration of lunch counters.

Similar sit-ins occurred in Nashville, Tennessee, when some 200 young African Americans were mobilized to stage sit-ins at the city's lunch counters. After the first sit-in, the police came and arrested the demonstrators, ignoring the attacks on the African Americans by European Americans who threw them off the counter stools. After much violence and a great deal of lost revenue, the lunch counters were finally integrated.

Later, during the American Civil Rights Movement, the tactic was used in universities by students who wished to make changes in administrative policies. While most of the sit-ins occurred large universities, such as the University of California (Berkeley) and the University of Wisconsin (Madison), sit-ins were also undertaken at smaller colleges with mostly European-American students, such as Eastern Washington University. Often, the sit-ins would occur in the university president's office and students would present the president with a list of demands.

References: Sharon Harley, *The Timetables of African-American History* (New York: Simon and Schuster, 1995); Juan Williams, *Eyes on the Prize: America's Civil Rights Years, 1954–1965* (New York: Viking Press, 1987).

SITTING BULL (CHIEF) (1831–1890), leader of the Lakota Sioux, was chief of the tribe during the famous Battle of the Little Big Horn in which the Sioux nation destroyed the forces of General George Custer. Born in the early 1830s, Sitting Bull (Tantanka Lyotanka) was called Hunkesni (Slow) because of his deliberate manner that became a lifelong characteristic. He became known as an excellent hunter at the age of 10 when he killed a buffalo. When he was 14, he again exhibited unusual courage and was given the name "Sitting Bull" in a special ceremony.

Later, he distinguished himself in doing battle with enemy tribes such as the Crow, Hidatsa, Gros Ventre, and Assinboine. He became part of the Strong Hearts Warrior Society at the age of about 20 years. He was a sash wearer, and only the very bravest were allowed to wear sashes. By 1856, he had become such an outstanding warrior that he was awarded a membership in the Midnight Strong Heart Society, an honor reserved for the bravest of the brave. During a battle with the Crow tribe, he was wounded in the foot, causing him to limp the rest of his life.

About this time, the European-American encroachments occurred in the northern section of the Great Plains. Sitting Bull gained national recognition for his effective attacks on settlers and soldiers at Fort Buford, located at the juncture of the Yellowstone and Missouri Rivers.

By 1872, the encroachments by European Americans increased in the Black Hills area after a government-sponsored Black Hills expedition that verified substantial gold deposits in the region. Soon, hordes of gold-seekers poured into the area in search of riches. Moreover, the Federal government failed to enforce a 1868 treaty and refused to negotiate a purchase of the Black Hills region that had been the homeland of the Sioux.

In 1876, Sitting Bull had a vision during a Sun Dance. He saw many soldiers coming into camp. On June 26, 1876, the Sioux destroyed Custer's Army at Little Bighorn. After that the Sioux army broke up into small bands, which were pursued aggressively by U.S. soldiers.

After a less than successful period of about four years in Canada, Sitting Bull surrendered with about 200 people, surrendering his horses and weapons to the federal government. In spite of government promises to quarter him and his followers at the Standing Rock Agency, they were imprisoned at Fort Randall in South Dakota for 2 years. In 1883, he was allowed to join the rest of his people at Standing Rock.

References: Usher Burdick, *The Last Days of Sitting Bull, Sioux Medicine Chief* (Baltimore: Wirth Brothers, 1941); James McLaughlin, *My Friend the Indian* (Lincoln: University of Nebraska Press, 1989); Robert M. Utley, *The Lance and the Shield: The Life and Times of Sitting Bull* (New York: Henry Holt, 1993).

SKINHEADS, a term used in referring to youth gangs whose members have shaved their heads, are usually young European-American males who believe strongly in Aryan supremacy. Some skinheads are members of gangs that harbor racist views and openly discriminate against African Americans and Jews. Sometimes they are sponsored by adult groups of Supremacists. The activities of skinhead groups and other racist organizations are closely monitored by the Southern Poverty Law Center in Montgomery, Alabama.

For teachers, skinheads can cause problems because of their racist attitudes. Often sporting tattoos and wearing bizarre clothing, they have caused problems in the disruption of the educational process. Thus, educators must take steps to ensure that gang activities are not carried on in the schools. Many schools throughout the country have adopted strict dress codes, which disallow gang regalia in any form.

Reference: *Teaching Tolerance* (Montgomery, AL: Southern Poverty Law Center, 1997).

SLAVERY, a societal phenomenon based on power and the exploitation of human beings, is an age-old practice that has destroyed the lives of millions of people throughout history. It has occurred throughout the entire world and among people of virtually every cultural tradition. Moreover, it has been found in a variety of economic and religious systems. For example, during the Crusades, Christians enslaved Muslims, while Muslim pirates enslaved Christians, who were captured passengers.

Spain and Portugal had practiced slavery throughout the Middle Ages. With the European discoveries of the New World, an enormous demand for cheap labor resulted. When the Spanish and Portuguese commenced to enslave African people from West Africa, they discovered that slavery already existed on that continent. European slave traders enlisted African chiefs to provide young, healthy people who would bring the highest prices and would have a better chance of reaching their destination alive.

The first slaves arrived in the English colonies in North America in 1619 and were categorized as indentured servants, similar to the Europeans who came as a result of work contracts. As the plantation system developed, the need for cheap labor intensified, resulting in a dramatic increase in the number of Africans who were sold into slavery in the English colonies. Between the sixteenth and nineteenth centuries, an estimated 8 to 15 million slaves reached the Americas.

Opposition to slavery was orchestrated in the American colonies by religious groups, including the Quakers, Methodists, and Congregationalists. The Quakers (Society of Friends) made their first formal statement opposing slavery in 1724. While individual states abolished slavery, the U.S. Constitution allowed slave trade until 1808. However, even after that time, some illegal slave trade occurred.

Because of anti-slavery sentiment, the British Parliament outlawed slave trade in 1807. As South American countries acquired their independence, slavery was outlawed, as was slave trade in Spain and Portugal in 1840. However, some Portuguese ships were involved in illegal trade throughout the nineteenth century.

Anti-slavery sentiment in the United States intensified with: the publication of William Lloyd Garrison's abolitionist newspaper, *The Liberator*; the creation of the Underground Railway in 1840; the Fugitive Slave Act of 1850; the Dred Scott Decision of 1857; the John Brown Raid on Harper's Ferry in 1859; and literary works, such as *Uncle Tom's Cabin* by Harriett Beecher Stowe.

The resulting Civil War was a bloody confrontation that produced approximately 900,000 casualties. Slaves in the Confederacy were declared to be free as a result of The Emancipation Proclamation enacted in 1863 during the presidency of Abraham Lincoln. The Thirteenth Amendment to the U.S. Constitution officially abolished slavery.

References: W.E.B. Du Bois, *The Suppression of the African Slave Trade to the United States of America, 1638–1870* (New York: Russell and Russell, 1965); Herbert S. Klein, *African Slavery in Latin America and the Caribbean* (New York: Oxford University Press, 1986); Ronald Takaki, *A Different Mirror: A History of Multicultural America* (Boston: Little, Brown, 1993).

SLEEPY LAGOON CASE, resulting from a 1942 incident involving Jose Diaz, a Latino youth found dead in south-central Los Angeles, was one of the incidents responsible for creating a public reaction against Mexican-American youth during World War II. The Sleepy Lagoon was a water-filled gravel pit that had been used by Mexican-American children as a swimming hole. Police reports stated that Diaz was killed in a gang altercation between two groups of Mexican Americans.

The Los Angeles Police charged that Diaz, a member of a group called the Downey Boys, had been murdered by members of a gang referred to as the 38th Street Club. Police arrested 22 club members on charges of conspiracy and murder. In January 1943, an all European-American jury convicted 17 members of the gang of assault and battery and/or first degree murder.

During world War II, Zoot Suit Riots erupted between servicemen and Mexican-American youth. Zoot suits were stylish outfits consisting of baggy trousers with tight pant cuffs and jackets with greatly padded shoulders. The outfit also included a chain decorating the pantleg and a wide-brimmed hat.

The confrontations consisted of a number of violent acts between young Mexican Americans and U.S. servicemen. The Sleepy Lagoon case and the Zoot Suit Riots inflamed the Los Angeles community, stirring up anti-Latino sentiments among the European-American community. Another source of friction was the manner in which two of the Los Angeles newspapers reported the incidents. Such story headlines as "Young Hoodlums Smoke 'Reefers,' Tattoo Girls and Plot Robberies," along with "Grand Jury to Act in Zoot Suit War," helped to fan the flames of racial hatred against Latino youth in the Los Angeles community.

The Sleepy Lagoon Defense Committee was an advocacy organization that functioned in Los Angeles during this period of time. As a result of its efforts, the convictions of the 38th Street Club Defendants were overturned through the legal appeal process.

References: David G. Gutierrez, *Walls and Mirrors: Mexican Americans, Mexican Immigrants, and the Politics of Ethnicity* (Berkeley: University of California Press, 1995); Mauricio Mazon, *The Zoot Suit Riots: The Psychology of Symbolic Annihilation* (Austin: University of Texas Press, 1984); Ricardo Romo, *East Los Angeles: History of a Barrio* (Austin: University of Texas Press, 1983).

SNYDER ACT, also known as the Indian Citizenship Act, granted U.S. citizenship to all Native Americans born within the territorial limits of the United States. However, the legislation did not apply to all Native Americans. For example, persons who were members of tribes or nations with negotiated U.S. government treaties, while they were independent political units, had great difficulty in securing citizenship.

By the late 1800s, many persons concluded that Native Americans should be granted citizenship, and the 1887 General Allotment Act offered citizenship in return for adopting "the habits of civilized life." World War I rekindled the rhetoric for granting citizenship to Native Americans. Consequently, in January 1924, Congressman Homer P. Snyder of New York introduced House Resolution 6355, which granted citizenship to Native Americans without diminishing their right to also become members of their tribal units. The legislation was signed into law by President Calvin Coolidge.

Reference: Vine Deloria, *American Indian Policy in the Twentieth Century* (Norman: University of Oklahoma Press, 1985).

SOCIAL ACTION refers to programs, many of them federally-funded, to help poverty powerless clients become more upwardly mobile. One of the more successful federal efforts was University Year for Action (UYA). The funding legislation was passed early in the Nixon Administration and was designed to utilize the talents of college and university students, who wished to make a difference in the lives of the American underclass.

Receiving grants were schools such as Eastern Washington State College, Western Washington State College, Kent State University, and the Universities of Kentucky and Nebraska. Students were placed in social service agencies that attempted to meet the needs of their low-income clients. They served as quasi-tutors, counselors, teachers, and consultants. Under the supervision of professional social workers, counselors, psychologists, attorneys, and educators, they worked with the clients in various types of social action enterprises.

All of the placements had to involve clients from the culture of poverty. The expertise of the student volunteers was derived through experiential learning courses in given disciplines, along with practical instructional strategies that would facilitate their work with the clients. Some of the agencies in which students were placed consisted of schools, social service agencies, jails and prisons, mental health clinics, and juvenile detention/parole centers.

Participating schools received grants that were awarded for periods of from three to five years. At the end of that time, the schools agreed to institutionalize their social action efforts to continue the program after the withdrawal of Federal funds. Students were paid minimal stipends, which were used for room, board, tuition, and books. Because of the skewed proportion of persons of color in low-income circumstances, students were able to work with clients from a wide variety of racial and ethnic backgrounds.

Reference: James A. Banks, *Teaching Strategies for Ethnic Studies*, 6th ed. (Boston: Allyn and Bacon, 1997).

SOCIETY, a concept pertaining to organized groups of human beings, is normally used by multicultural educators in a rather specific sense. For example, a microcultural society might be identified as a group of affluent, European-American, Chief Executive Officers of the Fortune 500 companies. On the other hand, a macroculture might be identified as the pluralistic, socioeconomically different subgroups that comprise the population of the United States.

As can be seen from this description, the word itself only refers to the fact that a group of people has banded together. To identify the nature of the people, other descriptions must be used. For example, a religious society would consist of persons all subscribing to the same spiritual tenets. In all societies, regardless of how large or small, human beings tend to reside in a structured climate that offers protection, along with economic, intellectual, and moral stimulation.

For educators, it is often useful to describe the nature of a given society. A pluralistic society would refer to a group of human beings representing a plethora of racial and ethnic subgroups. For this reason, it is incumbent on teachers to understand the societal value systems in which students from the various subgroups function.

Reference: Daniel U. Levine and Robert J. Havighurst, *Society and Education* (Boston: Allyn and Bacon, 1992).

SOCIOECONOMIC STATUS (SES), a sociological concept referring to the social structure and economic patterns of people, has been used by sociologists and anthropologists to describe societal groups accurately. Socioeconomic influences have a profound effect on students and their parents. Numerous studies reveal a correlation between per capita income and school performance.

The U.S. Census Bureau measures the economic condition of an individual based on occupation, educational attainment, and income. Two other factors used in determining socioeconomic status are wealth and power. Income is measured by determining the amount of money earned in wages and/or salaries in a year.

Wealth is more difficult to determine. It is computed by determining the net worth of a family, which consists of the money remaining after computing all of the property owned by a family and subtracting the debts. ''Properties'' consist of such things as real estate holdings, stocks and bonds, bank accounts, and notes owned.

Occupations, as classified by the U.S. Bureau of Labor Statistics, consist of: managerial and professional specialties; technical, sales, and administrative support, including secretaries and clerks; service occupations, including private household work and protective service; precision production, craft, and repair, including mechanics, repairers, and construction trades; operators, fabricators, and laborers, including machine operators, assemblers, inspectors, transportation and material-moving occupations, handlers, equipment cleaners and helpers; and farming, forestry, and fishing.

Education is based on number of grades completed and degrees earned. Salaries for persons with Bachelor of Arts degrees have been dramatically different from non-degreed persons. For example, European-American heads of the household with less than an eighth-grade education average $14,470 a year, while the average European-American college graduate earns $47,175 (based on 1988 Bureau of Census figures). Power is measured by such factors as being members of boards that determine local and state policies, boards of colleges and universities, and boards of corporations. There is usually a strong positive correlation between power and income/wealth.

References: Donna M. Gollnick and Philip C. Chinn, *Multicultural Education in a Pluralistic Society* (Columbus: OH: Merrill, 1990); Daniel U. Levine and Robert J. Havighurst, *Society and Education* (Boston: Allyn and Bacon, 1992).

SOUTHEAST ASIAN AMERICANS, one of the fastest-growing ethnic minorities in the United States during the 1980s and 1990s, have provided the United States with one of its vital new ethnic minority groups. A great deal of the growth occurred as a result of the conflicts in Southeast Asia connected with the Vietnam War. The displaced persons from Southeast Asia included Cambodians, Vietnamese, and Laotian Hmong.

Situated between Thailand and South Vietnam, Cambodia was an innocent bystander during the war. The government of Cambodia allowed North Vietnamese personnel to move their military units and supplies through the country. In 1975, the Kmer Rouge forces assumed power and changed the name of the country to Kampuchea. This regime initiated a campaign of genocide against supporters of the Lon Nol government which had been supported by the United States. Many Cambodians fled to Thailand, and about 100,000 Cambodians eventually settled in the United States.

The Laotian Hmong were recruited by the U.S. Central Intelligence Agency to fight the North Vietnamese during the Vietnamese war. Because of their loyalty to the United States, Hmong were allowed to emigrate to the United States. Thousands of Hmong persons settled in the United States because of Vang Pao, a noted Hmong leader who was instrumental in assisting the Hmong-Americans to function effectively in the United States. After settling on a ranch in Montana, Vang Pao moved to Southern California, where a large population of Laotian-Hmong-Americans still reside.

However, in addition to large population clusters, such as the Southern California enclave, smaller groups of Laotian Hmong exist in such American communities as Spokane, Washington. Receiving teaching certificates from Eastern Washington University, Hmong students have become role models in the Hmong community by virtue of their English language acquisition and their successes as professional educators. Although the Hmong-American community in the United States is small, it has distinguished itself by its tenacity and work ethic, both of which appeal to the American macroculture.

Prior to World War II, Vietnam had been a French protectorate. During World War II, Ho Chi Minh started a campaign to help the Viet Minh acquire Vietnam's independence from France. While the efforts of Ho Chi Minh were supported by the Communist Russians and Chinese, the United States backed the South Vietnamese government. When the South Vietnamese government collapsed in 1975, many Vietnamese people fled to the United States.

After these South Vietnamese refugees reached the United States, the children tended to perform well in American schools. Sociologists have posited the reason for this was that the early immigrants were persons who were relatively affluent and could pay bribes to get on planes bound for the United States. Because of their affluence and the corresponding educational successes in Vietnam, these children tended to perform well in American schools as well.

References: Keith Quincy, *Hmong: History of a People* (Cheney, WA: Eastern Washington University Press, 1988); Joan Thrower Timm, *Four Perspectives in Multicultural Education* (Belmont, CA: Wadsworth, 1995).

SOUTHERN POVERTY LAW CENTER, located in Montgomery, Alabama, was founded by attorney Morris Dees to provide free and/or low-cost legal services for low-income clients. Over the years, the organization has expanded its efforts to combat racism through the surveillance of hate groups, such as White Supremacist Organizations. In addition to its legal enterprises on behalf of their poverty clients, the Southern Poverty Law Center has created computer data bases that monitor the activities of America's hate groups.

Another service of the Southern Poverty Law Center is the Klanwatch, which monitors the hate crimes of the Ku Klux Klan. In recent years, the Klanwatch has uncovered numerous attempts to commit acts of violence, such as a plan to blow up the First African Episcopal Methodist Church in Los Angeles and a neo-Nazi's attempt to bomb the National Afro-American Museum in Wilberforce, Ohio, on Martin Luther King Day. The organization also monitors the activities of Skinheads.

The Southern Poverty Law Center makes available educational materials designed to help classroom practitioners teach tolerance toward the pluralistic microcultures in the United States. The materials consist of video tapes, lesson plans, and meaningful activities for students.

Reference: *Intelligence Report* (Montgomery, AL: Southern Poverty Law Center, 1993).

SPANISH AMERICANS, a term referring to persons from Spain who reside in the United States as United States citizens, is not a generic term that can be used in referring to a wide variety of Spanish-speaking groups. On some occasions, the term is used as an alternative to such concepts as Mexican American or Puerto Rican American, since some persons tend to place a higher value on this microculture compared to persons representing other Latino groups. However, the term can only apply to Spaniards who have acquired citizenship in the United States.

STANFORD, LELAND (1824–1893), a former U.S. Senator, governor, and entrepreneur who was involved in the creation of the Central Pacific Railroad, was one of the most important figures in the westward expansion. He was the first Republican governor in the State of California, founded Stanford University, and was the president of the Central Pacific Railroad.

Leland Stanford's story in the creation of the Central Pacific Railroad involves the actions of Charlie Crocker, Colis Huntington, and Mark Hopkins, the other instigators of one of the country's most ambitious undertakings. An English American, Stanford's ancestors came to the United States in the middle of the seventeenth century. His father, Josiah Stanford, grew up near Albany and joined an Albany law firm after finishing his education at Cazenovia Seminary in 1845. He moved to California with his brothers after the California gold strike.

During 1856 he assisted in the organization of the Republican Party in Sacramento and was elected as governor of California in 1861. Previously, he had been a Whig but joined the Republican Party because of his disbelief in slavery. His gubernatorial tenure, starting in January 1861, occurred during the Civil War. At this time in history, the mode of travel from the West Coast to the East Coast was by steamship through the Isthmus of Panama.

Theodore Judah lobbied for railroad funding and eventually the 1862 Pacific Railroad Act by Congress provided the funding for the railroad. Stanford, Crocker, Huntington, and Hopkins became the owners. By 1865, an advertisement for 5,000 laborers appeared in the *Sacramento Union.* A large labor force was recruited from China, thereby creating a large microculture of Chinese Americans who added to the pluralistic nature of the nation.

After the completion of the railroad, Stanford turned to the development of his university. Located on a portion of his Palo Alto farm, it became one of the nation's most prestigious institutions of higher education.

For teachers, the story of the development of the nation's Transcontinental Railroad is one of the more exciting events in the country's history. The acquisition of Chinese laborers and the resulting problems can help students to understand the ethnic groups that comprised the nation's cheap labor pool.

References: George T. Clark, *Leland Stanford* (Stanford, CA: Stanford University Press, 1931); Oscar Lewis, *The Big Four: The Story of Huntington, Stanford, Hopkins and Crocker and the Building of the Central Pacific* (New York: Knopf, 1938).

STEREOTYPING, from a multicultural education perspective, pertains to the attitudes and values that students bring to the schoolroom regarding the beliefs they harbor about entire groups of people, based on only limited or faulty information. Stereotypes can pertain to virtually any topic, but one of the biggest concerns on the part of classroom teachers relates to the stereotypes about race, ethnicity, and gender.

One of the most common problems for educators is teaching children what the use of the term ''they'' can mean insofar as stereotyping is concerned. For example, if a person refers to Latinos as "they," it might mean that the person is drawing conclusions about an entire group, based on the actions of one or two persons. Regardless of the group, stereotyping can occur if the person making judgments fails to understand the nature of individual differences.

Words themselves can lead to stereotyping. Color words such as "black" and "white" can lead to subtle stereotyping. Phrases such as "blackmail," "blackball," and "black sheep" portray negative images of the color "Black" which is used (although inaccurately) to designate a group of human beings. On the other hand, phrases such as "white lies," "good guys in white hats," and "that's mighty 'white' of you" tend to portray positive images. Likewise, the color "White" is used (also erroneously) to characterize a group of human beings. These colors can have dramatic effects on the lives of children. Psychologists, such as Kenneth Clark, found that African-American children and European-American children opt for "white" dolls rather than "black" dolls when given a choice.

References: Pamela L. Tiedt and Iris M. Tiedt, *Multicultural Teaching: A Handbook of Activities, Information and Resources* (Boston: Allyn and Bacon, 1995); Juan Williams, *Eyes on the Prize: America's Civil Rights Years, 1954–1965* (New York: Viking Press, 1987).

STEW THEORY, a multicultural term which surfaced during the American Civil Rights Movement, refers to the notion of cultural pluralism as opposed to the idea of assimilation. The "melting pot theory," which emerged during Colonial times and again at the turn of the century, suggested that the United States was a giant crucible. When people came to the country, they should leap into the pot and adapt the value system of the dominant culture.

However, the notion of the stew theory brought forth the idea that the uniqueness of the United States depended on the diversity of the different groups throughout the land. Like the stew, each ingredient offered something important for the total product. If any single ingredient was subtracted, the total product would be lacking. Thus, the metaphor implies that each microculture offers something special and that is what constitutes the greatness of the United States. *See also* SALAD BOWL THEORY.

Reference: George E. Pozzetta (Ed.), *Assimilation, Acculturation, and Social Mobility* (New York: Garland, 1991).

STORYVILLE, a segment of New Orleans designated as a legally established red-light district, existed from 1898 until it was officially closed in 1917 by the Department of the Navy. Jazz historians sometimes make the argument that Storyville was the birthplace of American Jazz. The boundaries were Claiborne Avenue, St. Louis Street, Basin Street, and Canal Street. Ironically, the region was named after Sidney Story, a New Orleans alderman who hated jazz and loved Johann Strauss.

Racist practices were prevalent in Storyville. For example, it was against the law for African-American and European-American prostitutes to work in the same premises. African-American customers were not allowed to frequent the houses on Basin Street. One of the most famous sporting houses was Lulu White's on the corner of Basin and Bienville Streets. Some of the Madames, such as Madame Piazza, became extremely wealthy, and she retired to France, marrying a Gaelic nobleman.

Musically, Storyville was a perfect place for New Orleans musicians to perform. One of the most famous early jazz musicians, Jelly Roll Morton, got his first piano-playing job at Hilma Burt's Mirror Ballroom at 209 North Basin Street. Another famous jazz pioneer, Joe (King) Oliver, started his career in 1920 as a member of the Eagle Brass Band. He later replaced the great Freddie Keppard in the band that performed at Pete Lala's Café in the District.

The original art form, created in Storyville by African Americans, went through a number of evolutionary changes, and musicians such as Jelly Roll Morton took advantage of the Mexican influences, injecting some elements of "salsa" in their music. But the fact that Storyville existed for partying and there was a plethora of extremely talented African-American musicians on hand, helped in the creation of this American musical art form.

However, even with the closing of Storyville in 1917, jazz continued to flourish elsewhere in the French Quarter and "up the river" all the way to Chicago. But without the advent of Storyville in New Orleans, it is probable that jazz may never have acquired its initial popularity and might even have surfaced in an entirely different format.

Forty-four years after the closing of Storyville, during a period when jazz lost a lot of its popularity due to the creation of "rock 'n roll," Preservation Hall opened in a building on St. Peters Street in the French Quarter. Originally constructed about 1750, the structure served as a tavern during the War of 1812. The present building was re-built after a fire in 1816. Preservation Hall provided New Orleans musicians, such as Jim Robinson (trombone), George Lewis (clarinet), and Sweet Emma Barrett (piano), the opportunity to help perpetuate the original art form which had its roots in Storyville.

References: William Carter, *Preservation Hall* (New York: W. W. Norton, 1991); Al Rose, *Storyville, New Orleans* (Tuscaloosa: University of Alabama Press, 1974).

STOWE, HARRIETT BEECHER (1811–1896), the author of *Uncle Tom's Cabin*, became known as one of the key persons who motivated much of the anti-slavery sentiment that led up to the start of the Civil War. Published in 1852, the book portrayed the predicament of African-American slaves. In the first year of publication, the book sold more than 300,000 copies. She wrote it to illustrate the evils of the fugitive slave law.

Stowe's book portrayed the life of African-American slaves in a very negative sense. Their ill-treatment created a sentimental reaction to the concept of slavery in the United States. The book supposedly was based on an autobiography of the life of Josiah Henson, an inhabitant of Canada, who was formerly a slave in the United States.

The daughter of a Congregationalist minister, her first book was *The Mayflower; or Sketches of Scenes and Characters Among the Descendants of Pilgrims* published in 1843. This and other works revealed her interest in New England personalities. After the Civil War, she continued writing novels, essays, and poetry based on New England issues.

Reference: Sharon Harley, *The Timetables of African-American History* (New York: Simon and Schuster, 1995).

STUDENT NON-VIOLENT COORDINATING COMMITTEE (SNCC), founded in 1960 on the campus of Shaw University in Raleigh, North Carolina, was formed to combat segregation in the South. The SNCC was a grassroots organization run by college students who attempted to increase their numbers by recruiting other high school and college students. They attempted to develop their own leaders rather than relying on credentialed persons who were professional leaders.

One of the SNCC's first efforts was an attempt to desegregate the Trailways bus terminal in Albany, Georgia. In 1961, the Interstate Commerce Committee had ruled that a 1960 U.S. Supreme Court decision banning segregation must be carried out in the country's transportation facilities. However, this had not yet occurred in Albany. In November 1961, a group of African-American students sat down in the "Whites Only" waiting room and refused to leave. The Albany police arrived, ordering them out. They left peacefully.

In addition to the sit-ins, the SNCC also participated in freedom marches and voter registration. Initially, their attempts to register African Americans to vote were often rebuffed because of the fear of retaliation by racist European Americans. Moreover, they were often accused of being Communists. However, this group had a profound effect on the American Civil Rights Movement because of its integration of African-American and European-American young people, who worked together to end segregation in the South.

References: Sharon Harley, *The Timetables of African-American History* (New York: Simon and Schuster, 1995); Ronald Takaki, *A Different Mirror: A History of Multicultural America* (Boston: Little, Brown, 1993); Juan Williams, *Eyes on the Prize: America's Civil Rights Years, 1954–1965* (New York: Viking Press, 1987).

STUDENTS OF COLOR, a generic term used to designate students in American schools who were not European Americans, came into existence well after the end of the American Civil Rights Movement. Many educators became skeptical about the accuracy of the term "minority students," since the enrollment projections show that European Americans will also become members of a "minority group" sometime during the first half of the twenty-first century.

SUFFRAGE MOVEMENT, the attempt to secure voting rights for women, first became a strong voice for women's rights at the Seneca Falls Convention held in 1848. Some of the efforts for the acquisition of women's suffrage was a result of the women's anti-slavery movement, an international effort that held a major convention in London in 1840. Several U.S. women attended, and some of the impetus for women's rights was due to the motivation acquired through women taking an active stance against slavery.

After the Seneca Falls Convention, women became more active to reform American education. Modest improvement in education occurred, along with an increased number of women entering the labor market. However, the enormous gap between the rights of European-American men and women persisted through the Civil War.

When the Fifteenth Amendment was enacted, women were hopeful that this piece of legislation would result in their enfranchisement. However, the final document read: "The rights of the Citizens of the United States to vote shall not be denied or abridged by the United States or any State, on account of race, color, or previous condition of servitude." The word "sex" was not included in the wording.

By 1896, states such as Wyoming, Utah, Colorado, and Idaho included women's suffrage in their constitutions. In 1917, members of the Congressional Union and Workers' Party picketed the White House to secure suffrage. The more aggressive tactics seemed to have their effect and by 1920, 75 percent of the state legislatures had ratified the Nineteenth Amendment that finally granted women the right to vote.

References: Alexander Rippa, *Education in a Free Society* (New York: Longman, 1988); Daniel Selakovich, *Schooling in America* (New York: Longman, 1984).

SUPREME COURT OF THE UNITED STATES, composed of eight associate justices and a chief justice, is the cornerstone of the American judicial system. Article Three of the U.S. Constitution provided the basic ingredients for the establishment of the Supreme Court.

Supreme Court Justices are appointed by the president and confirmed by the Senate. Consequently, the composition of the Court is politicized. Each president has been anxious to appoint as many Supreme Court Justices as possible to perpetuate his political agenda. Originally, the Supreme Court had just six members, but the size was augmented between 1863 and 1866. President Franklin Roosevelt unsuccessfully attempted to add to the number of Justices during his time in office.

The Supreme Court's roots extend well back into history. As a court of law, its history can be traced to twelfth century England. Its decisions are final, and the Supreme Court becomes judge for every lawyer and judge in the United States. It is also political, since its decisions affect the policies of the entire nation.

Primarily a Court of Appeals, cases are brought before the U.S. Supreme Court from either the lower federal courts or from the state supreme courts. The Supreme Court only hears cases that relate to constitutional questions. Quite frequently it hears cases relating to measures passed by states that are thought to be unconstitutional. For example, the 1896 *Plessy v. Ferguson* case pertained to a Louisiana law requiring the segregation of railway cars. Also, the Supreme Court declared two abortion statutes in Texas and Georgia to be unconstitutional in the 1973 *Roe v. Wade* and *Doe v. Bolton* cases.

The Supreme Court commences hearing cases in October each year. If at least four justices opt to hear a case, it is placed on the docket and about 150 cases are heard each year. Adjournment usually occurs in June. Attorneys submit written briefs in regard to the cases, and then oral arguments allow the justices to ask additional questions about an individual case. Opinions are then written after the cases are researched and discussed in conference behind closed doors.

Historically, the Supreme Court has had a profound effect on United States history. During the tenure of the Warren Court, the famous *Brown v. Board of Education* decision was passed, and life in the United States would never be the same as the walls of racial desegregation finally came down. This 1954 decision occurred in a Court that was probably the most liberal in the nation's history. The resulting social revolution caused massive changes in the social fabric of the nation.

In addition to the termination of racial segregation in the schools, the U.S. Supreme Court has had an enormous effect on public education in general. Because of Supreme Court decisions, compensatory education programs are undertaken in the schools for the provision of special help for children with limited English proficiency. Organized prayer in the schools is not allowed, nor is religious indoctrination. Students and parents are not allowed to infringe upon the process of instruction, and due process of the law is a constitutional guarantee for educators and students alike.

References: Louis Fischer, David Schimmel, and Cynthia Kelly, *Teachers and the Law* (New York: Longman, 1995); Robert G. McCloskey, *The American Supreme Court* (Chicago: University of Chicago Press, 1960); David Selakovich, *Schooling in America* (New York: Longman, 1984); Samuel Walker, *In Defense of American Liberties* (New York: Oxford University Press, 1990).

SWANN v. CHARLOTTE-MECKLENBURG BOARD OF EDUCATION became a landmark Supreme Court decision, since it related directly to the manner in which desegregation could be implemented. The decision was that mandatory busing programs used to desegregate schools were constitutional. The decision also suggested a number of desegregation options such as pairing, clustering, and grouping schools to facilitate the transfer of European-American students to schools that previously had been populated with African-American students.

The decision had the effect of weakening the long revered concept of the "neighborhood school," because the reform plan articulated in *Swann* called for students residing closest to suburban schools to be bused to inner-city schools to create desegregated school environments. Buses could be used legally to accomplish this. While the Supreme Court did not totally outlaw racially segregated schools, it did create certain conditions that would make segregated schools difficult to maintain.

The decision was extremely controversial. President Nixon opposed the busing of American children to achieve racial balance. Various anti-busing groups attempted to generate Congressional support for passing a constitutional amendment. Angry parents in Michigan dynamited and burned buses and ugly anti-busing rallies occurred throughout the United States. At the time, the anti-busing rallies were carried out primarily by European-American parents.

Another effect of the *Swann* decision was the growth of the private school movement and the so-called "White Flight," an exodus of European Americans to areas of the country where forced busing was not an issue because of certain population demographics.

References: Alexander Rippa, *Education in a Free Society* (New York: Longman, 1984); Daniel Selakovich, *Schooling in America* (New York; Longman, 1984); *Swann v. Charlotte-Mecklenburg Board of Education*, 402 U.S. 1 (1971).

SWEATT v. PAINTER, a University of Texas case heard by the U.S. Supreme Court in 1950, was instrumental in leading up to the famous *Brown v. Board of Education* decision in 1954. Interestingly enough, the case had to do with racial restrictions at the University of Texas Law School.

Herman Sweatt, an African-American postal employee, applied for admission to the University of Texas Law School. Since the University of Texas was racially segregated, the school officials offered to create a law school program for Herman Sweatt. The new "law school" was to be housed in three basement rooms, and the faculty would have consisted of part-time faculty members.

At issue was the question of whether the facilities at the segregated law school for one African-American student (Herman Sweatt) were equal in quality to the facilities for European-American students. The concept of "separate but equal" facilities being constitutionally acceptable had been established by the U.S. Supreme Court as a result of the 1896 *Plessy v. Ferguson* case.

Prior to the Sweatt case, the American Civil Liberties Union (ACLU) had been battling to overturn the 1896 Plessy decision. Sweatt was one of the major cases since it forced the justices to rule on the issue of equality. At question was whether the newly-constructed school for Sweatt was equal in quality to the main law school for European-American students. Ruling in favor of Sweatt, the Court ordered the University of Texas to admit him to the regular University of Texas Law School, since the new one for only one African-American man was decidedly inferior. All of the Supreme Court members during this case had been appointed by Presidents Roosevelt and Truman.

References: Daniel Selakovich, *Schooling in America* (New York: Longman, 1994); Juan Williams, *Eyes on the Prize: America's Civil Rights Years, 1954–1965* (New York: Viking Press, 1987).

T

TAKAKI, RONALD (1939–), a key figure in multicultural history, has become known as one of America's most important multicultural scholars. A professor in the Ethnic Studies Department at the University of California, Berkeley, Takaki has made important contributions in his historical studies that focus on the multicultural contributions of all of the American microcultures, many of which have been omitted from a great deal of the historical literature of the United States.

The grandson of Japanese laborers in the state of Hawaii, Takaki received his Ph.D. from the University of California in American History. During his work, which he undertook in the pursuit of his advanced degree, he became concerned about the lack of attention historians paid to the historical contributions of non-European Americans. He has rewritten history to include the important contributions of Native Americans, European Americans, African Americans, Latinos, Asian Americans, and all of the microcultures that added their influences to create the exciting cultural diversity which has made the nation great.

His books include *A Pro-Slavery Crusade: The Agitation to Reopen the African Slave Trade; Violence in the Black Imagination: Essays and Documents; Iron Cages: Race and Culture in Nineteenth-Century America; Pau Hana: Plantation Life and Labor in Hawaii; From Different Shores: Perspectives on Race and Ethnicity in America*; and *Strangers from a Different Shore: A History of Asian-Americans*. He has received the Distinguished Teaching Award from the University of California, Berkeley, and Cornell University honored him as the Messenger Lecturer in 1993.

References: Ronald Takaki, *A Different Mirror: A History of Multicultural America* (Boston: Little, Brown, 1993); Ronald Takaki, *From Different Shores: Perspectives on Race and Ethnicity in America* (New York: Oxford University Press, 1987).

TALMUD, a body of rabbinic literature, consists of the Mishnah (a collection of laws) and the Gemara (analytical accounts of the Mishnah). The Palestinian Talmud and the Babylonian Talmud have different Gemara but the same Mishnah. The Babylonian Talmud is the most famous. After being finished about 200 A.D., the Mishnah became the primary text in the Babylonian and Palestinian rabbinical schools.

The Talmud is the Oral Law of Orthodox Jews. Mosaic in origin, the teachings of the Oral Law have been handed down by word of mouth throughout history. Talmudic law has occurred through Biblical law and reflects the mores and customs of the times. The codes of Jewish law are incorporated in the Talmud, which is of paramount importance in Jewish religious practices.

The Talmud has been important to students of religion, law, history, language, and literature. Throughout history, the Talmud has been the primary text of Orthodox rabbinical scholars. However, reformed Jews and other groups, such as the Karaites in the Middle Ages, have sometimes questioned parts of the Talmud, particularly in regard to religious observance.

It is acceptable for teachers to educate students about contemporary religions. Discussing the characteristics of the Talmud and its effects on the ethnic values of Jewish people is important in order for students to acquire more accurate insights about the role of religion in the lives of people all over the world.

References: M. Herbert Danzer, *Returning to Tradition: The Contemporary Revival of Orthodox Judaism* (New Haven, CT: Yale University Press, 1989); Mordecai M. Kaplan, *Judaism as a Civilization: Toward a Reconstruction of American-Jewish Life* (New York: Reconstructionist Press, 1957).

TAYLOR, MILDRED (1943–), an outstanding author of children's books, won the 1973 Council on Interracial Books award in the African-American category. An African American who grew up in Toledo, Ohio, after her birth in Jackson, Mississippi, she graduated from Toledo University, joined the Peace Corps, and served in Ethiopia. Later she returned to the United States to become a recruiter for the Peace Corps.

As a student in the School of Journalism at the University of Colorado in Boulder, she helped the University of Colorado create a Black Studies program. She received her Master of Arts Degree at the University. Becoming a highly-regarded author, she won the 1977 Newberry Award for her *Roll of Thunder, Hear My Cry*, and her *Song of the Trees* won the *New York Times* Outstanding Book of the Year award in 1975.

References: Mildred Taylor, *Roll of Thunder, Hear My Cry* (New York: Dial Press, 1976); Mildred Taylor, *Song of the Trees* (New York: Dial Press, 1975).

TEACHING ENGLISH TO SPEAKERS OF OTHER LANGUAGES (TESOL), a program designed to improve the English skills of students who speak English as a second language, has a national organization of teachers who are involved in the language development of students for whom English is not their native language. TESOL conducts national conferences that attempt to help teachers acquire sophisticated strategies to help English as a Second Language (ESL) students become more proficient English speakers.

The movement developed because of an "English Only" movement initiated by ex-California Senator S. I. Hayakawa in the 1980s. Hayakawa and his followers argued that there was no need for bilingual education or special programs to help the Limited English Proficiency (LEP) student. The National Council of the Teachers of English (NCTE) has denounced Hayakawa's "English-only" position.

References: National Council of the Teachers of English, 1600 Cameron St., Alexandria, VA: Pamela Tiedt and Iris M. Tiedt, *Multicultural Teaching: A Handbook of Activities, Information, and Resources* (Boston: Allyn and Bacon, 1995).

TEACHING TOLERANCE is the name of the excellent teaching materials published by the Southern Poverty Law Center in Montgomery, Alabama. Founded by current leader, attorney Morris Dees, the Southern Poverty Law Center publishes multicultural education teaching materials for classroom teachers. As the title implies, the original goal of the Center was to provide legal services for low-income clients. However, in recent years the goals have been expanded to deal with teaching tolerance issues.

The goal of the *Teaching Tolerance* effort is to provide teachers with suitable materials that are designed to help students acquire positive attitudes about the diverse populations constituting the macroculture in the United States. Materials are provided to the schools free of charge, and the kits have both student and teacher manuals. *See also* DEES, MORRIS; SOUTHERN POVERTY LAW CENTER.

References: Sara Bullard (Ed.), *Free at Last: A History of the Civil Rights Movement and Those Who Died in the Struggle* (Montgomery, AL: Southern Poverty Law Center, 1989); Kevin Blocker, *Spokesman Review*, October 1966.

TECUMSEH (1768–1813), the son of a Creek woman, was born in western Ohio in a Shawnee village. His name means "Shooting Star" in the Shawnee language. During his life, he was involved in a number of skirmishes with European Americans, notably in a conflict with European-American forces led by Colonel William Crawford and an attack on Kentucky with the British in 1782. During the early 1800s, Tecumseh allied himself with the British and organized several tribes, including the Senecas, Wyandots, Shawnees, and Ottawas, into a coalition which he believed would be successful in stopping the encroachments of European-American settlers into their lands.

After some limited successes against the Americans, Tecumseh's Native

American/British coalition suffered a huge defeat in the 1813 Battle of Thames. Many coalition participants grew tired of the hostilities and dropped out of the ongoing conflicts. Eventually, Tecumseh received a fatal wound. Without his leadership the Native American resistance waned. For teachers, the study of Tecumseh's life can help students to understand the political complexities involved in the War of 1812. Native Americans were forced to choose sides with Britain or the United States, and sometimes life was difficult for Native Americans who backed the losing side. Such studies can help students develop better insights into the historical interactions between the nation's microcultures.

References: James A. Banks, *Teaching Strategies for Ethnic Studies*, 6th ed. (Boston: Allyn and Bacon, 1997); David R. Edmunds, *Tecumseh and the Quest for Indian Leadership* (Boston: Little, Brown, 1984); Alec Gilpin, *The War of 1812 in the Old Northwest* (Lansing: Michigan State University Press, 1958).

TEJANO, a term relating to Mexican Americans who have resided in the present state of Texas for many generations, were native Mexicans, many of whom lost their land to European Americans. This occurred because of high legal fees, unethical legal practices, and turbulent markets. These three practices helped to negate Spanish land grants, which eventually became invalid.

After the termination of the Mexican War, a combination of drought and enormous volatility in the cattle market caused many Tejanos to give up their land. Consequently, by 1900 the Mexican upper class had virtually disappeared and about two thirds of the Tejanos were involved in unskilled labor positions. Early in the 1900s, European Americans had gained control of Texas voting areas that had a large Mexico-Texan ethnic population. Moreover, Tejanos were forced to relocate into Latino barrios.

Tejanos, like other Mexican Americans, were subjected to intense racial discrimination. For example, the schools for Tejano children and other Mexican-American children became segregated, and the children received a decidedly inferior education. However, these actions resulted in Tejanos developing an intense pride, which was often referred to as "Mexicanness."

References: Arnaldo de Leon, *The Tejano Community, 1836–1900* (Albuquerque: University of New Mexico Press, 1982); David G. Gutierrez, *Walls and Mirrors: Mexican-Americans, Mexican Immigrants, and the Politics of Ethnicity* (Berkeley: University of California Press, 1995); Earl Shorris, *Latinos* (New York: W. W. Norton, 1992).

TERMINATION POLICY, instigated by the U.S. government, was an attempt to assimilate Native Americans into the American macroculture. The effort intensified at the close of World War II when federal policies moved away from tribal self-determination to the goal of assimilation. Commencing in 1950, the Bureau of Indian Affairs (BIA) began drafting policies that were designed to terminate existing tribes and force Native Americans to become assimilated in the American macroculture.

Between 1954 and 1962 Congress passed 12 pieces of termination legislation that affected more than 100 tribes and bands in 8 different states. However, these new laws did not succeed in assimilating Native Americans into the American macroculture. Instead, the attempts proved ineffective and extremely more costly than the previous system.

Two tribes that approved termination acts were the Klamath of southern Oregon and the Menominees of Wisconsin. Public opinion gradually turned against the concept of termination, and after a well-orchestrated and well-publicized effort to reverse their termination proceedings, the Menominees were able to overturn their original termination orders.

References: Harvey Markowitz (Ed.), *American Indians* (Pasadena, CA: Salem Press, 1995); Nicholas C. Peroff, *Menominee Drums: Tribal Termination and Restoration, 1954–1974* (Norman: University of Oklahoma Press, 1982).

THIRTEENTH AMENDMENT, which outlawed slavery in the United States, occurred in 1865. The groundwork for the enactment of the Thirteenth Amendment took place during that same year, when slavery officially ended in Texas and President Lincoln approved a plan to utilize the services of a Black regiment in the Civil War. The plan was never carried out because the war ended. Also, during that year, the "672nd U.S. Colored Troops" and two European-American regiments fought in the last Civil War battle at White Ranch in Texas. By the end of the war, more than a quarter of a million African Americans had served in the Civil War conflicts. Thirty-eight thousand of them lost their lives.

Section One of the Amendment reads: "Neither slavery or involuntary servitude, except as a punishment for a crime whereof the party shall have been duly convicted, shall exist within the United States, or any place subject to their jurisdiction." Section Two stated that: "Congress shall have the power to enforce this article by appropriate legislation."

Following the enactment of the Thirteenth Amendment, Congress established the Bureau of Refugees, Freedmen, and Abandoned Lands (known as the Freedmen's Bureau) to aid refugees and newly-emancipated African Americans. Also, the Congress overrode a veto by new President Andrew Johnson that allowed citizenship to newly freed slaves. The legislation also nullified "Black codes."

For teachers, the Thirteenth Amendment is a crucial part of U.S. history. Works of literature, such as Paula Fox's *Slave Dancer*, can help students learn to appreciate the significance of the Thirteenth Amendment. This work is suited for students in grades five to nine.

References: *1994 Deskbook Encyclopedia of American School Law* (Rosemount, MN: Data Research, 1994); Sharon Harley, *The Timetables of African-American History* (New

York: Simon and Schuster, 1995); Pamela Tiedt and Iris M. Tiedt, *Multicultural Teaching: A Handbook of Activities, Information, and Resources* (Boston: Allyn and Bacon, 1995).

THOMAS, CLARENCE (1948–), nominated by President George Bush as a replacement for the Honorable Thurgood Marshall on the U.S. Supreme Court, became a center of controversy during his Senate hearings. Marshall, appointed to the High Court by President Lyndon Johnson, was the former attorney for the NAACP National Defense Fund and U.S. Solicitor General.

Marshall had come to represent the left-leaning wing of the U.S. Supreme Court and President Bush, anxious to create a strong right-leaning Supreme Court in the spirit of Ronald Reagan, appointed Thomas, an African American. However, the hearings became extremely volatile when Anita Hill, an African-American attorney who had worked with Hill, testified against him, arguing that he had been guilty of sexual harassment against her when the two lawyers worked for the Equal Employment Opportunities Commission years before.

During the hearings, conservative Republican Senator Orrin Hatch of Utah argued vigorously in favor of Thomas' confirmation and attempted to discredit the testimony of Anita Hill. The Republican-controlled U.S. Senate voted in favor of the confirmation of Clarence Thomas, the second African-American Supreme Court Justice in United States history. As a result, the United States Supreme Court became far more conservative than it had been for many years.

Teachers who are responsible for the social studies curriculum can use these highly politicized hearings to illustrate the effects of Supreme Court appointments on the social milieu in the United States. For example, if the same Justices who ruled on the 1896 *Plessy v. Ferguson* case had been sitting on the bench during the 1954 *Brown v. Board of Education* case, it is possible that a different ruling would have occurred.

References: Albert R. Hunt, ''Tales of Ignominy: Beyond Thomas and Hill,'' *Wall Street Journal*, October 28, 1991; Toni Morrison, *Race-ing, Justice, and Engendering Power* (New York: Pantheon, 1992); William Raspberry, ''Southern Conservatives Change Their Stripes,'' *The Oregonian*, October 18, 1991.

THORPE, JIM (1888–1953), a Native American of Sauk and Potawatomi ancestry, was born near Prague, Oklahoma. He was proud of his Native American heritage and that his great-grandfather was Black Hawk, a war chief of the Chippewa. Thorpe's athletic career commenced to improve during his involvement with coach Glenn ''Pop'' Warner at Pennsylvania's Carlisle Institute. He ran for 75 yards on his second carry for Carlisle.

Thorpe was also an extremely versatile athlete. In addition to his football prowess, he also excelled in baseball, playing professionally for two years. He returned to Carlisle where he was an all-American in 1911 and 1912. Competing in the Stockholm Summer Olympic Games in 1912, he won the pentathlon and decathlon. However, his Olympic medals were confiscated because of his involvement in professional baseball. Years later, in 1982, the medals were returned to his family.

Thorpe's athletic fame was well known, and he was considered to be one of the most outstanding athletes in American history. In his honor, many athletic facilities were named after him. After playing professionally in baseball and football, he retired from athletics in 1929. He died in Lomita, California, in 1953.

Reference: Harvey Markowitz (Ed.), *American Indians* (Pasadena, CA: Salem Press, 1995).

TILL, EMMETT (1941–1955), a 14-year-old boy from Chicago, was brutally murdered in LeFlore County, Mississippi in 1955 by European-American racists. Allegedly he had whistled at a European-American woman in a store. As a youth, Till had attended a segregated (African Americans only) elementary school in Chicago. His mother decided to send him south for a visit, and she warned him to have nothing to do with European-American people down south.

Emmett, described as a prankster by his cousin, Curtis Jones, spoke to a European-American woman named Carolyn Bryant, allegedly saying, ''Bye Baby'' as he was exiting the Bryant's Grocery and Meat Market in Money, Mississippi. Allegedly, Emmett Till was showing off a picture of a European-American girl who was a friend of his in Chicago.

According to some accounts, Roy Bryant (Carolyn's husband) and his brother-in-law, J. W. Milam, decided to get the boy ''who done the talkin.'' Apparently, Roy Bryant decided to retaliate for the supposed transaction between Emmett Till and Carolyn Bryant. Allegedly, Milam and Bryant drove Till to the Tallahatchie River, requiring the boy to carry a 75-pound cotton-gin fan from the truck to the bank of the river, ordered him to strip, and then murdered him by shooting 14-year-old Emmett Till in the head.

Till's body was found three days after the shooting. Milam and Bryan were charged with kidnapping and murder. However, after a short five-day trial, the jury ruled that the plaintiffs were ''not guilty.'' The all European-American jury had deliberated for a bit over an hour. Reactions to the verdict were quick to erupt, and African-American demonstrations occurred in Baltimore, Cleveland, New York, Detroit, and Los Angeles.

From a multicultural teaching perspective, teachers can use the Emmett Till incident to illustrate the deep anti-African-American sentiments that existed in the South during this era. The episode was one of the major events during the American Civil Rights Movement. It would serve as a reminder of the racist attitudes that have plagued the nation throughout its history.

Reference: Juan Williams, *Eyes on the Prize: America's Civil Rights Years, 1954–1965* (New York: Viking Press, 1987).

TIME PERCEPTIONS of different microcultures are key issues for educators. For example, teachers who work with Native Americans and Latinos need to be sensitive to the differences in time perceptions of these two microcultures compared with the time perceptions of European Americans. While European Americans are sometimes extremely concerned with time factors such as promptness and adhering to precise schedules, Native Americans and Latinos often adopt a more casual attitude about time.

For example, in some Latino microcultures, people see the past, present, and future differently than European Americans, particularly Anglos. While European Americans value the future, Latinos often feel that life should be lived for the "here and now" since the future is too indefinite. In fact, some Latinos define the future as *"mañana."* The present (*actualidad*) is what exists concretely, and the future may be unpredictable. Native Americans often view the world similarly. What is important happens now, and the future is impossible to predict. Time is not too important. The term "Indian time" has sometimes been used to make a statement about human beings needing to become more relaxed about time. Time should not control the person.

Some sociologists have observed that there are differences between urban and rural dwellers with respect to time. In addition to the ethnic differences, urban residents tend to be more concerned with schedules and other time factors. On the other hand, rural dwellers have often assumed a more casual attitude about the importance of time.

References: Arthur L. Campa, "Manãna Is Today," *New Mexico Quarterly*, February 1939; "Everything in the Past Was Better Back in My Day," *El Nuevo Mexicano*, February 9, 1939; Mario T. Garcia, *Mexican-Americans: Leadership, Ideology, and Identity, 1930–1960* (New Haven, CT: Yale University Press, 1989).

TITLE IV, a federal funding source for achieving desegregated schools. *See* SCHOOL PROGRAMS FOR INTERCULTURAL COMMUNITY EDUCATION (SPICE).

TITLE IX, based on the education Amendments of 1972, states that "no person in the United States shall, on the basis of sex, be excluded from participation in, be denied the benefits of, or be subjected to discrimination under any education program receiving federal assistance." Title IX has had an effect on most aspects of public education, except for curriculum materials and textbooks.

Many lawsuits have occurred over the issue of girls competing on boys' athletic teams. Boys and girls are entitled to equal access to noncontact sports. Equal access is also guaranteed for separate teams that may be provided by the schools. Coaching, scheduling, and other support, such as equipment, must be guaranteed for both genders.

Admission requirements for boys and girls must be equal to be considered constitutionally acceptable. Married students and/or pregnant students may not be required to participate in segregated classes. Moreover, the courts require that pregnancy be treated as a disability like any other type of disability.

The issue of equal pay for coaches has been less clear. Disparate treatment refers to actions taken by employers that result in less favorable treatment due to gender, race, ethnicity, or national origin. In such cases, the burden of proof is always with the plaintiff. Disparate impact occurs when a particular employment practice appears to be neutral but in actuality excludes a particular group protected by the Civil Rights Act.

References: Robert Cole, "Title IX: A Long Dazed Journey into Human Rights," *Phi Delta Kappan* (May 1976); Charlotte B. Hallam, "Legal Tools to Fight Sex Discrimination," *Phi Delta Kappan* (October 1973); Fred Rodriguez, *Equity in Education: Issues and Strategies* (Dubuque, IA: Kendall/Hunt, 1990).

TLINGIT TRIBE, a northwest coastal group of Native Americans and Native Canadians, has resided from northern California to southern Alaska in the coastal regions. According to the 1990 census, the U.S. population was nearly 14,000 persons. Recently, the tribe has tended to drop the first "T" in the tribal name, since it represents a European attempt to modify the original pronunciation of the tribal name.

Anthropologists believe that the Tlingits first inhabited the area between 6,000 and 5,000 years B.C. Russian ships made contact with the Tlingits in 1741 A.D. after the tribe had taken advantage of the mild climates of present-day Sitka. Russian missionaries introduced the Russian Orthodox religion. However, Tlingit spirituality is still evident in the tribal mythology. The belief is that the animals have spirits, which are able to communicate with human beings. The Tlingit religion is organized around the maintenance of life, nature, and order. The raven is an important spiritual animal, a crucial part of the tribal mythology.

The Tlingits are well known for their cultural artwork, particularly their wood carvings, decorated boats, baskets, and their exquisite "Chilkat" blankets. The Tlingit art influences are strong among other northwest tribes, particularly the Haida.

Educators can use the Tlingit tribe as an example of the ever-growing ethnic pluralism of the peoples of the United States. After Alaska achieved statehood, social studies teachers revised their curriculum to help students understand that the peoples of this new state were also an important part of the American mosaic.

References: Nora M. and Richard D. Dauenhauer (Eds.), *Haa Shuka, Our Ancestors: Tlingit Oral Narratives* (Seattle: University of Washington Press, 1987); Aurel Krause, *The Tlingit Indians* (Seattle, WA: University of Washington Press, 1956); Mary Helen Pelton and Jacqueline DiGennaro, *Images of a People: Tlingit Myths and Legends* (Englewood, CO: Libraries Unlimited, 1992).

TOCQUEVILLE, ALEXIS DE (1805–1859), who visited the United States in 1830, commented on what he perceived to be an inordinate American emphasis on the acquisition of material wealth. He argued that the democratic way of life in America accounted for a great deal of the emphasis on materialism. European-American males were no longer bound by the restrictions they had encountered in the old country.

This emphasis on material wealth, coupled with the transformation of the United States into an industrial society, created a great need for cheap labor. While slavery had served the purpose for a number of years, new cheap labor sources became necessary. Thus, laborers from virtually all parts of the world helped to create the pluralistic society that the country enjoys in modern times.

Reference: Ronald Takaki, *A Different Mirror: A History of Multicultural America* (Boston: Little, Brown, 1993).

TOTEM POLES, trademarks of the Pacific Northwest coastal tribes, are carved wooden columns that portray the ethnic identity, family history, and social position of Native American peoples from this region of the United States. The totems were the animal spirits that helped the people cope with life's problems. The poles are among the most spectacular wood carvings in the United States.

Sometimes specific events are depicted on a totem pole, such as an account of the manner in which one clan had outwitted another one. Other totem poles might depict a mythical or historic event of some sort. Several different forms of totem poles have been used in the past. ''Free standing'' poles are sometimes constructed along the beach or in front of a home. Other totem poles are used as part of the basic construction of a home.

Reference: Harvey Markowitz (Ed.), *American Indians* (Pasadena, CA: Salem Press, 1995).

TOUSSAINT L'OUVERTURE, FRANCOIS DOMINIQUE (1746–1803) led about 100,000 Haitian slaves in a major revolt against their French masters in 1791. By 1802 the revolution and other events led to France's termination of slavery and Toussaint L'Ouverture became Haiti's first governor. The situation in Haiti was one of the major world events that led to the termination of slavery. When slavery was ended in Haiti, the population of U.S. African-American slaves was more than 1 million persons, constituting about 19 percent of the American population.

Reference: Sharon Harley, *The Timetables of African-American History* (New York: Simon and Schuster, 1995).

TRADING POSTS, economic trading sites between Native Americans and European Americans, were particularly prominent during the height of the fur trade period. The first permanent trading posts were established by the Hudson's Bay Company, which made use of all the tributaries emptying into that body of water.

Furs were exchanged between European Americans and Native Americans from the late 1700s until the 1870s. They were the most common form of exchange between the two groups. In 1796, the U.S. Congress appropriated funds to create trading posts to improve the economic well-being of the Native Americans in the trading process. However, by 1822, John Jacob Astor was successful in persuading Congress to allow private enterprise to participate in the process, and his American Fur Company created trading posts.

However, over the years the trading posts became places where Native Americans would spend a great deal of their time. As a result, some Indians were afflicted with European-American diseases such as smallpox and whooping cough. The consumption of alcohol, forbidden on the government trading posts, was available at the private trading posts, and alcoholism soon became a problem as well. Eventually, the supply of buffalo waned because of the railroads and increased numbers of European Americans who moved west. Due to tremendous hunting pressures, the beaver population diminished greatly. As a result, the trading posts gradually gave way to the reservation system.

Reference: Harvey Markowitz (Ed.), *American Indians* (Pasadena, CA: Salem Press, 1995).

TRADITIONAL JAZZ, also called "vintage jazz," "New Orleans jazz," or "Trad Jazz," was created at the turn of the century in the vicinity of New Orleans. The roots combined the West African influences, particularly the rhythmic patterns, with the European influences, such as the French quadrille. Much of the early experimentation occurred in Storyville, a red-light section of New Orleans. It has been argued by jazz historians that jazz represents America's most significant contribution to the world's music.

While the original art form was performed entirely by African-American musicians such as King Oliver, Freddie Keppard, Jelly Roll Morton, and Buddy Bolden, European Americans copied the music. Jazz eventually became integrated with the European-American groups featuring such talented musicians as Benny Goodman on clarinet, Lionel Hampton on vibraphone, Gene Krupa on the drums, and Teddy Wilson on piano.

In the 1940s and 1950s, traditional jazz resurfaced when New Orleans jazz legends such as Kid Ory (trombone), Alton Purnell (piano), Jim Robinson (trombone) and George Lewis (clarinet) played in Southern California, rejuvenating the interest in traditional jazz among European-American musicians. Eventually, during the 1970s, 1980s, and 1990s, traditional jazz festivals became popular with older European-American musicians who traveled to Sacramento, San Diego, Los Angeles, and numerous other locales to hear outstanding traditional jazz bands such as the New Black Eagles from Boston, the Golden Eagles from

Southern California, the Uptown Lowdown Jazz Band from Seattle, and numerous other talented groups playing traditional jazz.

While most of the festival band musicians were European Americans, the traditional jazz art form gained popularity throughout the world in countries such as Canada, England, Germany, Japan, Argentina, and Australia. The musicians tried to emulate the traditional jazz numbers in their original form.

Teachers can make use of this theme in planning curriculum units to showcase the unique racial and ethnic diversity of the American macroculture. History and social studies units can investigate the development of American jazz through a study of the history of segregation as a function of racism.

References: Rudi Blesh, *Shining Trumpets: A History of Jazz* (New York: Knopf, 1946); Dave Dexter, Jr., *The Jazz Story from the '90s to the '60s* (Englewood Cliffs, NJ: Prentice-Hall, 1964); Marshall Stearns, *The Story of Jazz* (New York: Oxford University Press, 1963).

TRAIL OF TEARS, the result of the Removal Act of 1830, caused major problems for the Chickasaw, Seminole, Choctaw, Creek and Cherokee Tribes after it went into effect. Signed into law by President Andrew Jackson, the legislation authorized the federal government to relocate Native Americans away from their native lands. Thus, it had the affect of completely altering some of the key ethnic traditions of the southeast's five major tribes and bands. Native Americans were forced to leave their ancestral territories and move to Indian Territory, west of the Mississippi River.

The saga of the Cherokees is probably known the best, and social studies teachers often use their story to help students acquire more sophisticated perceptions about the atrocities connected with the encroachment into the lands occupied by Native Americans. The actions occurred after gold was discovered on native Cherokee lands. The Georgia legislature incorporated a large portion of the Cherokee lands and nullified Cherokee laws. After squatters occupied much of the Cherokee lands, a case was filed. The U.S. Supreme Court Chief Justice John Marshall ruled in favor of the Cherokees, but President Jackson did not enforce the Supreme Court's decision.

In 1838, the forced removal began, and the Cherokees were removed to Indian Territory. An estimated 3,000 Cherokees died during the "Trail of Tears" expedition, and approximately 1,000 of their numbers managed to escape and flee to the southern Appalachian mountains.

The Choctaws were left in a vulnerable position when the tribe incurred trading post debts which they were unable to pay. As a result, they were coerced into ceding about 4 million acres of their land in return for the cancellation of their debts. The State of Mississippi, like Georgia, also extended Mississippi law to the Choctaws, abolished their government, and acquired all of the Choctaw land as a result of the 1830 Treaty of Dancing Rabbit Creek. Most of the 23,000 Choctaws migrated to Indian Territory during the next 20 years.

The Creeks in eastern Alabama strongly resisted removal. They eventually decided to sign the Treaty of Washington in 1832, which ceded their land to the United States. After a few small parties of Choctaws moved west in 1835 and 1836, reprisal raids were conducted by the Creeks, who were finally removed forcibly in 1837 and 1838.

The Chickasaws withdrew quietly in 1832 as a result of the Treaty of Pontotoc Creek. Residing in northern Mississippi, their tribe numbered about 5,000. After their land was ceded to the United States, they were able to take their possessions with them on their forced removal.

Descendants of the Creeks who moved to Florida during the 1700s, the Seminole population reached about 67,000 by 1800. Included in this number were escaped slaves and freed slaves. Efforts to remove the Seminoles began after the United States acquired Florida from Spain in 1819. By the middle of the nineteenth century, most of the Seminoles had been driven to Indian Territory, except for a large group which found refuge in the Everglades.

References: Arthur H. DeRosier, *The Removal of the Choctaw Indians* (Knoxville: University of Tennessee Press, 1970); John Ehle, *The Trail of Tears: The Rise and Fall of the Cherokee Nation* (New York: Doubleday, 1988); Grant Foreman, *Indian Removal* (Norman: University of Oklahoma Press, 1932); Charles Hudson, *The Southwestern Indians* (Knoxville: University of Tennessee Press, 1976).

TRANSITIONAL BILINGUAL EDUCATION, one of the major strategies of bilingual education, has been among the most popular approaches to bilingual instruction since the passage of the Bilingual Education Act of 1968. The philosophy behind this approach is instruction should be provided to students in their native language as long as necessary. The ultimate goal is to help students become proficient in English to the extent that the need for instruction in the their native language disappears. This is a popular approach in many countries around the world.

The maintenance approach to bilingual education instruction offers instruction in the students' native language throughout their schooling. The two major goals of this strategy are: to help students become proficient in English and to maintain competence in the native language so that the learner is truly bilingual and hopefully, bicultural.

Most of the bilingual education programs are transitional in nature. Moreover, some educators defend the use of this approach on the grounds that it is the cheapest to implement. Critics have pointed out that the lack of maintenance strategies might well result in pupils losing their native tongue due to an overemphasis on the quick acquisition of English.

Bilingual education is not without its critics, some of whom argue that bilingual education strategies may work against the maintenance of English as the nation's "legal language." In fact, some states have passed "English-Only" laws, and there is a national organization pushing for federal legislation that would abolish all bilingual education programs. However, it is important to understand that the bilingual education concept is not only found in the United States. International studies in multicultural education have revealed that at least sixteen countries use bilingual education approaches, and others use more than one language as a general principle.

It is also important to remember that the 1974 *Lau v. Nichols* decision was centered around the need for bilingual education approaches and/or other teaching strategies that would help language-different students become more proficient learners.

References: Donna M. Gollnick and Philip C. Chinn, *Multicultural Education in a Pluralistic Society* (Columbus, OH: Merrill, 1990); Bruce M. Mitchell and Robert E. Salsbury, *Multicultural Education: An International Guide to Research, Policies, and Programs* (Westport, CT: Greenwood Press, 1996); Joan Thrower Timm, *Four Perspectives in Multicultural Education* (Belmont, CA: Wadsworth, 1996).

TREATY OF GUADALUPE HIDALGO was signed in 1845 between the United States and Mexico. In 1836 a group of Texas Americans revolted against the Mexican government. The center of the conflict was a San Antonio mission called the Alamo. Under the leadership of General Antonio Lopez de Santa Anna, the Mexican army attacked the Alamo in which 175 Texas rebels had become encamped. Most of the Alamo rebels were killed, including Jim Bowie and Davy Crockett. However, a counterattack led by General Sam Houston resulted in the surrender of Santa Anna, and the Lone Star Republic was created under the leaderhsip of Sam Houston, who became its president.

By 1845, the United States had severed diplomatic relations with Mexico, and the Mexican War began. With an army of about 40,000 men, the American forces (many of them Texas Americans) reached Mexico City, which they occupied; the result was the Treaty of Guadalupe Hidalgo between the United States and Mexico. The American forces were accused of murder, robbery, and rape. The notion of ''manifest destiny'' played a role in these events assuming the Anglo-Saxon superiority of the European-American immigrants in North and South America.

The Treaty of Guadalupe Hidalgo resulted in the acquisition of the present-day states of California, Texas, New Mexico, Nevada, and parts of Utah, Colorado, and Arizona. For these lands, which represented about half of the country's original boundaries, Mexico received 15 million dollars.

In teaching about the history of these events, several issues are important. One of them relates to the Civil War that started just a little over a decade later. Since the Mexican War was the last conflict in which many Civil War participants had been engaged in active combat, it has been posited by some historians that one reason for the errors in Union strategy in the early stages of the Civil War were related to the lack of combat experience during the period between the two wars. A second concept directly focused on multicultural, educational issues relative to the perceptions of Mexican Americans. Many considered themselves to be "Native Americans" since they were residing within the present boundaries of the United States before the arrival of the Europeans. A third notion relates to one of the major issues that precipitated the Mexican War—slavery and the fact that Americans had commenced settling in the Texas portion of northern Mexico. They were looking for new areas to grow cotton and wanted to use African slaves as a form of cheap labor. In 1830, Mexico refused to allow these European-American incursions, and slavery was outlawed in Mexico that year. These two actions infuriated the illegal American aliens who continued to defy the Mexican decrees.

References: Rodolfo Acuna, *Occupied America: The Chicano's Struggle Toward Liberation* (San Francisco: Canfield Press, 1972); Carey McWilliams, *North From Mexico: The Spanish-Speaking People of the United States* (Westport, CT: Greenwood Press, 1990); David Montejano, *Anglos and Mexicans in the Making of Texas, 1836–1986* (Austin: University of Texas Press, 1987); David J. Weber (Ed.), *Foreigners in Their Native Land: Historical Roots of the Native-Americans* (Albuquerque: University of New Mexico Press, 1973).

TRIBE, a term used in referring to large groups of Native Americans, was brought to the United States by the Europeans. Originally, the word is thought to have come from the Etruscans and was altered by the French and English. Some social scientists believe that a tribe consisted of several bands, who have been organized into large self-sufficient groups of people with a common language and an organized system of decision making.

However, the term "tribe" has become somewhat convoluted throughout history. It is a European word brought by settlers, who were encroaching on the territories of indigenous persons. Originally it referred to a rather primitive group of people with limited technology. The European-American notion of manifest destiny meant that the original persons inhabiting the areas were not important, and the land was there for the taking. Therefore, the original meaning of the word "tribe" in the United States had racist connotations, since it referred to large groups of native people who were deemed to be "uncivilized" and "inferior" by the new European residents.

Before the arrival of the Europeans, there were numerous tribal communities throughout North America. As the United States evolved into a nation controlled by European Americans, it became necessary to define indigenous persons according to their tribal affiliation. Elsewhere in the world, the word "tribe" often referred to a political unit and did not necessarily denote persons who were considered to be "primitive" or "uncivilized."

Some Native Americans still object to the term "tribe," viewing it as an attempt by the European Americans to "civilize" them or force them into assimilating into the European-American macroculture. But legally, numerous treaties have been signed between the U.S. government and Native American ''tribes.'' Moreover, tribes today are considered to be ''domestic dependent nations'' with limited sovereignty. Therefore, from a legal standpoint, it is necessary to identify tribes according to their ethnic history. Native Americans can be ''enrolled'' as tribal members, which sometimes entitles them to certain benefits.

Thus, it can be seen that the word ''tribe'' is difficult to define and is ambiguous at best. Depending on one's point of view, it can be perceived both as a legal necessity and a further manifestation of racism. Obviously, teachers must be willing to define the word in terms of its many complexities, its history, and its perception by Native American persons.

References: Vine Deloria, Jr. and Clifford M. Lytle, *The Nations Within: The Past, Present and Future of American Indian Sovereignty* (New York: Pantheon, 1984); Morton H. Fried, *The Notion of Tribe* (Menlo Park, CA: Cummings, 1975); Max Gluckman, *Politics, Law, and Ritual in Tribal Society* (New York: Blackwell, 1977).

TUBMAN, HARRIET (1829–1913), known for her involvement in the Underground Railway, was instrumental in helping an estimated 300 African-American slaves gain their freedom. Born in 1829, she escaped from slavery in Maryland and became heavily involved in the Underground Railroad. The Underground Railroad included a number of ''conductors'' (like Harriett Tubman), who would help escaped slaves on their way north. There also were designated stopping points where runaways would be safe.

By 1860, Tubman had become involved in anti-slavery and women's rights. She also was a guerrilla, a spy, and scout for the Union Army. One time she even led a Union Army raid against Confederate forces in a battle occurring along the Combahee River in South Carolina. It was the only military mission in U.S. history which was planned by a woman.

Harriett Tubman was truly one of the significant African-American women who became involved in the women's movement and the anti-slavery movement. Teachers can use her accomplishments in the construction of multicultural calendars, that commemorate the accomplishments of persons from all racial and ethnic backgrounds throughout the nation's history.

References: James A. Banks, *Teaching Strategies for Ethnic Studies*, 6th ed. (Boston: Allyn and Bacon, 1997); Sharon Harley, *The Timetables of African-American History* (New York: Simon and Schuster, 1995).

TURE, KWAME. *See* CARMICHAEL, STOKELY.

TURNER, NAT (1800–1831), thought to be a rather docile and even humble slave, led 70 fellow slaves on a revolt against their masters on August 22, 1831, in Virginia. During the 2-day battle, nearly 60 European Americans died. The incident was terrifying to southern slave owners, because suddenly it meant that any of their docile slaves might be involved in leading such a revolt.

Turner claimed to have received the idea through a religious experience. A vision of his pictured African Americans and European Americans engaged in a battle resulting in a bloody confrontation. After his arrest, Turner professed that his master had been kind to him, but the vision made it necessary for him to execute his battle plan.

References: Herbert Aptheker, *American Negro Slave Revolts* (New York: International Publishers, 1963); John Hope Franklin, *From Slavery to Freedom: A History of Negro-Americans* (New York: Vintage Books, 1980); Kenneth Stampp, *The Peculiar Institution: Slavery in the Antebellum South* (New York: Harper and Row, 1956).

TUSKEGEE AIRMEN, formally known as the Ninety-Ninth Pursuit Squadron, were trained through the Tuskegee Training Program. The 99th Pursuit Squadron was involved in over 500 missions and better than 3,700 sorties during a single year of combat. Eventually the unit became united with the 332nd Fighter Group.

TUSKEGEE INSTITUTE, founded by Booker T. Washington in 1821, stressed a practical and useful curriculum for African-American students. Located in Alabama, Tuskegee Institute was one of the important segregated school facilities for African-American students who were forbidden to matriculate into European-American universities or colleges because of the state's segregation laws. Moreover, the goal at Tuskegee was to generate attitudes of self-respect and confidence. Washington was influenced by his mentor, General Samuel C. Armstrong, from Hampton Institute.

Washington created a philosophy at Tuskegee Institute that if students could make themselves become useful and important cogs in the economic recovery of the South, they could help to reduce the hostile racial tensions that existed in that portion of the United States. He felt that through these actions, they could also become respected by the European-American power structure. In addition, he wanted his Institute to become a place of hope for freed African-American slaves.

An excellent orator, Washington became a highly efficient fund-raiser. His well-crafted, articulate orations were successful in persuading wealthy philanthropists, such as Andrew Carnegie and H. H. Rogers of Standard Oil, to make sizable donations to the Institute. The funds were used primarily for scholarships and for the improvement of instruction.

Not everyone agreed with Washington about his goals for African-American education in Alabama. Probably his most severe critic was W.E.B. Du Bois, the renowned African-American scholar. He argued that the industrial-based curriculum served to verify the common European-American notion of the supposed inferiority of African Americans.

However, Washington and Du Bois came from quite different backgrounds.

Washington, raised in slave quarters during his very early years, understood the ravages of slavery and poverty. On the other hand, Du Bois, who grew up in Great Barrington, Massachusetts, after the Civil War, attended Fisk University, studied in Germany, and received his doctorate from Harvard University.

References: Addie Louise Joyner Butler, *The Distinctive Black College: Talladega, Tuskegee, and Morehouse* (Mutuchen, NJ: Scarecrow Press, 1977); Louis R. Harlan, et al. (Eds.), *Booker T. Washington Papers* (Champaign, IL: University of Illinois Press, 1972); Louis R. Harlan, *Booker T. Washington, the Wizard of Tuskegee, 1901–1915* (New York: Oxford University Press, 1983); Booker T. Washington (Ed.), *Tuskegee: Its People, Their Ideals and Achievements* (New York: Appleton, 1905).

TWENTY-FOURTH AND TWENTY-FIFTH INFANTRY REGIMENTS. *See* BUFFALO SOLDIERS.

U

UMATILLA TRIBE, part of the Plateau Native American culture, has resided in the Mid-Columbian Plateau in the states of northeastern Oregon and southeastern Washington. Their reservation is located in northeastern Oregon. When European-American settlers arrived, the Umatillas had established a culture based primarily on the plentiful supply of salmon, which they harvested from the Columbia River. They also gathered wild fruits and berries, and the horse was part of their culture.

Originally, the encroachments of the European Americans did not result in an epidemic of smallpox and other diseases. In spite of the fact that their villages were constructed close to the Emigrant Road, or Old Oregon Trail, they did not suffer from the usual diseases until the 1840s. When the Cayuse War broke out, some of the Umatillas were involved.

Originally, the Umatilla Reservation consisted of nearly 247,000 acres. However, at the present time (1997), it has about 85,322 acres. The tribe presently enjoys an economy of farming and grazing. Wheat is the primary crop, and there are some small industries on the reservation. The population of the Umatilla Tribe is approximately 1,159 persons.

Reference: Harvey Markowitz, *American Indians* (Pasadena, CA: Salem Press, 1995).

UNCLE TOM, a term which had its origins in Harriett Beecher Stowe's work, *Uncle Tom's Cabin*, became commonly used during the American Civil Rights Movement to designate African-American persons who purportedly had rejected their African heritage and became assimilated into the dominant European-American macroculture. However, the term is a complicated one and according to some scholars, has been based on efforts to promote a more submissive style of behavior on the part of African-American people. Thus, the phrases such as "Toms" or "Uncle Toms" sometimes referred to African Americans who "sold out" to European Americans. In doing so, they were often viewed as persons who had rejected their Africanness.

Harriett Beecher Stowe, in her novel *Uncle Tom's Cabin*, characterized Uncle Tom as a man who was civilized, sympathetic, and assimilative. He had acquired refined tastes and feelings, and his acculturation involved learning how to read the Bible. He accepted his status as a slave and somehow felt that his predicament was part of God's plan. Even when he learned that he would be sold away from his family, he somehow decided that it was part of God's plan and things would be better in his next life. Uncle Tom harbored a profound sense of loyalty and did not try to escape to the North. However, in spite of these characteristics, he refused to administer a beating to Cassy when ordered to do so by his master.

Thus, Uncle Tom became a metaphor during the American Civil Rights Movement. He symbolized the African Americans who refused to take a stand against European-American oppression, because they did not want to lose the special relationships they enjoyed with those who were in positions of power.

Reference: Wilson Jeremiah Moses, *Black Messiahs and Uncle Toms* (University Park, PA: The Pennsylvania State University Press, 1982).

UNCLE TOM'S CABIN, a novel by Harriett Beecher Stowe, had a powerful effect on the psyche of the nation prior to the start of the Civil War. In fact, President Abraham Lincoln referred to Stowe as "the little lady who started this great war." The book's protagonist, Uncle Tom, was murdered by Simon Legree because he lied about the whereabouts of fellow slaves, Cassy and Emmeline. And while Stowe painted Uncle Tom as a noble character, whose self-sacrificing love was a noble Christian virtue, Tom also has been characterized by critics as being either neurotic and/or deceitful.

Tom was motivated by Christian love, a manifestation of Stowe's religious upbringings. However, her Calvinistic parents, the Beechers, believed that people were inherently evil; moreover, Stowe was subjected to her parents' religious dogma on a daily basis. While people were free to be good, they were inherently bad. Most humans were certain to be subjected to eternal hellfire. Her marriage to Calvin Stowe resulted in the development of her writing prowess because of their financial circumstances. While Calvin Stowe probably would have preferred that Harriett become the typical Calvinistic housewife, she was forced to help supplement the family income by writing.

Uncle Tom's Cabin, her most famous work, turned out to be a piece of writing which vilified slavery. Tom, a bright African-American slave, was sold down the river. Eliza, one of Tom's fellow slaves, her child, and husband fled to Canada, taking advantage of the Underground Railway. But while Stowe revealed her unbridled disgust for the concept of slavery, she was a very private person and did not join any of the groups (such as the Quakers) which were lobbying for government intervention against slavery. However, her behavior changed in 1850 when she became involved in the northern reaction against the Fugitive Slave Law.

This piece is one of the classic works of literature used in middle schools and high schools all over the country. However, the story requires careful interpretation by English teachers. The many metaphors and powerful messages contained in the book's passages can be useful tools for teachers who wish to help students understand the egregious damage that African-American people have had to contend with due to the country's history of slave exploitation.

References: John R. Adams, *Harriett Beecher Stowe* (Bloomington: University of Indiana Press, 1989); Alice Crozier, *The Novels of Harriett Beecher Stowe* (New York: Oxford University Press, 1969).

UNCONSCIOUS CULTURAL CONFLICTS, a crucial element of the multicultural education curriculum, refers to the beliefs, attitudes, and values that people have. While some people are able to articulate these values well, others have never bothered to analyze their beliefs and harbor certain prejudices against some groups. These prejudices can develop into unconscious cultural conflicts.

Social-distance research, while showing a change in attitudes, also reveals a general unwillingness for human beings to accept interactions with members of other groups. For example, European Americans have been found to be most accepting of Native Americans, African Americans, Mexican Americans and Japanese Americans (in that order). Studies have also shown that more than one in ten Americans would not welcome Koreans, Hispanics, Indians, Pakistanis, or Vietnamese as neighbors. Also, European Americans from the South are less tolerant of African Americans, Latinos, and Asian-American groups. Many of the subjects in such studies have not even been aware of the attitudes they harbored about other cultural groups.

A useful tool for teachers is James Banks' six levels of racial tolerance. Level one is referred to as ethnic psychological captivity, where students have internalized negative attitudes about their ethnicity. Level two, ethnic encapsulation, describes persons who believe in the superiority of their own microculture. Moreover, they purposefully avoid any contacts with individuals from any other ethnic group and believe in the superiority of their own cultural group, for example, "skinheads."

Stage three, ethnic identity clarification, refers to the capacity of the person to commence relating more positively to other groups, because they have developed a psychologically healthy view of their own ethnicity. Stage four, biethnicity, refers to the interest a person has in functioning equally within a second ethnic group. The fifth stage, multiethnicity, means that a person can function within several ethnic environments and prefers to do that. The final stage, globalism and global compentency, refers to the person who seeks out cultural relationships all over the world.

The Banks model is a useful tool for teachers who wish to acquire better information about unconscious cultural conflicts. It also can be used as a device for helping students move to higher levels of cultural acceptance.

References; Christine I. Bennett, *Comprehensive Multicultural Education: Theory and Practice*, 3d ed. (Boston: Allyn and Bacon, 1995); Carl A. Grant (Ed.), *Educating for Diversity: An Anthology of Multicultural Voices* (Boston: Allyn and Bacon, 1995).

UNDERCLASS, a sociological term synonymous with phrases such as "culture of poverty," refers to persons who find themselves below the poverty line. The underclass in the United States has struggled to provide the basic food, clothing, and shelter necessities throughout the history of the country. Unfortunately, there are skewed proportions of persons in the American underclass who are not European Americans; this has sometimes turned poverty issues into racial problems.

For educators, the problem has been particularly critical, and it cuts to the heart of multicultural education. Perhaps no other single issue has created more misperceptions for the American public and more hardships for the American underclass than testing. Research has persisted in showing powerful correlations between the test scores of American school children and their socioeconomic status. For example, school districts such as Mercer Island in Washington State have enjoyed fourth-grade reading scores at the 80th percentile, while some schools in south-central Los Angeles, one of the poorer communities in the United States in terms of per-capita income, have had extremely low test scores.

Starting in the early 1980s, the proportion of children from the underclass has been increasing rapidly, along with persons from upper socioeconomic levels. On the other hand, the American middle-class has been shrinking in size. Partly because of this change in demographics, many affluent families have been placing their children in private schools, arguing that the public schools are inferior in quality. In many communities, this has resulted in the public schools being populated by increasing numbers of children from the underclass.

The reasons for lower school performance by children from the underclass are many. There is a stronger likelihood that they have had poor pre-natal care, which can result in brain-cell damage. In their early years, they may not have seen role models to provide them with the idea about the importance of learning. Some underclass children live in houses where the adults have also experienced their own educational problems, which may make it difficult to help their own children with their school work. If the child has grown up without being exposed to standard English, his or her verbal skill-development in English may be retarded. These are just a few of the many problems which children from America's underclass must face in school.

However, another major problem is related to funding. Since the United States is one of the few nations in the world that does not have federally-funded equalization formulas, the problem of school funding often means that more money is available for schools in affluent communities compared to the communities with large populations of children from poverty backgrounds. For example, in East Saint Louis, Missouri, one of the poorer communities in the United States, physical education classes had to be cancelled because there were no funds to fix leaking pipes in the gym. But while the problem of providing an adequate education for children from the American underclass is severe, there is hope. In some districts, attempts to provide extra funds for the physical improvement of the school environment have been successful: keeping libraries open before and after school; purchasing computers and other teaching aids; providing special tutors; creating bilingual education programs, which have the acquisition of bilingualism as the ultimate goal; and instituting special programs, which focus on broad-based community education and more community involvement in the schools.

References: Jonathan Kozol, *Savage Inequalities* (New York: Crown, 1991); Daniel U. Levine and Robert J. Havighurst, *Society and Education* (Boston: Allyn and Bacon, 1992): Bruce M. Mitchell, et al., *The Dynamic Classroom*, 5th ed. (Dubuque, IA: Kendall/Hunt, 1995).

UNDERGROUND RAILROAD, an elaborate network of havens for runaway slaves who were attempting to escape to the northern United States or Canada, enabled thousands of African-American persons in bondage to gain their freedom. The Underground Railroad was established in 1815 by Levi Coffin, a Quaker, who learned about the possibility of attaining freedom in Canada for African slaves from soldiers returning from the War of 1812.

A number of abolitionists were prominent for their assistance in maintaining the Underground Railroad. Among them were William Wells Brown of Lexington, Kentucky, who escorted 69 escaped slaves to Canada in 1849. Also that year, Harriett Tubman escaped from slavery and was instrumental in assisting more than 300 persons escape slavery in 19 different successful attempts.

The stopping points were often established by abolitionist groups, often under the sponsorship of several Protestant churches such as the Quakers, Congregationalists, and Unitarians, among others. Runaway slaves were housed in a variety of buildings, often including houses and churches, on the Underground Railroad to the Canadian border.

The system was called the Underground Railway because of the secret way in which the slaves escaped. They traveled mostly at night, usually walking. The hiding places were referred to as *stations* and the persons, such as Harriett Tubman, who led them to safety in the North, were known as *conductors*. The most heavily used routes of the Underground Railroad ran through Ohio, Indiana, and western Pennsylvania. The runaways often reached Canada by going through Detroit or Niagara Falls. Others sailed across Lake Erie to Ontario.

References: Charles Blockson, *The Underground Railroad* (Berkeley, CA: Berkeley, 1994); Virginia Hamilton, *Many Thousand Gone: African-Americans from Slavery to Freedom* (New York: Knopf, 1993); Benjamin Quarles, *Black Abolitionists* (New York: Oxford University Press, 1969); William Still, *The Underground Railroad* (Chicago: Johnson, 1970).

UNDOCUMENTED WORKERS, a term referring to persons who have entered the United States illegally to become engaged in employment, most often refers to persons who have crossed the border from Mexico. The terms used to identify such persons have often been controversial. For example, ''wetback'' was used originally to describe Mexican nationals who illegally crossed the Rio Grande to gain access to the U.S. job market. The term often has carried negative connotations with it.

Other terms used when referring to undocumented laborers from Mexico are ''fence jumpers,'' ''illegal aliens,'' or *mojados*, meaning ''wet ones'' in Spanish. While these terms also are often viewed negatively, it is important to remember that even though undocumented workers are illegal, huge numbers of them come from Mexico to provide a source of cheap labor for American employers who are happy to take advantage of their need for even minimal wages.

The need for cheap farm labor developed during the first half of the twentieth century due to the irrigation projects in the southwest which created tens of thousands of new arable acres in California, Arizona, Washington, Oregon, Idaho, and Texas. Mexico, being right next door, was a logical source for acquiring new laborers.

One of the early attempts to meet the growing labor needs during World War II was the Bracero Program, which lasted from 1942 to 1964. This was an agreement between the United States and Mexico that allowed American farmers to take advantage of the available labor resources. However, the working and living conditions were sometimes less than desirable, and the salaries were very low. It was terminated under the Johnson Administration. Also, there was a growing resentment against the Latino laborers, partly due to racist sentiments, and also due to the false perception that the Mexican Braceros were taking jobs away from European Americans.

In recent years, undocumented workers have continued to cross the border in search of higher-paying jobs in the United States. The equation of a very poor country being right next door to one of the world's wealthiest has resulted in Mexican workers being willing to run the risk of getting arrested in order to take advantage of the more lucrative economic system of the United States.

For educators, this has created a need for more bilingual, educational programs and English as a Second Language (ESL) programs for the children of both documented and undocumented workers. The courts have ruled that all children in a given public school district within the United States have a right to an education. This legal ruling applies to the children of both documented and undocumented workers.

References: Mario T. Garcia, *Mexican Americans, Leadership, Ideology and Identity 1930 to 1960* (New Haven, CT: Yale University Press, 1989).

UNITED STATES COMMISSION ON CIVIL RIGHTS, established under the Eisenhower Administration in 1964, is a unit within the federal government's Executive Branch. Public Law 85–315 of the 1957 Civil Rights Act stipulated that the Civil Rights Commission is required to: "investigate allegations that certain citizens of the United States are being deprived of their right to vote and have that vote counted by reason of their color, race, religion, or national origin; study and collect information concerning legal developments constituting a denial of equal protection of the laws under the Constitution; and appraise the laws and policies of the Federal Government with respect to equal protection of the laws under the Constitution."

Subject to the advice and consent of the Senate, the President appoints six members to the Civil Rights Commission. The Commission is able to hire a full-time staff director, subpoena witnesses, and create advisory committees. The role of the Civil Rights Commission was broadened under the Civil Rights Act of 1964, which included the investigation of individual civil rights in the use of public facilities, housing, transportation, the administration of justice, and education.

The new interest resulted in the Civil Rights Commission reviewing matters pertaining to such issues as racial discrimination in the schools, school segregation, and the rights and responsibilities of teachers and students. Of particular interest to educators is the issue of equal educational opportunities, a constitutional guarantee and a topic of prime importance to the United States Commission on Civil Rights.

References: Public Law 85–315, *United States Statutes at Large*, 1957 (Vol. 71) (Washington, DC: U.S. Government Printing Office, 1958); Public Law 88–352, *United States Statutes at Large*, 1964 (Vol. 78) (Washington, DC: U.S. Government Printing Office, 1965); Thomas Sowell, *Civil Rights: Rhetoric or Reality* (New York: William Morrow, Inc., 1984).

UNITED STATES DEPARTMENT OF EDUCATION, formerly part of the Department of Health, Education, and Welfare, became a separate cabinet position in October 1979. The landmark legislation was enacted during the Carter Administration. Ronald Reagan successfully campaigned for the 1980 presidency, and part of his campaign platform argued for reversing the Congressional decision and returning the Department of Education to the Department of Health, Education, and Welfare.

Aggressively seeking to carry out this wish, he lobbied for the abolishment of the Department of Education. However, even though the Reagan agenda for this change became a goal of many conservative Republicans, the efforts to abolish this Cabinet position have been unsuccessful.

Since education is only a federal interest, not part of its mission, the Department of Education has very little direct authority over educational programs in the 50 states. However, past Commissioners of Education, such as Ernest Boyer, argued that the body should be something other than a pipeline for federal funding. It is the responsibility of the Department of Education to provide vigorous leadership and provide the states with needed support.

One example of this role was articulated by Secretary of Education Richard W. Riley, who strongly opposed Republicans' education proposals for making vouchers available for private education. He argued that making private school vouchers available for students would likely result in siphoning off badly needed funds for public schools. While a small percentage of low-income students might be able to attend private schools, which historically have been for affluent children, the vast majority of low-income students would not be able to attend private schools because of a lack of available space. Another potential problem with the Republican proposal is that such practices might violate the Constitution's principle of separation of church and state if vouchers were used to attend religion-based schools. The First Amendment of the Constitution reads: "Congress shall make no law respecting the establishment of religion or prohibiting the free exercise thereof."

Thus, it can be seen that the Department of Education is highly politicized. While Republicans have generally supported such voucher proposals, Democrats, on the other hand, have tended to rally against them.

References: Gerald L. Gutek, *Education and Schooling in America* (Englewood Cliffs, NJ: Prentice-Hall, 1983); Melissa Healy, "Schools Chief Riley Calls Voucher Programs a 'Fad,' " *Los Angeles Times*, September 24, 1997; James A. Johnson, et al., *Introduction to the Foundations of American Education* (Boston: Allyn and Bacon, 1996).

UNITED STATES OF AMERICA v. STATE OF SOUTH CAROLINA is a 1978 U.S. Supreme Court case related to teacher certification or pay. The state of South Carolina used the National Teacher Examination (NTE) as a screening device for determining certification for potential teachers. All candidates were required to achieve a minimum score to become legally certificated to teach in the state.

At issue was the greater number of African-American candidates who failed the test compared to European-American candidates. In addition, teacher salaries were partially predicated on the scores they received on the NTE. Since a larger number of African Americans failed to pass the test, it was alleged that this constituted the creation of a racial classification that violated the Fourteenth Amendment and Title VII of the Civil Rights Act of 1964.

The Supreme Court determined the NTE to be a valid and reliable test that was not created to discriminate against African-American candidates. Moreover, the Court ruled that using the NTE to determine pay levels was a rational and reasonable use of the instrument. They further ruled that the state's interest in improving the quality of instruction through the use of the NTE was proper and within the bounds of the U.S. Constitution. Consequently, the Court upheld the policy of the State of South Carolina.

References: Louis Fischer, David Schimmel, and Cynthia Kelly, *Teachers and the Law* (White Plains, NY: Longman, 1995); *United States of America v. State of South Carolina*, 434 U.S. 1026 (1978).

UNITED STATES SUPREME COURT. *See* SUPREME COURT OF THE UNITED STATES.

UNIVERSAL DECLARATION OF HUMAN RIGHTS, initially adopted by the General Assembly of the United Nations in 1948, is a document that is useful for any professional educator who is interested in improving multicultural, educational efforts. The Declaration was reaffirmed in 1948 at the Vienna, Austria, Human Rights Conference. The Universal Declaration of Human Rights declares that all persons are equal in dignity and born free. The basic economic, civil, political, and all social rights of humans are then defined. These values are as follows:

Human life on our planet is in jeopardy.

It is in jeopardy from war that could pulverize the human habitat.

It is in jeopardy from preparations for war that destroy or diminish the prospects of decent existence.

It is in jeopardy because of the denial of human rights.

It is in jeopardy because the air is being fouled and the waters and soil are being poisoned.

If these dangers are to be removed and if human development is to be assured, we the peoples of this planet must accept obligations to each other and to the generation of human beings to come.

We have the obligation to free our world of war by creating an enduring basis for worldwide peace.

We have the obligation to safeguard the delicate balance of the natural environment and to develop the world's resources for the human good.

We have the obligation to make human rights the primary concern of society.

We have the obligation to create a world order in which man neither has to kill or be killed.

In order to carry out these obligations, we the people of the world assert our primary allegiance to each other in the family of man. We declare our individual citizenship of the world community and our support for a United Nations capable of governing our planet in the common human interest.

Life in the universe is unimaginably rare. It must be protected, respected, and cherished.

We pledge our energies and resources of spirit to the preservation of the human habitat and to the infinite possibilities of human betterment in our time.

An examination of these values can lead to valuable curriculum development opportunities in the area of multicultural education. Teachers can discuss and evaluate domestic policies that are enacted by Congress in terms of their potential for addressing the human rights values of the United Nations and can also evaluate the policies of other countries, using these human rights criteria.

Reference: Christine I. Bennett, *Comprehensive Multicultural Education: Theory and Practice*, 3d ed. (Boston: Allyn and Bacon, 1995).

UNIVERSITY OF CALIFORNIA v. BAKKE. *See* BAKKE, ALLAN.

UPWARD MOBILITY, a phrase that refers to the capacity of people to improve themselves educationally and/or economically, became a popular concept during the American Civil Rights Movement. The sociological meaning of the phrase refers to attempts by persons from the culture of poverty to move from one socioeconomic level to the next.

The concept represented the core philosophy of the Johnson War on Poverty efforts during the 1960s. Special grants were available for social service agencies to help persons leave their poverty status. The federal, state, and local programs that were crafted to accomplish this generally offered compensatory educational opportunities for poverty persons based on the belief that the more education a person had, the better the job he or she could obtain. And as occupations improved, so did income. However, for many, becoming upwardly mobile was extremely difficult. Large numbers of Americans had coped with poverty for many generations. Consequently, some of them had little understanding of how to go about improving their living circumstances. Thus, compensatory social programs sought to upgrade educational competence in order for such people to acquire higher paying jobs and improve their lives in the process.

Reference: Daniel U. Levine and Robert J. Havighurst, *Society and Education* (Boston: Allyn and Bacon, 1992).

URBAN INDIANS, a name for more than half of the Native Americans who live in urban areas on at least a part-time basis. This statistic belies a common notion that most Native Americans live on reservations. The fact that the stereotypical view of Native Americans has them residing on reservations has made it difficult for people to understand the needs of Native Americans, who make their homes in urban areas of the United States.

During the mid-1950s, the Bureau of Indian Affairs (BIA) initiated a program that provided funding for Native Americans to move from reservations to urban areas. Native American people who agreed to be relocated were given a subsistence allowance for a period of six weeks. After that time, they were expected to be on their own. However, after becoming urban residents, many Native Americans went back to their reservations for a variety of reasons.

Most Native American urban residents did not go to the cities because of the Congressional legislation. Rather, they moved there to secure employment or to live closer to friends and relatives. Many quickly became disillusioned when they discovered that affordable housing was often located in the poorest parts of the city, and many of the jobs were unskilled and often offered minimal compensation. As a result, many moved back to their reservations.

One major set of lessons learned by Native Americans, who have moved to urban areas, has been their interest in learning how to deal with national, state, and local governments. Since a 1988 ruling that allowed gambling on reservation lands, Native Americans have become far more sophisticated negotiating with urban bureaucracies. Many Native American microcultures have taken advantage of legislative actions to establish gambling reservations that have improved the economic lives of Native American persons. Many tribes have started gambling operations in hopes of improving their fiscal status. Others are carrying on heated debates in hopes of determining the best approach.

References: Jeanne Buillemin, *Urban Renegades* (New York: Columbia University Press, 1975); Michael T. Kauffman, "A James Bond with $100 Tries out a Tribal Casino," *New York Times*, March 18, 1994.

UTE TRIBE, belonging to the Great Basin culture and the Ute-Aztecan language group, have been located primarily in the Utah and Colorado sectors of the United States. The 1990 census revealed a population of 7,272 persons. Historically, the Utes (who actually called themselves "the people") were nomadic hunters and gatherers, who traveled with their extended families in search of game for their sustenance.

Living in brush huts or skin-covered tipis, Utes were considered by some to be "warlike," and raiding sometimes became a companion activity to their hunting. Sometime during the seventeenth century it is believed that the Utes first came into contact with the Europeans when Spaniards came into the region. Through trading enterprises, the Utes acquired horses and arms in return for buckskins and Indian captives.

European Americans commenced encroaching on Ute territory when the Mormons came to Utah the Mexican War in 1848. In 1849, a treaty was signed between the Utes and the U.S. government, and new treaties were negotiated when the discovery of precious minerals in the Rockies brought a new influx of European-Americans into Ute territories. Chief Ouray became a prominent figure in many of these negotiations because of his bilingual abilities.

Two decades later, in 1879, a new agent at the White River Agency irritated members of the northern Utes when he ordered the agency to be moved. Moreover, he plowed up a race track and some of the Utes' best pasture land. Believing he needed protection from the Tribe, the agent also called up troops under the command of T. T. Thornburgh. They were sent to the Utes Reservation, which made the Tribe fear that they were to be removed forcibly to Indian Territory in Oklahoma. More than 300 Utes attacked the U.S. troops when they entered the reservation. Because of the uprising, the Utes were removed to the Uintah Reservation in the present state of Utah.

The Indian Reorganization Act enabled the Utes to establish tribal entities that were self-governing. As a result, the Uintah-Ouray Ute Tribe, the Southern Ute Tribe, and the Ute Mountain Ute Tribal units were formed. The three tribal units, organized as the Confederated Ute Tribe, were successful in reparation claims against the federal government, resulting in the establishment of the Indian Claims Commission in 1946.

References: Robert Delaney, *The Ute Mountain Utes* (Albuquerque: University of New Mexico Press, 1989); Robert Emmitt, *The Last War Trail: The Utes and the Settlement of Colorado* (Norman: University of Oklahoma Press, 1954); Wilson Rockwell, *The Utes: A Forgotten People* (Denver: Sage, 1956).

V

VICTORIO (1825–1880), a Membreno Apache, became a leader of his band in raids against Mexican miners and European-American prospectors and ranchers who persisted in encroaching on their lands. While he has sometimes been painted as a warlike leader of his people, most of his life was spent in relative peace. In fact, he signed a provisional compact with the United States and attempted to procure a reservation for his people in 1869.

The Mimbrenos were brought to Ojo, Caliente, in 1874. But three years later, an attempt to unite the Apache groups on the San Carlos Reservation brought the Mimbrenos there against their will. As a result, they encountered neglect and engaged in conflict with the Chiricahua Apaches. Later that year, Victorio petitioned that he and 200 of his tribal members be allowed to return to New Mexico after he led them away from the Reservation. However, the U.S. government refused, deciding instead to force them to return to San Carlos. This action motivated Victorio to flee, along with 50 of his warriors and for the next year led raids in southern New Mexico, northern Mexico, and southeast Arizona.

These actions resulted in the pursuit of Victorio by U.S. government troops. But Victorio's military exploits baffled the U.S. troops for a year, and many of them were killed in the ensuing skirmishes. His numbers swelled when a number of other Apache groups joined his ranks. Geronimo also joined him for a time. However, Victorio was surprised by Apache scouts who ambushed his band, resulting in the loss of about 50 of Victorio's best warriors.

In 1880, tired of his attacks on Mexican troops, the Mexican government organized a force of some 300 soldiers, who attempted to thwart Victorio's raids. Finally, on October 15, they found him at Tres Castilios. He and his forces were ambushed and trapped. He committed suicide rather than having to return his band back to the reservation. The overwhelming numbers of his enemies resulted in the defeat of his band.

The exploits of the Apaches in the southwestern United States can provide students with accurate insights into the reasons for the conflicts between Native Americans and European Americans as they repeatedly invaded sacred Native American territories in their search for gold and other riches. The fact that Mexicans were also involved in these skirmishes can help teachers develop important learning concepts pertaining to the meaning of land ownership, boundaries, and the like.

References: John C. Cremony, *Life Among the Apaches* (Tucson, AZ: Arizona Silhouettes, 1954); Frank C. Lockwood, *The Apache Indians* (New York: Macmillan, 1938); Harvey Markowitz (Ed), *American Indians* (Pasadena, CA: Salem Press, 1995).

VIETNAMESE AMERICANS, a term pertaining to persons from North or South Vietnam who live in the United States. Following the fall of Saigon in 1975, approximately 138,000 Vietnamese people migrated to the United States Many of the Vietnamese refugees came from relatively affluent families. About 20 percent of this number were ethnic Chinese people.

During the presidency of Gerald Ford, the U.S. government was supportive of Vietnamese immigration, and special programs were established to assimilate the new Vietnamese into the American macroculture. On the whole, Vietnamese children easily made the adjustment to American schools and out-performed many other immigrant groups.

Originally, the Vietnamese immigrants were placed in states which had less than 3,000 other Vietnamese residents. The government felt that there would be less resistance that way. Then, after they were established, they were free to move as they wished. Many Vietnamese refugees eventually settled in Southern California, especially in the Los Angeles area. A neighborhood known as "Little Saigon" became known as a Vietnamese enclave. More than 25 percent of the Vietnamese population now reside in Southern California.

With help from their sponsors, Vietnamese people have been successful in securing employment, resulting in a very low unemployment rate for this group. More than 20 percent of all Vietnamese persons over 18 years of age have had some college experience, and since many of the immigrants fled to the south from North Vietnam, most of the immigrants are strongly anti-Communist. However, in recent years, many Vietnamese youth have become involved in gangs, which sometimes have erupted into violent confrontations with their own and other groups.

Teachers must be sensitive to the needs of Vietnamese students. One way teachers can motivate Vietnamese students is through the use of appropriate literature. Excellent works are available by Vietnamese authors such as: Huynh Quang Nhuong *The Land I Lost: Adventures of a Boy in Vietnam* (Harper, 1982); Vuong Thuy, *Getting to Know the Vietnamese and their Culture* (Ungar, 1976);

and L. D. Vuong, *The Brocaded Slipper and Other Vietnamese Tales* (Addison-Wesley, 1982). Works such as these help students to stay in touch with their microcultural ethnicity.

References: Robert M. Jiobu, *Ethnicity and Assimilation* (Albany: State University of New York Press, 1988); Pamela L. Tiedt and Iris M. Tiedt, *Multicultural Teaching: A Handbook of Activities, Information, and Resources* (Boston: Allyn and Bacon, 1994).

VIKINGS, claimed by many historians to be the first Europeans to reach North America, landed in Vinland about 1000 A.D. The term "Vinland" is Norse in origin and means grassland or pasture land. Now the area is known as Newfoundland, a Canadian province east of Quebec. The exploration was led by Thorvald Eriksson, the son of Erik the Red. It is believed that they sailed from Greenland.

However, most of the Norsemen did not stay because of the violent confrontations with Native Greenlanders. In 1960, archaeologists found Norse tools and artifacts. Carbon dating verified that they were created about 1000 A.D. Prior to 1969, the explorations of the Vikings were known only through oral history created through tales that had been handed down for nearly 1,000 years.

The explorations of the Vikings can be used by teachers to illustrate the multicultural influences of the Europeans on the development of the United States. While it is not believed that the Norse explorers ever reached the present boundaries at that particular time in history, it is important for students to understand the significance of the European explorations. By the time Columbus succeeded in his explorations, the printing press had been invented and ordinary people had better access to such information.

Reference: Ronald Takaki, *A Different Mirror: A History of Multicultural America* (Boston: Little, Brown 1993).

VISION QUEST, a personal experience involving fasting in secluded places, was a ceremony conducted by Native Americans in search of knowledge or help from the spiritual world. Although most of the Native American vision quests were carried out by Native American males, females occasionally participated, as well. The vision quests were sometimes conducted in secluded locations some distance away from the village.

The vision quest required the participant to fast for a period of approximately four days. During the experience, participants might ask for courage or health, or even for assistance in helping them provide the basic necessities for their family. Following the event, a holy man would help to interpret the meanings derived from the vision quest experience.

Among Native American tribes, it was common for young men to have significant religious experiences before they reached puberty. These religious events would usually involve seeing a vision. A religious member of the tribe, sometimes a shaman or medicine man, would help the young man to interpret the vision which he encountered.

At the present time, if Native American men or women wish to participate in an evening journey to sort out their callings in life, they sometimes present a prayer instrument to a holy person and solicit his advice. The holy man then escorts the person to a holy place where the fasting person remains until the holy person returns. The vision circle is often a pit. However, if a pit is not used, sometimes prayer flags are placed around the participant.

Teachers can use descriptions of the vision quests in comparing the religious traditions of American microcultures. James Banks recommends having students produce data retrieval charts for cultural comparisons. These retrieval charts can compare other variables such as economy, family, government, clothing, shelter, and food.

References: James A. Banks, *Teaching Strategies for Ethnic Studies*, 6th ed. (Boston: Allyn and Bacon, 1997); Joseph Epes Brown (Ed.), *The Sacred Pipe: Black Elk's Account of the Oglala Sioux* (Norman: University of Oklahoma Press, 1989); Thomas E. Mails, *Fools Crow: Wisdom and Power* (Tulsa, OK: Live Oak Press, 1989).

VISTA, an acronym standing for Volunteers in Service to America, was one of President Lyndon Johnson's "War on Poverty" programs designed to eliminate poverty in America. While the issue of poverty had been addressed vigorously during the administration of President Franklin Roosevelt in the post-depression era, it resurfaced in the 1960s. As a result, VISTA was created in 1964 to deal aggressively with poverty problems. In 1971, VISTA and the Peace Corps, its companion program, were combined under a newly-established agency called ACTION.

VISTA volunteers worked in several different areas according to their levels of expertise. Included in their volunteer activities were programs of: community service; economic development; improvement of learning, such as involvement in bilingual/bicultural education; health and nutrition; legal rights; housing; and energy conservation. University Year for ACTION volunteers were involved in many of the same activities, only the volunteers were all college students.

Volunteers in the VISTA program had to possess the required skills and had to be at least 18 years of age. After a brief training program, the VISTA volunteers spent one year in a designated agency. They received a minimal monthly allowance to cover nominal living expenses along with a small stipend, which they were awarded at the termination of their involvement in the program.

Much of the training related to multicultural factors in order for the volunteers to be more effective in meeting the needs of their clients. The basic issues of poverty were addressed also in the training sessions. For example, in America, poverty exists in virtually every microculture, but there is a highly skewed proportion of persons below the poverty line who happen to be persons of color.

VISTA volunteers worked in social service agencies such as juvenile detention centers, free legal advice programs, schools, Boys and Girls Clubs, juvenile and adult probation centers, food and clothing banks, senior centers, and a host of other private and public agencies designed to meet the needs of poverty persons.

References: *Loving, Caring, Sharing, Living: Older American Volunteers in Action,* Pamphlet No. 4500.7 (Washington, DC: ACTION, September 1977); *Put Yourself Where You're Needed,* ACTION Flyer No. 4301.5 (Washington, DC: ACTION, August 1978).

VOTING RIGHTS, historically a problem for some American microcultures, were finally granted by the Voting Rights Act of 1965 to all persons who were able to satisfy citizenship and age requirements, regardless of their race or ethnicity. The act was modified in 1975, requiring states to provide bilingual ballots in 24 states in which Alaskan, Spanish, Indian, and Asian languages and dialects were spoken by large numbers of voters.

Since the states have had the power to determine who could vote, barring any federal constitution stipulations, a number of non-European-American microcultures were not able to vote until the enactment of the Fifteenth Amendment to the Constitution, in 1870. Prior to that time, African-American slaves were disenfranchised. It should be noted also that large numbers of freed slaves were still disenfranchised because of the poll taxes and literacy laws. Also disenfranchised were all American women who were not allowed to vote until the passage of the Nineteenth Amendment in 1920.

In spite of the Fifteenth and Nineteenth Amendments, some Native Americans were disenfranchised until the passage of the Voting Rights Act of 1965. In 1924, Congress passed legislation that granted voting rights to all Native Americans who had served in the armed forces during World War I. This Indian Citizenship Act granted full citizenship to all Native Americans who were born in the United States, regardless of their reservation status or tribal affiliation. However, some were still disenfranchised because of certain pre-existing clauses, literacy tests, and poll taxes. Some states argued that since the state had no power to regulate Native Americans who resided on reservations, they were not legal residents of the state. These barriers were finally terminated after passage of the Voting Rights Act of 1965.

References: Daniel U. Levine and Robert J. Havighurst, *Society and Education* (Boston: Allyn and Bacon, 1992); Felix S. Cohen, *Handbook of Federal Indian Law* (Washington, DC: U.S. Government Printing Office, 1942), Vine Deloria, Jr. and Clifford M. Lytle, *American Indians, American Justice* (Austin: University of Texas Press, 1983); Monroe E. Price and Robert N. Clinton, *Law and the American Indian; Readings, Notes, and Cases* (Charlottesville, VA: Michie, 1983).

W

WALLACE, GEORGE (1919–1998), four-time, anti-integration governor of Alabama during the American Civil Rights Movement, first attracted attention in 1963 in his inauguration speech in which he stated, "Segregation Now! Segregation Tomorrow! Segregation Forever!" During the late spring of 1963, demonstrations in Birmingham, Alabama, intensified as a result of desegregation efforts by civil rights activists, the jailing of Dr. Martin Luther King, and the aggressive tactics of Theophilus Eugene "Bull" Connor, public safety commissioner of Birmingham.

After a federal judge ordered the University of Alabama to admit African-American students, Connor joined forces with Governor George Wallace. Later that spring, on June 11, 1963, Wallace stood in a doorway at the University of Alabama, personally blocking the entrance of Vivian Malone and James Hood, two African-American students who were trying to register for classes. He argued that the edict by the federal court violated the Constitutions of the United States and Alabama. Backed by federal marshals, the two students were admitted to the university after Wallace left the campus.

Wallace also attempted to block the enactment of the Voting Rights Act of 1965, which finally terminated all literacy tests and made provisions for utilizing federal examiners in many southern communities to protect the voting rights of African-American people. He was committed to the concept of "states rights" and was opposed to federal involvement in what he considered to be state problems.

Born in Clio, Alabama, in 1919, Wallace ran unsuccessfully for president in 1968, 1972, and 1976. In 1968, he ran against Republican Richard Nixon and Democrat Hubert Humphrey. He carried five states and received close to 10 million votes. During his 1972 candidacy for the presidency, he was shot and seriously wounded in an assassination attempt by Arthur H. Bremer. The shooting left his legs paralyzed. During a 1978 speech, he apologized for his segregation stance, stating that his opposition to integration had been wrong. He retired from politics in 1987.

His life illustrates how persons who have harbored bigoted attitudes about racial matters can change. In addition, it provides teachers with a powerful reason for utilizing multicultural teaching approaches to change the negative racial attitudes that students sometimes acquire from their parents.

Reference: Juan Williams, *Eyes on the Prize: America's Civil Rights Years, 1954–1965* (New York: Viking Press, 1987).

WAMPANOAG TRIBE, part of the Algonquian language group, is a northeastern Native American tribe known for its deep historical roots. Archaeologists believe that the tribe resided in the area at least 12,000 years ago. Moreover, they were prominent participants in the various interactions between the Europeans and the Native Americans. The Wampanoag played a major role in the lives of English colonists who landed in present-day Plymouth.

Probably the most famous Wampanoag was Massasoit, the supreme sachem, along with his two sons and eventual successors, Wamsutta and Metacomet. The sachems traded with the English colonists and signed a number of treaties, as well. They relied on farming and fishing for food and lived in wigwams in the summer and longhouses in the winter months.

Massasoit, supreme sachem of the Wampanoag during the early days of the Pilgrims colonization, had two sons, who also became sachems. Successors to his leadership, Wamsutta (Alexander) and Metacomet (King Philip) signed treaties with the Pilgrims. As sachems, they governed through consensus and charisma.

However, the loss of their native lands to the Pilgrims became increasingly irritating to King Philip. He attempted to establish a confederation of Native American tribes in the New England area hoping to take back their tribal lands. The issue came to a head in 1675 with the outbreak of the so-called King Philip War. The Pilgrims prevailed and King Philip lost his life in the conflict.

Some social studies textbooks used by teachers in the United States have painted inaccurate pictures of the eastern tribes. Sometimes the Squanto/Massasoit stories have been sugar coated without pointing out that the European encroachments went far beyond the stories about the eastern tribes showing settlers how to plant corn by putting fish in seed holes. Native American lands were taken over by Europeans as a result of the "manifest destiny" concept, and this ultimately led to the violent conflicts.

References: Jack Campisi, *The Mashpee Indians: Tribe on Trial* (Syracuse, NY: Syracuse University Press, 1991); Russell M. Peters, *The Wampanoags of Mashpee* (Mashpee, MA: Indian Spiritual and Training Council, 1987); Aurie Weinstein, "We're

Still Living on our Traditional Homeland: The Wampanoag Legacy in New England,'' in Frank W. Porter III (Ed.), *Strategies for Survival* (Westport, CT: Greenwood Press, 1986).

WAR ON POVERTY, an attempt to address the needs of the millions of Americans who were below the poverty line, was initiated during the mid 1960s as an element of the American Civil Rights Movement. The ''War'' involved an infusion of federal funds into the Office of Economic Opportunity (OEO) and passage of the Elementary and Secondary Education Act of 1965.

One of the more successful school programs of the War on Poverty was Head Start. Between 1965 and 1990, Head Start programs for low-income children served approximately 11 million children. Unfortunately, this figure represents less than 24 percent of the eligible low-income children. Other War on Poverty programs were designed for adults and older Americans.

However, while War on Poverty programs helped to curtail hunger problems and assist many persons in becoming upwardly mobile, the latest studies reveal a shrinking middle class and a widening gap between the ''haves'' and the ''have nots.'' For example, the *Forbes* 400 list of the richest persons in the United States included 170 billionaires; the ''poorest'' person on the top 400 list was worth $475 million. On the other hand, about 36 million persons in the United States live below the poverty line. Also, U.S. Census Bureau figures revealed that an examination of the top 5 percent of household incomes ($119,540) increased their national share of the United States' income from 15.6 percent in 1981 to 21.4 percent in 1996.

The new increases in the percentages of people in poverty have placed added burdens on public school teachers attempting to meet the needs of a burgeoning number of poverty students, a disproportionate percentage of them coming from non-European families. Problems encountered in poverty environments have often resulted in low test scores and high dropout rates. The problems for teachers are obvious. Without lower class sizes and specially-prepared educators, it may be difficult to address the complicated needs of poverty students.

References: Daniel U. Levine and Robert J. Havighurst, *Society and Education* (Boston: Allyn and Bacon, 1992); Molly Ivins, ''Accelerating in the Wrong Direction,'' *Spokesman-Review*, October 19, 1997.

WASHINGTON, BOOKER T. (1856–1915), educator and African-American leader, became a staunch supporter of vocational education for African-American students during the Reconstruction period following the termination of the Civil War. At the age of 35, he was appointed to become the head of Tuskegee Institute in Alabama. Under his leadership, the school became one of the leading educational centers for African-American students.

During his youth, he worked in the coal mines and attended school for three months out of the year. He managed to work his way through Hampton Institute, where he graduated in 1875. During his presidency at Tuskegee, he made it possible for young African Americans to acquire trades that would make them employable at a difficult time in history. The school was segregated in compliance with the Jim Crow segregation policies of the State of Alabama.

In an 1895 speech at the Atlanta Exposition, he attracted the attention of African Americans; eventually African Americans were appointed to federal jobs. In addition, Washington became an adviser on racial issues to Presidents Theodore Roosevelt and Howard Taft. He died in 1915.

Washington was not without his critics. Probably his most severe adversary was W.E.B. Du Bois, the African-American intellectual. Du Bois accused him of not encouraging African Americans to acquire four-year degrees in colleges and universities to pursue professional occupations. However, Washington was totally committed to the Tuskegee programs, which he felt would help African Americans become economically upwardly mobile.

References: Louis R. Harlan, et al. (Eds.), *Booker T. Washington Papers* (Champaign: University of Illinois Press, 1972); Louis R. Harlan, *Booker T. Washington, The Wizard of Tuskegee, 1901–1915* (New York: Oxford University Press, 1983); Booker T. Washington, *Tuskegee: Its People, Their Ideals and Achievements* (New York: D. Appleton, 1905).

WASHINGTON, KENNY (1919–1971), a three-sport athlete at the University of California at Los Angeles (UCLA), was one of the first African Americans to break the color barrier. He opted to matriculate at UCLA because at the time, his two favorite schools, USC and Notre Dame, would not enroll African-American athletes. Along with teammates Jackie Robinson and Woody Strode, Washington enjoyed enormous success at UCLA in football, baseball, and track. Because of his dignity, courage and mental toughness, he made an excellent role model for other African-American athletes.

He went to UCLA in 1936 at a time when the school was attempting to join the ranks of the major university football teams. Shortly before he joined the team, UCLA had suffered embarrassing losses to much smaller schools, such as Whittier College. When he first entered Los Angeles' Lincoln High School, he was 6'1" tall but weighed about 135 pounds.

In his sophomore year, he became the signal caller and with his accurate passing to Woody Strode, they became known as the ''Gold Dust Twins.'' During his junior year, Washington became part of the ''Gold Dust Trio'' when Jackie Robinson was recruited to play football at UCLA. Washington became well known for his great speed and his incredible throwing arm. In his senior year, under the new UCLA coach ''Babe'' Horrell, Washington helped his UCLA team go undefeated. He was UCLA's first All-American. He graduated from UCLA with an AB degree in Letters and Science.

George Halas, coach of the Chicago Bears, wished to sign Washington to a pro contract, but other owners prevailed in refusing to allow racial integration in the sport. Since he was rejected by the National Football League, he went to work with the Los Angeles Police Department. He played for several years in the semi-pro Pacific Coast League. After a major knee operation, he became the first African American to become an NFL player when the Cleveland Rams moved to Los Angeles in 1946.

He was a warm, articulate man who did a great deal of charity work in the Los Angeles community and served as a mentor for athletes such as Hank Aaron, Willy Mays, and Tank Younger. He died in 1971 at the age of 52 of a blood disease. His enormous popularity as an athlete and his position as a highly respected public figure resulted in the Los Angeles Coliseum torch being lit in his honor.

His story provides teachers with an excellent example of the problems encountered by persons of color because of racist segregation practices.

References: David Falkner, *Great Time Coming: The Life of Jackie Robinson from Baseball to Birmingham* (New York: Simon and Schuster, 1995); Erik Brady, ''Pioneer Found Pain, Not Fame in Pro Football,'' *USA Today*, September 20, 1995; UCLA News Bureau, *Kingfish: The Kenny Washington Story* (Los Angeles: University of California at Los Angeles, 1997).

WATTS RIOTS, occurring during the American Civil Rights Movement, took place in the south-central areas of Los Angeles during the summer of 1965. They served to underscore the frustration experienced by low-income African-Americans who perceived themselves to be victimized, poverty-powerless members of the American macroculture.

The riots were precipitated by an incident that occurred on August 11, 1965, which typified the frustration experienced by young ghetto-dwelling African Americans. By 1965, the Civil Rights issues had been articulated well by Dr. Martin Luther King, Jr., and many young African Americans became convinced that because of their race they did not have the same access to social and economic opportunities available to European Americans.

On that date, a member of the Los Angeles Police Department arrested a young African American for speeding and intoxication. According to eyewitness stories, an innocent bystander was erroneously struck by a patrolman and a young woman, who was believed to have spit on the police, was brought to the middle of the street. August 11 was a very hot day, and the incidents provoked local residents to throw rocks at the police cars. This motivated a number of vandalization acts in the community.

Despite the efforts of community leaders, the problems became more acute. The crowds increased in size, and the incidents became more violent. Fire bombings resulted in major conflagrations, and African Americans threw firebombs at buildings. When Los Angeles firemen attempted to put out the blazes, they sometimes were fired upon. Rocks were thrown at cars, and European-American owned buildings were assaulted and looted. After the Los Angeles Police Department, under Chief Parker, lost control, the National Guard was called. Finally, the riots were terminated after 34 people lost their lives. Property damages exceeded 35 million dollars.

While European Americans deplored the violence and often failed to understand its origin, some African Americans, particularly male prisoners, looked upon it as justified; their "brothers" had lashed out against the European Americans who had enslaved and terrorized them ever since they had been brought to the United States against their will.

References: Leonard Dinnerstein, et al., *Natives and Strangers* (New York: Oxford University Press, 1990); Ronald Takaki, *A Different Mirror: A History of Multicultural America* (Boston: Little, Brown, 1993); Juan Williams, *Eyes on the Prize: America's Civil Rights Years, 1954–1965* (New York: Viking Press, 1987).

WETBACKS. *See* UNDOCUMENTED WORKERS.

WHEELER–HOWARD ACT. *See* INDIAN REORGANIZATION ACT of 1934.

WHITE FLIGHT, a term that originated during the American Civil Rights Movement, referred to the relocation of European Americans to the suburbs as persons of color moved into their neighborhoods. As a result of *Brown v. Board of Education* in 1954, the nation changed its residential patterns. When "redlining" and "sundown laws" became unconstitutional, it became possible for African Americans and other non-European-American groups to move into neighborhoods that originally were composed of European-Americans only.

In addition to the racist attitudes of some European Americans, the perception that persons of color might bring down their property values provided additional motivation for European Americans to relocate. As a result of these desegregation practices, many European Americans moved to newer suburban areas. This "white flight" phenomenon resulted in the resegregation of America.

These resegregation practices caused enormous problems for school districts that were under court orders to desegregate. Many districts discovered that because of White Flight, it became impossible to integrate schools to comply with the *Brown v. Board of Education* Supreme Court decision.

Reference: Daniel U. Levine and Robert J. Havighurst, *Society and Education* (Boston: Allyn and Bacon, 1992).

WILEY, LEE (1915–1975), of Cherokee/Scotch/English heritage, grew up in a small town in Fort Gibson, Oklahoma. As a young girl, she dreamed of becoming a singer. She and her boyfriend would sometimes skip school and play records at a music store. The records she enjoyed were referred to as "race records,'' meaning records created by African-American musicians. Her favorites were the works of Bessie Smith and Ethel Waters Her mother disapproved.

However, Wiley could not be deterred, and at the age of fifteen she left home, moving to Saint Louis, Chicago, and New York to make her way into the music world. For awhile she was a prime-time featured singer on the Kraft Music Hall with Paul Whiteman. She became famous for the sensuality of her voice and was enamored with Cole Porter's tunes.

Establishing a connection with the Liberty Music Shop in New York, she recorded several Cole Porter tunes on two 1939/1940 albums. Cole Porter was thrilled with her work saying, ''I can't tell you how much I like the way she sings these songs.'' Her ''laid back'' style, coupled with her sweet voice, became a favorite for all jazz lovers.

For teachers, her work illustrates the value of using American jazz as an example of the value of intercultural interaction. The fact that Lee Wiley, part Cherokee, part European-American, developed her love for jazz singing by listening to great African-American jazz singers can be used to help students learn to appreciate the great value of American pluralism.

Reference: Nat Hentoff, *Listen to the Stories* (New York: HarperCollins, 1995).

WILKINS, ROY (1910–), the grandson of a slave, graduated from the University of Minnesota and went on to become a newspaperman for the *Kansas City Call*, an African-American newspaper. In 1934, he became the editor of *The Crisis*, the magazine for the National Association for the Advancement of Colored People (NAACP).

In 1955 he became the executive secretary for the NAACP. His leadership in the organization continued until 1977. During that time, he became known as ''Mr. Civil Rights,'' helping to acquire civil rights for African Americans. Wilkins believed strongly in using constitutional means to acquire racial equality and opposed both White supremacy and African-American separatism. He was awarded the Springarn Medal in 1974 for his work in civil rights.

Reference: Juan Williams, *Eyes on the Prize: America's Civil Rights Years, 1954–1965* (New York: Viking Press, 1987).

WILLIAMS, DANIEL H. (1856–1931), an African-American son of a barber, became an important pioneer in open-heart surgery. After being apprenticed to a shoemaker, his interest in medicine motivated his involvement in a two-year medical apprenticeship that led him to formal study in Northwestern University Medical School. It was known as the Chicago Medical School when he graduated in 1883.

After practicing medicine on Chicago's south side, he founded Provident Hospital and Medical Center in 1891. It was one of the nation's first hospitals open to all racial groups. His leadership made it possible for African-American nurses and doctors to join the medical profession. In 1883 he conducted a successful operation to repair a tear in a patient's pericardium that was injured by a knife wound. The patient outlived him. From 1893 to 1898, he served as chief surgeon of the Freedmen's Hospital in Washington, D.C. Later, he became an attending surgeon at St. Luke's Hospital in Chicago. Williams also was one of the organizers of the National Medical Association and the Medico-Chirurgical Society. The American Medical Association barred African-American doctors.

In addition to his enormous contributions to the field of medicine, he also is well remembered for making it possible for other African Americans to enter the medical profession. He believed in racial integration, and his example made it possible for people of non–European-American backgrounds to become involved in the various facets of the medical profession.

References: Sharon Harley, *The Timetables of African-American History* (New York: Simon and Schuster, 1995); L. Mpho Mabunda (Ed.), *The African-American Almanac*, 7th ed. (Detroit: Gale, 1997); Louise Merriwether, *The Heart Man: Dr. Daniel Hale Williams* (New York: Prentice-Hall, 1972).

WISCONSIN LEARNING ASSISTANCE PROGRAMS consist of several educational strategies that were designed to deal with equity and multicultural education. The legislation was enacted in May 1993 and relates to such topics as: non-discrimination against students; provisions for local school boards to utilize instructional materials that adequately reflect the cultural diversity and pluralistic nature of American history; provision of bilingual/bicultural educational programs for Limited English Proficiency students; learning assistance programs for Limited English Proficiency students; provisions for teaching Native American history in grade three; scholarships for minority-groups students; and Japanese language and culture programs.

These and other learning assistance programs have helped make Wisconsin one of the nation's leading educational systems for encouraging and nurturing strong multicultural, educational programs. Moreover, Wisconsin has pioneered equity programs in the schools that have become models for the other states to follow.

Reference: *Wisconsin Laws and Administrative Rules Related to Equity and Multicultural Education* (Madison: State Department of Public Instruction, 1993).

WOMEN'S MOVEMENT, a phrase referring to equality issues pertaining to women's rights, became powerful during the American Civil Rights Movement. Two of the organizations that championed these causes were the National Organization for Women (NOW) and the Women's Equity Action League (WEAL). While the Women's Movement has addressed numerous topics pertaining to the equal rights of women, three primary issues have been; equal pay for equal work; equal access to employment opportunities; and abortion rights.

Equal pay for equal work has long been a nagging issue for the Women's Movement. As late as the decade of the 1950s, some school districts in the United States had separate salary schedules for men and women. The rationale for paying women less was that teaching for women amounted to a supplemental income and, therefore, they should be paid less then men. Also, studies have revealed that despite efforts to address the disparity, American women, on the average, make 50 percent of the salaries of American men. And the Fortune 500 Chief Executive Officers are nearly all European-American males.

Other concerns of those involved in the Women's Movement relate to such educational topics as the kinds of messages girls and women receive from curriculum materials and textbooks. Often, boys have been pictured in more adventuresome roles than girls, and pictures have also placed girls in stereotypical occupations such as housewives, nurses, secretaries, and waitresses. On the other hand, boys have been pictured as doctors, attorneys, corporate heads, and in other professional pursuits.

The main goal of the Women's Movement has been to create equal social and economic opportunities for women. Some of the changes since the Civil Rights Movement have occurred as a result of Title IX legislation that mandated equal expenditures in athletics for boys and girls and special school programs to encourage girls to become interested in math and science.

The Women's Movement has even become politicized. In general, the Republican Party, particularly its conservative Christian faction, has opposed many of the ideas of the Women's Movement. On the other hand, the Democratic Party has viewed many of the Women's Movement ideas favorably. This has been reflected in recent presidential elections in which the women's vote helped elect Bill Clinton to his two terms.

References: Chip Berlet (Ed.), *Eyes Right! Challenging the Right Wing Backlash* (Boston: South End Press, 1995); Linda K. Kerber and Jane Sherron De Hart, *Women's America* (New York: Oxford University Press, 1991).

WOODSON, CARTER G. (1875–1950), regarded as one of the leading writers of African-American history, is also viewed as the originator of the African-American History movement in the United States. He founded the Association for the Study of Negro Life and History in 1915; the name of the organization now is the Association for the Study of Afro-American Life and History. The organization started publishing *The Journal of Negro History* in 1916.

Born in New Canton, Virginia, his parents were former slaves. Woodson received his Ph.D. in history from Harvard University and was the recipient of the Spingarn Medal in 1926. Perhaps his best known work is *Negro in Our History*, published in 1922. Many history scholars have argued that it is one of the two or three most scholarly works on African-American history.

Harvard University was among the first American universities to grant advanced degrees to African-American students. Many of the nation's universities still practiced *de jure* or *defacto* racial segregation until after the 1954 *Brown v. Board of Education* Supreme Court decisions. However, Woodson and W.E.B. Du Bois were two of the University's most famous scholars during the first two decades of the twentieth century.

Reference: Sharon Harley, *The Timetables of African-American History* (New York: Simon and Schuster, 1995).

WOUNDED KNEE MASSACRE, occurring in South Dakota in 1890, resulted in the deaths of several hundred members of the Sioux Tribe. The incident occurred as a result of western migration by European Americans after the Civil War. From 1870 to 1880, the population of the United States west of the Mississippi River grew from an estimated 7,000,000 to nearly 17,000,000. The population of Native Americans, an estimated 280,000, resided on about 180 reservations. The Sioux were among the last tribes to relocate to a reservation.

The incident was a result of Ghost Dances. While they were performed peacefully for many tribes, for the Sioux they were used as a method for stirring up resentments against European Americans. A special shirt was worn. Painted with magic symbols, it was believed that if the warriors wore the shirt, not even bullets could harm them. The Ghost Dance was upsetting to the European Americans who understood very little about it. An order to stop dancing was not heeded by the Sioux.

At Standing Rock, the army attempted to arrest Sitting Bull, thinking that he was the instigator of the Ghost Dance. During the arrest attempt, he was killed, which infuriated the Sioux people. Many members of the Sioux Tribe left Standing Rock to find Chief Red Cloud (also called Spotted Elk). Along with Big Foot, the Sioux went back toward Pine Ridge. However, only about 20 miles away, the soldiers decided to disarm the relatively peaceful Sioux tribal members who carried weapons.

The resulting massacre was exceptionally bloody, because the Army soldiers used Hitchkiss guns that were capable of firing 50 rounds a minute. Very few escaped, and the women and children were killed along with the men. Some of the wounded were taken by wagon to Pine Ridge. The battle was considered to be the last major confrontation between the Native Americans and European-American settlers.

References: Alan Axlerod, *Chronicle of the Indian Wars: From Colonial Times to Wounded Knee* (New York: Prentice-Hall, 1993); Dee Brown, *Bury My Heart at Wounded Knee* (New York: Bantam Books, 1972); James Mooney, *The Ghost Dance Religion and the Sioux Outbreak of 1890*, Reprint (Washington, DC: U.S. Government Printing Office, 1986).

X

XENOPHOBIA literally refers to a human condition resulting in a fear of foreigners, differences, or languages that a person cannot understand. For classroom teachers working on multicultural issues, xenophobia is a key issue as it relates to language. The term originated shortly after the turn of the century. Since many children inherit the condition, it is a critical problem for multicultural, educational educators to address.

Throughout history, xenophobia has been a persistent problem insofar as it pertains to language. Many people are extremely uncomfortable and even annoyed when they hear persons conversing in a language that they are unable to understand. For some, the situation creates a type of paranoia, because they assume others may be talking about them. Other persons simply object to a language that sounds different from their own.

Prior to the Civil Rights Movement of the 1960s, a number of English-only laws were passed to exhort people to learn the language of the country, English. For example, in 1889, a Wisconsin law, known as the Bennett Law, stipulated that certain school subjects must be taught in English. In general, these English-only laws were passed to help immigrants become fluent in English as quickly as possible.

However, one of the key arguments among English as a Second Language (ESL) groups was that to maintain a person's ethnicity, one should be encouraged to maintain his or her native language. During recent years, many American schools commenced to put bilingual education programs in place, based on the theory that children could learn faster in their native language. The 1974 *Lau v. Nichols* Supreme Court decision even mandated that children who spoke a language other than English should receive compensatory educational programs designed to facilitate their learning.

Since the 1980s, a national shift away from bilingualism and multilingualism has occurred. Criticisms of the schools' bilingual educational programs increased and by 1993, fifteen states made English their official language through constitutional amendments or legal statutes. In the absence of a legal national language, a number of states have passed "English-only laws," which, among other things, prohibit the use of bilingual ballots and other state documents.

To combat the nation's xenophobic tendencies, teachers have created curriculum materials that teach children the value of pluralistic groups living together. These curriculum materials encourage the development of positive attitudes about ethnic, racial, and linguistic diversity and the value of becoming bilingual or multilingual.

References: James A. Banks, *Multiethnic Education: Theory and Practice*, 3d ed. (Boston: Allyn and Bacon, 1994); Chip Berlet (Ed.), *Eyes Right! Challenging the Right Wing Backlash* (Boston: South End Press, 1995); Sara Bullard, *Teaching Tolerance* (Montgomery, AL: Southern Poverty Law Center, 1995).

Y

YAKAMA TRIBE, located in the Columbia Basin Plateau in Washington State, has been identified as Plateau Indians belonging to the Sahaptin language group. The Yakamas first encountered European Americans in 1805 during the explorations of the Lewis and Clark Expedition. By that time in history, the Yakamas had already been using horses for about 75 years.

While the land they inhabited in eastern Washington was semi-arid, they relied on the Yakima River flowing from the Cascade range for their water supply. The tribe subsisted on fishing, hunting, and gathering of roots and berries. Fishing is still a major source of food for the tribe, and in the early 1990s the tribe was involved in several lawsuits over water rights and catch limits.

During the middle 1800s, European-American adventurers made their way through Yakama lands on their way to the gold fields of the north. Gradually, relations between the two groups deteriorated and Isaac Stevens, governor of the Northwest Territory, attempted to persuade the Yakamas to give up their land and move to a reservation. A treaty council was organized in the Walla Walla area and attended by approximately 1,000 Yakamas, in addition to members of other tribes and bands. Chief Kamiakin was the main spokesman for the Native Americans. While a treaty was signed in 1855, Kamiakin refused to agree to the treaty.

The Yakama Wars began soon after the treaty was signed when Major Granville O. Haller was sent to the area to avenge the death of Andrew Bolen, an Indian agent. The first battle took place at Toppenish Creek. The European-American forces were forced to withdraw after suffering a defeat, and Major Gabriel Rains was sent to the area in order to avenge the defeat. Colonel George Wright was in command of the Northwest forces at the time, and the campaign against the Yakamas became more vigorous. A treaty was signed in 1856, after Wright had established control of the lands west of the Cascade range.

The Yakama tribe has always had the status of a sovereign nation, which led to their title of the "Yakama Nation." The Tribe was granted 1,250,000 acres for their reservation. However, due to the provisions of the General Allotment Act, the tribe lost about 500,000 acres, some of which were recovered later in the century. The current tribal government was established in 1935 and consists of a fourteen-member tribal council.

Reference: Harvey Markowitz (Ed.), *American Indians* (Pasadena, CA: Salem Press, 1995).

YELLOW WOLF (1856–1935), a young Nez Perce warrior who exhibited his bravery in the war with United States forces, was a second cousin of Chief Joseph. He received his name from a dream in which he saw a wolflike form standing in front of him. However, his given name was actually Hainmot Hikkih, which means "White Thunder" in the Nez Perce tongue.

During the battles of the Nez Perce Tribe, Yellow Wolf established himself as a loyal, brave, and courageous warrior. In September of 1877, Yellow Wolf became the advance guard due to his prowess in dealing with struggling soldiers. It was believed he was such a skilled warrior that he could take care of the enemy by himself. However, two days before the Nez Perce were to arrive in Canada, the tribe was forced to surrender to the U.S. forces.

However, Yellow Wolf refused to surrender. He and several other warriors fled to Sitting Bull's Sioux camp in Canada. After wintering there, they decided to return to the Wallowa Valley, thinking that it would then be safe. However, after arriving in June 1878, Yellow Wolf realized that he would be forced to reside in the midst of his former enemies, so he went to the Nez Perce agency. After resettlement in Oklahoma, he returned to the Colville Reservation in Washington state, where he resided until his death in 1935.

Teachers can use this story of Yellow Wolf to help students learn to appreciate the problems encountered by Native Americans due to the encroachments of the European-Americans who took over their land. It also offers the opportunity to teach students about the Native American reservation system, in general, and the Colville reservation, in particular.

References: Norman B. Adkison, *Indian Braves and Battles with More Nez Perce Lore* (Grangeville, ID: Idaho County Free Press, 1967); Merrill D. Beal, *I Will Fight No More Forever: Chief Joseph and the Nez Perce War* (Seattle: University of Washington Press, 1963); Harvey Chalmers II, *The Last Stand of the Nez Perce* (New York: Twayne, 1962); Don C. Fisher, *The Nez Perce War* (Thesis) (Moscow: University of Idaho, Department of History, 1925).

YOUNG, ANDREW (1932–), born in New Orleans in 1932, graduated from Howard University and the Hartford Theological Seminary. In 1955, he became

Z

ZAHARIAS, "BABE" DIDRICKSON (1914–1956), one of the pioneer athletes to gain notoriety in the United States, first became famous for her performances in the 1932 Olympic Games held at the Los Angeles Coliseum. She became one of the early international celebrity athletes because of her unbelievable performances in that Olympiad. In addition to her gold medals in the javelin throw and the hurdles, she also tied for first in the women's high jump. Prior to the Olympic Games in 1932, she won five gold medals at the Amateur Athletic Union championships, resulting in her acquisition of the nickname, "The Texas Tomboy."

After her successes in track and field, this amazing track and field athlete turned to golf. Because of her extraordinary athletic ability, she later demonstrated her talents as a golfer. She was instrumental in helping to originate the Ladies' Professional Golf Association in 1948. By the year 1950, she was recognized as the greatest female athlete during the first half of the twentieth century.

However, at an early age she developed cancer. After learning that she had contracted the disease in 1953, she decided to go public with the news to attract attention to the need for treatment and research. She died 3 years later at the age of 42.

One of the important pioneers in women's athletics, she opened the door for many other female athletes during a time in history when athletics was primarily the domain of European-American males. Teachers can use her story to help young women appreciate the sacrifices that women and persons of color were forced to endure during the first half of the twentieth century.

Reference: Irene M. Franck and David M. Brownstone, *Women's World: A Timeline of Women in History* (New York: HarperCollins, 1995).

ZANGWILL, ISRAEL (1864–1926), a Jewish-American playwright during the turn of the century era, became well known for his play, *The Melting Pot*, which opened in New York City in 1908. Zangwill, himself an immigrant, described his perception of the new nation with its cultural diversity. It was his notion that the ethnic groups would mix, ultimately creating a new person who would be superior to all.

The classic speech from Zangwill's play is as follows: "America is God's crucible, the great Melting Pot, where all races of Europe are melting and re-forming! Here you stand, good folk, think I, when I see them at Ellis Island, here you stand in your fifty groups with your hatreds and rivalries, but you won't be long like that, brothers, for these are the fires of God. A fig for your feuds and vendettas! Germans and Frenchmen, Irishmen and Englishmen, Jews and Russians—into the Crucible with you all! God is making the American . . . the real American has not arrived. He is only in the Crucible, I tell you—he will be the fusion of all races, the coming Superman."

While the notion of the melting pot was articulated during the 1700s, this time it received greater attention due to the success of the play. It stirred up a great controversy between the assimilationists and those who believed in maintaining their traditional ethnicity. However, it should be noted that Zangwill seemed to be arguing for only European Americans being allowed to jump into the crucible. No mention was made of the original residents—the Native Americans, African Americans, Asian Americans, or Latinos. Thus, the argument has continued.

References: James A. Banks, *Multiethnic Education: Theory and Practice*, 3d ed. (Boston: Allyn and Bacon, 1994); Donna M. Gollnick and Philip C. Chinn, *Multicultural Education in a Pluralistic Society* (Columbus, OH: Merrill, 1990); Robert M. Jiobu, *Ethnicity and Assimilation* (Albany: State University of New York Press, 1988); Fred Rodriguez, *Equity in Education: Issues and Strategies* (Dubuque, IA: Kendall/Hunt, 1990).

ZIONISM, a Jewish nationalist movement, refers to efforts for establishing the state of Israel as the Jewish homeland. The Jewish homeland was finally created following World War II through efforts by the United Nations. The Jewish *Diaspora*, which refers to the Babylonian exile during the sixth century B.C., precipitated the term *Zionism*, which has to do with the Jewish yearning for Zion, or Jerusalem. During the Diaspora, pseudo messiahs such as Sabbatai Zevi claimed that they would return the Jews to Zion. Another failed attempt to return Jews to their homeland was orchestrated by the Italian Nasi family. They obtained a permit from the Turks to establish a Jewish community in Galilee during the late 1500s. This ploy was also unsuccessful.

Prior to 1791, when Jews were emancipated during the French Revolution, they were unable to return to Zion. However, in the nineteenth century, an increased national sentiment in Europe provided ample motivation for David

Luzatto, Leo Pinkser, Zvi Kalischer, and Yehudah Alkalai to raise the consciousness of the ghetto Jewry. During the 1894 World Zionist Congress, held in Basel, Switzerland, an effective worldwide political organization was established. Convened by Theodor Herzl, an Austrian journalist, the organization published an official weekly newspaper, *Die Welt (The World).* After his death in 1904, the Zionist Movement's center moved to Germany.

During the worldwide congress in 1905, the British proposed the establishment of a Jewish homeland in Uganda. This attempt was thwarted. However, a Jewish homeland was finally created in Palestine as a result of the Balfour Declaration in 1917. Prior to that time, many Russian Jews moved to Palestine and the United States as a result of the failed Russian revolution and the subsequent persecution of the Jews. Unfortunately, hostilities between the Jewish settlers and the Palestinian Arabs increased.

During World War II, Zionist leadership moved to the United States, and a 1941 conference in New York City demanded the establishment of a Jewish state in all of Palestine with unlimited immigration. In 1947, the United Nations voted to partition Palestine, leading to the creation of the State of Israel in May 1948.

ZOOT SUIT RIOTS, involving violent confrontations between Mexican-American youth and European-American servicemen, took place during a 10-day period in 1943. One of the first incidents leading to the riots occurred at the Aragon Ballroom in Venice, California. The term "zoot suit" referred to the coats with padded shoulders, pegged pants, broad-brimmed hats, thick-soled shoes, and long watch chains worn by the Mexican-American youth in downtown and East Los Angeles. Sensationalized press releases portrayed the Mexican-American young men as "marauding Latin gangs" and "roving wolf-packs," which exacerbated the hostile feelings between the two groups.

Actually, the "riots" were racial in nature and at least, in part, manifestations of a xenophobic perception of Mexican Americans by many European Americans in the Los Angeles basin. A 1943 report issued by the Foreign Relations Bureau of the Los Angeles County Sheriff's Department characterized Mexican Americans as having innate proclivities toward violence with biological urges "to kill or at least to let blood." This unfortunate report, obviously unsubstantiated by research data, had a chilling affect on the Mexican-American communities in the Los Angeles area. Military police units were forced to quell the riots.

The Sleepy Lagoon Defense Committee was organized to defend the constitutional rights of Latino people, some of whom were zoot suiters. The defense committee was accused of being a Communist front organization by Los Angeles Police Chief, C. B. Horrall. The Los Angeles Police Department had been accused by some of harboring racist attitudes against Mexican-American people, particularly zoot suiters.

For social studies and history teachers and other professional educators involved in multicultural education, the newspaper stories can be used as examples of how the media can unwittingly stir up public sentiment against a particular group of people through writing styles, word choices, and headline writing. For example, referring to Mexican-American youth as "marauding Latin gangs" and "roving wolf packs" can incite people to violent behaviors. Using colors as adjectives for minority group members involved in crime can contribute to the development of damaging stereotypes.

References: Carey McWilliams, *North from Mexico: The Spanish-Speaking People of the United States* (Westport, CT: Greenwood Press, 1990); Maruricio Mazon, *The Zoot Suit Riots: The Psychology of Symbolic Annihilation* (Austin: University of Texas Press, 1984).

ZORACH v. CLAUSON, a 1952 Supreme Court decision relating to religious instruction in public schools, resulted in a verdict that upheld religious instruction for public school children as long as the instruction was carried on away from public school systems. A prior decision, *McCollum v. Board of Education*, had been declared unconstitutional in 1948. In the McCollum case in Champaign, Illinois, religious instruction had been carried on in the public schools. The court ruled that this practice violated the Establishment Clause of the First Amendment of the United States Constitution. It was also ruled that the Illinois compulsory attendance law provided a captive audience for the religion classes.

In New York State, students were excused from their classes to participate in religious education classes that were held off the school grounds for a few hours each day. Moreover, church officials provided the school district with attendance forms to verify the students' attendance in the religious instruction classes. Since there was no evidence that the school district was aiding or abetting the religious instruction programs, the Supreme Court ruled that the public schools were only accommodating religion and not directly aiding it.

Reference: *Deskbook Encyclopedia of American School Law* (Rosemount, MN: Data Research, 1994).

ZUNIS, classified as a microculture of the Western Pueblo tribes, have approximately 7,000 tribal members. During the 1980s the Zunis created their own tribal school system that incorporated a strong Zuni cultural component into their educational curriculum. Each year in August, the tribe conducts a fair that includes a parade with floats and dancing, along with a rodeo. At every event, Miss Zuni is selected; the winner is not necessarily the most beautiful young woman but the entrant who knows the most about the Zuni culture. Moreover, she must be fluent in the Zuni language. It is believed that, in this manner, the culture can be carried on.

Part of the Western Pueblos in the Southwest, the Zunis belong to the Desert

Culture believed to have inhabited the area for about 10,000 years. The current Zuni pueblo is located at the village of Halona wa, one of six villages that existed prior to 1700. Five other villages were vacated, perhaps because of raids by other tribal groups or diseases. Some historians believe that the legends of the *Seven Cities of Cibola* may have pertained to the Zuni villages. Vasquez de Coronado explored the area in 1540 when he heard about the legend.

The Zuni language is highly valued in the tribe and is the favored language of communication. However, most Zunis are also fluent in the English language. In the 1930s, Ruth Bunxel published the first Zuni grammar book, along with a number of Zuni texts. Linguistically, the Zuni language is thought to be unique, since it has not been related to any of the other language groups. The word order of the Zuni language is subject-verb-object.

References: Henry F. Dobyns and Robert C. Euler, *Indians of the Southwest* (Bloomington: University of Indiana Press, 1980); Edward P. Dozier, *The Pueblo Indians of North America* (New York; Holt, Rinehart, and Winston, 1970); T. J. Ferguson and Richard E Hart, *A Zuni Atlas* (Norman: University of Oklahoma Press, 1985); Dorothea Leighton and John Adair, *People of the Middle Place: A Study of the Zuni Indians* (New Haven, CT: Human Relations Area Files Press, 1966); Matilda C. Stevenson, *The Zuni Indians: Their Mythology, Esoteric Fraternities, and Ceremonies*, Bureau of American Ethnology, Annual Report 23 (1901–1902) (Washington, DC: U.S. Government Printing Office, 1904).

Selected Bibliography

Abalos, David T. *Strategies of Transformation Toward a Multicultural Society: Fulfilling the Story of Democracy*. Westport, CT: Praeger, 1996.

Abbey, Nancy, et al. (Eds.). *Family Life Education in Multicultural Classrooms: Practical Guidelines*. Santa Cruz, CA: Network Publications, 1990. [microform]

Adams, Maurianne, et al. (Eds.). *Teaching for Diversity and Social Justice: A Sourcebook*. New York: Routledge, 1997.

Adler, Sol. *Multicultural Communication Skills in the Classroom*. Boston: Allyn and Bacon, 1993.

Alvermann, Donna E., and Phelps, Stephen E. *Content Reading and Literacy: Succeeding in Today's Diverse Classrooms*. Boston: Allyn and Bacon, 1994.

American Indian Studies Center. *Multicultural Education and the American Indian*. Los Angeles: University of California, 1979.

Baker, Gwendolyn C. *Planning and Organizing for Multicultural Instruction*. Menlo Park, CA: Addison-Wesley, 1994.

Baloche, Lynda A. *The Cooperative Classroom: Empowering Learning*. Upper Saddle River, NJ: Prentice-Hall, 1998.

Banks, James A., (Ed.). *Multicultural Education, Transformative Knowledge, and Action: Historical and Contemporary Perspectives*. New York: Teachers College Press, 1966.

Banks, James A., and Banks, Cherry McGee (Eds.). *Handbook of Research on Multicultural Education*. New York: Macmillan, 1995.

Baptiste, H. Prentice. *Multicultural Education: A Synopsis*. Washington, DC: University Press of America, 1979.

Baruth, Leroy G. *Multicultural Education of Children and Adolescents*. Boston: Allyn and Bacon, 1992.

Benjamin, Michael. *Cultural Diversity, Educational Equity, and the Transformation of Higher Education: Group Profiles as a Guide to Policy and Programming*. Westport, CT: Praeger, 1996.

Bowser, Benjamin P., et al. *Confronting Diversity Issues on Campus.* Newbury Park, CA: Sage, 1993.

Bull, Barry L., et al. *The Ethics of Multicultural and Bilingual Education.* New York: Teachers College Press, 1992.

California, State Department of Education, Office of Intergroup Relations. *Planning for Multicultural Education as a Part of School Improvement.* Sacramento: California State Department of Education, 1979.

Campbell, Duane E. *Choosing Democracy: A Practical Guide to Multicultural Education.* Englewood Cliffs, NJ: Merrill, 1996.

Carlson, Dennis. *Making Progress: Education and Culture in New Times.* New York: Teachers College Press, 1997.

Cassara, Beverly (Ed.). *Adult Education in a Multicultural Society.* New York: Routledge, 1990.

Colangelo, Nicholas, et al. (Eds.). *Multicultural Nonsexist Education: A Human Relations Approach.* Dubuque, IA: Kendall/Hunt, 1979.

Cordeiro, Paula, et al. *Multiculturalism and TQE: Addressing Cultural Diversity in Schools.* Thousand Oaks, CA: Corwin Press, 1994.

Cox, Carole, and Boyd-Batstone, Paul. *Crossroads: Literature and Language in Culturally and Linguistically-Diverse Classrooms.* Upper Saddle River, NJ: Merrill, 1997.

Crawford, Leslie W. *Language and Literacy Learning in Multicultural Classrooms.* Boston: Allyn and Bacon, 1993.

Darder, Antonia. *Culture and Power in the Classroom: A Critical Foundation for Bicultural Education.* Westport, CT: Bergin & Garvey, 1991.

Davidman, Leonard. *Teaching with a Multicultural Perspective: A Practical Guide.* New York: Longman, 1994.

Davidson, Florence, and Davidson, Miriam. *Changing Childhood Prejudice: The Caring Work of the Schools.* Westport, CT: Bergin & Garvey, 1994.

De Gaetano, Yvonne, et al. *Kaleidoscope: A Multicultural Approach for the Primary School Classroom.* Upper Saddle River, NJ: Merrill, 1998.

De Melendez, Robles, Wilma, and Ostertag, Vesna. *Teaching Young Children in Multicultural Classrooms: Issues, Concepts, and Strategies.* Albany, NY: Delmar Publishers, 1997.

Devillar, Robert A., et al. (Eds.). *Cultural Diversity in Schools: From Rhetoric to Practice.* Albany: State University of New York Press, 1994.

Diamond, Barbara J. *Multicultural Literacy: Mirroring the Reality of the Classroom.* White Plains, NY: Longman, 1995.

Dilworth, Mary E. (Ed.). *Being Responsive to Cultural Differences: How Teachers Learn.* Thousand Oaks, CA: Corwin Press, 1998.

Donaldson, Karen. *Through Students' Eyes: Combating Racism in United States Schools.* Westport, CT: Praeger, 1996.

Elder, Pamela S. *Worldways: Bringing the World into the Classroom.* Menlo Park, CA: Addison-Wesley, 1987.

Eldridge, Deborah. *Teacher Talk: Multicultural Lesson Plans for the Elementary Classroom.* Boston: Allyn and Bacon, 1998.

Epps, Edgar (Ed.). *Cultural Pluralism.* Berkeley, CA: McCutchan, 1974.

Ferguson, Henry. *Manual for Multicultural Education.* Yarmouth, ME: International Press, 1987.

Fradd, Sandra, and Weismantel, Jeanne. *Meeting the Needs of Culturally and Linguistically Different Students: A Handbook for Educators*. Boston: Little, Brown, 1989.

Garcia, Eugene, et al. *Meeting the Challenge of Linguistic and Cultural Diversity in Early Childhood Education*. New York: Teachers College Press, 1995.

Gay, Geneva. *At the Essence of Learning: Multicultural Education*. West Lafayette, IN: Kappa Delta Pi, 1994.

Glazer, Nathan. *We Are All Multiculturalists Now*. Cambridge, MA: Harvard University Press, 1997.

Grant, Carl (Ed.). *Educating for Diversity: An Anthology of Multicultural Voices*. Boston: Allyn and Bacon, 1995.

Grant, Carl (Ed.). *Research and Multicultural Education: From the Margins to the Mainstream*. Washington, D.C.: Falmer Press, 1992.

Grant, Carl, and Gomez, Mary. *Making Schooling Multicultural: Campus and Classroom*. Englewood Cliffs, NJ: Merrill, 1996.

Gumbert, Edgar (Ed.). *Different People: Studies in Ethnicity and Education*. Atlanta: Center for Cross-Cultural Education, Georgia State University, 1983.

Hamm, Mary, and Adams, Dennis. *The Collaborative Dimensions of Learning*. Norwood, NJ: Ablex, 1992.

Hawley, Willis, et al. *Achieving Quality Integrated Education*. Washington, DC: National Education Association, 1986.

Howe, Kenneth Ross. *Understanding Equal Educational Opportunity: Social Justice, Democracy, and Schooling*. New York: Teachers College Press, 1997.

Jorgensen, Karen, et al. *New Faces in Our Schools: Student-Generated Solutions to Ethnic Conflict*. San Francisco: San Francisco Study Center, 1992.

Kendall, Frances. *Diversity in the Classroom: A Multicultural Approach to the Education of Young Children*. New York: Teachers College Press, 1983.

King, Joyce, et al. (Eds.). *Preparing Teachers for Cultural Diversity*. New York: Teachers College Press, 1997.

Klassen, Frank H., and Gollnick, Donna M. (Eds.). *Pluralism and the American Teacher: Issues and Case Studies*. Washington, DC: Ethnic Heritage Center for Teacher Education of the American Association of Colleges for Teacher Education, 1977.

Kohls, Robert L. *Developing Intercultural Awareness: A Learning Module Complete with Master Lesson Plan, Content, Exercises, and Handouts*. Washington, DC: Society for Intercultural Education, Training and Research, 1981.

La Belle, Thomas, and Ward, Christopher. *Ethnic Studies and Multiculturalism*. Albany: State University of New York Press, 1996.

La Belle, Thomas, and Ward, Christopher. *Multiculturalism and Education: Diversity and its Impact on Schools and Society*. Albany: State University of New York Press, 1994.

Long, Robert E. *Multiculturalism*. New York: H. W. Wilson, 1997.

Longstreet, Wilma S. *Aspects of Ethnicity: Understanding Differences in Pluralistic Classrooms*. New York: Teachers College Press, 1978.

Los Angeles Unified School District, *Incorporating Multicultural Education Into the Curriculum: Grades Four Through Eight*. Los Angeles: Los Angeles Unified School District, Office of Instruction: Elementary and Secondary, 1981.

Manning, M. Lee, and Baruth, Leroy G. *Multicultural Education of Children and Adolescents*. Boston: Allyn and Bacon, 1996.

Martin, Renee J. (Ed.). *Practicing What We Teach: Confronting Diversity in Teacher Education.* Albany: State University of New York Press, 1995.

Massaro, Toni Marie. *Constitutional Literacy: A Core Curriculum for a Multicultural Nation.* Durham, NC: Duke University Press, 1993.

Matiella, Ana Consuelo. *The Multicultural Caterpillar: Children's Activities in Cultural Awareness.* Santa Cruz, CA: Network Publications, 1990.

McCarthy, Cameron, and Crichlow, Warren (Eds.). *Race, Identity, and Representation in Education.* New York: Routledge, 1993.

McCormick, Theresa Mickey. *Creating the Nonsexist Classroom: A Multicultural Approach.* New York: Teachers College Press, 1994.

McIntyre, Alice. *Making Meaning of Whiteness: Exploring Racial Identity with White Teachers.* Albany: State University of New York Press, 1997.

McLaren, Peter. *Revolutionary Multiculturalism: Pedagogies of Dissent for the New Millennium.* Boulder, CO: Westview Press, 1997.

Miller-Lachmann, Lyn, and Taylor, Lorraine. *Schools for All: Educating Children in a Diverse Society.* Albany, NY: Delmar Publishers, 1995.

Montalto, Nicholas V. *A History of Intercultural Education Movement.* New York: Garland, 1982.

Norby, Shirley, and Ryan, Gregory. *Multicultural Children's Literature: Authors, Illustrators and Activities.* Minneapolis, MN: T. S. Denison, 1994.

O'Hair, Mary, and Odell, Sandra (Eds.) *Diversity and Teaching.* Fort Worth, TX: Harcourt Brace Jovanovich, 1993.

Ovando, Carlos Julio, and Collier, Virginia. *Bilingual and ESL Classrooms: Teaching in Multicultural Contexts.* New York: McGraw-Hill, 1985.

Perry, Theresa, and Fraser, James (Eds.). *Freedom's Plow: Teaching in the Multicultural Classroom.* New York: Routledge, 1993.

Pignatelli, Frank, and Pflaum, Susanna. *Experiencing Diversity: Toward Educational Equity.* Thousand Oaks, CA: Corwin Press, 1994.

Protheroe, Nancy. *Culturally Sensitive Instruction and Student Learning.* Arlington, VA: Educational Research Service, 1991.

Ramsey, Patricia G., et al. *Multicultural Education: A Source Book.* New York: Garland, 1989.

Ramsey, Patricia G., et al. *Teaching and Learning in a Diverse World: Multicultural Education for Young Children.* New York: Teachers College Press, 1987.

Reissman, Rose. *The Evolving Multicultural Classroom.* Alexandria, VA: Association for Supervision and Curriculum Development, 1994.

Rényi, Judith. *Going Public: Schooling for a Diverse Democracy.* New York: W. W. Norton, 1993.

Rhodes, Robert W. *Nurturing Learning in Native American Students.* Hotevilla, AZ: Sonwai Books, 1994.

Rivlin, Harry, et al. *Advantage, Disadvantaged, Gifted: Presentations from the Third National Conference on Disadvantaged Gifted.* Ventura, CA: Ventura County Superintendent of Schools Office, 1978.

Roberts, Helen, et al. *Teaching from a Multicultural Perspective.* Thousand Oaks, CA: Sage Publications, 1994.

Roberts, Patricia, et al. *Developing Multicultural Awareness Through Children's Literature: A Guide for Teachers and Librarians, Grades K–8.* Jefferson, NC: McFarland, 1993.

Rodriguez, Fred. *Mainstreaming a Multicultural Concept into Teacher Education: Guidelines for Teacher Trainers*. Saratoga, CA: R & E Publishers, 1983.

Rothstein, Stanley (Ed.). *Class, Culture, and Race in American Schools: A Handbook*. Westport, CT: Greenwood Press, 1995.

Sanborn, Michelle, et al. *Teaching About World Cultures: Focus on Developing Regions*. Denver, CO: Center for Teaching International Relations, University of Denver, 1986.

Saravia-Shore, Marietta, and Arvizo, Steven (Eds.). *Cross-Cultural Literacy: Ethnographies of Communication in Multiethnic Classrooms*. New York: Garland, 1992.

Scarcella, Robin C. *Teaching Language Minority Students in the Multicultural Classroom*. Englewood Cliffs, NJ: Prentice-Hall, 1990.

Schlesinger, Arthur. *The Disuniting of America*. New York: Norton, 1992.

Schoem, David, et al. *Multicultural Teaching in the University*. Westport, CT: Praeger, 1993.

Seelye, H. Ned (Ed.). *Experiential Activities for Intercultural Learning*. Yarmouth, ME: Intercultural Press, 1996.

Seller, Maxine, and Weis, Lois (Eds.). *Beyond Black and White: New Faces and Voices in U.S. Schools*. Albany: State University of New York Press, 1997.

Shade, Barbara (Ed.). *Culture, Style, and the Educative Process*. Springfield, IL: C. C. Thomas, 1989.

Shade, Barbara, et al. *Creating Culturally Responsive Classrooms*. Washington, DC: American Psychological Association, 1997.

Siccone, Frank. *Celebrating Diversity: Building Self-Esteem in Today's Multicultural Classrooms*. Boston: Allyn and Bacon, 1995.

Sleeter, Christine E., and Grant, Carl. *Making Choices for Multicultural Education: Five Approaches to Race, Class, and Gender*. New York: Merrill, 1994.

Sleeter, Christine E. and McLaren, Peter (Eds.). *Multicultural Education, Critical Pedagogy, and the Politics of Difference*. Albany: State University of New York Press, 1995.

Sleeter, Christine E. *Multicultural Education as Social Activism*. Albany: State University of New York Press, 1996.

Spring, Joel H. *Deculturalization and the Struggle for Equality: A Brief History of the Education of Dominated Cultures in the United States*. New York: McGraw-Hill, 1997.

Stoodt, Barbara D. *Exploring Cultures Through Literature*. Greensboro, NC: Carson-Dellosa, 1993.

Sutman, Francis X., et al. *Educating Personnel for Bilingual Settings, Present and Future*. Washington, DC: American Association of Colleges for Teacher Education, 1979.

Thompson, Becky, and Tyagi, Sangeeta. *Beyond a Dream Deferred: Multicultural Education and the Politics of Excellence*. Minneapolis: University of Minnesota Press, 1993.

Trueba, Henry, et al. (Eds.). *Culture and the Bilingual Classroom: Studies in Classroom Ethnography*. Rowley, MA: Newbury House, 1981.

Washburn, David E., and Brown, Neil L. *The Multicultural Education Directory*. Philadelphia, PA: Inquiry International, 1996.

Weiss, Bernard (Ed.). *American Education and the European Immigrant, 1840–1940*. Urbana: University of Illinois Press, 1982.

Williams, Leslie, and DeGaetano, Yvonne. *ALERTA: A Multicultural, Bilingual Approach to Teaching Young Children*. Menlo Park, CA: Addison-Wesley, 1985.

Wilson, John K. *The Myth of Political Correctness: The Conservative Attack on Higher Education*. Durham, NC: Duke University Press, 1995.

Winzer, Margret, and Mazurek, Kasper. *Special Education in Multicultural Contexts*. Upper Saddle River, NJ: Merrill, 1998.

Wlodkowski, Raymond, and Ginsberg, Margery. *Diversity and Motivation: Culturally Responsive Teaching*. San Francisco: Jossey-Bass, 1995.

Wyner, Nancy B. (Ed.). *Current Perspectives on the Culture of Schools*. Cambridge, MA: Brookline Books, 1991.

Yeo, Frederick L. *Inner-City Schools, Multiculturalism, and Teacher Education: A Professional Journey*. New York: Garland, 1997.

York, Stacey. *Roots & Wings: Affirming Culture in Early Childhood Programs*. St. Paul, MN: Gryphon House, 1991.

Index

Note: **bold** page numbers indicate main entries.

About the Authors

BRUCE M. MITCHELL is Professor Emeritus of Education at Eastern Washington University. While he taught there he directed and facilitated school desegregation projects in the Northwestern states and California. He is coauthor, with Robert E. Salsbury, of *Multicultural Education: An International Guide to Research, Policies, and Programs* (Greenwood, 1996).

ROBERT E. SALSBURY is Professor of Education at Eastern Washington University. He has extensive experience participating in school desegregation programs in California and the Northwest. He is coauthor, with Bruce M. Mitchell, of *Multicultural Education: An International Guide to Research, Policies, and Programs* (Greenwood, 1996).